English Literature:

1900 TO THE PRESENT
Second Edition

Arthur H. Bell, Donald Heiney, and Lenthiel H. Downs

BARRON'S

All inquiries should be addressed to:
Barron's Educational Series, Inc.
250 Wireless Boulevard
Hauppauge, New York 11788

Library of Congress Catalog Card No. 94-1567

International Standard Book No. 0-8120-1837-0

Library of Congress Cataloging-in-Publication Data
Bell, Arthur, 1946–
    English literature : 1900 to the present / by Arthur
H. Bell, Donald W. Heiney, and Lenthiel H. Downs.
        p.   cm. — (College review series)
    Includes bibliographical references.
    ISBN 0-8120-1837-0
    1. English literature — 20th century — Outlines,
syllabi, etc.   I. Heiney, Donald W.
II. Downs, Lenthiel Howell.   III. Title.   IV. Series.
PR471.H36   1994
820.9'0091 — dc20   94-1567
                                                              CIP

PRINTED IN THE UNITED STATES OF AMERICA
4567 9770 987654321

CONTENTS

Part 1
BRITISH LITERATURE TO THE BEGINNINGS OF MODERNISM

Part 2
THE REALISTIC MOVEMENT

Part 3
THE REACTION TO REALISM

Part 4
THE REALM OF IDEAS: INTELLECTUAL AND IDEOLOGICAL LITERATURE

Part 5
TRADITION AND REVOLT IN POETRY

PREFACE

Literature, it has been said, is a mirror of social and personal concerns. To a remarkable extent, the literature of England in the twentieth century can be described as, at least in part, a shattered mirror. In Yeats's phrase, "the center will not hold." This is said simply to explain the organization and manner of development of this volume. Authors included here have been grouped under only the broadest of categories because, frankly, they defy more narrow classification. Perhaps a later age will see these writers in a more unified (or less distinct) way. For the present, we are too aware of what makes each of these writers unique.

If in our descriptions we allow modern British authors breathing room to be themselves rather than a movement, we must do no less for their works. The course of works over a writer's lifetime is not necessarily held in an ideal or even consistent order merely by the connection of the works with that life. People change, as do their poems, novels, and plays.

In this volume, it has been our goal, therefore, to particularize wherever possible in descriptions and assessments of writers and works. Among the authors treated here are not only the recognized pillars of the temple — Yeats, Joyce, Lawrence, and so forth — but also relatively new voices: Molly Holden, Seamus Heaney, Elaine Feinstein, Donald Davie, Thom Gunn, Stevie Smith, and many others. Also included in this edition are "Historical Background" sections to help the reader interpret literature within the climate of its time. An up-to-date bibliography has been provided for each author treated here as well as a glossary of literary terms useful in discussing twentieth-century literature. Review questions appear frequently as an aid to study.

The opportunity to write about the literature of one's own period is inevitably a stimulating and at times daunting experience. It goes without saying that our selection of and commentary upon authors included here should not be interpreted so as to exclude in importance other modern writers who move, delight, and challenge contemporary readers.

San Francisco, California
February 1994

Arthur H. Bell
University of San Francisco

CHRONOLOGY OF HISTORICAL AND

HISTORICAL EVENTS

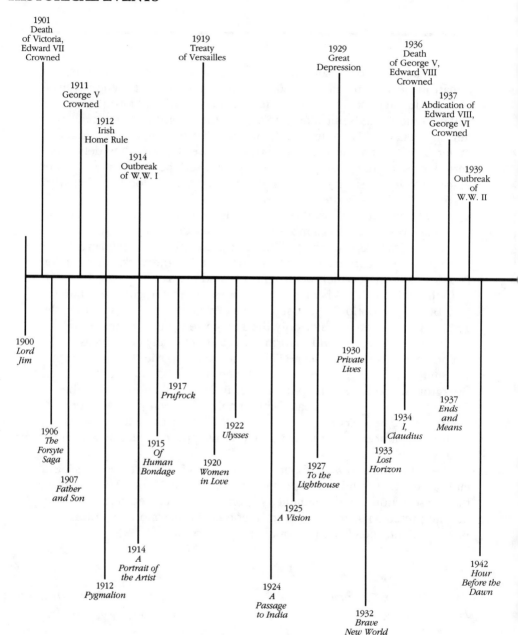

1901
Death
of Victoria,
Edward VII
Crowned

1911
George V
Crowned

1912
Irish
Home Rule

1914
Outbreak
of W.W. I

1919
Treaty
of Versailles

1929
Great
Depression

1936
Death
of George V,
Edward VIII
Crowned

1937
Abdication of
Edward VIII,
George VI
Crowned

1939
Outbreak
of
W.W. II

1900
Lord
Jim

1906
The
Forsyte
Saga

1907
Father
and Son

1915
Of
Human
Bondage

1917
Prufrock

1914
A
Portrait of
the Artist

1912
Pygmalion

1920
Women
in Love

1922
Ulysses

1924
A
Passage
to India

1925
A Vision

1927
To the
Lighthouse

1930
Private
Lives

1933
Lost
Horizon

1934
I,
Claudius

1932
Brave
New World

1937
Ends
and
Means

1942
Hour
Before the
Dawn

LITERARY EVENTS

LITERARY EVENTS 1900 TO THE PRESENT

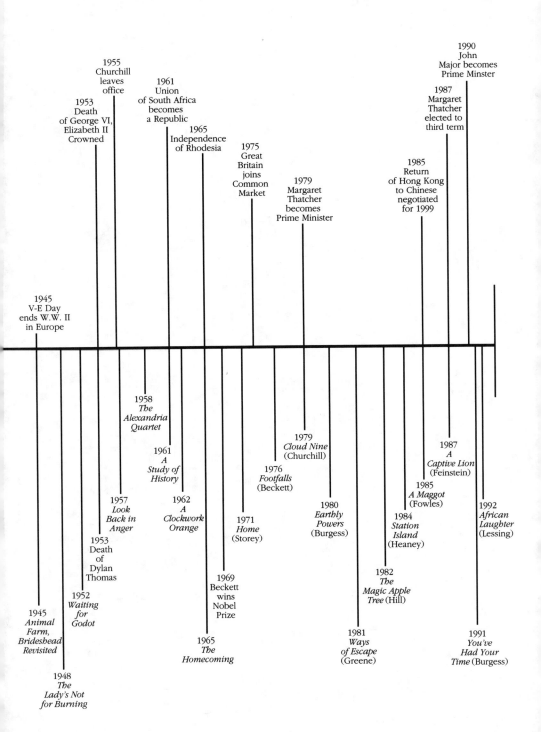

1990
John
Major becomes
Prime Minster

1987
Margaret
Thatcher
elected to
third term

1955
Churchill
leaves
office

1961
Union
of South Africa
becomes
a Republic

1953
Death
of George VI,
Elizabeth II
Crowned

1965
Independence
of Rhodesia

1975
Great
Britain
joins
Common
Market

1979
Margaret
Thatcher
becomes
Prime Minister

1985
Return
of Hong Kong
to Chinese
negotiated
for 1999

1945
V-E Day
ends W.W. II
in Europe

1958
The
Alexandria
Quartet

1979
Cloud Nine
(Churchill)

1987
A
Captive Lion
(Feinstein)

1961
A
Study of
History

1976
Footfalls
(Beckett)

1957
Look
Back in
Anger

1962
A
Clockwork
Orange

1971
Home
(Storey)

1980
Earthly
Powers
(Burgess)

1985
A Maggot
(Fowles)

1984
Station
Island
(Heaney)

1992
African
Laughter
(Lessing)

1953
Death
of
Dylan
Thomas

1982
The
Magic Apple
Tree (Hill)

1969
Beckett
wins
Nobel
Prize

1952
Waiting
for
Godot

1945
Animal
Farm,
Brideshead
Revisited

1981
Ways
of Escape
(Greene)

1991
You've
Had Your
Time (Burgess)

1965
The
Homecoming

1948
The
Lady's Not
for Burning

Part 1

BRITISH LITERATURE TO THE BEGINNINGS OF MODERNISM

The literature of Great Britain began as a bridge literature connecting Continental cultures with the traditions, manners, and mores emerging in the British Isles. Even Britain's first literary language, Anglo-Saxon, owes its origins to Germanic tribes, the Angles and the Saxons. Students turning to Beowulf *for the first time are often surprised to find this early monument of English literature reading more like Old High German than modern English.*

Certainly after the Norman Conquest (1066 and following) the materials and modes used by British writers were deeply influenced, even dictated, by Continental literary developments. In his major works, for example, Chaucer openly and frequently pays tribute to his "sources" or "masters" in French and Italian literature. The "Matter of Britain" (stories of King Arthur and the Knights of the Round Table) may have been written down by Geoffrey of Monmouth (c. 1100–54), Sir Thomas Malory (c. 1394–1471), and others, but its narrative development assuredly was shaped by French and German writers and storytellers. More often than not, young English writers (including Milton, Byron, Shelley, and Browning) undertook prolonged Continental journeys in an effort to return to classical sources.

This early and sustained interaction between English and Continental literatures makes the point that English literature did not grow up in isolation, notwithstanding the island geography of its base. At the same time, the influence of Continental sources should not be misunderstood to mean that English literature is merely imitative and derivative. If Chaucer, Spenser, Shakespeare, and Milton owe some debt to Continental sources, it is no less true that Voltaire, Lessing, Stendhal, and Proust acknowledged their own education via the works of English authors.

1
ROMANTICISM, REALISM, NATURALISM, AND SYMBOLISM

ROMANTICISM

The Romantic Period in England (approximately 1800 to 1830) reveals the many ways in which English authors made use of Continental cultural and literary resources. At the beginning of the Romantic era, William Blake wrote *Europe: A Prophecy* (1790). Wordsworth and Coleridge spent their meager earnings from *Lyrical Ballads* to travel to Germany to gain what they hoped would be a deeper understanding of Goethe, Kant, Schelling, and others. Byron and Shelley lived as virtual expatriates, writing many of their major works from and about the Continent.

REALISM

Similarly, the rise of Realism in English fiction cannot be told without significant reference to Continental writers. In its social aspect, Realism was a manifestation of the faith in science and liberalism that grew constantly in England during the nineteenth century and only began to waiver toward 1900. The literature of Realism concerned itself with the affairs of middle and depressed classes, economic and social matters, and the "local color" of daily life. In France, the major influences upon English Realism were Stendhal, Honore de Balzac *(Comedie Humaine),* and Gustave Flaubert *(Madame Bovary).* A bit later, the Realistic movement was given further impetus in England by the popularity of the works of the Norwegian dramatist Henrik Ibsen and the works of the great Russians — Fyodor Dostoyevsky, Ivan Turgenev, Leo Tolstoy, and Anton Chekhov.

In England the realistic movement, latent in Defoe, Fielding, and Richardson and emergent in Jane Austen, begins in earnest with Charles Dickens (1812–70). Although Dickens had no such semisociological vision as Balzac's *Human Comedy* in mind, he nevertheless created a similar panorama of early nineteenth-century Britain. William Makepeace Thackeray (1811–63) and Anthony Trollope (1815–82) are the chief remaining figures of British Realism as it manifested itself in their century, although George Eliot (pseudonym for Mary Ann Evans, 1819–80) and George Meredith (1828–1909) made significant contributions as well.

NATURALISM

In drama, Ibsen's harshly realistic domestic plays found champions in William Archer and George Bernard Shaw. With the help of their exegesis of the movement, Realism gradually metamorphosed by the end of the century into Naturalism, which tended to be more militantly pseudoscientific in its approach and even more concerned with degraded and often sordid levels of human existence. The novelist Emile Zola (1840–1902) and the critic Hippolyte Taine (1828–93) share the honor of founding the French naturalist school, so influential on their English contemporaries. Zola sought to make literature into a branch of social science; the novel was to study social behavior just as the chemist studies the behavior of compounds in a test tube. His extensive *Rougon-Macquart* series purported to present "a natural and social history of a family under the Second Empire"; the second novel in the series, *Germinale,* vividly described the plight of coal miners in northern France and the problems of laborers on strike. Zola was deeply interested in the operation of heredity, which he considered the dominant motivating force in human destiny. Taine took a similar direction in his proposal that human destiny is a product of race, place, and time. In these writers we see early seeds of the "Nature versus Nurture" (heredity versus environment) debate that continues to rage. These themes are nowhere explored more passionately and pitilessly than in the works of Thomas Hardy (1840–1924), the earliest English Naturalist. His many novels and poems are marked by a deep deterministic pessimism. Except for the works of Hardy, the full flower of Naturalism would not appear in Britain and America until the twentieth century.

SYMBOLISM

Another literary current in the nineteenth century was Symbolism, especially as connected with the decadent movement, which included such British figures as Algernon Swinburne (1837–1909) and Oscar Wilde (1856–1900). Its starting point was the rejection of bourgeois-capitalistic materialism and the realistic literature growing out of it. Foreshadowings of the movement are to be found in the British Pre-Raphaelites, headed by John Ruskin (1819–1900), who favored a revival of medievalism. The Symbolist school began to form about 1880 and reached its climax in the 1890s in a circle in Paris around its leading poets, Stéphane Mallarmé (1842–98) and Paul Verlaine (1844–96). The Symbolists had three broad agendas for the reform of art. First, they sought to eradicate all narrative, exposition, and didacticism from poetry. Second, they tried to form each poem (or other work of art) around a single image or sensation (which is their appeal for the later Imagists). Third, they endeavored to utilize the newly discovered subconscious associations of the human mind to lead the reader along the path from the concrete to the intangible. In so doing, the Symbolists stood for a conscious cult of Beauty for its own sake, and an obsession with sensory or erotic experience. Several of the leading poets of the twentieth century, including William Butler Yeats, T. S. Eliot, Rainer Maria Rilke, W. H. Auden, and Stephen Spender, were clearly influenced by these French Symbolists.

NONLITERARY INFLUENCES

Many of the major influences upon English literature prior to the twentieth century were not specifically literary in nature. Charles Darwin (1809–82), with his theories of evolution by natural selection and their devastating implications for fundamentalist religion, gave great impetus to the growth of both Realism and Naturalism. The socialist-radical movement, culminating in the work of Karl Marx (1818–83), found its way into more and more late nineteenth-century literary plots, themes, and characters. In addition to the leftist authors frankly professing Marxism, there were a large number who more generally presented such Marxist dilemmas as the conflict of social classes or the intransigence of the bourgeois-capitalistic ruling classes.

Just as influential were the lectures and writings of Viennese psychoanalyst Sigmund Freud (1856–1939), who interpreted human motivation in terms of subconscious forces, including suppressed sexual impulses. Finally, Albert Einstein (1879–1955) opened up a Pandora's box with his theory of relativity and the idea of time as a fourth dimension. There is scarcely an author in the twentieth century who can be said to have escaped the influence of Darwin, Marx, Freud, or Einstein.

As the influence of these thinkers combined with the Realism and Naturalism to define the modern spirit and temper, some nineteenth-century English authors seem to have anticipated the intellectual and emotional climate of the twentieth century. With the advantage of hindsight, it may now seem to us that Robert Browning, Gerard Manley Hopkins, Thomas Hardy, and perhaps Samuel Butler were decidedly anti-Victorian in their deepest motives and literary impulses.

2
MAIN CURRENTS OF THE TWENTIETH CENTURY

The year 1900 is more than an arbitrary chronological milestone in literary history. It marks the onset of a new period in literature—a sea change in thought and feeling—just as it does in the field of social activity. In Britain, Queen Victoria's death in 1901 marked the official close of an era. Of course the doors had been closing for some time, and there is no sudden about-face at the century's end in literature or social life. But the voices of the Empire grow weaker as the tight little island loses one outpost after another—and, in the process, firms up its own identity.

The literature that springs from this moment of change is marked first by its utter diversity. There is no one single school, no one tendency, which can be said to typify the age. Never before in literary history have there been so many schools, circles, and movements existing simultaneously. This diversity is naturally only an aspect of a wider heterogeneity in social development. The twentieth century has no one dominant social philosophy or religion and so cannot hope for unanimity of approach or even interest in literature. The two World Wars and other world events struck serious blows to British traditions and idealism, including the traditions of a somewhat stable literary heritage.

Such fragmentation allowed, and even encouraged, the tendency of some twentieth century authors to lose themselves in obscurantism and esotericism. Literature has never, except in rare instances, been the preoccupation of the great masses of the population, but never before has literature been written for such a small and clannish group of cognoscenti. Comparatively speaking, the public that enjoys the poetry of T. S. Eliot or Ezra Pound is infinitely smaller than the public that read the poems of Tennyson or Kipling, or even that attended the plays of Shakespeare. Certain schools of poetry in the twentieth century tend to be difficult, heavy with allusion, and highly technical in construction.

At the same time, the opposite tendency is discernible: Many twentieth-century authors seek deliberately to create a literature for the masses, literature that sacrifices none of its artistic quality in being presented in terms that are comprehensible to the man or woman in the street. This experiment has, of course, been carried forth on a wide scale and in a highly organized manner in Russia, but the attitude is also apparent in the work of such contemporary English writers as Somerset Maugham, Rudyard Kipling, G. K.

Chesterton, and Graham Greene. Along with the tendency to broaden the bases of all the arts — music, opera, drama, and painting — to make them available to the mass of the population, there has been a comparable effort to democratize literature. Perhaps one can best see this tendency in terms of protest songs, both American and British; John Lennon of the Beatles turned out poems which have commanded world-wide attention across age groups.

But amid the complex diversity of twentieth-century literary schools it is possible to discern two basic tendencies. The first of these, the Realistic-Naturalistic movement, continues the current that began in the nineteenth century with Stendhal, Balzac, Ibsen, Tolstoy, Dickens, Thackeray, Trollope, and Hardy. In the twentieth century this movement tends to become more political, more liberal in outlook, and at the same time more consciously scientific in technique. Representative authors include George Gissing, Arthur Morrison, G. E. Moore, and Arnold Bennett.

The second great movement might be roughly labeled "the Reaction to Realism." It comprises the various forms of repudiation of strictly external objectivity: psychological literature, Neo-Romanticism, Impressionism, and other forms of antirealistic experimentation. Of particular note in this movement are such authors as D. H. Lawrence, Virginia Woolf, James Joyce, George Bernard Shaw, Brendan Behan, Mary Lavin, Graham Greene, William Golding, Lawrence Durrell and others.

The realm of ideological or intellectual literature is treated in Part 4. The authors in this section agree more in content than in technique, and in general the chief importance of their work lies in its ideological content.

It is remarkable that England in the twentieth century has produced a large number of very good, thoroughly competent, and literate writers in the traditional modes, who make good reading but who have not been outstandingly or creatively original. Indeed, if it were not for the inclusion of Irish authors and such adoptive English writers as Joseph Conrad, the list of British creative literary talent might be much smaller — as the Irish often like to point out.

A special case of sorts is T. S. Eliot, who is claimed by both English and American literature. A poet and critic of Eliot's stature regularly gets double exposure in both British and American anthologies. Was Eliot English or American? One can make either answer, depending upon criteria. Eliot was born in St. Louis, Missouri, of a New England family and lived there until he was eighteen. His college work, including graduate studies, was done chiefly at Harvard (which granted him bachelor's and master's degrees in 1909 and 1910), with additional study at the Sorbonne in Paris and at Oxford. Only at the age of twenty-six did he take up what was to become permanent residence in England. He married an Englishwoman, Vivienne Haigh, the following year and became a British citizen in 1927 at the age of thirty-nine. The accident of birth seems as insufficient to establish national character as does the choice of citizenship; perhaps schooling and the formative years have more to do with it. The British can point to Eliot's declared preferences for royalism in politics, classicism in literature, and Anglicanism in religion; but perhaps these represent an American's nostalgia for "our old home." At any rate, Eliot in these volumes has been grouped with the Americans. Time will tell where he best belongs.

One of the sources of the genius and strength of English literature as of the English language itself is its ability to assimilate, ingest, break down, and make peculiarly its own such foreign materials as the *Beowulf* legends, Church Latin, forms of blank verse and sonnetry from Italy, and Noh plays imported from Japan by Yeats. The Nobel Prize was given to some half-dozen British writers of this century, but some of the most influential and significant literary talents of our time who escaped that distinction brought even greater honors to the British empire; these writers include Lawrence, Conrad, and Joyce. More recently, Joyce Cary, William Golding, and Lawrence Durrell among others have carried British fiction forward or at least in new directions. Beginning in the 1960s, London again became a center of exciting playwrights and productions.

In all, then, there is much rich territory to explore in contemporary British literature. It would be a mistake to view the literary vigor of Britain as a phenomenon of past centuries alone.

Part 2

THE REALISTIC MOVEMENT

WORKS AT A GLANCE

Thomas Hardy

1871	*Desperate Remedies*	1903, 1905,	*The Dynasts*
1873	*A Pair of Blue Eyes*	1908	
1876	*The Hand of Ethelberta*	1909	*Time's*
1878	*The Return of the*		*Laughingstocks*
	Native		*and Other*
1880	*The Trumpet Major*		*Verses*
1882	*Two on a Tower, A*	1914	*Satires of*
	Laodicean		*Circumstances,*
1886	*The Mayor of*		"Ah, Are
	Casterbridge		You Digging
1891	*Tess of the d'Urbervilles*		on My Grave?"
1896	*Jude the Obscure*		"Channel
1898	*Wessex Poems and Other*		Firing."
	Verses		"The Subalterns"
1902–	*At Casterbridge Fair*	1928	*Winter Words*
09			(posthumous)

Arnold Bennett

1898	*A Man from the North*	1910–	*Clayhanger* trilogy
1908	*The Old Wives' Tale*	15	

W. Somerset Maugham

1897	*Liza of Lambeth*	1921	"Rain"
1915	*Of Human Bondage*	1930	*Cakes and Ale*
1919	*The Moon and Sixpence*	1946	*Then and Now*

John Galsworthy

1904	*The Island of Pharisees*	1921	*To Let*
1906	*The Silver Box, The Man of*	1924	*The White Monkey*
	Property	1926	*Escape, The Silver Spoon*
1909	*Strife*	1928	*Swan Song*
1910	*Justice*	1931	*Maid in Waiting*
1916	*The Apple Tree*	1932	*Flowering Wilderness*
1920	*In Chancery*	1933	*Over the River*

3
REALISTIC STORYTELLERS AND NATURALISM IN TRANSITION

In British literature the dominant realistic movement that began in the middle of the nineteenth century reached well into the twentieth century. Although some novelists had turned to naturalism and subsequently reacted against it in the early nineteen hundreds, an important minority, including figures of the stature of Arnold Bennett, continued to write in the traditional and realistic style of the mid-nineteenth century.

As a group these writers manifest a strong feeling of artistic vocation; they consider themselves professional authors whose business it is to write books, and they are generally wary of engaging in politics, lending their services to groups, or promulgating doctrines. At the same time they tend to be broadly liberal and humanitarian in outlook. Generally speaking, these authors can be classed as antagonistic to bourgeois conventions of morality or respectability; they frequently portray sensitive and artistically talented young persons whose lives are devoted to the struggle against middle-class Philistinism. As artists all of them are concerned with the delineation of character, especially eccentric, impassioned, or sensitive character. Many realists demonstrate an almost devout respect for the art of writing; they are consecrated craftsmen who construct books with a careful and perspicacious attention to detail. Of the group treated, Bennett and Maugham are primarily storytellers whose work contains no dominant or consistent message, while Hardy and Galsworthy, influenced by Naturalism, have something of an axe to grind, or at least relatively consistent thematic materials.

A further word about Emile Zola's central position in the promotion of self-conscious Naturalism may be useful. Inspired by Claude Bernard's *Introduction to the Study of Experimental Medicine* (1865) and by Hippolyte Taine's deterministic and socio-eugenic theories, Zola published in 1880 *The Experimental Novel,* a long essay or manifesto calling for the creation of a new scientific literature. The influence of heredity upon character was to be demonstrated with scientific exactitude; literature was to observe and record life rather than to interpret it or to create a world of the imagination. Vice and virtue were "products like sugar and vitriol"; they were to be utilized as a chemist uses reagents for the discovery of scientific truth. In his *Rougon-Macquart* series Zola actually created a vast cycle of novels dissecting the rise, triumph, and degeneration of a single family and the operation of the principles of heredity on its members. Several units of this cycle, especially

L'Assommoir (*The Dram Shop,* 1877), *Nana* (1880), *Germinal* (1885), and *La Terre* (*Earth,* 1887), must be grouped with the greatest novels of the nineteenth century. The cycle, comprising twenty volumes in all, was widely imitated in the twentieth century. Around Zola formed a school of young authors determined to avoid the literature of the past and create an idiom "worthy of the age of the locomotive."

Spreading from France, the naturalistic movement reached its height in Germany and Russia around the turn of the century; Gerhart Hauptmann and Maxim Gorky became the champions about whom the disciples rallied. In the Anglo-Saxon countries the movement caught on somewhat more slowly. Although Thomas Hardy and George Gissing are usually considered Naturalists, English literature during the fin-de-siècle was actually dominated by the Pre-Raphaelite revival and by the "cult of decadence" of Swinburne and Wilde. The height of British Naturalism was to occur in the twentieth century with John Galsworthy and his contemporaries.

In America the Anglo-American counterpart of European Naturalism was to reach its climax, after beginnings in Frank Norris (1870–1902) and Stephen Crane (1871–1900), in Theodore Dreiser (1871–1945), Upton Sinclair (1878–1968), James T. Farrell (1904–1979), F. Scott Fitzgerald (1896–1940), Ernest Hemingway (1898–1961), John Dos Passos (1896–1970), John Steinbeck (1902–68), and many others, actually a dominant mode of our century. Back in England there was a resurgence of Naturalism in the fifties and sixties, particularly in the novels of the generation of Angry Young Men: John Wain, John Braine (*Room at the Top,* 1957), Kingsley Amis (*Lucky Jim,* 1954), who won the Somerset Maugham Award in 1955 and more recently has been seen as a satiric successor to Evelyn Waugh, and perhaps especially Alan Sillitoe with *Saturday Night and Sunday Morning* (1958) and *The Loneliness of the Long-Distance Runner* (1959). These angry young writers depicted working-class life with sharp criticism of the established order and lip service to traditional virtues, revealing a contemporary society with no interests but the flesh and money. The new hero was an anti-hero in revolt against the Establishment but without much belief in social programs or progress, disillusioned to the point of breakdown.

Naturalism differs from Realism in several aspects, none of which is clear-cut and definitive. It tends to be more doctrinaire in its exposition of pseudo-scientific principles, it is less interested in character and more in the conflict of social forces, and it is concerned to a greater extent with the sordid, the shocking, and the depressing sides of existence. By these criteria, however, there are Naturalistic elements in Dostoevsky; and Galsworthy, Hemingway, and Scott Fitzgerald demonstrate many qualities of typical Realists. Some further suggested qualities of literary Naturalism are as follows:

1. Naturalism is scientific or pseudo-scientific in its approach; it attempts to treat human beings as biological pawns rather than agents of free will. The author does not attempt to judge the characters or to comment on their

actions, but merely inserts them into a crucial situation and then pretends to stand back and watch them with the impassivity of the scientists. Although Zola applied this principle with some success, it has generally remained a synthetic theory and has only infrequently been applied to actual literary works.

2. The Naturalist attempts to make literature into a document of society, and writes "novel cycles" purporting to cover every aspect of modern life, or creates characters who are personifications of various social classes. Many Naturalists gather copious data from actual life and include it in their literary works: They write novels around specific occupations such as railroading or textile manufacturing in which they utilize technical details of the trade for story interest. This aspect of Naturalism represents an attempt to remove literature from the realm of the fine arts into the field of the social sciences.

3. Because of the above-described documentary nature of Naturalism, the technique often involves the conscious suppression of the poetic elements in literature. The prose style is flat, objective, and bare of imagery; it includes copious details and explanations, and is wary of highly literary metaphors. Like the pseudo-scientific dogma described above, this quality is often more theoretical than practical. The best Naturalists are those who do not totally abandon the literary traditions of the past. On the other hand, some Naturalists are merely writers lacking in the poetic instinct; they avoid a highly literary prose because they have little feeling for style and imagery. Others like Hardy are essentially poets who achieve highly poetic effects in their prose.

4. Naturalistic literature tends to be concerned with the less elegant aspects of life; its typical settings are the slum, the sweatshop, the factory, or the farm. Where the Romantic author selects the most pleasant and idealistic elements in his experience, the Naturalistic author often seems positively drawn toward the brutal, the sordid, the cruel, and the degraded. This tendency is in part a reaction against earlier literature, especially against the sentimentalism of the Dumas school, where vice is invariably made to appear romantic. The real motivating forces in a Naturalistic novel are not religion, hope, or human idealism; they are alcohol, filth, disease, and the human instinct toward bestiality. It will be seen immediately that there are important exceptions to this principle. Galsworthy's scenes are middle class, and Scott Fitzgerald prefers to do his slumming at the Ritz.

5. Naturalism is sometimes, but not always, socialist or radical in attitude. The sympathy of the typical Naturalist lies with the proletariat, who sees social evolution mainly in terms of the conflict of classes. Industrial strife plays a large part in the Naturalistic novel, as does the description of the exploitation of the worker, male and female, by the boss. Many critics have held that there is a strong Romantic element in Naturalism, and the liberalism of the Naturalist, when it occurs, tends to be of an intellectual, quixotic, and impassioned variety. In spite of their purported objectivity, in fact, many

Naturalists seem less detached than angry. Naturalism is the literature of revolt, both political and literary. Zola and Hardy share this Romantic element in their Naturalism.

6. Freedom of the will tends to disappear in the Naturalist's philosophy. Human life is controlled by the modern fates of heredity and environment. Blame is not usually assigned in a deterministic universe (to understand the individual's background is to forgive) unless the accusing finger is pointed at the universe itself.

Again it must be remembered that particularly in English literature individual practitioners of Realism and Naturalism are not always so far removed one from the other. Perhaps it is because they are less doctrinaire and more devoted to the arts of poetry and fiction apart from philosophical stance.

THOMAS HARDY (1840 – 1928)

Hardy represents the climax of nineteenth-century English Realism-Naturalism both in the novel and in poetry and its transition into the twentieth century. Albert Guerard points to Thomas Hardy and Joseph Conrad as transitional figures who no longer belong to the old order of the realistic novel and "our old plausible world" of Anthony Trollope and George Eliot but can tell us something of what has happened between them and Kafka and Faulkner and Joyce as representative of the ironic distortions, psychological explorations, and dislocations of form of more contemporary fiction.

As a novelist Hardy seems to be more interested in "storytelling" than most other Naturalists. His first love had been poetry, but he turned to fiction in order to find avenues of publication and profit. When he had achieved recognition and some financial security, he dropped the writing of novels after publishing some fourteen of them and returned to poetry as his preferred medium of expression. It was Hardy himself who divided his novels into three groups: (1) the novels of ingenuity, which emphasized plot, like *Desperate Remedies* (1871), *The Hand of Ethelberta* (1876), and *A Laodicean* (1882), (2) romances and fantasies, like *A Pair of Blue Eyes* (1873), *The Trumpet Major* (1880), and *Two on a Tower* (1882); and (3) novels of character and environment, those dealing with his semifictional and native countryside of Wessex, including among seven titles his generally recognized best novels, *The Return of the Native* (1878), *The Mayor of Casterbridge* (1886), *Tess of the D'Urbervilles* (1891), and *Jude the Obscure* (1896).

It is certainly true that Hardy's most interesting novels (and poetry) deal with his fictional Wessex, a territory including the shire of Dorset, with Casterbridge for Dorchester, but reaching as far as Oxford, which becomes Christminster. This region of Hardy's imagination (and why not Wessex, since we have Sussex south of London and Essex east of it?) is as tied to his effective creative writing as Yoknapatawpha County is to Faulkner's. When either writer moved from his home base in search of a master work — Hardy's *The Dynasts,* Faulkner's *A Fable* — he never really made it. There is a growing feeling that *Jude the Obscure,* the novel that caused the greatest consternation among Victorian readers and critics, has the most to say to readers of the present. In many ways, in its bitter criticism of marriage as an institution and divorce English-style and the repressive inadequacies of Christian views of sex and society, *Jude* paves the way for D. H. Lawrence and his attacks on such established concepts. Lawrence's fictional focus on sex itself is not in Hardy, but the scorn of accepted social conventions is remarkably alike in the two men.

Hardy the poet has been undergoing even more extensive revaluation in this century. As a matter of fact his literary reputation has been something like a yo-yo in its movements during the past fifty years, neither a tremendous surge nor ebbing but still up and down. The poetry, beginning with *Wessex Poems and Other Verses* in 1898, through *Time's Laughingstocks and Other Verses* (1909), *Satires of Circumstance* (1914), and *Winter Words* (published posthumously), offers difficult barriers to many readers: its pessimism; its plain, naked, bleak, angular style; its economy, concentration, and intensity of expression; its satiric barbs. It is highly dramatic (lyric, monologue, or dialogue), stripped-down Browning at its best. But surely these factors, rather anti-Victorian in sum, indicate a rough, modern appeal. John Crowe Ransom, admitting that most of Hardy's verse was written after the end of the Victorian period, with something like the modern temper, that of a "disaffected religionist," makes him nevertheless a late Victorian poet. To others Hardy sounds more like Wilfred Owen than like Tennyson.

Hardy in his advancing years was certainly not unaware of the world around him and the impact of ideas. A few stanzas from "Drinking Song" (with an overall A. E. Housman flavor and appearing in *Winter Words*) make this clear:

> *Once on a time when thought began*
> *Lived Thales: he*
> *Was said to see*
> *Vast truths that mortals seldom can;*
> *It seems without*
> *A moment's doubt*
> *That everything was made for man.*

> CHORUS: *Fill full your cups: feel no distress*
> *That thoughts so great should now be less!*

After the progress of time and the appearance of Copernicus and Hume we reach Darwin:

> *Next this strange message Darwin brings,*
> *(Though saying his say*
> *In a quiet way);*

> *We all are one with creeping things;*
> *And apes and men*
> *Blood-brethren,*
> *And likewise reptile forms with stings.*

CHORUS: *Fill full your cups: feel no distress;*
> *'Tis only one great thought the less!* . . .

> *And now comes Einstein with a notion—*
> *Not yet quite clear*
> *To many here—*
> *That's there's no time, no space, no motion,*
> *Nor rathe nor late,*
> *Nor square nor straight,*
> *But just a sort of bending-ocean.*

CHORUS: *Fill full your cups: feel no distress;*
> *'Tis only one great thought the less!*

No Victorian ever heard of Einstein, much less thought to place his ideas in this context.

It is true that Hardy's forms are for the most part traditional, even conventional. Technically the novels contain no new story-telling devices. The verse meters and stanzaic structures are also generally not those of an innovator but rather based on old ballad and hymn measures; however, Hardy does bend them to his uses, having decided that too regular a beat was bad art. Speaking of himself in the third person, he wrote of his own approach to poetic form "that in architecture cunning irregularity is of enormous worth, and it is obvious that he carried on into his own verse, perhaps in part unconsciously, the Gothic art-principle in which he had been trained—the principle of spontaneity found in mouldings, tracery, and suchlike—resulting in the 'unforseen' . . . character of his meters and stanzas, that of stress rather than of syllable, poetic texture rather than poetic veneer; the latter kind of thing, under the name of 'constructed ornament', being what he . . . had been taught to avoid as the plague. He shaped his poetry accordingly, introducing metrical pauses and reversed beats. . . ." Critics have been offended, according to Kenneth Marsden, by Hardy's semiconservative practice mixed with vague revolutionary theory.

IMPORTANCE

The real crux of Hardy's modernity is in his content. The determinism and pessimism that so offended the early twentieth century fall on much more sympathetic ears as the century grows older. Inconsistency bothers us less than equanimity. G. K. Chesterton in *The Common Man* has pointed to "the fine literature and very confused cosmic philosophy of Thomas Hardy who tried to say (at the same time) that God did not exist, and that He ought to be ashamed of existing; or possibly that He ought to be ashamed of not existing." It might be more accurate to say that Hardy saw the blind urge toward life of the universe as completely indifferent to man's consciousness and the values he has developed that make life worth living. He shows man caught by his surroundings, particularly in rural Wessex, and determined by his inheritance both individual and social.

Life

Thomas Hardy was born in 1840 in the village of Higher Bockhampton, near Dorchester (his later Casterbridge) and grew up with rural people, their stories, customs, and songs. Apprenticed at sixteen to a local architect and rebuilder of churches, he continued in this profession for some time, studying Latin and Greek on the side and, after removing to London, began to write poetry and fiction. There is some evidence that his knowledge of architecture contributed to his narrative construction. In any event he eased himself into full-time literary labors, beginning with serial publication in magazines. From his first novel, *Desperate Remedies,* published in 1871, through the fourteenth in the mid-nineties, he devoted his efforts to fiction but always hoping to free himself for poetry.

Hardy was twice married, first to Emma Lavinia Gifford in 1872, and following her death, to Florence Emily Dugdale in 1914. He began to publish his poetry in 1898, the *Wessex Poems,* and continued to work in this medium until his death in 1928. His most ambitious effort, a philosophical verse drama, an unstageable closet drama, *The Dynasts,* dealing with the Napoleonic wars, was published in 1903, 1905, and 1908. He called it an epic-drama in three parts, nineteen acts, and one hundred and thirty scenes. Supernatural beings called phantom intelligences, including the Pities and Spirits Sinister and Ironic, discuss the delusions of doomed men caught in the forces of history as they hover over a huge cast of great persons and unknown citizens. In 1923 another venture into drama, *The Queen of Cornwall,* was produced.

Siegried Sassoon has given us this picture of Thomas Hardy in his eighties:

> *Old Mr. Hardy, upright in his clair,*
> *Courteous to visiting acquaintance chatted*
> *With unaloof alertness while he patted*
> *The sheepdog whose society he preferred.*
> *He wore an air of never having heard*
> *That there was much that needed putting right.*
> *Hardy, the Wessex wizard, wasn't there.*
> *Good care was taken to keep him out of sight.*

In recent times there have been attempts to view Hardy's philosophy as existential. He might, indeed, have been a precursor here as well.

Chief Novels

***The Return of the Native* (1878):** Probably the most widely read of Hardy's major novel series, the Wessex fiction. Its most important character may be Egdon Heath, that desolate stretch of land that the author liked to connect with King Lear. The native, of course, is Clym Yeobright, who has been working with a diamond merchant in Paris but returns to Egdon to become a schoolmaster. Clym's failing eyesight forces him to become a furze-cutter on the heath to the distress of his bride, the selfish but beautiful Eustacia Vye, who had married him in the hopes of escape to Paris. She resumes relations with Damon Wildeve, a former lover, who in spite had married Clym's cousin, the selfless, gentle Thomasin. After Eustacia contributes to the death of Clym's mother, she and Damon plan to run away together but are drowned in a weir. In despair Clym becomes a traveling open-air preacher, and Thomasin is allowed to marry the faithful, honest reddlemen Diggory Venn, although Hardy tells us that was not his original intention. Fate, aided by chance and circumstance, makes this a grimly tragic story; the pagan, Greek fates are simply translated into more modern terms.

Albert Guerard has pointed to some interesting parallels between Eustacia Vye and Flaubert's Emma Bovary. Both are romantic young women lost in a realistic, naturalistic, world, married to dull, sleepy husbands, and longing to escape monotonous country existence, both possessed by alternate force and langour. The difference is that "Hardy never treats Eustacia with irony," although he might have done so had she appeared in his subsequent poetry.

***The Mayor of Casterbridge* (1886):** Considered by some critics the least flawed of Hardy's novels, it is the tightly woven story of six characters and their tangled lives: Michael Henchard (who becomes the mayor of Casterbridge/Dorchester), his wife Susan Henchard, the daughter Elizabeth Jane, Richard Newson, Donald Farfrae, and Lucetta. Michael, getting drunk at a county fair, sells his wife and child for five guineas to Richard, a sailor. The next day with morning-after clarity and despair he tries to find them but fails, and takes a solemn vow to keep away from liquor for twenty years, during which time by tremendous effort he becomes rich and respected as a merchant and eventually Mayor of Casterbridge. After eighteen years of work and triumph, Henchard falls to quarrelling with his assistant, the able Farfrae, for whom he has a hidden affection, driven by the faults of his own nature: impulsive anger, stubbornness, and pride. Farfrae becomes his rival in business and love, marrying Lucetta, whom Henchard had pursued. Elizabeth Jane turns out to be not his child but Newson's, and he sets himself against her, although there is a subsequent reconciliation. A business disaster brings ruin, his past is revealed, and he takes again to drink in poverty and loneliness. Physical and emotional torture drive him to the end. After Lucetta's death Farfrae marries Elizabeth Jane, but the wedding present sent by Henchard goes unnoticed. Later nobody knows how the new birdcage with the body of a goldfinch that had evidently starved to death came to be in a corner behind a screen. The bird's death parallels that of Henchard in a hut on Egdon Heath. Henchard was a man with strength, vigor, and greatness in him, but he falls like the Greek tragic hero, "not eminently good or just, yet whose misfortune is brought about not by vice but by some flaw in character or error in judgment." He seems ultimately to be more sinned against by things as they are, a malignant fate, than sinning.

Tess of the d'Urbervilles **(1891):** A seduced girl is the heroine, obviously in direct opposition to Victorian assumptions in such matters. When the ne'er-do-well Jack Durbeyfield learns that he may be descended from the noble d'Urberville line, he finds it beneath him to continue supporting his family. His wife therefore sends their daughter, Tess, to find work of some kind with the *nouveau riche* relations, the Stoke-d'Urbervilles. In a purposely ambiguous scene, Tess is either raped or seduced by Alec d'Urberville. She bears a child by Alec, but the baby soon dies. Thereafter, she takes on work at a distant dairy farm owned by the Talbothays. She meets and marries Angel Clare, the free-thinking son of a conservative minister. For all his liberalism and frankness about his own past sexual experiences, he cannot hide revulsion at learning of Tess's relations with Alec. Clare leaves immediately for Brazil, and Tess returns to a laborer's life. When her frequent letters to Clare go unanswered, she falls again into the clutches of Alec. A repentant Clare eventually returns to "forgive" her, at which point Tess in a moment of madness kills Alec and flees with Clare. Pursuing police apprehend her at Stonehenge, and she is later executed. Clare and Tess's cousin watch from a nearby hillside, and then go off hand-in-hand.

Jude the Obscure **(1896):** In some ways this is the most modern in its content of all of Hardy's fictional narratives. Jude Fawley, the orphan boy brought up by his great aunt in the hamlet of Marygreen and under the influence of Richard Phillotson, the schoolmaster, dreams of Christminster (Oxford), which can be seen in the distance on a clear day if you get high enough, and of the life of service and scholarship it represents. Helping his aunt by delivering her bakery products with horse and cart while teaching himself Latin and Greek from books sent by Mr. Phillotson from Christminster, until he found apprentice work with a stonemason in nearby Alfredston, Jude continues until his twentieth year dreaming of eventual removal to Christminster and the study of divinity in one of its colleges. But his plans are interrupted by the wiles of Arabella Donn, who stirs his physical lust and traps the properly honest young man into marriage by pretended pregnancy. Standing before the parson, "the two swore that at every other time of their lives till death took them, they would assuredly believe, feel, and desire precisely as they had . . . during the few preceding weeks," and "nobody seemed at all surprised at what they swore." The marriage breaks up very soon when Arabella leaves for Australia with her parents; Jude was not as good a catch as she had hoped.

Some three years later Jude makes his way to Christminster to work as a full-fledged stonemason, to dream still of eventual college study, and to meet his cousin, Sue Bridehead, a "liberated" young woman working in an "ecclesiastical establishment" and apparently separated from her father in London, alone and increasingly attractive to her cousin. Although freely pagan, a worshiper of Venus and Apollo, and an easy companion to Jude, Sue, slim and breastless, is rather frigid sexually. She resists all her cousin's advances and marries the much older (by eighteen years) Richard Phillotson without allowing him to consummate the marriage. She later leaves her husband to live with her cousin without "living" with him as the world thinks. Jude at the request of Arabella and Richard ostensibly to free Sue get divorces from their wives.

In the beginning Jude had been the orthodox, conservative, dogma-reverencing Christian while Sue had been the modern pagan Hellenist (at least in talk and general attitude), but as Jude, largely through Sue's influence, moves toward liberation, she falls into the strictest kind of Christian self-abnegation and narrowness. Jude, in the middle of his story, feels that he was checked in his first ambition to become an ordained minister by a woman, Arabella, and that his second aspiration, to become a simple licentiate in the church without degree, was checked by Sue. He wonders, "Is it that the women are to blame; or is the artificial system of things, under which the normal sex impulses are turned into devilish gins and springes to noose and hold back those who want to progress?"

It is only when Arabella seems to threaten to take Jude from her that Sue gives in to sexual intercourse with him. They talk about marrying but can't bring themselves to more than pretending to have carried through the ceremony. When Arabella, now legally married to her second husband, Cartlett, with whom she had lived as his wife, announces to Jude the arrival of his own son who had been born in Australia, Jude and Sue agree to bring him up. "The beggarly question of parentage—what is it after all? What does it matter, when you come to think of it, whether a child is yours by blood or not? All the little ones of our time are collectively the children of us adults of the time, and entitled to our general care."

The child, called Father Time or young Jude, seems to be another reason for Sue and Jude to marry but they can't face the contract that would substitute duty for love. Sue says, "Everybody is getting to feel as we do. We are a little beforehand, that's all. In fifty, a hundred years . . ." Arabella and Carlett, who *do* marry, are seen "in the antipathetic, recriminatory mood of the average husband and wife of Christendom." But tragedy relentlessly pursues Jude and Sue. Two little children of their own are killed by Father Time, who then hangs himself with the note, "Done because we are too menny." Sue, broken in spirit and in spite of Jude's plea, "Do not do an immoral thing for moral reasons," returns to remarry Richard and breaks her body in that almost flagellated loveless union. Jude sickens and dies miserably, alone, although the widowed Arabella hovers about.

Representative Poems

"The Subalterns," one of the early poems frequently coupled with "God-Forgotten," which is often anthologized, presents in five stanzas Hardy's disaffected religious ideas and an almost stoic reaction. The junior officers, represented in the military metaphor, only carry out the Commandant's orders; they are, in one stanza for each, the leaden sky, the North Wind, Sickness, and Death, but they bear no spite since they too are slaves. And "we smiled upon each other then," since they do not represent active malignancy. Each of the subalterns has a speaking part in Hardy's characteristically dramatic approach to the lyric.

A series of poems called *At Casterbridge Fair* (1902–09) presents two highly effective dramatic lyrics. In one, "After the Club-Dance," a young girl talks about leaving the party and drinking wine at dawn with her young man. Why does nature make her feel ashamed when she has done only what the birds who look at her do? In "A Wife Waits" the woman who speaks is older and wiser and sadder as she waits outside the clubroom for her husband, Will, who is inside drinking and carrying on with another woman. Before they were married in June, he had promised his complete devotion and sobriety. Now she waits "to steady him home." "The Curate's Kindness," subtitled "A Workhouse Irony," is another dramatic lyric spoken by an old man on his way to the poor house. His one happy thought in the distress of the removal had been that regulations there would have placed his wife in one wing and himself in another with the men. He might thus get free of his forty years' chain. But an apparently well-meaning Parson works hard to get the authorities to suspend the rule in this one case so that husband and wife can remain together. "To get freed of her there was the one thing/ Had made the change welcome to me." Now he might just as well jump out of the wagon and drown himself. "The Man He Killed," also of 1909 vintage, may be considered a dramatic monologue in which an old soldier, a common Wessex fellow, tries to explain to an acquaintance how he happened to kill a man in a war, although obviously he doesn't understand it himself. Had they met in any other way than as infantry, face to face, they would have treated each other to a drink in a bar. The worry is in finding an adequate reason: "I shot him dead because— / Because he was my foe, / Just so— my foe of course he was; / That's clear enough; although . . ." And there's the rub. The army's propaganda of "Why We Fight" is insufficient for the modern, thinking soldier, even if he can't think very much. Many Vietnam veterans might find this a modern poem.

In "Channel Firing" (1914) the speaker is one of the clerical dead, disturbed in their churchyard repose by the firing of gun in practice at sea. They think it must be Judgment Day. But God obligingly reassures the ghosts that this is men's doing, not His. "It will be warmer when/ I blow the trumpet (if indeed/ I ever do; for you are men,/ And rest eternal sorely need)." The guns continue to disturb the land, the hour, and the dead. And within months of the writing of the poem, the First World War broke out.

From *Satires of Circumstance* (1914) we have another of the ghostly dead, a woman, speaking in "Ah, Are You Digging on My Grave?" (often compared with Housman's "Is My Team Ploughing," although not necessarily for influence; both are good independent poems.) This is a dialogue between the dead woman and her little dog who reveals his identity in the fourth stanza, after the departed has assumed it was her lover (no, he married another yesterday), her nearest relatives (no), her enemy (no, she thinks the dead not worth her hate). "Ah, yes! You dig upon my grave . . ./ A dog's fidelity!" But the dog admits he was only burying a bone, "I am sorry, but I quite forgot/ It was your resting-place."

ARNOLD BENNETT (1867–1931)

Bennett is a professional author of a type peculiar to modern times: he considered writing to be a business like any other, and wrote frankly to sell books and make money. At the same time he constantly conserved that respect for his craft which distinguishes the true artist from the hack writer. Although some of his novels seem a little superficial today, he never wrote trash; and at least one of his works, *The Old Wives' Tale,* seems destined to take its place with the classic novels of English literature.

IMPORTANCE

In one sense Bennett tends toward the Naturalism of the French school. His novels are carefully documented, and he shows a certain pseudo-scientific preoccupation with the effects of commerce and industrialization on the inhabitants of the pottery towns of the Midlands. His real interest, however, is in the internal struggles of his characters and the efforts they make to adjust themselves to an unsatisfactory environment. Frustrated in their search for love, for money, and for human recognition, they struggle through life blindly seeking some meaning in existence, and usually manage to arrive at some compromise that lends them the illusion of happiness. Bennett has too much optimism to be a Naturalist, but he is too clear-sighted to be a romantic in the manner of Robert Louis Stevenson.

Life

Bennett's life is almost synonymous with his literary career. He was born in 1867 near Hanley, an industrial settlement of the "Five Towns" area, the pottery center of England. He worked as a journalist and editor, and from time to time wrote book reviews, drama criticism, and literary columns. His serious novels commenced with *A Man from the North* (1898). In 1900 he abandoned journalism definitely and went to write on a farm in Bedfordshire. He lived part of his life in France, where he married Marguerite Soulié in 1907. In 1922, after separation from his wife, he became intimate with the actress Dorothy Cheston, who bore him his only child. He died in 1931.

Chief Works

The Old Wives' Tale (1908): This novel is often stated to have been partly inspired by Maupassant's *Une Vie* (1883). The Bennett novel is laid in the Five Towns, where we are introduced to a Bursley draper and his two daughters, Sophia and Constance ("wisdom" and "constancy" respectively). Sophia, the more romantic and courageous of the two, attempts to break out of her dull middle-class existence, but comes only to hardship and grief. She elopes with the dashing Gerald Scales, who abandons her in Paris and leaves her to live out a life of grubby and monotonous insecurity. Constance, the more conventional of the two sisters, envies Sophia, whom she imagines to be leading an adventurous life in Paris. Constance herself marries a dull clerk, Mr. Povey, and goes on dragging out her days tediously in the Five Towns. Her life is little changed by the death of her husband; her only interest is her brilliant son, Cyril. Toward the end of her life Sophia returns, and Constance realizes that Sophia's life has been as unsatisfactory as her own. At last Sophia dies, leaving Constance a lonely and unhappy old eccentric abandoned even by her own son. This novel is a study of a peculiarly depressing sort of middle-class life: its futility and monotony, and the ruthlessness with which it punishes the romantic aspirations of the young.

The *Clayhanger* trilogy (1910–15): This series comprises three novels: *Clayhanger, Hilda Lessways,* and *These Twain.* The first is the study of young Edwin Clayhanger, a sensitive youth born, like the Sophia of *The Old Wives' Tale,* into a narrow middle-class family of the Five Towns. His artistic talent is ruthlessly suppressed by his father, and he seems doomed to a life of intolerable tedium. At twenty-three, however, he meets Hilda Lessways, a vigorous, aggressive, and fascinating woman who dominates his entire life. Although she becomes engaged to Edwin, she abandons him to marry another man. This marriage comes to nothing, and Edwin later discovers her living in misery in a Brighton rooming house. *Hilda Lessways* drops back to begin the story of Hilda's life from her girlhood. Her only sin is her desire to live an exalted and adventurous life; but this leads her into her union with her faithless husband and finally into vice and degradation. *These Twain* describes the marriage of Edwin and Hilda. Unfortunately, the marriage occurs too late in the careers of both; Edwin is disillusioned by the frustrations and disappointments of the past, and Hilda is demoralized by her former life of vice. The pair quarrel incessantly and manage to make each other thoroughly miserable. Edwin has now found that to achieve one's heart's desire does not always bring happiness. Although he achieves material success and eventually attains the status of a country gentleman, he is able to enjoy peace only by submitting to Hilda's neurotic tyranny. In its analysis of the artistic temperament persecuted by a materialistic family, the *Clayhanger* trilogy resembles Mann's *Buddenbrooks,* but its real theme is closer to that of *The Old Wives' Tale:* the gradual disillusionment of a sensitive hero isolated in a sordid and materialistic society.

W. SOMERSET MAUGHAM (1874 – 1965)

Most critics are inclined to treat Maugham as a facile and competent storyteller rather than a major novelist, and Maugham himself has made statements supporting this view. An examination of his work shows that the majority of it is competent rather than profound. At his best, exemplified in *Of Human Bondage* and, *Cakes and Ale,* he is a careful student of human nature with a flair for dramatic and original human types. At his weakest, he is a commercial magazine author who has produced superficial popular magazine fiction in tremendous quantities. One of his last novels, *Then and Now* (1946), was book-club fiction; most critics consider that the best Maugham stories and novels are those written before 1930.

Although Maugham gives the illusion of objectivity and detachment toward his characters, most of his fiction is based in some way on personal experience. His own boyhood and career contribute to many of his works *(Of Human Bondage, Cakes and Ale),* and his travels in the Orient and long residence in Southern France have also provided him with material.

Life

William Somerset Maugham was born in 1874 in Paris, where his father was an attaché of the British Embassy; he was virtually bilingual from the time he began to speak. Orphaned at ten, he was sent to live with his uncle, a Kentish clergyman; here he acquired the experiences he was to fictionalize in *Of Human Bondage.* In lieu of Philip Carey's club foot, Maugham had a less visible but equally burdensome disability: a pronounced stammer, which perhaps resulted from the confusion of learning French and English simultaneously in his early childhood. He was educated at King's School in Canterbury (the Tercanbury of the novel) and later boarded in Heidelberg, where he learned German and acquired his first taste of the artistic and literary life. Returning to England, he entered medical school in London and received his degree in 1898. Except for his internship, he never practiced; during this time he was working on his first novel, *Liza of Lambeth.* When it was finished, he had definitely decided to become a writer. From 1898 to 1907 he lived in Paris on very little money, turning out stories and plays at a steady rate. With *Lady Frederick* (drama, 1907) some success began to come his way, and thenceforth he was able to earn a comfortable living as an author.

He travelled widely, especially in the Orient, the Pacific islands, the United States, and Spain. He married in 1915 and was divorced in 1927; after that he remained single. In the early thirties he settled in a villa at Cap Ferret, on the French Riviera, which continued to be his headquarters thereafter except for a brief exile during the Second World War.

Maugham died at the end of the year 1965 at the age of ninety-one, having become almost as well known for his quips and misanthropy as Shaw. "Only a mediocre writer is always at his best," he said, and added, "In my twenties the critics said I was brutal; in my thirties they said I was flippant; in my forties they said I was cynical; in my fifties they said I was competent; and now they say I am superficial." But Bette Davis as Mildred Rogers, and Leslie Howard as Philip Carey will remain a long memory for those who saw the first filming of Maugham's one indisputable classic.

Chief Works

Of Human Bondage (1915): This is Maugham's best novel; most of what he wrote afterward is superficial in comparison. Its power of authenticity derives from the fact that Maugham is writing from personal experience; the novel is autobiographical in its outline and chief details. As for literary influences, it owes something to Butler's *The Way of All Flesh* (1903).

The protagonist is Philip Carey, a young man of artistic bent who eventually becomes a physician, and the story centers around his revolt against his austere middle-class family background. In 1895 Philip, only nine, is orphaned and sent to live with his Uncle William Carey, a sanctimonious and stingy vicar in the village of Blackstable in Kent. His uncle stifles the boy's natural development through his unnatural Puritanism and austerity, but his Aunt Louisa, childless, secretly lavishes upon him all her frustrated maternity. Under these two influences he grows up sensitive but repressed and timid.

Sent away to school at Tercanbury, Philip is ridiculed and tormented by the other boys because of his club foot; although he has great scholastic ability he detests school life. As soon as he is eighteen, he goes to Heidelberg to study; he takes a room in a boarding house and begins to sample the intellectual life of the university town. He shares discussions with Weeks, an intense young American Unitarian, and Hayward, a clever English youth with modern "radical" ideas. This experience, the beginning of his real education, results in Philip's losing the rickety faith his uncle has forced upon him.

Returning to Blackstable, Philip engages in a transitory affair with Miss Wilkinson, a woman much older than himself; this serves as his initiation into physical love. Thenceforth his passions, especially the erotic, begin to come to the fore; he commences a long quest for sexual satisfaction, which continues for many years. He presently resolves to become a painter, and embarks for Paris to take up quarters on the Left Bank. Here he meets a fascinating array of Bohemian students: Lawson, Clutton, the desperately poor Fanny

Price, who commits suicide, and the insouciant hedonist Cronshaw, whose motto is, "Follow your inclinations, with due regard to the policeman round the corner." Although Philip temporarily accepts Cronshaw's standards, he begins to realize he can never be more than a second-rater in the world of art; when he returns to England for the funeral of his aunt, he decides not to go back to Paris.

He next turns toward a medical career; he enrolls in medical school in London and for a time feels he has found his vocation. But at this point he encounters Mildred Rogers, a waitress who is to dominate the next epoch in his life. Mildred is totally unworthy of him; she is selfish, vulgar, and promiscuous, and moreover she is rudely cold to his overtures. But he is swept away by a fierce physical obsession with her; he despises her intellectually but knows he must have her at any cost. She grants him nothing, even though he offers to marry her to have his way; and presently she marries another man who offers a promise of a better income. Although Philip is for a time disconsolate, he soon meets Norah Nesbit, a young writer who is struggling to support herself; he is relieved to have extricated himself from Mildred. But after a time Mildred appears on the scene again; her "husband," who never married her, has deserted her and left her pregnant and destitute. Weakly Philip turns back to her, and Norah goes her way. He spends so much of his money taking care of Mildred that he is forced to drop out of medical school, and she repays him by using his money to run off with another man.

But a new friend, the middle-aged Thorpe Athelny, comes to his aid at this point and finds him a steady job. He becomes intimate with Athelny's family, especially his children, and begins to hanker after a stable family life for himself. When his uncle dies, he uses the inheritance to go back to medical school; he takes his degree, marries Athelny's daughter Sally, and settles down happily to a practice in a small fishing village.

The dominant theme of this novel lies in Philip's effort to find his own nature; in this respect it is a typical *Entwicklungsroman,* or novel of personal development. Many passions torment the young Philip; his sexual frustration, his resentment at a world that mocks him for his club foot, his ambition to gain fame as an artist, and his reaction against the domination of his uncle. As the novel ends, his bondage to Mildred, to ambition, and to the Puritanical conscience inculcated by his uncle is over; he has freed himself from the Human Bondage into which every person is born. He becomes a free man partly by accepting the limitations his own abilities impose on his ambitions; in the end he chooses a happy obscurity over a frantic battle for fame. The novel is unique in that it begins as a typical novel of the artist struggling against a hostile world and ends with the hero accepting a serene and obscure domesticity; Maugham here is no devotee of the cult of the divinely gifted and consecrated artist.

The Moon and Sixpence (1919): This novel is based on the life of the French painter Paul Gauguin. Charles Strickland, an English stockbroker, at the age of forty abandons business, wife, and children to become a painter. The true character he has suppressed for years begins to come to the surface, and his personality appears to alter completely. He is encouraged and aided by a friendly Dutch painter, Dirk Stroeve; in return he seduces and abandons Stroeve's wife with utter cynicism. To outsiders he appears a creature of terrible ego, but actually he is driven by a deep compulsion to create through his painting and resolutely sets aside any temptation that does not contribute to this. At last, dissatisfied with European civilization, he travels to Tahiti, and there he finds a native wife who will alleviate his physical desires without interfering in his art. He is scornful of fame; he paints only to satisfy himself and his inner ideal. Before he dies of leprosy, he has covered the walls of his hut with paintings of an exquisite beauty; but on his orders his native wife burns them after his death. In contrast to *Of Human Bondage,* Maugham here shows a more conventional picture of the romantic artist-figure who feels himself an alien in society.

Cakes and Ale **(1930):** Maugham himself declared this to be his favorite work, although not his best. Edward Driffield, a talented young author, marries a barmaid, Rosie. She is pleasantly sensual, gracious, and generous to others; so generous, in fact, that she is unable to resist the attentions of "Lord" George Kemp, a Blackstable coal merchant who runs off with her to America. Deserted, Driffield is at first monopolized by Mrs. Barton Trafford, a superficial socialite, then falls prey to an attack of pneumonia and marries his nurse, Amy, during his convalescence. Through the combined efforts of Mrs. Trafford, who publicizes him, and Amy, who guides him and keeps him presentable for the public, Edward is made into a great author; but his fame is in great part a legend created by his public and by the social machinations of his patroness. *Cakes and Ale* is a study of a modern literary career and of the factors that go to make up popular literary success.

"Rain" (1921): This short story relates an epic encounter between Sadie Thompson, a prostitute who has just been banished from Hawaii, and Alfred Davidson, a rigorously Puritanical missionary who is destroyed when he cannot resist her attractions. The scene is laid in the South Seas; the chief interest lies in the progressive degeneration of Davidson's morality. This story has been widely reprinted and made into a successful motion picture.

JOHN GALSWORTHY (1867–1933)

Galsworthy is an aristocrat by background and inclination; he shows none of the preoccupation with poverty and degradation that distinguishes many Naturalists. He is nevertheless from a technical point of view a Naturalist in the scientific tradition. The great work of his life is the *Forsyte* series, a chain of novels illustrating the degeneration and decline of a bourgeois family in the period from 1886 to the advent of the 1920s. In structure and intent the *Forsyte* series is no different from Martin du Gard's *Les Thibaults* or Zola's *Rougon-Macquart* series; the principal difference is one of style or treatment.

IMPORTANCE

Unlike some Naturalists, Galsworthy is an author of wide education. He read extensively in Turgenev and in the French Realists, and his work has a certain cultivated sophistication natural in a product of the British public school system and a member of the European intellectual aristocracy. From Tolstoy and Turgenev he learned compassion, a quality lacking in the great French Realists. Like Dreiser, he views his characters not with the cold objectivity of a scientist but in the manner of a father who reluctantly throws his children into the world and then observes their struggles in helpless anguish. There are no totally despicable characters in Galsworthy, and no characters whose degradation is so great as to excite only our disgust. For this reason Galsworthy's novels, tragedies as they are, achieve a certain cathartic exaltation lacking in more callous works.

In style Galsworthy's work is not succinct in the manner of, for example, Hemingway. He has little use for the hard-boiled school of literature; he prefers to tell his story in the discursive and leisurely manner of an English gentleman. At the same time he is not rambling; his work is tightly knit even though long, and every paragraph contributes to the final effect. In this respect he resembles Joseph Conrad, with whom he had an important personal relationship. In religion and philosophy Galsworthy is a skeptic; he lacks the transcendental fervor of Romain Rolland or Tolstoy, and he is unable to share the faith in human perfectibility of such reformers as Bernard Shaw and H. G. Wells. Temperamentally he is an Epicurean; he is resolved to enjoy the best that life can offer him in a vulgar and materialistic civilization, and to endure what afflictions heaven may send him with fortitude.

In the *Forsyte* novels Galsworthy is chiefly interested in the bourgeois fetish of private property and its effects on human character. He is not a socialist; he does not propose to abolish private property because he can see no satisfactory device to replace it. He is simply interested in the psychological and moral impact of property on the middle class, and the gradual decline of bourgeois fiber over a span of generations. His attitude here is that of the artist, and in this respect it is to Thomas Mann that he must be compared.

As a dramatist Galsworthy is more concise, and somewhat more concerned with human justice, than he is in his novels. Such plays as *The Silver*

Box (1906), *Strife* (1909), and *Escape* (1926) might be the work of a careful and adept socialist playwright; they are not only studies of human character but analyses of the causes and results of human inequality. Additionally one might mention a single, almost perfect, little novella, *The Apple Tree* (1916).

Life

Galsworthy was the son of a prominent attorney of cultured Devonshire stock. His youth was provided with every advantage; he attended Harrow and went on to New College, Oxford, where he became something of a fop. He began practicing law in a perfunctory fashion in 1890. His literary interests were stimulated shortly after this during a sea voyage to Africa, when he met the young Joseph Conrad, then a ship's officer. Conrad showed him a draft of part of *Almayer's Folly,* and the meeting encouraged both Conrad and Galsworthy to undertake writing in a serious fashion. The friendship continued through the lives of the two authors. In 1905 Galsworthy married the former Ada Cooper, a young woman whom he had aided in extricating herself from an unhappy marriage with his cousin Arthur. The litigation, divorce, and subsequent marriage gave Galsworthy a firsthand experience of British and martial law, as well as a sympathy for those unfortunate individuals whose personal happiness conflicts with the legal machinery of society.

From 1897 to 1901 Galsworthy published four immature and transitory novels. *The Island of Pharisees* (1904) was similarly embryonic, although it contained the germ of the idea he was to develop more expertly in the *Forsyte* novels. The first of these, *The Man of Property,* appeared in 1906, and the series continued throughout his career. His interest in drama began with *The Silver Box* in 1906; the play was immediately successful, and helped to turn the English stage toward the drama of social problems.

Immediately after the First World War Galsworthy was offered a knighthood, which he refused. He did, however, accept the Nobel Prize for Literature in 1932. He made two successive trips to America, in 1926 and 1930 respectively. In 1933 he died at his Dartmoor estate; by his own instructions his ashes were scattered to the wind.

Critical reception of Galsworthy's novels, especially in America, was cool before 1918. In the period after the war, however, he was widely read. When one of his later novels revealed the death of Soames Forsyte, British newspapers featured the event as the obituary of a living person. The awarding of the Nobel Prize and the publication of a single-volume edition of *The Forsyte Saga* in the 1930s completed his triumph; and since his death he has been accepted as one of the great British writers of the twentieth century. By 1970 a televised series of *The Forsyte Saga* offered a renewal of interest in Galsworthy.

Chief Works

The *Forsyte* series (note the symbolic name suggesting foresight and acumen) is actually a double trilogy. The first trilogy, *The Forsyte Saga,* consists of *The Man of Property* (1906), *In Chancery* (1920), and *To Let* (1921). At the time of the writing of *The Man of Property* Galsworthy did not conceive of the novel as the beginning of a series; this notion seems to have come to him only much later. Thus the long lapse of time before the second novel appeared.

The Forsyte Saga: The story begins in 1886 as the Forsyte clan gathers at the home of old Jolyon Forsyte; the occasion is the engagement of Jolyon's granddaughter, June, to Philip Bosinney, a talented but somewhat Bohemian young architect. Also a member of this third generation, is Soames Forsyte, the "man of property," the son of James Forsyte and grandson of old Jolyon. Soames is the central figure of the trilogy: his fierce ambition to succeed and his tendency to equate success with property are the major themes of the work. Soames is married to Irene, a sensitive and romantic young woman who fits rather poorly into the Forsyte clan because of her willfulness. Irene is the antithesis of Soames; a symbol of "Beauty impinging on a possessive world," she stands for the realm of love, of emotion, and of art that Soames cannot appreciate. By an unlucky chance Soames commissions June's fiancé, Bosinney, to design a country house. Bosinney and Irene fall in love in spite of the honest efforts of both to avoid this catastrophe, and the situation soon becomes obvious to the entire family. June reluctantly agrees to abandon her lover; but Soames, driven not by sexual jealousy but by a frenetic obsession that his property—his wife—is being tampered with by a member of the unpropertied Bohemian class, forces his marital rights onto Irene, torments her physically and mentally, and completely breaks off her relations with Bosinney. He further manages to ruin Bosinney by suing him over the contract for the house. Bosinney, wrecked emotionally and financially, is run over by a bus in a London fog. Irene, as we learn in the interlude *Indian Summer of a Forsyte,* actually escapes from Soames, supports herself by giving music lessons, and devotes herself to caring for Old Jolyon in his last years. The portrayal of the decline and death of Old Jolyon is one of the high points of the trilogy.

In *In Chancery* the narrative is taken up again after the war. Soames, now driven by a desire to procreate a son to inherit his property, seeks a reconciliation with his wife. She, however, is attracted to Young Jolyon, June's father; she divorces Soames and marries Jolyon, and they produce a son, Jon. Soames desperately seeks a marriage with a French girl, Annette, who obligingly presents him with a child, Fleur.

In *To Let,* which opens almost a generation later, Jon, Irene's son, and Fleur, daughter of Soames and Annette, meet by chance and, in a manner reminiscent of Romeo and Juliet, fall in love in spite of the antagonism between their respective branches of the family. When Fleur learns the true extent of the quarrel, she is still determined to marry Jon. Soames, however, has picked out another suitor for his daughter: Michael Mont, a young aristocrat. To avoid Michael's attentions, Fleur tries to persuade Jon to an early marriage. She fails, however, because Young Jolyon reluctantly gives his son a letter revealing the origin of the hatred between Soames and Irene. Jon now realizes that the marriage is impossible; Soames' greedy machinations have ruined the lives of the family even to the second generation. Thus the true extent of the evils proceeding out of Soames' obsession with property are revealed; Fleur reluctantly marries Michael and Jon goes off to America.

It can be seen that, taken generally, *The Forsyte Saga* is concerned with the inevitable and endless conflict between two processes: Soames' effort to acquire and cherish his property, and the efforts of the Forsyte clan to incorporate new blood through exogamy. These two principles are basically incompatible, and thus arises the repetitive conflict of the novel.

A Modern Comedy: This second trilogy, consists of *The White Monkey* (1924), *The Silver Spoon* (1926), and *Swan Song* (1928). The history of Fleur is continued after her marriage with Michael Mont. Wilfrid Desert, a child of the Jazz Age who seems to have wandered in out of a novel of Scott Fitzgerald, attempts to seduce her from her husband. In the end, however, morality and the family triumph; Fleur's Forsyte blood has made her essentially upstanding. In the last novel of the series Fleur encounters a more dangerous temptation: Her old passion for Jon, only partly submerged through her marriage with Michael, rises to the surface again. At length this infatuation destroys the last remnants of the Forsyte clan; Soames, in his old age, witnesses the final tragedy of the course of events his own possessiveness has set into motion. *A Modern Comedy* is somewhat different in style from *The Forsyte Saga,* but this is partly due to the difference in content of the two trilogies. The latter work, dealing with the callous and amoral era of the twenties, seems slightly more superficial in its analyses of character and social situation. It is also likely that Galsworthy, by this time approaching old age, did not properly understand the 1920s, and saw them only with the weary and disapproving eye of a superannuated Edwardian.

End of Chapter: Galsworthy wrote a third trilogy on the Forsyte theme toward the end of his career, but *End of a Chapter* is generally conceded to be an inferior work. It consists of *Maid in Waiting* (1931), *Flowering Wilderness* (1932), and *Over the River* (1933). The work chiefly concerns Dinny Charwell, a relative of Fleur's husband Michael Mont, and her romance with Wilfrid Desert, who had previously attempted to break up the marriage of Fleur and Michael. There are in addition several other Galsworthy works connected with the Forsyte material. The interludes connecting several of the novels, of which *Indian Summer of a Forsyte* has already been remarked, are really short stories or sketches; they might easily stand on their own as separate works. A volume of short stories concerned with the Forsytes was published in 1930 under the title *On Forsyte Change;* and several non-Forsyte novels, especially *Villa Rubein* (1900), contain passing references to the clan.

***Justice* (1910):** Galsworthy's most famous play, *Justice* exposes the ruthless savagery of the English legal system toward an essentially honest young man who has committed a minor offense. The hero, Falder, is a clerk in a law firm; he is in love with Ruth Honeywell, who is unhappily married and brutalized by her husband. In order to take Ruth out into the country Falder commits a small forgery. It is detected and he is sent to prison, although his counsel protests to the court that an excellent young man's life is being ruined over a triviality. After two years he is released on probation. He applies for a job at his old firm, but is told he must first give up Ruth. Since she has waited faithfully for him while he was in prison, he refuses to do this. At last, unable to get a job and harassed by the probation officials, Falder commits suicide rather than return to jail.

The message of this drama is that the true malefactors in society (Ruth's husband and Falder's employer) are often rewarded while the minions they enslave are punished for following their normal inclinations.

HISTORICAL BACKGROUND (1900 – 14)

In the years shortly after the death of Victoria in 1901, the Liberal party consolidated its influence and, in 1905, come into power as the governing party. Pledging a program of internal reform, the Liberals, with strong House of Commons constituencies, turned to questions of education, fair taxation, and other thorny matters. The legislative struggles in the period 1905 to 1910 yielded two significant changes in British government. The House of Commons assumed control of money measures as well as the ability to pass laws against the will of the Lords if the measures were passed at three successive sessions within a period of two years.

Important laws during this period included limitation of working hours, worker's compensation provisions, minimum wages in certain industries, and an old-age pension plan.

Consolidated also during this period into a more formal union was the British Commonwealth of Nations. Member states included Canada, which had gained self-government as a Dominion in 1867; Austrailia, which became an independent Commonwealth in 1901; New Zealand, which Parliament recognized as a Dominion in 1907; South Africa, formed as a Union in 1910; Ireland, which was given home rule in 1920 by a bill dividing the country into Northern and Southern Ireland, each with its own government (changed thereafter, in 1922, with the creation of the Irish Free State); India and Pakistan, given a degree of self-rule in 1919 but not granted full Dominion status until 1948; Egypt, a protectorate at first but, in 1936, given sovereignty; and many other British possessions (or former possessions), including Gibralter, Malta, British Malaya, Ceylon, North Borneo, Sarawak, Cyprus, British Guiana, the Falkland Island, and others.

Political Parties

In the last decades of the nineteenth century, the Social Democratic Federation was founded on Marxist principles by H.M. Hyndman. The party attracted some of the English intelligentsia, including Henry George (noted for his single tax theory) and the members of the Fabian Society (Sidney Webb, Shaw, and others). Although the Socialists had a strong voice in the English media, the party never developed into a major political power.

The Labour Party had grown in influence and membership since the time of Disraeli. The Independent Labour Party was organized in 1893. The courts tried to suppress the growing labor movement by ruling that unions were liable for damages done to an employer during strikes or by unlawful picketing. Such efforts only motivated the Labour Party to further gains. By 1906 the Labour Party had twenty-nine members in the House of Commons, and in later decades grew to be England's most powerful party.

The early years of the twentieth century also saw a dramatic shift away from the Conservative party to the Liberals. The social programs of the latter group included meal and medical programs for school children, city-planning provisions, and minimum wages. The Liberals remained in power until World War I began in 1914.

A note must be added about the question of the relevance of historical events to literary events. Although literature can hardly be said to exist in a vacuum apart from history, few authors would subscribe to the idea that history directly provokes literary art or that literature is little more than an imaginative reenactment of history. The influence of the First World War on Hemingway's fiction, for example, is undeniable; yet such novels as *For Whom the Bell Tolls* and *Farewell to Arms* are certainly more important to us as works about the influence of war in general than of a particular war or period.

Therefore, through the volumes of English, American, and World literature in this series we have chosen to present historical information without specifying the often dubious causal links to particular authors' intentions and achievements suggested by some critics. History, in other words, is treated here as one of several backdrops for literature, not as its prime mover.

REVIEW QUESTIONS

THE REALISTIC MOVEMENT

Multiple Choice

1. _____ Writers of the Realist movement tended to consider themselves
   a. humanitarians
   b. professional writers
   c. apolitical
   d. all of the above

2. _____ Realism can best be described as
   a. interested in the social conflicts of the day
   b. intentionally shocking
   c. interested in character
   d. interested in the impact of technology on society

3. _____ Thomas Hardy
   a. experimented with original verse forms
   b. wrote of characters unable to overcome the forces of circumstance
   c. set his novels in exotic locales
   d. considered poetry an idle recreation

4. _____ Thomas Hardy is known for
   a. his romantic poetry
   b. his optimistic philosophy
   c. his adventurous plots
   d. none of the above

5. _____ Arnold Bennett's novels are characterized by
   a. their meticulously documented backgrounds
   b. their idealized characters
   c. their melodramatic plots
   d. all of the above

6. _____ Naturalism differs from Realism in its emphasis on
   a. rural settings
   b. use of upper-class characters
   c. reliance upon pseudo-science
   d. political activism

7. _____ Realist authors
   a. tend to be optimistic about the future
   b. try to maintain an objective view of their characters
   c. deal only with the sordid aspects of life
   d. all of the above

8. _____ A connected series of novels was written by
   a. Maugham and Bennett
   b. Maugham and Galsworthy
   c. Bennett and Galsworthy
   d. none of the above

9. _____ Hardy's most successful novels are set in
   a. London
   b. exotic locales
   c. Wessex
   d. a wide variety of locales

10. _____ Marital unhappiness is a theme in
    a. Galsworthy's *Forsyte* saga
    b. Bennett's *Clayhanger* books
    c. Hardy's *Jude the Obscure*
    d. all of the above

True-False

11. _____ W. Somerset Maugham's most successful novel is based on his personal experiences.

12. _____ Arnold Bennett's novels deal with hopeless romantic love.

13. _____ Naturalistic style tends to be flat and documentary.

14. _____ *The Forsyte Saga* covers several generations of the same family.

15. _____ Naturalism and Realism were both a reaction against romantic sentimentality.

16. _____ *Tess of the d'Urbervilles* has one of Thomas Hardy's more melodramatic plots.

17. _____ W. Somerset Maugham has never visited any of the exotic settings he uses in some of his books.

18. _____ Thomas Hardy's poetry has always been more highly regarded than his novels.

19. _____ John Galsworthy was a staunch conservative who decried the efforts of the lower classes to ape their betters.

20. _____ Arnold Bennett was more comfortable writing about rural than urban life.

Matching

21. _____ Naturalism   a. *Clayhanger*
22. _____ Realism   b. *Of Human Bondage*
23. _____ Angel Clare   c. "Rain"
24. _____ Soames Forsyte   d. pseudo-scientific approach
25. _____ Philip Carey   e. *The Return of the Native*
26. _____ Sadie Thompson   f. dealt with ordinary life
27. _____ Eustacia Vye   g. *The Old Wives' Tale*
28. _____ Sophia Scales   h. *The Mayor of Casterbridge*
29. _____ Michael Henchard   i. *The Man of Property*
30. _____ Helen Lessways   j. *Tess of the d'Urbervilles*

Fill-in

31. W. Somerset Maugham used the life of Paul Gaugin in his novel _____.

32. A major influence on the English Naturalists was the French writer _____.

33. The French influences on English Realism were Stendhal, Balzac, and _____.

34. Thomas Hardy's long narrative poem on the Napoleonic Wars was _____.

35. The impact of property on character is a major theme in John Galsworthy's _____.

36. Thomas Hardy's poetry, though modern and pessimistic in its themes and tone, is basically _____ in its prosody.

37. Injustice is a frequent theme in _____ plays.

38. Bennett's *The Old Wives' Tale* is set in England and in _____.

39. The author in this group who is generally considered a "popular" novelist is _____.

40. Of this group of authors, the one who wrote most frequently about wealthy characters is _____.

Answers

1.	d	15.	T	29.	h
2.	c	16.	T	30.	a
3.	b	17.	F	31.	*The Moon and Sixpence*
4.	d	18.	F		
5.	a	19.	F	32.	Emile Zola
6.	c	20.	F	33.	Flaubert
7.	b	21.	d	34.	*The Dynasts*
8.	c	22.	f	35.	*Forsyte* saga
9.	c	23.	j	36.	conventional
10.	d	24.	i	37.	Galsworthy's
11.	T	25.	b	38.	France
12.	F	26.	c	39.	Maugham
13.	T	27.	e	40.	Galsworthy
14.	T	28.	g		

Part 3

THE REACTION TO REALISM

WORKS AT A GLANCE

E. M. Forster

1905	*Where Angels Fear to Tread*	1924	*A Passage to India*
1907	*The Longest Journey*	1927	*Aspects of the Novel*
1908	*A Room with a View*	1951	*Essays*
1910	*Howards End*	1953	*The Hill of Devi*

D. H. Lawrence

1911	*The White Peacock*	1928 –	*Lady Chatterley's*
1913	*Sons and Lovers*	29	*Lover*
1915	*The Rainbow*	1931	*The Man Who Died*
1921	*Women in Love*	1926	*The Plumed Serpent*
1923	*The Fox*		

Christopher Isherwood

1928	*All the Conspirators*	1954	*The World in the Evening*
1932	*The Memorial*	1958	*All the Conspirators*
1935	*The Last of Mr. Norris*	1964	*A Single Man*
1939	*Goodbye to Berlin*	1966	*Exhumations*
1945	*Prater Violet*	1967	*A Meeting by the River*

(For collaborations, see W. H. Auden)

Ivy Compton-Burnett

1911	*Dolores*	1947	*Manservant and*
1925	*Pastors and Masters*		*Maidservant*
1929	*Brothers and*	1949	*Two Worlds and Their Ways*
	Sisters	1963	*A God and His Gifts*

Rudyard Kipling

1886	*Departmental Ditties,* poetry		"Fuzzy-Wuzzy," "Danny Deever," "Mandalay"
1888	*Plain Tales from the Hills*	1899	*Stalkey and Co.*
1892	*Barrack-Room Ballads,* poetry: "Gunga Din,"	1901	*Kim*

Joseph Conrad

1895	*Almayer's Folly*	1907	*The Secret Agent*
1897	*The Nigger of the Narcissus*	1911	*Under Western Eyes*
1900	*Lord Jim*	1912	*The Secret Sharer, A*
1902	*Youth, Heart of Darkness*		*Personal Record*
1903	*Typhoon*	1915	*Victory*
1904	*Nostromo*		

Ford Madox Ford

1915	*The Good Soldier*
1924	*Some Do Not*
1925	*No More Parades*
1926	*A Man Could Stand Up*
1928	*Last Post*

In collaboration with Joseph Conrad:

1901	*The Inheritors*
1903	*Romance*
1924	*The Nature of a Crime*

Christopher Fry

1935	*She Shall Have Music*
1937	*Siege, The Boy with the Cart*
1946	*A Phoenix Too Frequent*
1948	*Thor, with Angels; The Lady's Not for Burning*
1950	*Venus Observed*
1951	*A Sleep of Prisoners*
1954	*The Dark is Light Enough*
1961	*Curtmantle*

Virginia Woolf

1915	*The Voyage Out* (written 1909)
1919	*Night and Day*
1921	*Monday or Tuesday*
1922	*Jacob's Room*
1925	*Mrs. Dalloway*
1927	*To the Lighthouse*
1928	*Orlando*

Katherine Mansfield

1911	*In a German Pension,* "The-Child-Who-Was-Tired"
1914	"At the Bay"
1918	*Prelude*
1919	*Je ne parles pas français*

James Joyce

1914	*Dubliners*
1916	*A Portrait of the Artist as a Young Man*
1922	*Ulysses*
1939	*Finnegans Wake*

Joyce Cary

1932	*Aissa Saved*
1940	*Charley Is My Darling*
1941	*Herself Surprised, A House of Children*
1942	*To Be a Pilgrim*
1944	*The Horse's Mouth*
1952	*Prisoner of Grace*
1953	*Except the Lord*
1955	*Not Honour More*
1959	*The Captive and the Free*

Lawrence Durrell

1935	*Pied Piper of Lovers*
1937	*Panic Spring*
1938	*The Black Book*
1945	*Prospero's Cell*
1946	*Cities, Plains and People*
1948	*On Seeming to Presume*
1950	*Sappho*
1952	*Keys to Modern British Poetry*
1953	*Reflections on a Marine Venus*
1957	*Bitter Lemons, Justine*
1958	*Balthazar, Mountolive*
1960	*Clea*
1963	*An Irish Faustus*
1965	*Acte*
1968	*Tunc*
1970	*Nunquam*

William Butler Yeats

1890	"The Lake Isle of Innisfree"	1927	"Among School Children"
1892	*The Countess Cathleen*	1928	*The Tower*
1894	*The Land of Heart's Desire,* "The Cap and Bells"	1929	*The Winding Stair,* "A Dialogue of Self and Soul," "Byzantium"
1907	*Deirdre*	1930–	"Crazy Jane" poems
1916	"The Wild Swans at Coole"	33	
1921	*Calvary*	1931	*Resurrection*
1923	"Leda and the Swan"	1939	*Purgatory*
1925	*A Vision*		
1926	"Sailing to Byzantium"		

Augusta, Lady Gregory

1902	*Cuchulain of Muirthemne*	1907	*The Workhouse Ward, The Rising of the Moon*
1904	*Spreading the News*	1909	*Seven Short Plays*

John Millington Synge

1903	*The Shadow of the Glen*	1907	*The Playboy of the Western World*
1904	*Riders to the Sea*	1909	*Deirdre of the Sorrows*
1905	*The Well of the Saints*		

Sean O'Casey

1923	*The Shadow of a Gunman*	1940	*The Stars Turn Red, Purple Dust*
1924	*Juno and the Paycock*	1943	*Red Roses for Me*
1926	*The Plough and the Stars*	1955	*The Bishop's Bonfire*
1928	*The Silver Tassie*	1958	*The Drums of Father Ned*

Lord Dunsany

1909	*The Glittering Gate*

Paul Vincent Carroll

1931	*The Watched Pot*	1934	*Shadow and Substance*

James Stephens

1912	*The Crock of Gold* "The Goat Paths" "Buile Said in a Pub"	"The Red-Haired Man's Wife" "Righteous Anger"

Brendan Behan

1956	*The Quare Fellow*	1963	*Hold Your Hour and Have Another*
1958	*The Hostage, Borstal Boy*	1965	*Confessions of an Irish Rebel*

Frank O'Connor

1932	*The Saint and Mary Kate*	1968	*My Father's Son*
1940	*Dutch Interior*		"My Oedipus Complex"
1956	*The Mirror in the Roadway*		"The Drunkard"
1961	*An Only Child*		"News for the Church"
1962	*The Lonely Voice*		

Mary Lavin

1938	"Miss Holland"	1958	"The Living"
1945	*The House of Clewe Street*	1970	"Happiness"
1950	*Mary O'Grady*		

4
LITERATURE OF PSYCHOLOGY AND ANALYSIS

Today the term *psychological literature* is used in many different senses. In the France of the seventeenth century it referred to the analysis of moral sentiments and the conflict of ideas of right and wrong in the minds of tragic heroes. In the nineteenth century the term *psychological novel* was applied to novels of the type written by Stendhal, in which the hero's inner conflicts and motivations were examined for the reader, where the hero thought about his own actions and emotions. Later in the century the works of Poe, Baudelaire, and Dostoevsky were termed "psychological" because these authors were preoccupied with unusual or abnormal states of mind. Psychology in Henry James came to mean a minute examination of character motivation and point of view. All of these elements are reproduced in the literature of the twentieth century as a part of the broader reaction against external Realism. E. M. Forster treats moral problems from the psychological point of view; Ivy Compton-Burnett concerns herself chiefly with analysis of the motivations of her characters as revealed almost exclusively and advertently or inadvertently in their own dialogue; and D. H. Lawrence and Christopher Isherwood concentrate their attention on the sexual and neurotic complexes popularized by the Freudian and other schools of psychoanalysis.

These authors differ widely in content and technique, but they are essentially alike in their purpose: to present human motivation from the inside, from the point of view of the mind concerned, rather than from the point of view of an external observer. Some are influenced by modern psychiatry, others react strongly against it, and still others seem to ignore it entirely. They agree, however, that it is inside the human brain that significant battles of life take place, and that mental conflicts have a subtlety, and intensity, and an importance far beyond what might be expected from mere external examination of a human being. Miss Compton-Burnett may seem the stranger in the group, but she would be a stranger in any group.

E. M. FORSTER (1879–1970)

E. M. Forster was a careful and conscientious author who wrote slowly and had a fervent respect for his craft. His social attitudes were those of a cultivated and liberal English gentleman; he was simultaneously moderate in temperament and faithfully consecrated to liberal humanism. His novels are carefully worked studies of emotional conflict between individuals, and the often-remarked social content in them is latent and secondary. His characters seek above all understanding, brotherhood, kinship, and broader experience, but are frustrated by human conventions: the proprieties of university life in *The Longest Journey,* racial prejudices and stereotypes in *A Passage to India,* and conventions of a half-dozen types in *A Room with a View.*

IMPORTANCE

Forster is not a moralist. He is, in fact, opposed to morality in the ordinary sense and believes that clear thinking and understanding between men are more important than all the social taboos in the world. At the same time he possesses a definite ethic and incorporates it into each of his novels. He believes the most basic human impulse is the desire of individuals to understand one another; he believes as well that it is the duty of each person to seek out his true nature and then pursue it fearlessly in spite of social censure, and he thinks the individual rather than the group must be our ultimate measuring-stick. These ideas are neither striking nor original, but Forster presents them with a faithful and convincing perspicacity.

Forster's characterization is entirely internal; he has little interest in the outward semblance of the person. Nevertheless, like André Gide, he likes to present a character as he appears to various friends in succession, or under a variety of aspects. He begins by describing one character of a novel, allowing us to enter into the man's thoughts, and simultaneously treats us to the character's evaluation of his friends and intimates. Then he enters into the mind of a second character; we see the same scenes, the same persons, from another vantage. Thus Forster demonstrates the relativity, not only of moral systems, but of our very estimates of human character.

Forster's prose is terse and economical without being laconic. There is very little exposition; he allows us to see the events taking place instead of merely telling us about them. He has a delicate feeling for images and metaphors, and his flair for dialogue is remarkable, especially in the case of aristocratic Britons. (His Indians and Americans do not come through quite so well.) His novels are structurally perfect; Forster is a painstaking workman of the type of Henry James in this respect. If Forster has faults, they are his paucity of original ideas and his lack of positive criticism; he seldom offers a solution to the lack of understanding and intolerance he demonstrates, which may also be construed as an artistic strength rather than a weakness.

Life

Edward Morgan Forster was born in England in 1879; his ancestry was partly Welsh on his father's side. He attended Tonbridge School as a day boy and went on to King's College, Cambridge, where he formed an important friendship with the professor, critic, and author G. Lowes Dickinson. He wrote a biography of Dickinson in 1934, and the older man's aesthetic and literary ideas undoubtedly influenced his early experiments in technique. He began writing as a young man; his first short stories appeared shortly after the turn of the century and his first novel, *Where Angels Fear to Tread,* in 1905. He continued to produce novels, one of the best, *Howards End,* appearing in 1910, and in addition turned out literary essays, travel notes, and reviews at a steady rate that gradually slowed down to a halt. He spent several years in Italy and made two trips to India (1911 and 1921); he used these two countries as the locales of two important novels, *A Room with a View* and *A Passage to India.* In 1927 he was invited to deliver the annual Clark Lectures at Cambridge, and produced the important essays published as *Aspects of the Novel,* which appeared later the same year.

A Passage to India (1924) was Forster's last novel, but there were additional short stories and essays, a fine history and travel guide on *Alexandria* (published in 1922 and in enlarged form in 1938), which makes an excellent companion to the reading of Lawrence Durrell's *Alexandria Quartet,* and *Abinger Harvest—A Miscellany* (1936). During these years he made his home for a time in a village in Surrey. Following the Second World War his last two books appeared: *Two Cheers for Democracy* (essays, 1951) and *The Hill of Devi* (1953), a last travel book on India. Forster moved into quarters at King's College, Cambridge, where he lived as an honorary fellow, receiving a steady flow of admirers, including Eudora Welty, until his death on June 7, 1970 in Coventry. The *New York Times* in its next day's tribute remarked on the unusual fact that although he had published no novel for over forty years, his reputation as a novelist had not diminished but, if anything, had reached classic status.

Chief Novels

***The Longest Journey* (1907):** This is a study of marriage, especially of the breakdown of the institution in modern western society. Rickie Elliott, the protagonist, is a physically weak but spiritually sensitive young man reared in a broken family; his highly cultured father scorned his mother and eventually drove her into a liaison with a lover. From this union was born Rickie's half-brother, Stephen, who becomes important later in the novel. The action follows Rickie through Cambridge, where he forms a binding intellectual attachment with the philosophy student Stewart Ansell; as his sexual nature develops, he seeks to find the same sort of companionship with a woman. He marries Agnes Pembroke, a robust girl whose athlete fiancé, Gerald Dawes, has been killed in a football accident, but the marriage is doomed from the beginning. Agnes provides little intellectual companionship for Rickie, and she finds him insipid after the virile Gerald. She, the stronger, begins to dominate the marriage; she finds Rickie a job assisting her brother Herbert in a grubby private school. Rickie appears to be doomed to a life of monotonous compromise. At this point he encounters his half-brother Stephen, and in the dissolute and romantic child of his mother's illicit affair he sees a symbol of escape. He runs off with Stephen and is eventually killed performing what is virtually his first overt physical act: he attempts to rescue the drunken Stephen at a grade crossing and is run down by a train. His death is a sort of victory, since he has demonstrated his courage and overcome his lack of will power. The incident is also the making of Stephen; he marries and begins a useful life as a farmer.

A Room with a View (1908): This complex study of social conventions and their effect on individual human beings opens in the Pension Bertolini in Florence, where Lucy Honeychurch, a well-bred young British girl, has just arrived with her elder cousin and chaperone, Charlotte Bartlett. They soon discover their room has no view; the concept of the "room with a view" is presented throughout the novel as a symbol of the life with broader aspects of experience. Young George Emerson and his father, guests in the pension, surrender their room and provide Lucy with her view, both in the literal and the symbolic sense. Shortly after this, Lucy happens to witness a murder in a Florentine square; she swoons, and George happens along to carry her to a nearby church. The combination of violence and intimacy in this experience awakens Lucy to an entirely new vista; her emotional windows have been opened. She temporarily forgets Cecil Vyse, her fiancé in England, and allows herself to be kissed by George in a bed of violets. When she ill-advisedly mentions this incident to her chaperone, it finds its way into a novel written by Eleanor Lavish, a silly female author. Later in England Cecil unwittingly reads this passage to Lucy and George, to their intense embarrassment. Lucy, impatient with the superficial Cecil, turns definitely to George and finally marries him in spite of the objections of her family.

The plot of *A Room with a View* is actually a complex pattern impossible to synopsize. Lucy, before she is done, revolts against at least three sorts of conventions: she rejects Miss Lavish's Bohemian clichés, she becomes bored with Cecil's British respectability, and she rejects Charlotte's bourgeois and hypocritical morality. George likewise rejects the convention of middle-class marriage; he seeks in Lucy a woman who can love a man and at the same time retain her independence.

Howards End (1910): Among other things this novel studies the strangling encroachments of industrial wealth, the creeping outward of the metropolis (in this case London) threatening to engulf the good life of country estates like Howards End, which represents the old values of manners, tolerance, and understanding. Its theme, stated as an epigraph, is "Only connect . . ."; two separate worlds are seen in two families: the Schlegel sisters (half German, half English), Margaret and Helen, who live for the inner life of personal relationships and culture, and the Wilcox family, tough but limited, efficient but unimaginative, Henry and his sons Charles and Paul. The woman between is the first Mrs. Wilcox who, after her death, becomes a kind of goddess symbolizing female and illocial wisdom (her counterpart appears subsequently as Mrs. Moore in *A Passage to India*). Other symbols include the music of Beethoven's Fifth Symphony, an elm, the King's Cross railway station, six Danish tumuli, a painting; but the story moves with subtlety and complexity through considerable action — Margaret's marriage with the widower, Helen's love affair with Leonard Bast of the lower classes and the illegitimate child, the killing of Leonard by Charles Wilcox and his prison term — on the whole a good deal of violence. And all is not well at the end; there is a kind of uneasy truce. But many critics, including Lionel Trilling, feel that this is Forster's masterpiece. Problems are placed in a very clear light.

A Passage to India (1924): Less complex structurally than some of the preceding novels, it achieves even more subtlety in its characterizations. It is usually considered Forster's masterwork. The scene is laid in the Indian city of Chandrapore. Cyril Fielding, a young British visitor, makes friends with Dr. Aziz, an Indian physician who has tried desperately to Anglicize himself and to gain acceptance into British society. Failing this, he has become outwardly scornful and inwardly resentful toward the whites. The remaining three important characters are Adela Quested, a supercilious but basically decent young British girl; her fiancé, Heaslop; and his mother, Mrs. Moore. Mrs. Moore, a worldly-wise and compassionate woman, tries to make friends with the Indians, especially with Dr. Aziz, but is puzzled by their stiff pride. The climax occurs when Adela, on an expedition to visit some nearby caves, is attacked by a mysterious Indian and is persuaded to accuse Dr. Aziz of the crime. The town is torn by the trial; Indian is set against Briton, and the whole fabric of British invulnerability is put into question. Adela, seized with an attack of conscience, retracts her charge, but the damage is done. Mrs. Moore departs for home and dies on shipboard; Aziz, terribly embittered, is freed. Later Fielding is married to Mrs. Moore's daughter Stella. In a final chapter Aziz and Fielding discuss their differences and try to arrive at a common understanding; their conversation ends in an argument, and nothing good comes of it.

The primary theme of this novel is the impossibility of true understanding between human beings, especially those of diverse backgrounds. Mrs. Moore represents Christianity; Dr. Aziz, the Moslem religion; a Professor Godbole, Hinduism. They meet in India, but each is inadequate. Godbole calls to his god: "Come, come, come," but he never comes. Mrs. Moore in the caves thinks of "poor little talkative Christianity," and all its words amount to nothing. One of the brilliant comments on racial intolerance is the coining of the phrase "pinko-grey" to denote more accurately the "white" man, and the unclean feeling it carries with it. Other themes treated are Anglo-Indian relations in India and the nature of the Indian personality, the flaws in the Western legal system with its heavy reliance on evidence of witnesses, and the awakening of understanding and character in the heroine, Adela, with whom, however, Fielding is not entirely happy. Forster consistently denies us a "lived happily ever after" ending.

D. H. LAWRENCE (1885–1930)

The novels of D. H. Lawrence are not very shocking today; it is difficult to appreciate the violent controversy they caused on their original publication in the twenties. More than any other single author, Lawrence has served to bring the subject of sexual relations into the open and admit it as a fit subject for conversation. Moreover, entirely apart from his contribution to the crusade against Puritanism, Lawrence made a valuable contribution to the art of the novel; the tumult over the subject matter of his novels has often obscured the fact that he is a talented and original novelist from the point of view of technique.

Lawrence is sometimes considered the novelist of Freudianism. It is true he shares many of Freud's concepts, especially the idea of the libido as a source of creative energy. To Lawrence, however, sexual satisfaction is only a part of a wider struggle toward self-realization. The goal of human life should be to come into an understanding of one's personality and energies. In a Puritan culture it is chiefly the sexual energies that society seeks to control or frustrate, and thus sexual revolt is the first action the individual must take in this process. Lawrence labored first of all, in his own words, "to make the sex relation valid and precious, instead of shameful." He did not, however, consider himself primarily an author of sexual problems. Naturally it is possible that he misjudged the significance of his own work in this respect.

IMPORTANCE

The male characters of Lawrence's novels fall roughly into three groups in their attitude toward sexual life. The first group, modern intellectuals, Puritans, and bourgeois, have intellectualized love and marriage to the point where these experiences become mere conventions. In Lady Chatterley's Lover, Clifford Chatterley, symbolically paralyzed from the hips down, is an overrefined intellectual who thinks only in words. The second type is epitomized in Michaelis, a déclassé Bohemian playwright who has rejected bourgeois and aristocratic morals but is capable of only a thin and artificial sensuality; he is a sort of amateur fin-de-siecle decadent. Naturally his attitude toward sex is no more valid and genuine than that of Chatterley. The third male of this novel, the gamekeeper Mellors, is the Lawrentian man *par excellence.* He has none of the inhibitions of the Puritan; he does not intellectualize love, but rather feels it through his blood. Neither is he a sex-obsessed decadent like Michaelis; he considers sexual satisfaction no more important than the satisfaction of any other natural drive. At the same time he is capable of real tenderness, since his tenderness is entirely unaffected. He has never been deluded by the tradition of literary or conventional love; thus he is free to follow the natural inclination to tenderness that every man has buried within him. Lawrence mistrusts rationality; it is not the overclever and sophisticated mind we must follow, but the blood, which can never err.

As a novelist Lawrence is little interested in technical innovation. He follows a conventional novel structure and his prose style is conservative. His chief originality lies in his use of symbols; there is almost no important action, no character, no salient object in Lawrence that does not have its levels of meaning. Clifford's paralysis *(Lady Chatterley's Lover)* is symbolic of the sexual inhibition of respectable society, and the submission of Kate to an illiterate but noble Indian in *The Plumed Serpent* symbolizes the defeat of the overintellectualized European woman before the overpowering force of the blood. He is little interested in tight plot; his novels are merely loosely linked conversations, emotional crises, and thinly connected incidents. Another technical device he shares with André Gide: He does not believe in the consistency of character, and prefers to show that human beings normally act in an inconsistent and even self-contradictory manner.

Life

David Herbert Lawrence was born in 1885 in the grimy colliery town of Eastwood in Nottinghamshire. His father was a miner and his mother, a woman of superior intellect and education, a teacher. Lawrence was one of five children, and his childhood was blighted by poverty, illness, and the drinking of his father. Encouraged by his mother, he passed through high school on a scholarship and eventually qualified himself as a teacher; in the years before his writing was recognized, he taught at an elementary school at Croydon, near London.

During this youthful period Lawrence was much influenced by "E. T.," a girl who figures as the Miriam of *Sons and Lovers.* Although Lawrence described this relationship, a purely platonic one, in *A Personal Record,* he preferred to keep the identity of his companion a secret. Meanwhile he began writing; his first novel, *The White Peacock,* appeared in 1911. In April of 1912 Lawrence met Frieda Weekley, née Frieda von Richthofen, wife of a Nottingham professor. The two were immediately attracted to each other and soon eloped; when Prof. Weekley was granted a divorce two years later, they were married. Although the couple sometimes quarreled, Frieda was in many ways a personification of the Lawrentian woman of fiction; she remained a great influence on Lawrence during the rest of his career.

After his marriage Lawrence began moving in British literary circles; his friends included Katherine Mansfield, J. M. Murry, and Sir Herbert Asquith. During the First World War Lawrence and his German-born wife, who did not seek to conceal their indifference toward the war, were closely surveyed by the police and ordered to leave a Cornwall town where they had been indiscreet in the showing of lights. The Lawrences travelled extensively in Europe both before and after the war; they lived in Italy from 1919 to 1922.

As early as 1915 Lawrence's novels were in trouble with the censors. The real tumult, however, came with the attempted publication of *Lady Chatterley's Lover* in 1928. First printed in Florenc, the book was banned by British and American censors, but was widely pirated. Bowdlerized versions were eventually admitted to both countries. Then in the spring of 1959 Grove Press of New York brought out the full text of *Lady Chatterley's Lover,* and Postmaster General Summerfield banned the book from the mails. This launched the second most famous court test of "obscenity" laws in this country (the first being the case of *Ulysses* in 1933). Judge Frederick Bryan of the U. S. District Court of New York handed down his opinion on July 21, 1959, that this novel "is not obscene, and that to ban it from the mails is illegal." *Lady Chatterley's Lover* was finally officially recognized as a work of art.

The Lawrences spent the winters of 1922 and 1924 in Taos, New Mexico, where they were presented with a ranch by a wealthy admirer, Mrs. Mabel Dodge Luhan. A visit to Mexico produced the novel *The Plumed Serpent* (1926). The next few years were spent in Italy, where Lawrence's health rapidly worsened. He had been subject to lung disease from his boyhood, and from 1929 on spent most of his time in sanatoriums. He died at Vence, in Southern France, in 1930. Mrs. Lawrence subsequently setttled permanently in New Mexico. The number of critical studies of D. H. Lawrence that have appeared in the fifties and sixties is phenomenal and bears comparison with those on Ford Madox Ford and F. Scott Fitzgerald, if not quite equal in number to those on Joyce and Faulkner. There is even something of a Melville-like revival, including a spate of new films like *The Fox, The Virgin and the Gipsy,* and *Women in Love.*

Chief Novels and Novellas

Sons and Lovers **(1913):** This was Lawrence's first widely successful book. The details are largely autobiographical, although Lawrence greatly reorganized his personal experiences and altered attitudes in some cases. The theme is the conflict in a young man's mind between affection for his mother and sexual attraction to two different women. Paul, the hero, is the son of the alcoholic coal miner, Walter Morel, and a refined and heroic schoolteacher, Gertrude Morel. Gertrude, turning in loathing from her husband, lavishes all her affection on her children, especially the sickly and sensitive Paul. She nurses him through a terrible illness caught while working in a garment factory; during this period the obsessive and quasi-sexual element in her love becomes apparent. During his convalescence Paul meets Miriam Leivers, spiritual and intense, who appreciates Paul's literary talents but is afraid of physical contact with him. The mother mistrusts Miriam because she threatens to dominate the whole soul of her son and leave nothing for the mother. Later Paul meets Clara Dawes, a married woman, and becomes intimate with her. During the remainder of the novel he vacillates between these two loves—one pure and spiritual and the other carnal—without gaining complete satisfaction from either. His mother dies of cancer, and Paul realizes that her smothering maternalism has forever inhibited his attitude toward women. In the final scene, however, Paul, wandering in the darkness on the outskirts of town, rejects the shadows that symbolize his mother's dominance over him and turns courageously away to walk toward the lights of the city.

Women in Love (1921): Somewhat more complex than *Sons and Lovers,* it involves two separate man-woman relationships. The central characters are Ursula and Gudrun Brangwen, intellectual young schoolteachers, and Gerald Crich and Rupert Birkin, their lovers. Ursula and Rupert marry, and Gerald and Gudrun accompany them to Basle. The married couple, suspicious of the complacency and monotony of conventional marriage, leave their companions and wander about Europe without fixing themselves in any one spot; their relationship is relatively satisfactory. As for Gerald and Gudrun, their extramarital relationship is more oppressive than marriage. Gerald is obsessed by his possessiveness toward Gudrun, and she is dismayed at his continual greedy importunacies. When Gudrun begins paying some attention to Loerke, a German sculptor, Gerald attacks Loerke and almost kills Gudrun; at the last moment he weakens and wanders off to fall to his death in a glacier. The dominant theme of the novel is the difficulty of real understanding between persons of the opposite sex. Gudrun and Gerald, dominated by their lusts, achieve a less satisfactory relationship than Ursula and Rupert, who manage to balance their passions and who avoid excessive possessiveness. The film based on this novel and released in the relatively permissive year of 1970 recreated some of the earlier controversy over Lawrence. It is a fine film and sensitively transfers the novel to the cinematic medium.

The Rainbow (1915): This novel, about the life of grandparents, parents, and the early life of Ursula, concentrates on the evolution of relationships between men and women through the three generations of that family, spanning the major cultural changes during the rise of the industrial age. Lawrence questions the ability of the self to survive the alarming social changes brought by urban industrialism and the decay of family structures. The first generation of the novel focuses on Tom and Lydia Brangwen, who live in a rural area. They feel their relationship to be moderately satisfying, though neither feels that they are living up to their marital obligations of intellectual intimacy. The next generation in the novel concentrates on Tom's stepdaughter, Anna, and her husband, Will Brangwen, Tom's nephew. They are disappointed to discover that they cannot live solely for each other. Their conflict comes primarily from her motherhood, which her husband feels deprives him of the lover he had married. Finally, they compromise, with her domination of their daytime lives and his domination during the night. He devotes his attention to their daughter, Ursula, to make up for his wife's lack of attention, and it is Ursula's life that is the third generation. Her love for a lieutenant is ruined by her possessiveness and independence, which drive him away. After reconciliations and proposals, they decide that they are not compatible. Too late she discovers she is pregnant and offers herself to him, but he is already married to another woman. She loses the child and while convalescing sees a rainbow, which she hopefully interprets as a good omen. The rainbow symbolizes the ideal relationship between a man and woman where fully realized communion is compatible with an actualized self.

In *The Rainbow,* Lawrence allows form to follow function. If we grant that the day-to-day experiences of human life are often both shifting and inexplicable, so we must be ready to grant Lawrence the freedom in the narrative structure of *The Rainbow* to eschew Edwardian stability, control, and predictability. Just as the English Romantic poet John Keats had argued for the necessity of "negative capability" for the modern artist fated to endure ambiguity and insecurity, so Lawrence suggests that the readers' ability to cope with narrative ambiguity and formlessness is a mark of philosophical and aesthetic maturity.

***The Fox* (1923):** This novella is representative of Lawrence's work in the middle genre. He has successes in all three (and relative failures): the short story ("The Rocking-Horse Winner," "The Prussian Officer," "The Lovely Lady"); the novella (including *St. Mawr, The Virgin and the Gipsy,* and *The Man Who Died*); and the novel. *The Fox* is the story of two women and a man and a fox, which represents male sexual dominance and insistence. As the story opens, the two women who call each other regularly by their last names, March and Banford, are trying to run a chicken farm; and the fox is a predator. Henry Grenfel, a soldier who joined up in Canada, is back from the war and has come to the farm, which had belonged to his grandfather before the old man died. Henry had not heard of his death. He is the intruder on what looks more and more like a lesbian menage, although apparently a latent, unacknowledged one. Henry falls in love with Nellie March, and she is fascinated by him since he looks so much like the fox. He stays at the farm, doing odd jobs, with the reluctant approval of the women. When he asks

March to marry him, there is open hostility between Banford and Henry, both pulling on March. Henry kills the fox and extracts a promise from March to marry him at Christmas time and go away to Canada with him. When he goes back to his army post, Banford manipulates March into changing her mind and telling him so by letter. On emergency leave he returns to the farm where the girls are trying to chop down a huge tree. Henry swings the axe and manages the fall of the tree so that it kills Banford. He hopes that March will now be emotionally free to become his real wife — and in time and in Canada, she may.

The Man Who Died **(1931):** This sensitive story is told with quiet and lyric beauty about Christ, who is never named, and what happened to him after he almost died and had been left for dead in the tomb; the story parallels the return of vitality of a magnificent cock who has been tied by the leg in a peasant's yard. Lawrence had one serious quarrel with Christianity: its asceticism, which taught that the flesh was unholy. The man who died has different attitudes toward life after his experience and his slow return to living in the house of the peasant. He meets Madeleine (Mary Magdalen) and tries to express to her (with a *noli me tangere* for all his followers) this difference, "A sermon is so much more likely to cake into mud, and to close the fountains, than is a psalm or a song. I made a mistake." He leaves them for a time, having bought the cock and given him his freedom, setting out into the "phenomenal world." In part two he arrives at a temple to Isis, facing Egypt, and meets the priestess of Isis, who waits to become the bride of the dismembered Osiris. The symbolism shifts to yellow and white, to pigeons, to the winter narcissus, and the lotus buds of Egypt. Slowly the priestess heals the deep wound of the man who died until he is full risen. "His soul smote him with passion and compassion." The priestess and her companion fulfill themselves in love, the one thing needful to complete the human experience, the harmony between flesh and spirit finally achieved; and the man who had died rows away in a boat. The tone and the message of this novella are much like those of Hauptmann's *The Heretic of Soana,* although the stories are worlds apart in place, time, and characters. D. H. Lawrence had left this narrative to be published posthumously.

Lady Chatterley's Lover **(1928–29):** Originally titled *The First Lady Chatterley,* this is Lawrence's most famous novel. Constance Reid, a young girl with conventional romantic and intellectualized ideas of love, marries Clifford Chatterley, an elegant young man who is shortly after paralyzed from the waist down by a war injury. After the war the couple live on Clifford's Midlands estate. Although their life lacks sexual passion, they imagine themselves happy at first. Soon, however, Connie becomes dissatisfied; she attempts a tentative affair with Michaelis, an Irish writer and amateur Casanova. Clifford, who is aware of this development, is not sexually jealous, and even suggests that she provide an heir to the family through intercourse with her lover. But Connie's affair with Michaelis is artificial and unsatisfactory. In her disappointment she becomes friendly with Oliver Mellors, a declassé farmer, former army officer, and at present gamekeeper on the Chatterley estate. Mellors is a perfectly natural man. He belongs to no class, is devoid of conventional artificiality, and is sexually uninhibited; he does not, however, overemphasize the rôle of love as Michaelis does. Eventually Connie becomes pregnant by Mellors. Their affair, however, is endangered by the return of Mellors' estranged wife, who finds evidence of her husband's "transgression" and succeeds in getting him dismissed from his position. Connie confesses all to Clifford and asks him for a divorce, but he, objecting to the social degradation of her relations with a gamekeeper, angrily refuses. In spite of this Mellors finds a job on a farm and the couple look forward to their eventual reunion.

CHRISTOPHER ISHERWOOD (1904 – 86)

During the late twenties and thirties Isherwood was an intimate of that brilliant circle of young British authors that included W. H. Auden, Stephen Spender, and C. Day Lewis. Since he was primarily interested in character, however, he turned to prose fiction rather than to verse. His association with the poets Spender and Auden is nevertheless apparent in the finished precision of his prose, in his careful choice of words, and in his feeling for concrete imagery.

Isherwood's first venture into prose was a rather colorless novel, *All the Conspirators* (1928). *The Memorial* (1932) was similar; both novels were written somewhat in the manner of Evelyn Waugh but lacking Waugh's suave and ironic pace. But in the so-called "Berlin Stories" growing out of his experiences in Germany during the thirties Isherwood came into his own. *The Last of Mr. Norris* (1935; in Britain *Mr. Norris Changes Trains*) is a colorful character study of Arthur Norris, a middle-aged British expatriate in Berlin. Mr. Norris, amateur spy, enthusiastic masochist, and incurable egotist, resembles a character of Dostoyevsky more than he does anything else in English literature. The chief themes of the story are Mr. Norris' mysterious negotiations with the German Communist Party and with the Nazis, resulting finally in his disgrace and deportation, and his epic conflict with his brutal valet Schmidt, to whom he is psychologically bound by his masochistic tendencies.

Goodbye to Berlin (1939) is a similar character study; this time the subject is the attractive but dangerous demimondaine Sally Bowles. The book is semiautobiographical; the narrator is named Christopher Isherwood, although an author's introduction warns the reader that this narrator is not necessarily identical with the author of the book. Sally is a curious mixture of sophistication and naivete. She is affectionate but egocentric; she has difficulty in remaining faithful to anyone for very long. The narrator courts her intermittently and half-heartedly, but eventually abandons her to more fervent swains. This novel was dramatized by John Van Druten as *I Am a Camera,* and in this form was produced on Broadway. Both *The Last of Mr. Morris* and *Goodbye to Berlin* must be regarded as studies in abnormal sexual character.

Isherwood continued to write and publish at a steady pace, including novels of more than passing interest like *Prater Violet* (1945), *The World in the Evening* (1954), *All the Conspirators* (1958), *A Single Man* (1964), and *A Meeting by the River* (1967). For the dramas written in collaboration with W. H. Auden, see the Auden entry. There have also been volumes of reminiscences and miscellany like *Exhumations* (1966).

IVY COMPTON-BURNETT (1884? – 1969)

The term "novelist's novelist" has perhaps been overused, sometimes to explain public resistance to those difficult writers who demand the active collaboration and attention of readers for effective appreciation. It has been applied to Henry James; to the curious Henry Green (pseudonym for Henry Vincent Yorke, born in 1905) whose novels bear the single-word titles often participial: *Living, Loving, Concluding, Nothing, Doting, Caught;* and to Ivy Compton-Burnett. But James' audience has extended well beyond the limits of fiction writers, aided and abetted by the academic world, no doubt, and Ivy Compton-Burnett's audience seems to be in the process of similar expansion. Her themes and style appear at this point less limited than Green's in width of interest. One has to live with strangeness for a while before it becomes familiar. It is true that other novelists, rather than more professional literary critics, have made the initial discoveries of her worth and originality: Arnold Bennett, Pamela Hansford Johnson, Elizabeth Bowen, Robert Liddell, Hugh Walpole, Victoria Sackville-West, and Nathalie Sarraute, among the more prominent.

When *Brothers and Sisters* appeared in 1929, Arnold Bennett wrote, "I am not sure, but I think it quite possible that a novel lying at the moment here will one day be the cause of research, envy, covetousness and other vices: *Brothers and Sisters,* by I. Compton-Burnett. I have never heard of the author, who, I am informed, is a woman. Though by no means easy to read, it seems to be an original work, strong, and incontestably true to life. I. Compton-Burnett may be a new star, low on the eastern horizon." And Pamela Hansford Johnson in 1951 calls this comment "an astonishing example of critical acumen and foresight."

Nathalie Sarraute, one of the creators of the *Nouvenu Roman* in France, has made some even more startling observations on Ivy Compton-Burnett (relating Henry Green to her in their new emphasis on dialogue in the novel) in an essay, "Conversation and Subconversation," published originally in the *Nouvelle Revue Francaise* in 1956: "The absolutely original solution, which has both distinction and power, that she has found for them [the problems of dialogue in fiction], would suffice for her to deserve the position unanimously accorded her by English critics and by a certain portion of the English reading public; that is, the position of one of the greatest novelists that England has ever had." The unanimity and even the place *may* be exaggerated. She goes on to say that Compton-Burnett's books have one absolutely new feature, "that they are nothing but one long continuation of dialogue. Here again, the author presents them in the traditional manner, holding herself aloof, very ceremoniously aloof, from her characters, and limiting herself as a rule, just as the behaviorists do, to simply reproducing their words and quietly informing the reader, without trying to vary her formulas, by means of the monotonous 'said X,' 'said Y.'"

The "dialogued novel" is perhaps not all that new (some critics carrying it back to the Spanish *La Celestina* of 1499), at least seeing it in Galdos and Unamuno (look at his *Abel Sanchez,* 1917, for a stripped-down conversational novel), and Compton-Burnett does have some connective passages between dialogues, but her dialogues, "upon which everything rests," *are* distinctive and "have nothing in common with the short, brisk, lifelike conversations" that resemble the clouds of comic strips. "These long, stilted sentences, which are at once stiff and sinuous, do not recall any conversations we ever heard. And yet, although they seem strange, they never give the impression of being spurious or gratuitous."

The reason, according to Sarraute, is that they are located not in an imaginary but a real place, "somewhere on the fluctuating frontier that separates conversation from sub-conversation. Here the inner movements, of which the dialogue is merely the outcome . . . try to extend their action into the dialogue itself. To resist their constant pressure and contain them, the conversation stiffens." But the pressure in this close, subtle, savage game between conversation and subconversation permits the inside to break through, disappearing, coming back again, threatening to make everything explode. The reader seems to be in the shoes of the person addressed, on the defensive, aware of hidden dangers and murderous impulses creeping into affectionate solicitude.

On occasion ordinary conversation seems to win, suppressing subconversational urges, but "the quotations, the metaphors, the ready-made, pompous or pedantic expressions, the platitudes, vulgarities, mannerisms and pointless remarks with which these dialogues are cleverly studded" are the result of "numerous, entangled movements that have come up from the depths." This is a remarkably astute analysis of the typical Compton-Burnett dialogue, the "burnished" dialogue, as others have noted, not what people really say but what they think and would like to say, or rather what they would like to have said (such perceptions coming late to most of us). It is important to observe the Freudian implications of id (up front the depths) and censor, although here instead of the occasional Freudian slip ("my wife's admirers — I mean advisers" of Leopold Bloom) the slippery id is more often in view.

In what has been called her remorseless study of mind and motive, Compton-Burnett uses her artificial, melodramatic, "'Victorian three-decker' plots simply as arbitrary framework upon which to build her histories of human motive and behavior," according to Pamela Hansford Johnson. These stories "tinged by insult" contain people who lie, murder, steal, deceive, and betray. Brother marries sister; children murder their father; a mother kills her daughter-in-law. Guy Davenport says in an obituary notice, "If Sophocles had written novels, these are the novels Sophocles would have written." For her, man's essential depravity is not modified by time or place; good is not rewarded and bad is not punished. Nor does the novelist make judgments. Her moral vision is strictly amoral. But the melodrama has movement to propel the reader through the most important thing, the talk with its clever sometimes oblique wit, "acute percipience, spiteful malevolence and angry satire." There are comic, grotesque values too in the artificialities of plot construction, a kind of theater of cruelty with enough distance to prevent identification.

The tone of Compton-Burnett's novels is not that usually associated with tragicomedy, although this has been suggested; the elements are too extreme and the endings are not all that happy. It is certainly not the smile-tear of Chekhovian realism or *vers de société;* there is too much outrage for that. But tragic elements and comic elements elbow each other constantly in the narratives. In *Mother and Son* characters comment:

> "So it is true that comedy and tragedy are mingled," said Adrian.
> "Really it is all tragedy," said his sister. "Comedy is a wicked way of looking at it, when it is not our own."

And a later exchange:

> "Your humour has been bitter, when I thought it was sound?"
> "I do not think humour is ever sound. If it is, it is something else."

The blend may be of nearly equal quantities, but as Frank Baldanza has pointed out in his book, "this seeming mistrust of the purely comic as wicked and unsound makes one incline slightly toward the view that Ivy Compton-Burnett's novels are meant as predominantly serious reflections of human experience."

The characters are more often character types rather than individuals drawn in the round, and a limited number is presented: the family tyrant, man or woman; the nagger; the children; the governess; the servants. But of the characters who remain memorable as individuals, no two readers will select the same ones; perhaps it depends too much upon which of them we have known and recognize from our living. Place and setting are slight and perfunctory (in only one novel, *Brothers and Sisters,* does the village have even a name, Moreton Edge). There is little if any character description. Costumes and accessories play so little a part that Elizabeth Bowen has said, "her characters sometimes give the effect of being physically, as well as psychologically, in the nude." There is neither description nor exposition. Of her putting people from the life around her into her novels, the author herself said, "People in life hardly seem to be definite enough to appear in print. They are not good enough, or bad enough, or clever enough, or stupid enough, or comic or spiteful enough." She views her created world without rancor but with detachment. If she refuses to mete out punishment to the bad and tyrannical, she can sympathize with a passive, defensive gesture with the put-upon companion or servant, with the children who are the victims of parental misbehavior, nagging, neglect, or odious comparison. She seems a little ashamed of showing emotion and holds herself sternly in reserve.

Her subjects (not her subject matter) and generalized settings certainly seem rather limited: the upper middle class and the petty English nobility (landed but often impecunious) with the dank and drafty houses of their country estates between 1880 and 1910. In nineteen novels and forty years of labor she has posed and solved in an almost identical manner the same problems. But this is oversimplification. The "classes" of characters are differentiated into elders and children, family and servants, home and school, manor house and village. Note that the elders and children make up the family as opposed to the servants, but the family and servants make up the home as opposed to the school or the village. There is always a dichotomy or what has been called a "diptych" structure at the base of the novels, to be seen usually in the disjunctive or conjunctive titles: *Parents and Children, Elders and Betters, Men and Wives, Pastors and Masters, More Women than Men, Two Worlds and Their Ways, A House and its Head,* and so on.

What is her subject matter? Baldanza talks about "a depiction of the most mannered civilization" combined with Gothic horrors like incest and infanticide, major concerns running against the bias of our age. "Aside from the precocious and articulate children, they represent the experience of a rural gentry in late middle age and in extreme old age, for whom the passions of the flesh are persistent ghosts of past mistakes that haunt their peace. Economically insecure, agnostic, committed to a family life, which is as exacerbating as it is inevitable, these gentlefolk pass leisured mornings and afternoons largely in protracted conversations about their lot." They certainly always seem to be at breakfast or at tea, only occasionally at luncheon or dinner. Of course that's where family talk takes place.

Tensions arise in taboo emotional attachments between unmarried persons, mother and son, father and daughter, brother and sister, man and man, woman and woman; with the countertensions of the proprieties and even of proper attachments without affection. The stability of society must be in control of family authority, but with control and authority comes power, and power as it corrupts produces tyrants, greed, cruelty, and a multitude of sins.

The subject matter is more specifically the dissection of the pre-1910 British family, more simply any family as a closed unit or system, somewhat like Sartre's hell, with no exit but with "other people." Divorce is not a viable escape in the Compton-Burnett world, and many of the marriages in her novels are pretty grim. But consider the family again. Parents and children are really caught (even in our times); they can't divorce each other. Brothers are trapped with sisters and there are always uncles, aunts, cousins, grandparents. Look at the grandmother or mother with matriarchal aspirations to power; how much can be done with invalidism as a tactic, with demands for love "for your poor mother" (Sophia in *Brothers and Sisters* is one of these). Look at the father and son (the generation or Oedipal gap), or husband and wife (the confidence gap or power struggle), with mutual hatreds, usually about little things in the enclosed home, even the way one squeezes toothpaste out of the tube. In March of 1971 according to Associated Press news releases, a University of Louisville coed expressed bitterness over an appeals court ruling that her father is not required to support her at school, frowning on her hippie life style which, he said, "stinks." We usually, if not always, repress our animosities. But Ivy Compton-Burnett lets it all hang out. Odd that the other characters when attacked never seem to flinch. They go on with their tea or breakfast and generally bat the ball back over the net in a sort of Greek tragic stichomythia. It does seem beautifully British, refined mayhem.

Of course the family is not only a horror; it is also a refuge, as the end of *Two Worlds and Their Ways* makes clear when Oliver says, "We can only hide our heads at home. Homes cause the shame, but they also provide a hiding place for it, and we have to take one thing with another." And the young half-sister Clemence answers, "You would hardly think homes would be so fair." This world is the better of the two worlds, the other being school. It is only that Ivy Compton-Burnett is too clinical and detached, not to say cynical, not to cut away sentimentality for the parasitic growth that it is. "Home truths" she gives us, says Hansford Johnson, with the accent on home. The family, whatever its current status, is still a relatively universal frame of reference. Aristotle in the *Poetics* said that the tragic complication or catastrophe was more effective when it took place, not with strangers, but in the family.

One of her admirers has said that Ivy Compton-Burnett "is the only writer since Joyce who is likely to be read one hundred years from now." It seems unlikely to a less partisan view that she will be the only one, but she may well be one among a small number. W. H. Auden is supposed to have said that "her prose has the beauty of a hand grenade," although others have apparently worked on the phrase as well. Edith Sitwell and Ivy Compton-Burnett have often been referred to as the *Grandes Dames* of contemporary British literature, both in literal and figurative senses. Different as they are, the term seems singularly appropriate.

Life

It was assumed until her death that Ivy Compton-Burnett had been born in 1892. Who made that original assumption is not known, but it was copied without much question, although it would have sent her to college at London University at the age of ten with Bachelor of Arts Honors in Classics at fourteen — not impossible but certainly worth special comment if true. According to the *New York Times* obituary account, Compton-Burnett kept her birth date secret, but it is believed to be June 5, 1884. If Jean Cocteau gained two years of youth in similar fashion, Ivy beat him by eight to two. The daughter of Dr. James and Katherine Rees Compton-Burnett, Ivy was brought up in well-to-do circumstances in the rural suburbs of Victorian London, educated at home before entering Royal Holloway College, which had been opened by Queen Victoria in 1886 for women of middle and upper classes, not to be considered a mere training for teachers and governesses.

Except for her writing Ivy Compton-Burnett led an uneventful life in public, as she insisted when pressed for information. For her first novel, *Dolores,* published in 1911, which is not yet vintage in that dialogue is not yet preponderant over commentary and narrative (there are even echoes of George Eliot's *Middlemarch*), Ivy had the help or hindrance of a literarily inclined brother. The thesis of *Dolores* is that to sacrifice oneself for the good of others is noble and beautiful. From the second novel, *Pastors and Masters* (1925), the thesis has changed: to sacrifice oneself for others is splendid for others and horrible for oneself. Seventeen more novels followed at almost regular two-year intervals, the series beginning with *Brothers and Sisters* in 1929 and ending with *A God and His Gifts* in 1963.

Living by preference as something of a recluse, she nevertheless shared digs with Margaret Jourdain, an authority on old furniture (a sort of Gertrude Stein-Alice B. Toklas arrangement, one gathers), for over thirty years. She is described as writing all of her novels in pencil, as wearing the coiffure of a Spartan matron and dresses that could come "only from the needle of a Mennonite." As relaxation from writing, she grew flowers — and became an expert on the wild flowers of Switzerland. She had conferred on her the Order of the British Empire in 1951, and in 1967 in additional royal honors became a Dame Commander. Something of a personality, she frequently entertained at tea in her South Kensington flat in London during her late years. On August 27, 1969, Dame Ivy died in her sleep, eighty-five years old, at home in Cornwall Gardens, London, leaving two sisters both of Hertfordshire.

Representative Novels

***Brothers and Sisters* (1929):** This novel, recognized by Arnold Bennett as significant, is already full-fledged Ivy. Six pairs of brothers and sisters figure in the story, not only underlining the plot and theme but shouting for attention in symmetrical groupings and regroupings with a variety of ironic contrasts. This suggests Shakespearian *dédoublement* pushed to comic limits as well as the Gidian inclusion of the "parody of itself." The daughter and adopted son of old Andrew Stace of Moreton Edge Manor, Sophia and Christian Stace, marry five months after the old man's death, despite his objections, showing "faith in his real understanding sufficient to do as he had forbidden them." Some twenty-six years later the family is celebrating the twenty-fifth birthday of Andrew, the eldest son, with his sister Dinah and the leftover (from the pairs) younger brother Robin: "Sophia sat in her father's seat at the head of his table, a place where he would have been baffled to see his only child. The seat was symbolic of Sophia's position in the household. Neither in outward nor inward things had the place of the head been Christian's. From old Mr. Stace's death it had simply been Sophia's."

Friends call for a birthday party: the Rector and his sister, Edward and Judith Dryden, pale and tall, at the end of their twenties — and other things as well; another brother and sister, Julian and Sarah Wake, somewhat younger and slightly more colorful although hardly more admirable; and Cousin Peter Bateman, rather mean and gossipy and poor but connected with *the* family, and his two children, Tilly and her nineteen-year-old brother, Latimer. Here are three pairs of brothers and sisters, but not much in the way of matrimonial prospects for Andrew and Dinah of the Manor. Into the village comes a widow, Mrs. Lang, a French woman, and her two children — Gilbert, a vigorous, charming man of thirty and his sister very like him, Caroline, who soon become engaged to Dinah and Andrew respectively.

Mrs. Lang becomes very ill and is attended by Dr. Christian Stace. Through an old photograph book brought by Miss Patmore or Patty, the nurse-governess-companion of the Stace family, she recognizes before she dies that Christian is her son by a liaison of her youth whom she (a visiting French governess in England at the time) had had to leave behind for adoption. The engagements have to be broken off to the regret of all, because of the impediment of the relationship. Christian, in poor health himself with a bad heart, tells Sophia of his condition; she, resolute, suddenly remembers some papers that her father locked in a desk before his death. She had always been afraid they might involve a will disinheriting her. Christian insists upon looking, prodded and then "held back" by Sophia. He finds the letter "To be opened after my death" and reads it. He and Sophia are half-brother and sister; and he dies in the chair at the desk as a result of the shock. Patty finds him and the letter but shuts it up quickly in the desk, after reading it.

After the funeral and the reading of the will, dinner is served, and Patty is invited to join the family. "No, I won't have anything to eat," says Sophia, "I will just try to drink a glass of wine." After silence, Sophia, "I don't know whether you all like sitting there, having dinner, with your mother eating nothing? On this days of all days!" "Oh, I understood that you wouldn't have anything," said Patty, rising and hurrying to her side with food. "I may have said those words," said Sophia. "It is true that I do not want anything. I hardly could, could I? But I may need it. . . . I don't think I should be left without a little pressing today. . . . I hardly feel you should let me depend quite on myself." And she browbeats Andrew and Dinah into pressing her. Robin doesn't respond and she asks, "You don't care whether your mother eats anything or not, Robin?" "Oh, come, you are not a child," said Robin. "You said you didn't want anything." "No, my son, I am not a child," said Sophia. "I am a grief-stricken old woman. That is what I am. But I should have thought that would make you the more concerned for your mother." "You made a very fair luncheon," said Robin. "There is no need to be anxious about you in that way. You are eating better than Dinah."

Andrew and Dinah become engaged to Edward and Judith, but the fatal letter is finally found and read by Sophia, who has been going into a slow decline but not for that reason. She says simply, "So I am Father's sister. Well, I am not troubled about that. It only seems to draw us closer." The children's reactions are matter-of-fact and pragmatic: "Could this happen to anyone but us?" said Robin. "It has not happened to us. It has made us," said Dinah. "Heaven help us!" said Robin. "Heaven helps those that help themselves," said Andrew. "There must not be a word of this." But Edward and Judith have to be told, and the news leaks out to the village via Peter. The engagements are off because of public knowledge. Julian and Sarah patch up projected marriages with Caroline and Gilbert; there seems to be no question of love. Even Tilly finds a marriage, but Andrew and Dinah leave the Manor for London, taking Grandfather's portrait. If anybody asks which grandfather, they can say quite simply, "Both."

***Manservant and Maidservant* (1947):** Published in the United States as *Bullivant and the Lambs,* 1948, it has been thought to be among the "lighter and more amiable" of the Compton-Burnett stories, therefore presumably easier for an American public to take. Hansford Johnson and others name this as "the peak of her achievement," the favorite. The main character may be Horace Lamb by name, but he's an old ram who is one of the most repelling tyrants in all the Compton-Burnett fiction. He tyrannizes over his wife Charlotte, his aunt Emilia, his cousin Mortimer; his servants, the butler Bullivant, the Cook Mrs. Seldon, and particularly George, the apprentice servant from the workhouse; and most especially over his children: Sarah, Jasper, Marcus, Tamasin, and the youngest child, Avery. He is parsimonious to the point of refusing to allow enough coal to be used to keep warm. As a villain he makes Scrooge look amiable. In exerting his tyranny he even goes so far as to make apparent reforms of character and conduct. The children are puzzled by the generous, kind, understanding surface of their scrimping, mean-souled father. One day Marcus and Jasper see him strolling toward a bridge which they know to be dangerous. Should they warn him? They hesitate. Horace is nice enough now, but suppose he returned to his old state and former self? It would be better for him to die now; he is so good that his soul would be safe. Nothing happens to Horace but the shock of realizing that his two nice little boys were willing to have him die. Some families might crack under this pressure, but not the Lambs. Later, under new austerity measures, Horace gets pneumonia, at the point of death is generous in forgiving and asking to be forgiven, but anticlimactically recovers. Bullivant is the man who always keeps things from falling apart, and his acceptance of Horace Lamb as he is with the butler's strong sense of loyalty to the family he serves produces almost the unwilling acceptance by the reader of his point of view. This is a fantastic *tour de force* and contains some of the strongest implied expressions of sympathy for helpless children and helpless servants in the entire range of novels.

Two Worlds and Their Ways (1949):

This was considered by the author one of her best books and had her marked preference. Surely Pamela Hansford Johnson is misreading the novel when she complains about the structure of it, that it could "have ended two-thirds of the way through, when the conflict between Home and School is resolved" with the mistake of introducing the complicated missing earrings subplot. For it is precisely this plot that reveals the misconduct of the elders in the family — mother, father, and grandfather — which balances very exactly the misconduct of the children, Clemence, Sefton, and their elder half-brother Oliver, the whole point of the novel.

The story in the main is not less complicated than the earrings. The father, Sir Roderick Shelley, has been twice married. His first wife, Mary, had died leaving her son, Oliver, and her father, old Mr. Firebrace, in the household being kept by Maria, wife number two (and the money she brought to the marriage). The names are deliberately and symbolically very similar. The children of the second marriage, fourteen-year-old Clemence and eleven-year-old Sefton, are to be sent to schools kept by the first Mrs. Shelley's sisters, Aunt Lesbia Firebrace and Aunt Juliet with her husband Lucius Cassidy, at the urging of the "aunts" on the theory that Miss Petticott (usually called Petticoat), the governess, can give them only an inadequate education. The Cassidy school for boys has need of a temporary music instructor, and Oliver, now in his thirties, volunteers for the post. Almost as distressing as leaving home for the unknown school world, as far as Clemence and Sefton are concerned, is the leaving of two remarkably entertaining servants, the irrepressible mimic Aldom and the almost maternal Adela.

When Clemence arrives at her school run by Miss Firebrace, she meets the quiet but insistent cruelties of her snobbishly dress-conscious companions, Maud, Gwendolen, Esther, and Verity, by lying about her home life, and is later pressured into cheating by her mother's expectations of her making superior grades. Sefton has a similarly distressing experience with his schoolmates, Bacon, Holland, Sturgeon, who think Sefton's mother must be a concubine since Mr. Shelley cannot have two wives and Oliver is revealed as only a halfbrother. Sefton also cheats, again in trying to measure up to a mother's unreasonable aspirations, and both he and Clemence are to be reported to their parents at Christmas holidays. Oliver gets into trouble by a too close friendship with Oliver Spode, the mathematics master at the school, which intimacy must be rebuked by Mr. Cassidy, the husband of his Aunt Juliet.

Home in disgrace, they are reproved by the family, but it is decided not to send them back to school. Old Mr. Firebrace discovers that Oliver Spode's mother is an old acquaintance of his (actually he is this Oliver's father and the other's grandfather, so the homosexual attachment is between half-uncle and half-nephew) and prepares to send her a valuable earring, companion to one he had given her years ago. But Maria has "lifted it" to sell in the shop where Spode had sold his mother's in order to give her husband the money to buy back a farm at the center of the estate (which he had transferred originally to cover an indiscretion). Juliet Cassidy has bought the pair and is able to substitute the missing earring. In the unravelling it becomes clear that Oliver Spode is Grandfather Firebrace's illegitimate son, (that Aldom is Sir Roderick's illegitimate son, fathered between Oliver Shelley and his second family), and all the elders have done worse things than Clemence and Sefton.

After a visit to the Shelley home of all the school companions of Clemence and Sefton, Maria's lapse in principles is accidentally revealed to Sir Roderick by Oliver Spode, everyone forgives and understands each other, and last references are made to the earrings. "It is a trivial sort of tale," said Mr. Firebrace. "What a shallow word!" said his grandson. "When the facts are trivial, and it is itself rooted in the depths. It is the sort of thing that is a test, and you have failed." And the reader may fail too, if he doesn't see Oliver Shelley's growth and superior insights. It is he who reassures the children, who have decided you cannot live in two places — it is better to be at home than in school. One is likely to feel ashamed, having been at school. "Now we think Mother is odd and shabby; and Father is simple;" Miss Petticott on the level of matrons; Aldom an awkward little manservant. The schoolgirls had thought Maria's dress a joke because they had seen it before. But when Clemence comes to see home as fair, Oliver says to her, "You see life whole, Clemence. [Echo of Matthew Arnold on Sophocles.] I leave you with a heavy heart, but with an easy mind." Miss Petticott equally reassures Maria about laughter from the children's room, "Relief, Lady Shelley. Relief that the aftermath of school is over, and home life stretches before them in happiness and peace." That is as much affirmation as Ivy Compton-Burnett has to offer, but it somehow seems a good deal.

HISTORICAL BACKGROUND (1914–39)

As the empire became ever more far-flung before the First World War, Britain felt the need to control the seas connecting its member states and colonies. A number of treaties were struck to support this endeavor, including the Anglo-Japanese Alliance of 1902, the *Entente Cordiale* with France in 1904, and the Russian Treaty of 1907. Opposing this loosely associated group of allies was the Triple Alliance (Germany, Austria, and Italy), founded by Bismarck in 1882.

A decade of diplomatic crises culminated on June 28, 1914, when the heir-apparent to the Austrian throne, Archduke Francis Ferdinand, was murdered by a Serbian sympathizer. A month later Austria declared war on Serbia. Russia supported Serbia, and Germany stood behind Austria. Germany, meanwhile, declared war on both Russia and France. When the German army invaded Belgium, England was drawn in the war, however reluctantly.

During the first two years of fighting, German armies advanced through Belgium and France until the resistance forced them into relatively stagnant trench warfare along the famed "Western Front," a battleline stretching from the European coast to Switzerland. European, Asiatic, and Middle Eastern countries associated themselves either as members of the Central Powers or the Allies.

Early in 1917 the German government began an all-out program of submarine warefare. The destruction of neutral ships brought the United States into the war in April, 1917. Meanwhile, the Bolsheviks gained control of Russia. The last major German offensive began in March, 1918, but was repulsed by the Allied powers under General Foch. Germany surrendered in the Armistice signed November 11, 1918. In the subsequent Treaty of Versailles the map of Europe was redrawn, and Germany lost territory, colonies, and the right to rearm.

In that settlement, Great Britain received large accessions of territory. Like Rome before her, Britain now faced the daunting task of managing and protecting such a geographically and culturally diverse empire. More than 2 million British soldiers had perished during the First World War and Britain has incurred huge war debts. The government therefore was eager to agree to the Washington Arms Limitation of 1922, which established a naval power ratio for Great Britain, Japan, and the United States. The Locarno Pact (1925) and the Briand-Kellogg Pact (1928) were similarly intended to reduce armaments.

Immediately after the First World War Great Britain faced the problem of restoring several million soldiers to the civilian job force. That transition was hampered by a severe recession in 1920. During the war, other nations had geared up as industrial competitors and struck protective trade agreements among themselves. Britain increasingly found herself cut out of world markets for machinery, clothing, and other manufactured goods. Massive war debts forced England to tax its industries heavily, putting them at a further competitive disadvantage.

In 1924 the first Labour government was elected, with Ramsay MacDonald as Prime Minister. He led the way toward more government control of mining, the railroads, and agriculture. Control vacillated between MacDonald and the Conservative Stanley Baldwin for the next decade. In 1936, King George V died and was succeeded by his eldest son, Edward VIII. But before he could be crowned, he abdicated the throne to marry the American divor-cee, Wallis Simpson, and enter private life as the Duke of Windsor. The second son of George V then became king as George VI.

In the years just prior to the outbreak of the Second World War in 1939, civil war broke out in Spain between the Leftists, who controlled the govern-ment, and the Fascists, led by Franco. Many of the old Central and Allied powers quickly chose sides in the struggle and began supplying munitions and volunteers. The ill-founded compromises of Neville Chamberlain with Mussolini eventually resulted in Franco's victory and consolidation of power.

5
THE NEOROMANTIC
MOVEMENT

Romanticism has had periodic recurrences in literary history, the most important of which occurred about 1800 in England and continental Europe. A revival of this movement began at the turn of the twentieth century, when it formed a part of the wider literary reaction against the Realism and Naturalism of the late nineteenth century.

The authors who participated in this romantic movement shared an interest in the exotic or unusual as opposed to the prosaic or ordinary, a certain flamboyance or ingenuity of language, a liking for fantastic, heroic, or superhuman characters, and an inclination toward fantastic plot material. Some, like Maeterlinck, sought to escape into an irrational world of dream; others, like Kipling, were attracted to exotic geographical settings. Although Neoromanticism tends toward the irrational and fantastic, not all of these writers were superficial; Conrad achieved great emotional and philosophical depths, and the content of such authors as Cocteau, Saint-Exupéry and Ford Madox Ford is far from trivial.

The aesthetic element is strong in this romantic revival. Romantic authors tend to be more interested in the sheer beauty of language than realists do; some, like Christopher Fry, make a virtual cult of verbal preciosity. Strong visual and other images also characterize these authors. The majority of Neoromantic writers are idealistic in attitude. The ideals of twentieth-century romanticism are the beautiful, the exotic, the strange, the heroic, and the mysterious — essentially the aspirations of a Schiller, Victor Hugo, Shelley, or Keats.

RUDYARD KIPLING (1865–1936)

IMPORTANCE

Kipling is an author of many facets: folklorist, dialect poet, adventure novelist, writer of juvenile literature, and champion of nationalism. Much of his work is dated today, and his political ideas seem hopelessly anachronistic. His dialect poetry is practically indestructible, however, and many of his short stories have lasting merit. As time goes on it appears that Kipling's children's stories are better, in their genre, than most of his adult prose. *Kim,* one of his best novels, lies on the line between the juvenile and the adult, and there is nothing in such tales as "The Man Who Would Be King" that a child cannot appreciate. There is a certain adolescent charm about Kipling that makes his books appeal to youth, and in this aspect he will probably remain a standard author for some time to come. His work also serves as a valuable source of information about nineteenth-century colonial India, especially the barracks life of the British colonial soldier.

Life

Kipling was born in Bombay in 1865; his father was a highly creative artist and professor. Educated in England at the school he was later to describe in *Stalky and Co.,* he returned to India at seventeen, dabbled in journalism, and soon turned to fiction writing. His first stories began appearing in newspapers around 1885, and his first verses, *Departmental Ditties,* in volume form in 1886. In 1888 he published *Plain Tales from the Hills,* including some of the earlier newspaper tales. As his literary fame began to grow, he settled in London; *Barrack-Room Ballads,* the first Kipling work to achieve world-wide recognition, appeared in 1892. The same year he married Caroline Starr Balestier, sister of an American writer, and shortly after went to live on his wife's property at Brattleboro, Vermont. Two daughters were born in America. Kipling returned to England in 1896, and in 1900 he served as correspondent in the Boer War. During the First World War he turned to anti-German propaganda; by this time he was a fervent, even fanatic British patriot. His only son was killed in the war. Many honors came to him in his old age; he was awarded the Nobel Prize for Literature in 1907, made a foreign associate of the French Academy in 1933, and endowed with numerous honorary university degrees. He died in London in 1936.

Chief Works

***Barrack-Room Ballads* (1892):** This collection of poetry contains the most famous of Kipling's dialect poems. There are actually two sections in the book, the first containing the serious ballads in conventional English and the second the semihumorous ditties in Cockney or soldier slang. In all cases the rhythms are strong, the rhymes ingenious, and the style salty. The most famous poems of the collection are "Gunga Din," about a dauntless native watercarrier who dies for his white comrades; "Fuzzy-Wuzzy," a tribute to the soldierly qualities of fanatic Sudanese tribesmen; "Danny Deever," a mock threnody on a British soldier who is hanged for murder; and "Mandalay," an unlettered soldier's paean to life in the Orient.

Kim (1901): This is generally considered Kipling's best novel. The hero, Kim, is an Irish orphan raised as an Indian in the native quarter of Lahore. As a young boy he encounters a mysterious Tibetan lama and follows him through India on a pilgrimage in search of the legendary River of the Arrow. Later Kim is claimed by the British and sent to a school in Lucknow. After his education he joins the British secret service and helps to capture a Russian spy in the Himalayas. The chief merits of the book are the absorbing interest of the plot and the first-hand pictures of Indian life at the time of the Crimean War.

JOSEPH CONRAD (1857–1924)

Conrad's reputation, which diminished somewhat during the socially conscious and liberal thirties, has since risen steadily. He is today recognized for what he wanted to be: a novelist of human character in its deeper and more thoughtful manifestations. Contrary to the reader's first impression, Conrad is not primarily a sea writer, nor is he a local colorist like Kipling. He laid his stories at sea and on remote oriental islands because these locales provided him with convenient microcosms where dramatic situations could be resolved to their utmost simplicity; it was a fortunate coincidence that his own experience provided him with a knowledge of such environments.

Conrad cannot handle a large cast of characters in the manner of Galsworthy or Martin du Gard; his highly dramatic talent is most at home with four or five characters whose wills bring them into intense conflict. Unlike the typical novelist of the twentieth century, he is idealistic in characterization, sparse in documentation, and romantic in his situations; yet he is too polished and careful an artist, too penetrating in his insight into character to be a typical romantic.

Some suggested qualities of Conrad's work are as follows:

1. Conrad's most characteristic stylistic device is his use of the *oblique point of view*. He is fond of tricky point-of-view devices: the narrating raconteur, the letter, the documentary report, or the story seen through the eyes of three or four persons. His favorite device is the narrator who relates a story from his past to an attentive circle of gentlemen in a club or aboard an anchored yacht *(Youth, Heart of Darkness)*. In many cases this narrator is the retired master mariner Marlow. Gentlemanly, discursive, basically serios but given to occasional pungent irony, Marlow is an *alter ego* of Conrad himself; he is Conrad as he conceived his better self to be or as he would like to have been. In other stories the narrator is not named; he moves through the narrative as a mysterious and unobtrusive "I." His attitude, however, remains that of Marlow, and thus of Conrad himself. Conrad occasionally utilizes a straight third-person narrative, but when he does so his point of view is likely to shift from external narration to internal stream of consciousness with confusing frequency. Conrad's action is never seen at first hand, always in

reflection. In the center of the work lies the plot, but we see it only at second and third hand through the eyes of others. These "others" each have their idiosyncrasies and blindnesses, and thus the reader never sees the matter in its straightforward clarity. This technique gives Conrad's novels and tales a curious contemplative mood which slows the action but which lends to the whole a strong air of authenticity.

2. *Experiments in chronology* also characterize Conrad's style. He is fond of the flashback, the story told in reverse, or the plot revealed in bits and snatches and fitted together only in the reader's mind. His rearrangement of chronology is of course connected with his use of oblique points of view; since the story is related by several characters, it often comes to us in mixed-up order. This technique has two advantages: It contributes to the air of authenticity, and it creates suspense and reader interest through withholding the most interesting parts of the story to the last. In this respect Conrad's novels and tales often resemble the detective story in construction, different as they may be in other respects.

3. Conrad effectively communicates *mood,* especially the mood of the sea or of exotic tropical settings. Here he shows himself to be a careful observer of the weather, of the shape of objects, and of the course of nature. He achieves mood not through a mere tabulation of observed phenomena, but through a sensitive poetic rearrangement of sensations. Often he animizes material objects: the jungle, the river, a ship at sea, a house, or a storm is invested with a mystical energy of its own.

In addition to his skill at place-mood Conrad is adept at communicating the mood of an action or incident; the best examples of these are storms and marine disasters. By carefully relating the emotional reactions of the characters and by avoiding an excessive mass of detail, he reconstructs the incident as it actually seemed at the time to the people who were participating in it. The best examples of place-mood occur in *Heart of Darkness* (the mood of the African river) and *Victory* (the island of Samburan). Examples of mood of action or incident are found in *Lord Jim* (description of the panic of the officers of the *Patna*), *The Secret Sharer* (escape of the fugitive from the narrator's ship), *Youth* (burning and abandonment of the *Judea*), and *Typhoon* (the storm at sea).

4. Conrad has a remarkable gift of *characterization;* his characters are real and vivid, and have the quality of coming to life on the printed page. But upon examination their motivation sometimes seems weak; this is especially true of his sinister or abnormal characters. He creates enigmatic and dramatic figures of the type of James Wait *(The Nigger of the Narcissus)* or Mr. Jones *(Victory)* who convince us as we read; but under cool analysis there is seen to be more mystery than psychology in their motivation. Conrad prefers to leave a veil around their inner thoughts, thus adding a mysterious stature to these characters that would be lacking if we understood them completely.

It is in his heroes that Conrad shows himself a master of psychology. His young masters and mates, usually projections of himself, he delineates with the skill of a great novelist. We see their inner thoughts in a way that makes them seem real, convincing, and sympathetic.

A third type of character found in Conrad is the grotesque: the vulgar, disgusting, psychologically twisted outcast of the tropics. The most typical of these is the hotelkeeper Schomberg, who appears both in *Lord Jim* and in *Victory*. Such characters are presented as pathological types rather than as true human beings; there is a mechanical quality about them that suggests the "originals" of Dickens or Dostoyevsky. They are like ridiculous but evil walking toys; their very lack of human quality makes them the more repugnant.

5. Conrad *abandons conventional plot* as a literary device; many of his works have no coherent plot at all *(Youth)* and others succeed without the conventional plot ingredients of classic fiction *(The Nigger of the Narcissus, Typhoon)*. The most remarkable innovation in Conrad's choice of plot is his lack of interest in the conventional love plot. His most typical works *(Typhoon, The Nigger of the Narcissus)* involve no women at all, and where a love theme does occur, it seldom has an essential part in the action. Frequently woman is the agency through which man is undone. Diverted by woman, the hero fails to give his total attention to the problem confronting him and is therefore destroyed. Examples of this are found in *Victory,* where Heyst would probably have been allowed to live in peace in his island Eden had he not eloped with Lena, and in *Lord Jim,* where Cornelius betrays Jim chiefly out of resentment against Jim's rescue and protection of Cornelius' ill-treated step-daughter. Conrad's characterizations of women are generally thin; he is interested in them only as foils for men.

6. Conrad is a *romanticist* chiefly in his nostalgia for exotic and striking settings. Born in northern Europe, he felt a deep nostalgia for the tropics. He is fascinated with place names, with odd nationalities, and with queer and primitive practices; he views these things not as an anthropologist but as a poet who uses them as stimuli to his imagination. For this reason he seeks not to understand the East and Africa but to absorb its mood of strangeness and to communicate it to the reader. In this respect his attitude is the opposite of scientific.

7. This romanticism is connected with the *insular and colonial attitude* of Conrad, an attitude that derives from his thoroughgoing assumption of British character. Born a Pole, he was "converted" to the British way of life; and like most converts he is more fervent than those born in the creed. He seems to make the tacit assumption that foreigners, especially Germans, Orientals, and polyglots, are "different from us" and lack the essential moral qualities of the British. With a few exceptions, such as Stein in *Lord Jim,* his Germans are all grasping merchants, rascals, or grotesques. It is significant that the evil Zangiacomo of *Victory,* who calls himself an Italian, is actually a German in disguise.

Conrad is a proponent of the "inscrutable Orient" concept; his Chinese, Siamese, Malayan, and Javanese characters do not possess the same kind of mentality as Westerners, and in fact seem to be imbued with some mysterious racial essence. They are by nature inscrutable, irrational, and a little sinister. Heyst in *Victory* explains to Lena that the actions of the "Chinaman" Wang are inexplicable, and that any attempt to understand them is doomed to failure. This view of foreign character contributes to the atmosphere of Conrad's fiction; his Orientals especially are effective additions to his décor.

Conversely, Conrad manifests and illustrates all the finer qualities of the British character: a respect for individuality, a neatness of body and mind, and especially a rigid sense of personal honor. The ideal of honor is most clearly presented in *Lord Jim*, where the hero devotes his life to an attempt to expiate a youthful breach of honor. Conrad sympathizes with Jim, yet both author and hero concede that the transgression against the code has been grave.

Another aspect of Conrad's insularity is his lack of socio-political consciousness. Beginning with the assumption that Orientals and Africans are totally different from the British, he naturally achieves little understanding of the true political and economic problems of these people. There is sympathy in his attitude toward the backward populations of the world, but almost no awareness of the political consciousness that even in his own time was beginning to manifest itself among these people. In *Nostromo* he views egalitarianism as a species of barbarism that threatens the finer values of civilization. Here Conrad stands in sharp contrast to his contemporaries Galsworthy, Wells, and Shaw, who recognized the politico-economic patterns of the century and incorporated them in their literature.

8. At the same time Conrad shows a *fascination with primitive character* that he would not have developed had he been more objective toward primitive races. He sees an elemental wisdom in the savage lacking in civilized man; even primitive superstition seems to him imbued with a mystical power. In several cases his heroes try to penetrate into this primitive wisdom in order to partake of its strength; to do this they must attempt to abandon civilization entirely. Usually they fail, and the attempt destroys them. There is a barrier around the primitive heart that no white man can breach. Kurtz in *Heart of Darkness* is one of the few who break through the barrier, and he emerges to die crying, "The horror!" Those who fail in this quest do so because they are unable to cut themselves off totally from civilization, as Heyst *(Victory)* tries to take the civilized Lena with him and is destroyed as a result. Conrad's mystique of the primitive, anthropologically inaccurate as it may be, nevertheless contributes greatly to the literary effect of his work.

Life

Joseph Conrad was born Josef Korzeniowski in 1857, the son of a Ukranian-Polish poet and revolutionist. As a boy he read Dickens and Shakespeare in translation, and soon developed two ambitions: to go to sea and to become an Englishman. He fulfilled both of these ambitions to perfection. Shipping out as a forecastle hand in 1874, he learned English laboriously and in 1880 passed his examination as a master in the British merchant service. He became a British subject in 1884. He took his first command in 1886, and during the next ten years sailed widely to America, to India, and to the Far East. His experiences in the Malay Archipelago and an arduous trip up the Congo in 1890 were especially important in providing him with literary material.

His first novel, *Almayer's Folly,* was written over a period of several years of sea duty; it appeared in 1895. He married in 1896 and passed the remainder of his career quietly on an estate in Kent, where his close acquaintances included Henry James, H. G. Wells, Stephen Crane, and Ford Madox Ford, the last a collaborator on three books. Conrad continued to write steadily up to his death in 1924.

An interesting autobiographical picture of his career up to 1896 is contained in *A Personal Record* (1912). Much admired in recent years are the novels, *Nostromo* (1904), *The Secret Agent* (1907), and *Under Western Eyes* (1911). We are not really "at sea" in these stories, and the last in particular says some pertinent things about the differences in psychology between the two sides of the Iron Curtain, the Russian East and the life of Western Europe.

Chief Works

The Nigger of the Narcissus **(1897):** This novel was Conrad's first widely successful work. It is a study of James Wait, a mysterious and melancholy black sailor, his deterioration and death from tuberculosis, and his influence on the other members of the crew of the *Narcissus.* The plot is not strong; the novel derives its chief interest from mood and characterization. Wait's character is suggested by the ship's name; he is excessively egocentric, almost narcissistic, in his interest in his own body. As the ship sails from Bombay, the huge black is unpopular with the crew, who nevertheless respect him for his strength and the mysterious power that seems to reside in him (an example of Conrad's interest in primitive character). When he turns sick, they suspect him of malingering, but he takes to his bunk seemingly deaf to their reproaches. His especial antagonist is the Cockney seaman Donkin, who reviles him sarcastically but subconsciously loves and admires him. As his health grows worse, Wait is moved to a midships deckhouse; now that he has a private cabin, he arrogantly begins to dominate the life of the whole ship. In a storm the *Narcissus* is thrown onto her beam ends, and Wait in his midships cabin is rescued only by heroic efforts of the cursing crew. The weather then turns hot and calm, and the crew's resentment smolders; they irrationally blame his presence on board for the calm. At last Wait dies. His final torments are so grim that the crew's hostility becomes mixed with awe and compassion; they do not know what to think of Wait. But as his body is consigned to the sea a fresh breeze comes up, and the *Narcissus* gratefully picks up speed for home.

Conrad's picture of the central figure of this novel is two-sided. To the other members of the crew, Wait is evil personified, and the ship is cursed until his body is committed to the sea. But as an individual Wait is depicted with great psychological skill, and the reader's sympathy is finally aroused through understanding of the feelings of loneliness and isolation that his color and his disease have produced in the man. The novel is one of Conrad's few straight third-person narratives.

Lord Jim (1900): This is probably Conrad's best-known novel. The hero, known only as "Jim," is endowed with a Puritanical conscience by his minister father, and is dogged all his life by a sense of guilt over a youthful transgression. This key incident occurs in the Red Sea on a ship called the *Patna,* loaded with Moslem pilgrims for Mecca. The ship strikes a floating object and begins to sink, and the white officers panic and think only of their own lives. Jim, at first disdainful of their pusillanimity, watches them launch a boat; but a moment later the panic catches him and he jumps after them. They drift off, abandoning the several hundred passengers, and are picked up by a passing ship. But the *Patna* perversely refuses to sink, and the officers are left in the humiliating position of having abandoned a sound vessel. This "sin" torments Jim all the rest of his life. He wanders aimlessly from one place to another in an effort to escape it, but finds that his reputation invariably catches up with him. Eventually he settles in Patusan, in the interior of a remote Malayan island, and becomes an adviser to Doramin, chief of a Moslem tribe and virtual ruler of the land. Aiding Doramin against the corrupt rajah of the region, Jim rapidly rises in prestige; at last he has found a land where no one knows his past. He becomes the close friend of Dain Waris, son of Doramin, but incurs the enmity of Cornelius, a renegade white trader, through rescuing his mistreated stepdaughter and taking her into his household. The girl, Jewel, becomes his "wife," and with her encouragement Jim sets out to make a new life for himself. He leads the bush people against a bandit group who have been terrorizing the countryside, defeats them through European methods of warfare, and is acclaimed by his followers as a divinely sent hero. For years he lives in productive happiness in the jungle. Then "Gentleman Brown," a wandering ne'er-do-well and pirate, comes to Patusan with the crew of his schooner in hope of terrorizing the town and making off with some loot. The pirates find the town in arms, and are soon surrounded on a fortified knoll. Jim, seeking to avoid bloodshed, decides to make a deal with Brown; the pirates agree to leave the region peaceably, and Jim stands before his people as a guarantee of this promise. But, inspired by the jealous Cornelius, Brown kills Dain Waris and several tribesmen as he makes his way to the coast. The blame is on Jim's head; the griefstricken Doramin shoots him in cold blood, and Jim accepts his death as a belated expiation for the transgression of his youth. In dying to preserve his honor, he has at last proven to himself that he is not a coward.

The theme of this mixed adventure yarn and psychological novel is the British concept of honor and its influence on the mind of a basically decent young man. The story is related secondhand by Marlow, who plays a minor part in the plot; minor sections of the book are written directly in the third person. Jim's point of view is never presented directly; we see his internal motivation purely through his actions and through the remarks he makes to Marlow.

Youth (1902): Again related by Marlow, this tale tells of an incident that occurred many years before when Marlow was a young ship's officer. Proud of his first berth as a second mate, he ships on the bark *Judea* for Bankok with a cargo of coal. The obsolete and rotten old ship is forced to turn back twice because of mutiny and leaks, but amid all his troubles Marlow exults over the adventure of sailing to the East as an officer on a bark. His youthful spirits continue to sustain him even when the cargo catches fire in the Indian Ocean. The crew fight the smoldering enemy for days without effect. Then, when the ship is only a day's sail from Siam, the gas in the hold explodes and blows out the decks. Refusing an offer of rescue by a steamer, the crew doggedly hold on until the flaming ship actually begins to sink. Then they take to the boats, and Marlow finds himself in charge of his "first command" —a fourteen-foot cockleshell. He brings his two crew members safely to land, and thus encounters for the first time the East of his dreams. This work is a remarkable exercise in fiction: The romanticism of youth is described with the detachment and perspective of maturity. The description of the explosion of the ship is masterful. Marlow, who in other Conrad works is a mere passive narrator, here is the central figure of the plot.

Heart of Darkness (1902): The story of the African trader Kurtz is related secondhand by Marlow. The true history of the protagonist is revealed only gradually and obliquely. When the pieces are put together, the story is seen as follows: Kurtz, a strange and brooding seeker after truth, goes to Africa and is hired by a French trading company as an agent at a remote upriver post. There, influenced by the spell of the surrounding primitive culture, he begins to lose his grip on civilization. Driven by an obsessive desire for power, he becomes a virtual god among the natives of the region. He participates in their superstitious rituals, leads them in war, marries one of their women, and at last achieves unity with the savage soul. But the experience kills him; Marlow, in command of a small river steamer, arrives to find him delirious and dying. As he dies he gasps, "The horror! The horror!" He has seen what no white man has seen before, but he dies without describing what it was.

This tale, a study in the contrast of civilization and primitive culture, is marked by an extensive use of symmetry and antithesis. Africa, the savage mind, and superstition are symbolically associated with darkness, and civilization with sunshine and brightness. Kurtz's African mate is balanced by a European girl he promises to marry before he leaves for Africa; she sees him as a normal European, not recognizing the depths of "darkness" in his soul, which lead him to death in the African jungle.

Typhoon **(1903):** This tale contains a superb picture of a tropical storm as well as a fine character study of Captain MacWhirr, the placid and unimaginative master of the *Nan-Shan*. Also important is the chief mate, Jukes, the young man through whose eyes the action is seen. The vessel, on its way to China with a load of homeward-bound coolies, is struck by the typhoon when the phlegmatic MacWhirr refuses to turn out of its path. The account of the typhoon, one of the greatest literary pictures of its kind, occupies the major part of the work. The storm is described chiefly through its effects on the crew and vessel; it is never directly portrayed. At the height of the storm the coolies in the 'tween-deck begin fighting over their money, which is spilled when their chests are smashed; Jukes is forced to enter the hold to restore order. Although most of the crew, including the narrator, give the ship up for lost, the storm is unable to ruffle MacWhirr perceptibly. He brings the half-wrecked *Nan-Shan* to port and placidly redistributes the scattered dollars among the Chinese. MacWhirr is a typical Conrad original; his motivation is not well established, and his inner thoughts are left in mystery to heighten the air of eccentricity that surrounds him.

The Secret Sharer **(1912):** The story is narrated by the captain of a British sailing ship in the East Indies. While he is anchored in the Gulf of Siam, his ship is boarded in the night by a mysterious swimmer. Alone on deck, only the captain knows of the visitor. This man is Leggatt, the mate of the brig *Sephora* anchored a few miles away. On the passage out from England, Leggatt has killed a mutinous crewman, and the *Sephora's* master has confined him preparatory to turning him over to the authorities. Escaping in the dead of night, Leggatt swims to the strange ship to throw himself upon the mercy of its captain. For several days the captain conceals him in his cabin, and gradually he develops a curious sensation that Leggatt is his "other self"—that he might have been in Leggatt's position, or Leggatt in his. This leads him to a participation in Leggatt's guilt. His sense of sin is increased through his furtive efforts to keep Leggatt's presence a secret from his crew. Thus the theme: The guilt of any man spreads in widening circles until all men are involved in it. Realizing Leggatt's guilt, the captain still cannot condemn him; he knows that he or any other man would have done the same under the same provocation.

In order to help Leggatt escape by swimming ashore, the captain is obliged to sail dangerously close to a Malayan island. His crew, apprehensive, only reluctantly obey his strange orders. As the ship approaches the dark beach and puts about, he hears a faint splash and knows that his "secret sharer" is safely in the water. Then the captain sees below in the water the hat he has loaned Leggatt; it is drifting forward, indicating that the ship has lost headway. The captain orders the helm shifted, thus saving the ship from destruction. His act of generosity in helping Leggatt has been repaid;

through Leggatt's "gift" of the hat seen in the water, he has avoided wrecking his first command.

***Victory* (1915):** This novel is one of Conrad's most complex. The protagonist is Axel Heyst, a Swedish adventurer, who comes to a strange end on an island in the Malay Archipelago. The story is related in a disconnected fashion, partly told by the narrator Marlow and partly seen at first hand. It is only at the end that the reader begins to see the course of Heyst's life clearly. The son of a baron, he is a contemplative, drifting person by nature; he has a loathing of tying himself down by steady employment. He therefore wanders aimlessly through the world until he settles in the region of Sourabaya, where he engages in odd ventures in the surrounding islands. He incurs the irrational hatred of the hotelkeeper Schomberg, who relates all manner of slander about him, but becomes the friend of the British sea captain Davidson. Then, in Timor, he encounters Morrison, skipper of a trading schooner that has been seized by the Portuguese authorities. Morrison is at the point of suicide over the loss of his ship, his only means of livelihood. Heyst helps him out of his difficulties, and the two become partners. Now that Heyst has someone "to look out after" (Morrison is hopelessly unbusinesslike), he reveals his real ability; in taking care of Morrison he achieves feats he would never have attempted by himself. The two plan a venture involving coal on the island of Samburan; Heyst sends Morrison to England to look after details of the financing. In England Morrison catches cold and dies. Schomberg whispers that Heyst has "squeezed him dry like a lemon" and then "sent him home to die"; and Heyst himself is dogged with a lurking guilt over Morrison's death. He decides he has betrayed his nature in interfering in Morrison's life, and resolves never to get into such a situation again. Now that Heyst has no interest in it, the company fails entirely. He determines to abandon civilization entirely, and retreats to Samburan, his last remaining possession, to spend the rest of his life as a hermit.

Later Davidson, whose ship passes the island, brings him to Sourabaya for a short visit. Stopping at Schomberg's hotel, Heyst meets Alma, a musician in an itinerant female orchestra led by the cruel Zangiacomo. The young English girl leads a miserable life; Zangiacomo and his wife threaten and mistreat her, and Schomberg menaces her with his lascivious overtures. Overcome by pity for the second time in his life, Heyst steals her secretly away and takes her back to Samburan.

As Schomberg, practically insane with rage and jealousy, is seeking some means of revenge, a new trouble appears. Three dubious characters — the mysterious "Mr. Jones," his sinister assistant Martin Ricardo, and his half-witted but strong servant Pedro (diabolical intelligence, instinctive savagery, and brute force respectively) — descend on the hotel and proceed to turn it into a gambling den. Terrified, Schomberg seeks to get rid of them by sending them to Samburan to murder Heyst for his money.

When the trio, obviously criminals, arrive at the island, Alma, now re-named Lena, exhorts Heyst to take some action against them to defend himself. But he seems to relapse into his old apathy; he is unable to engage himself against the powers of evil. In a sense he feels that civilization, personified in the three criminals, has arrived to punish him for his elopement; and Lena herself shares this presentiment. At the crucial moment Wang, Heyst's Chinese servant, steals his revolver and takes to the bush, leaving him weaponless. Lena, menaced by Ricardo, plays for time by pretending to become his ally. But Mr. Jones, who detests women and has not been told of Lena's presence, surprises his assistant with the girl and fires at him; he misses and kills Lena instead. Later he stalks Ricardo and kills him; Heyst takes his own life in despair over the fate he has brought to Lena, and Pedro is killed by Wang's revolver. Mr. Jones, finding his retreat cut off, also commits suicide. The ending resembles the catastrophic dénouement of a classic tragedy.

The chief theme of this intricate novel is Heyst's lifelong flight to escape responsibility for others, which is the price of participation in civilization. Schomberg's hotel, buzzing with intrigue and hatred, symbolizes to him the world in all its repulsive vulgarity. He is trapped, however, by his sense of compassion; twice he seeks to aid other human beings (that is, to participate in mankind) and twice tragedy results.

A second theme is Heyst's effort to penetrate into the primitive world, the same impulse that motivated Kurtz *(Heart of Darkness)*. But this penetration is virtually impossible for a Westerner; the Samhuran natives erect a barricade that Heyst cannot surmount. Had he not acquired Lena, the natives might have accepted him as one of their own. Wang, who has married a native woman, is admitted into the primitive circle. Thus Heyst fails in his life quest because his human emotion of compassion prevents him from leaving civilization entirely behind.

FORD MADOX FORD (1873–1939)

As late as 1949 Ben Ray Redman writing in *The Saturday Review* could disparage Ford and the Tietjens novels and say of a specific rereading of *The Good Soldier,* "I am convinced that anyone who considers it a great or even good novel is an injudicious critic." But the reaction to the long limbo for Ford was about to set in. Mark Schorer published an article in *Horizon,* "The Good Novelist in *The Good Soldier,*" in August of the same year. Robie Macauley was about to reintroduce the Tietjens tetralogy in a single American edition to be called *Parade's End* in 1950. And a dozen, more or less, American critics, professors, and graduate students were to launch as many books in the fifties and sixties devoted to critical analysis and revaluation of Ford's work. He seems to have become a minor industry.

IMPORTANCE

Somewhat difficult to classify (he himself wrote too much and too confusingly on the technique of fiction), portions of his work have been called impressionistic. Indeed there is a fine hallucinatory stream-of-consciousness sequence in Tietjens' shell-shock view of trench warfare. But the overall effect is in the combined realistic-romantic tradition; and his collaboration with Conrad on three novels — *The Inheritors* (1901), *Romance* (1903), and *The Nature of a Crime* (eventually published in 1924) — makes it convenient to consider him in the context of Conrad. He is reported to have admired particularly Flaubert, Turgeniev, Stendhal, and Maupassant.

Ford published well over sixty books in his lifetime, and most of them are comfortable in oblivion. But the accomplishment of *The Good Soldier* and *Parade's End* should be enough to give him more than simply biographical and historical significance. Often called a writer's writer, he has been associated with and exerted some influence on such other authors as Ezra Pound and Joseph Conrad, and, at the other end of his career, Ernest Hemingway, Robie Macauley, and Allen Tate.

Life

Ford Herman Hueffer, according to his birth certificate, was born in 1873 in Merton, England, the son of Dr. Francis Hueffer, German and one-time musical editor for *The Times*. His English mother, Catharine, was the daughter of Ford Madox Brown, the painter; and an aunt was married to William Rossetti, brother of Dante Gabriel and Christina, which gave him tenuous connection with the Pre-Raphaelite movement and *fin de siècle* poets like Swinburne. After his father's early death, Ford lived with the painter grandfather in the center of the circle. His first published writing was a fairy tale, *The Brown Owl*, written at seventeen and in press the following year. After several more books, including a novel, poems, and a biography of his grandfather, Ford, on the recommendation of William Ernest Henley, became the collaborator of Joseph Conrad for a series of novels written together.

By that time, near the end of the century, Ford had unwillingly entered the Roman Catholic Church to please relatives, and married a conservative Catholic, Elsie Martindale. The collaboration between Ford and Conrad ended in 1902, as Ford, becoming neurasthenic, toured German and Belgian spas for his health. Late in 1908 he began to edit *The English Review*, sponsored largely by a friend, Arthur Pearson Marwood, who later became the model for Christopher Tietjens. This was the period of a new association. Ezra Pound has said, "I don't know whether justice has *yet* been done to Ford. I went to England in 1908 to 'learn' from Yeats—and stayed to learn from Yeats *and*

Ford. From 1910 onwards, Fordie and I growled at each other for nigh on twenty years."

Hueffer changed his name to Ford Madox Ford in 1919 for reasons partly connected with tangled marital affairs. In 1909 he had left his wife Elsie, married in 1894, and two daughters; divorce was impossible because of her strongly Catholic position. Court action in 1910 put Ford in jail for ten days. Another court action in 1925 restrained Violet Hunt, his one-time secretary and collaborating novelist, from calling herself his wife. The scandal haunted Ford the rest of his life. He was prevented from seeing his children, although he continued to pay for their education; worse, things had cooled off with Hunt. When the First World War came, Ford, though forty, joined the army, served at the front, was shell shocked and gassed, which caused him to wheeze during his later years. After the war he founded the *Transatlantic Review* in Paris, publishing Joyce and Hemingway among others. Stella Bowen, an Australian painter, became Mrs. Ford, and they had a daughter, Juliet. In these years Ford wrote the four novels that became *Parade's End,* although he had earlier thought of *The Good Soldier* (1915) as his *last* novel. There were still others, not as good, to come in the thirties. Living mainly in France, Ford did come to America to become a writer in residence at Olivet College in Michigan. Robie Macauley talks about Ford in those years, walking on campus, leaning on his stick, in his introduction to *Parade's End.* Most of his students regarded him as colorful but somewhat *passé.* He died in Deauville, France, in June of 1939, and is buried there in an English cemetery.

Chief Works

***The Good Soldier* (1915):** This novel is not about a war, unless it be a war of passions, or rather a war between passions and morality or "good form." This novel has been called a *Madame Bovary* (Flaubert) told from the point of view of the deceived husband, John Dowell, narrator, an American of inherited wealth and New England background, whose wife, Florence, on the pretext of a bad heart deceives him with a number of men, finally Captain Edward Ashburnham, wealthy army officer from Hampshire — and *he* is the "good soldier." Dowell remembers and tries to understand his domestic tragedy: desultory courtship and elopement, an unconsummated marriage, the bondage of twelve years of feigned illness and cuckoldom. The Dowells associated with the Ashburnhams, the Captain and his wife, Leonora, and their ward, Nancy Rufford, the better sort of British people in the European spas. Leonora plays an ambiguous role in the melodramatic tale which includes lechery, adultery, gambling, blackmail, the suicide of Florence, Ashburnham's incurable infatuation with Nancy, her madness and his suicide, Leonora's remarriage to a decent sort of "chap," and Dowell's departure to take over the Hampshire estates.

There is more to the story, but everything that happens can be given several interpretations. One learns to distrust the narrator, not because he is a liar, but because, gradually revealed as incapable of sexual or moral passion, how can he react to such passions with understanding and justice? As Schorer wrote, "No simple inversion of statement can yield up the truth, for the truth is the maze, and, as we learn from what is probably the major theme of the book, appearances have their reality." So Dowell's view is both true and untrue. "Nothing is but what is not." Critics are about equally divided as to whether this is Ford's best work, or the tetralogy.

Parade's End (1924–28): This tetralogy — *Some Do Not,* 1924; *No More Parades,* 1925; *A Man Could Stand Up,* 1926; *Last Post,* 1928 — has one central character, Christopher Tietjens, a lumbering sort of man, fair hair patched with grey, clad in tweeds and some of the time in khaki uniform (for the setting is the First World War in England and France), the younger son of the squire of Groby, brilliant mathematician and Latinist, with intellectual arrogance, immense kindliness, and some sentimentality, above all a Tory and a Tory of the eighteenth century at that. As a war novel *Parade's End* has a special kind of validity; it is more mature and withdrawn than the First World War first novels of the Lost Generation (Dos Passos' *Three Soldiers,* Cummings' *The Enormous Room,* Faulkner's *Soldiers' Pay,* even Hemingway's *The Sun Also Rises*) and is a corrective to them; it is not a romantic view of the War, nor does it take the opposite approach as an antiwar novel; it rather views the War with detachment and disenchantment. Yet it is less about a single war than it is about a whole era, our world with a lament for the world destroyed by a series of events ostensibly beginning about 1914.

At the beginning of the novel series Tietjens and a friend, Macmaster, of the English public official class are riding first class on a train running from London to Rye as smoothly as British gilt-edged securities. It is just before the war, later than they think. Their train is on the wrong line, running from the past into the future; ahead of them are chaos and disorder — hysterical passengers, unpredictable stationmasters, troops, broken furnishings, disrupted schedules — eventually the wasteland. Christopher's character is synonymous with the harmonious past, ordered, humane, feudal, Christian, classical, Tory. His steadfastness is heroic in the world that changes; although amiable, he is persecuted by friends, fellow officers, superiors, but most of all and relentlessly through four volumes by his wife, Sylvia, as beautiful, reckless, arrogant, and morally chaotic as the new era. Her persecution of him is compulsive because he grows stronger under each assault, and this is a reproach to her. In the end he survives but understands there is no place in the modern world for a Christopher Tietjens.

Although Christopher and Sylvia are the most fully developed characters, well rounded and perfect antagonists, the novel series is full of splendidly drawn individuals: Valentine Wannop, the girl with whom Christopher does find, in his very slow, correct English way, some of the satisfactions of reciprocal love; his older brother, Mark, heir to Groby, and the central character in the *Last Post* until his death, with Sylvia's son, legally Christopher's, brought up by her as "a full-fledged Papist, pickled and oiled and wafered and all," the heir to follow him; the Old Squire of Groby, the father; the parson Duchemin; the Welsh private Morgan; the Roman Catholic priest, Father Consett; and a full supply of others.

The two middle novels provide a vivid but quiet picture of the war in France from trenches to headquarters, nothing harrowing, but the mud, blood, muddle, and heroism are real enough. The war changes Christopher in part. At a party celebrating the armistice he sees Valentine and thinks: "What he wanted he was prepared to take. What he had been before, God alone knew. A Younger Son? A Perpetual Second-in-Command? Who knew? But today the world was changed. Feudalism was finished; its last vestiges were gone. It held no place for him. He was going — he was damn well going! — to make a place in it for. . . . A man could stand up on a hill, so he and she could surely get into some hole together!" But the essential Christopher remains, an anachronism in the twentieth century world.

CHRISTOPHER FRY (1907 –   )

Fry's main contributions to the twentieth-century drama are two: He helped to turn the theater temporarily away from the preoccupation with social questions into which it fell at the beginning of the century, and he restored to the English drama something of the scintillating language of the Elizabethan stage. His interest in verbal fireworks has led some critics to view him as a mere manipulator of words, but this is probably unfair. His virtuosity in language is obvious, but there are serious ideas in his drama as well. Like Shaw, Fry stands for the Life-force and is opposed to an ingrown Puritanism, and like the Neo-Platonists of the Renaissance he believes in the ennobling force of sexual love. The heroes in his dramas are those who are moved by their physical urges; the villains are those who defend outmoded and synthetic social conventions. In this sense he is a traditional romantic poet, espousing natural action as opposed to artificial action.

In addition Fry is an experienced theatrical technician. Although he has been long associated with Oxford dramatic groups, he is not a university man; he owes his education and his literary development to the theater itself and to his private reading. The poetry and the "theater" in his plays are organically fused; Fry the playwright is indistinguishable from Fry the poet. His dramas are symmetrically constructed; they utilize all the stock tricks of the theater, and they invariably end with all the threads tied together and all the characters disposed of in an orderly manner.

As a poet he owes something to the twentieth-century imagists but even more to the Elizabethans; he uses the conceits, the soliloquies, and the far-fetched metaphors of the Renaissance stage, and is fond of archaisms in language. His mood and atmosphere are entirely modern; Fry writes, not Elizabethan drama, but modern drama in the Elizabethan vein.

Life

Born in Bristol in 1907, Fry received a brief schooling in the Bedford Modern School; he left at eighteen. He began his theatrical career before he was twenty. His experience in the theater has been broad; he has served as actor, director, producer, and general handyman, and early turned his hand to revising and adapting scripts. From 1932 to 1936 he served as director for the Tunbridge Wells Repertory Players. He wrote lyrics and music for *She Shall Have Music,* a sort of vaudeville produced at the Saville Theatre in London in 1935, and in 1937 wrote an unsuccessful play, *Siege. The Boy with the Cart,* a more successful drama, was produced in 1937 and published by the Oxford University Press in 1939. About the same time Fry became the director of the Oxford Playhouse, but was called up for military service in the winter of 1940. Upon his discharge in 1944 he turned to playwriting in earnest, and soon produced the plays that have made him famous: *A Phoenix Too Frequent* (1946), *Thor, with Angels* (1948), and *The Lady's Not for Burning* (1948). In 1950 four Fry plays were running simultaneously at London theaters.

He has translated and adapted several plays from the French, including two by Anouilh. His own plays since mid-century have included *Venus Observed* (1950); *A Sleep of Prisoners* (1951), which has been called Fry's best religious play; *The Dark Is Light Enough* (1954), his most recent comedy, written for Dame Edith Evans in the London production and played by Katherine Cornell and Tyrone Power in New York in 1955; and *Curtmantle* (1961), Fry's contribution to the dramatic treatment of Thomas à Becket. It has been said that T. S. Eliot's construction is focused and ritualistic, Fry's panoramic and historical, Anouilh's musical and choreographic, perhaps too conveniently placing *Murder in the Cathedral* in a theater of ideas, *Curtmantle* in a theater of characters, and *Becket* in a theater of situations. But this is oversimplification; Fry's play is just not as good theater as the other two. *A Phoenix* and *The Lady* remain Fry's best plays.

Chief Dramas

A Phoenix Too Frequent **(1946):** Laid in classic Rome, it is based on a tale of Petronius. Dynamene, a patrician lady, has resolved to starve herself to death in her beloved husband's tomb, and Doto, her faithful servant, has vowed to accompany her mistress into the Shades. As they wait in the underground tomb they are discovered by a young sentry, Tegeus. Soon the three enter into a melancholy but witty conversation during which they console themselves with Tegeus' wineflask and weigh the relative merits of life and death. Tegeus, falling in love with Dynamene, manages to convince her she should fly from death into his arms. Love seems to triumph; but at this point

Tegeus discovers that one of the hanged corpses he is supposed to have been guarding above the tomb has been stolen from its place. This neglect of duty, he knows, means certain death for him. Dynamene, however, in a triumphant flouting of convention, suggests that they substitute the body of her husband for the missing corpse. The Life-force conquers the Death-wish; the lovers depart, and Doto grows hilariously tipsy on the dregs of the soldier's wine.

The Lady's Not for Burning **(1949):** This play is laid in the fifteenth century in "the little market town of Cool Clary." Thomas Mendip, a young soldier just returned from the wars in Flanders, has been turned melancholy by his experiences and requests of the town clerk Richard that he be hanged; he even confesses to a couple of unsolved murders to expedite the matter. Meanwhile Alizon Eliot, an attractive young maiden, appears on the scene, and Richard falls in love with her. She is also loved by two brothers, Humphrey and Nicholas Devize; the brothers quarrel, and Nicholas knocks Humphrey cold. More complications ensue: the Mayor, Hebble Tyson, unearths an alleged witch, the beautiful Jennet, and preparations are made for her execution. Thomas tries to have himself condemned along with her, but he is instead sentenced to spend the evening joyously in the company of his fellowmen. Humphrey, attempting to force his attentions on Jennet through bribery, is thwarted by Thomas and Nicholas, whom Humphrey has unskillfully locked in a cellar to keep him out of the way. During the evening's celebrations everyone becomes so gay that the sentences are forgotten. "Old Skipps," the rag-and-bone man supposed to have been killed by Thomas, appears very much alive, and Thomas and Jennet, abetted by the tenderhearted Justice Tappercoom, escape together from the house of intoxicated guests. Richard and Alizon are also joined in the end. The theme of the comedy is the triumph of love, or the Life-force, over human perversion and despair. Thomas' description of his own person to Jennet, beginning "Just see me as I am, me like a perambulating vegetable," (Act II) is justly famous. The production featuring John Gielgud, Pamela Brown, and the then-young Richard Burton had notable success on both sides of the Atlantic.

6
IMPRESSIONISM AND STREAM OF CONSCIOUSNESS

As a part of the broader reaction against Realism, a number of authors in the twentieth century began to doubt the essential validity of "reality" as the term is understood by the Realists and Naturalists. To this new group, the "real" was not so much the external incident in the life of a character as the internal mental processes that developed in reaction to this incident. Among the devices invented by twentieth-century authors to depict this internal life were the techniques known as impressionism, stream of consciousness, and internal monologue. These techniques came into predominance in the period immediately after the First World War; by 1925 they had been practiced by four or five major authors and by a host of mediocre imitators.

Various authors utilized these devices differently; Joyce is far from Proust in his basic approach to the novel. Nevertheless these authors shared certain basic premises: (1) that the true existence of an individual lies in his mental processes, not in the external incidents of his life; (2) that the mental life of the ordinary person is disjointed, intuitive, and associative rather than sharply logical; and (3) that psychological association — that is, the mental linking of objects that have been encountered in juxtaposition — is one of the chief processes forming our emotional attitudes toward things. Thus a loved one's glove reminds us of the beloved person herself, and participation in a railway accident will cause us forever to associate train whistles with fear.

To portray this interior life on the printed page, these authors were obliged to invent new and radical narrative techniques. Proust is the most traditional of them and the most significant European of them all; he achieves his stylistic subtlety merely through endless ramification and examination of the problem from all sides. Joyce, on the other hand, is the most radical; following and outdistancing the interior monologue that he found in *Les Lauriers sont coupés* (1888) by Edouard Dujardin, he departs completely from the syntax and grammar of ordinary fiction and creates, not only a new literature, but virtually a new language. Durrell sometimes comes close to him here.

Both Joyce and Proust carry their new techniques to their logical climaxes; thus they are difficult to surpass in their genre. Nevertheless their would-be imitators are to be numbered by the hundreds, and countless other authors show their influence in one form or another.

Impressionistic authors, being chiefly concerned with the mental life of the individual, are generally somewhat detached from social, political, or ethical problems. Proust is the most intellectual of these authors, yet even he is curiously passive toward the problems of modern social evolution. Some of these authors have pretenses of metaphysics, but even this is not their chief interest. They are concerned with the way the human brain reacts to its external stimulations, even the most trivial. To them a cup of tea or a handclasp may be as important as the fall of an empire; their attitude is entirely an individual and subjective one. Virginia Woolf, following or perhaps accompanying Proust and Joyce in this, is a most notable example.

VIRGINIA WOOLF (1882–1941)

IMPORTANCE

Virginia Woolf is an important and significant author in at least two respects. She is a literary psychologist of the highest order, and she is the leading exponent of the stream of consciousness technique in the twentieth century. She demonstrates the method in its most effective form, and she brings to the task a rare and striking talent for portraying nuances of thought. For her the stream of consciousness is not a chain of organized logic, a ladder of thought leading to a definite conclusion, but a disorganized mass of impressions received from the environment mixed with chance notions culled from memory and recollection. She views the brain as a sort of target constantly being struck by diverse missiles from within and without. The brain has no control over the impact of these objects, and before it can attempt to organize and understand them another set arrives to distract and confuse it. Thus consciousness wanders through time weaving and halting, and only manages haphazardly to solve the problems the human will puts to it.

Naturally the portrayal of such a consciousness in its pure form would make poor literature, and Woolf is wise enough to impose a certain artificial pattern on the process to make it significant. Clarissa Dalloway's day in *Mrs. Dalloway* is carefully planned to include all the elements that go to make up her existence; thus the novel becomes a microcosm of her entire life. Moreover Woolf conventionalizes the gibberish of the unguided mind into a coherent and grammatical English style. She is no iconoclast; she has no desire to startle the reader with avant garde experimentation for its own sake. Her roots are firmly fixed in the tradition of the English novel, and she has a profound respect for classical style. She parodies the history of English literature in *Orlando*, but she is able to do so only because she has a copious knowledge of English literature and understands and respects its merits.

Woolf is not deeply interested in character. There are few memorable or striking personalities in her books, and often her characters seem cursed with a monotonous sameness. This is so partly because her writing is entirely subjective. She views the world through the eyes of a single character, who is essentially herself, and sees other characters only as dim reflections impinging upon her consciousness. Even in *The Waves*, which is related by six separate characters, it may be argued that each of these persons is only the author in a different form. The characters speak alike, think according to the same process, and even appear to have the same attitudes and opinions. In other books the stream of consciousness seems to switch aimlessly from one character to another without altering the basic style of thought. The switching, however, is seldom aimless; Woolf's novels are planned as carefully as those of Henry James or Gide.

Where ideas and opinions appear in Woolf's novels, they are usually latent. In her nonfiction works, however, she has given us a better key to her personal viewpoint. She is a fervent feminist *(A Room of One's Own)* who feels that women's poor showing in art and literature throughout the ages has been due to masculine conspiracy rather than to any lack of genius in the sex. She believes that life should be lived and enjoyed rather than understood, and she even doubts whether any understanding of it is possible. Lastly, she feels that humanity is linked by a sort of common consciousness, a community of the inner mind, and that the thoughts of any one person might serve as a symbol of the thoughts of all humanity.

Life

Virginia Stephen was born in 1882, daughter of the noted scholar, editor, and philosopher Sir Leslie Stephen. Her father in some respects formed the model for Professor Ramsay of *To The Lighthouse*. Virginia was privately educated, and read widely in classics and English literature while still a child. At thirty she married Leonard Woolf, a liberal historian and sociologist who had just returned from a tour of civil service in Ceylon. The same year, 1912, the Woolfs took a house in Bloomsbury and began to organize a sort of avant-garde literary salon; their intimates included E. M. Forster, the Sitwells, Clive Bell, Lytton Strachey, Victoria Sackville-West, and J. M. Keynes. T. S. Eliot and Katherine Mansfield were also occasional members of this "Bloomsbury group." As a hobby the Woolfs in 1917 began printing some of their own writings under the label "Hogarth Press"; this venture was so successful that they soon began to devote themselves seriously to the publishing business. The Hogarth Press printed early works by both Eliot and Mansfield.

Woolf's first novel, *The Voyage Out,* was first written about 1906 but did not appear until 1915. This work, along with *Night and Day* (1919) was conventional in style. *Monday or Tuesday,* a 1921 collection of stories, was more original in technique, and *Jacob's Room* (1922) was a fresh and daring experiment in the novel. Her best works appeared from 1922 to 1928, although she continued to write up to the time of her death.

During the First World War Woolf, greatly affected personally by the troubles of the times, suffered an attack of mental illness. In 1941, depressed by a new war and fearing that a recurrence of the disease would make her a burden on her husband, she quietly took her own life by drowning.

Chief Novels

***Mrs. Dalloway* (1925):** This book is probably Virginia Woolf's most significant work. The structure is reminiscent of *Ulysses,* and undoubtedly Joyce's novel, which Woolf read in serial form in *The Little Review* as early as 1919, had a stimulating influence on her.

Somewhat like *Ulysses,* the novel follows certain Londoners through a typical day of their lives in June of 1919. The chief character is Clarissa Dalloway, a successful but somewhat superficial British society woman; each of the other persons who passes through the novel is important as his life relates to hers. As the day passes and the time is marked by the striking of Big Ben, the novel passes successively through the minds of Mrs. Dalloway and her friends, and the pattern of their lives becomes apparent.

As the day begins Clarissa Dalloway is making preparations for an important dinner party; she is proud of her prestige as a hostess and of the important personages who are seen in her house. She meets an old friend, Hugh Whitbread, who has now become a rather stuffy Court official; this meeting turns her thoughts to the past and especially to the years before she was married. In the nineties she was courted by the romantic but somewhat unstable Peter Walsh; when she rejected him it was out of a vague and half-formed ambition to marry a man of importance. In the years since she has often secretly hoped for her husband to become Prime Minister, but now the chance seems slight. Peter, disappointed, parted from her in an emotional scene and went out to India, where he married another woman.

Leaving Clarissa temporarily, the novel introduces Septimus Smith, a young war veteran, and his wife Lucrezia (Rezia), whom he met in Italy shortly after the war. Woolf has indicated that Septimus is intended as a "double" for Clarissa herself; originally the two characters were merged in her mind. Both Clarissa and Septimus had literary talent in their youth; both are cold and unable to show the expected emotional reactions to crises, and both feel that their lives, especially their marriages, have turned out to be different from what they expected. In short, both feel a purposelessness in their lives that no amount of casual intercourse with other people can obliterate. But Clarissa is outwardly successful, while Septimus is tormented and miserable. He has threatened suicide and is under treatment at present for a nervous breakdown; but the bluff general practitioner Dr. Holmes who attends him has little comprehension of his mental predicament and tells him jovially that there is nothing wrong with him. Lucrezia is torn between her sympathy for Septimus and a resentment for the way, as she imagines, he has spoiled her life; she has no more comprehension of what is wrong with him than Dr. Holmes has. In desperation she takes him to an expensive and somewhat pompous specialist, Sir William Bradshaw, who makes arrangements to send him to a sanatorium in the country this very evening. Now the pattern begins to appear, for Sir William is to be a guest at Clarissa's party.

As Clarissa proceeds with her plans, a new element intrudes: Peter Walsh, who has come back to England to arrange for a divorce so he can marry a new love, calls on her, and Clarissa's thoughts are diverted for a second time to the days of her youth. She becomes aware that the dominant theme of Peter's life has been the pursuit of feminine love, and suspects that his unrequited affection for her is the root of it all. For his part Peter now feels somewhat superior to the superficial existence Clarissa leads; she senses this feeling, and begins to wonder whether she had not made a mistake in rejecting him.

Shortly before the party begins the novel returns to Septimus and Lucrezia, who are now in their lodgings. Septimus, brooding over the death of his friend Evans in the war and over his imminent confinement in the sanatorium, is in a black mood. Lucrezia tries to brighten him up, and even succeeds for a while. Then the boorish Dr. Holmes appears on the stairs and tries to force his way in to Septimus to jolly him out of his nonsense. Trapped, Septimus throws himself out the window and is killed.

The party is outwardly a success. The Prime Minister and other important personages arrive, and Clarissa feels very much the successful hostess. But the Bradshaws arrive late, and Sir William excuses himself by explaining that one of his patients — Septimus — has committed suicide. At first Clarissa feels a resentment that death has intruded its way into her party (she attempts to remain in an artificial world into which reality cannot intrude). But she shortly begins to feel an odd empathy with the unknown young man who has taken his own life; she even feels that Septimus has performed an act of courage of which she would never be capable. He has "reached the center" while she remains standing on the periphery of life. At last she knows herself for the superficial person she is. The novel ends, somewhat ironically, as Peter feels his old love for Clarissa returning; he wonders if the Clarissa he knew in his youth still lives beneath the successful hostess.

The chief theme of this novel is the effort of its middle-class Londoners to find some meaning in their lives, to tear away the superficial veil of convention and social intercourse that envelops them. In technique *Mrs. Dalloway* is striking and original. The chaotic pattern of the various characters' lives is tied together through a set of connective incidents: the passage of a motor car, a skywriting advertisement, and the striking of Big Ben. The point of view slips from one character's mind to another with a disconcerting subtlety; but the shifts are invariably meaningful, and the transitions from mind to mind are marked by carefully placed signposts. *Mrs. Dalloway* is an easier novel to follow than Joyce's *Ulysses*, but it is a no less penetrating portrait of human mental existence.

To the Lighthouse (1927): This novel follows the Ramsay family—Professor and Mrs. Ramsay, their son James, their daughter Camilla, and several other children—through a period of ten years. The novel is constructed of two sections connected by an interlude. In the first section, "The Window," the Ramsays, at a summer residence in the Hebrides Islands off the west coast of Scotland, are planning a boat expedition to an offshore lighthouse for the next day. Mr. Ramsay, an eminent philosophy professor, is not particularly respected by his children, who resent his sarcastic professional manner. His wife, a deeply intuitive and understanding woman, is the real force holding the family together. Six-year-old James especially has his heart set on going to the lighthouse, and when his father predicts that the weather will not permit the expedition, a great hate surges up in him. He carries this resentment, partly subconsciously, for ten years until another remark of his father's atones for it. A spectator of this family conflict is Lily Briscoe, a guest of the Ramsays and an amateur painter. She spends the day talking with the poet Carmichael, another guest, and trying to finish a landscape; but for some reason the proper pattern will not appear on her canvas. At the end of the day the weather turns stormy, and to the disappointment of the children the trip to the lighthouse is postponed.

The interlude, "Time Passes," describes the passing of ten years through picturing the effects of time on the summer house. As the paper peels from the walls and the books mildew, time eats away at the Ramsay family too. Mrs. Ramsay dies in her sleep; the youngest and prettiest of the daughters, Prue, succumbs in childbirth, and a son, Andrew, is killed in the war. The interlude closes as the remainder of the family come again to the island ten years after the events of the first section.

In the final section, "The Lighthouse," James, now sixteen, and his sister Camilla prepare for the long-postponed expedition. They expect little from the trip, since they have grown apart from their father and the whole subject of the lighthouse recalls unpleasant memories to them. But Mr. Ramsay is determined to make the trip. The expedition starts badly; the family oversleeps, and the preparations are botched. As Lily, again a guest in the house, watches the departure of the party, she feels vaguely sorry for Mr. Ramsay, but lacks the courage to express her sympathy. She goes back to the painting she had abandoned ten years before. As she works she tries to see some pattern in the events of the past ten years, but everything seems curiously unreal to her. She senses the intangibility, the transitory frailty, of everything that human beings call reality. For a moment she feels horribly alone, then suddenly she perceives the exact stroke needed to complete the painting in front of her. In her aesthetic "vision" she grasps the truth that art brings to our existence a permanence and significance that mere transitory reality cannot: "life is short, art is long." Whatever meaning there may be in the world about her, she has found a meaning in her painting; and this fact in itself imposes a meaning onto the chaotic pattern of life.

At this instant Mr. Ramsay, James, and Cam are approaching the lighthouse. When James first glimpses the lighthouse he has waited so long to see, he is disappointed; it does not equal the image he has carried in his anticipations. Presently he realizes that there are actually two lighthouses: the real one and the one he has cherished in his mind. It is perhaps the second one that is the more real of the two. After the fumblings and unhappiness of the past ten years, he grasps the truth that happiness exists in the region of the mind and is, in a sense, independent of external events. Thus, like Lily, he now knows that the meaning of life is not to be found in the pursuit of mere physical pleasure. As they near the dock Mr. Ramsay is moved to praise James' steering of the boat, and the resentment that James has carried for ten years against his father melts away. Both Camilla and James feel that a new life may be beginning for the family.

Lily Briscoe, who takes no overt part in the action of the novel, is actually a disguised transposition of the author herself. Like Lily, Woolf sees little meaning in life until it is organized into artistic form. The artist, who creates patterns out of chaos, imposes upon life the only meaning it will ever have. And like James, Woolf believes that the world of the imagination is more vivid and powerful, even more real, than what is ordinarily considered physical reality. A further autobiographical element in the novel is the figure of Professor Ramsay, who is partly drawn after Woolf's own father.

Orlando (1928): This whimsical and original work is quite different from Woolf's earlier novels. A number of elements, including the personality of the hero, are good-natured satires on Woolf's friend, the novelist Victoria Sackville-West. Orlando, the hero, is a romantic young man born in England in the sixteenth century. But his longevity is prodigious; he lives through the seventeenth and eighteenth centuries, changes to a woman midway through the book, and has arrived at the prime of life by 1928, when the novel closes. *Orlando* thus becomes a farcical survey of English literary history during the centuries covered. Woolf even attempts to write each section in the spirit, if not in the style, of the period treated. Notable incidents are the freezing over of the Thames in the Great Frost of 1604, Orlando's tour of duty as Ambassador to Turkey during the reign of Charles II, the portrayals of Addison and Pope in the period of Queen Anne, and Orlando's marriage to Marmaduke Bonthrop Shelmerdine, Esquire during the Victorian period.

KATHERINE MANSFIELD (1888–1923)

Katherine Mansfield, little recognized outside the English-speaking world, possessed one of the most sensitive literary talents of our time. She confined herself exclusively to the short story and sketch, and she contributed to this genre approximately what Virginia Woolf contributed to the novel. In fact, although the two women were never intimate, they recognized their essential kinship. "We have got the same job, Virginia, and it is really very curious and thrilling that we should both, quite apart from each other, be after so nearly the same thing," Mansfield wrote to Woolf.

IMPORTANCE

Like Woolf, Mansfield writes from the inside of her characters rather than the outside. She follows the wanderings of the human mind with fidelity, even when this leads her into divagations and digressions. She is even more likely than Woolf to skip from one character to another in the middle of a page; this gives her prose a curiously confused quality upon first reading. The trick has the merit of lending complexity to what would otherwise become a monotonous stream of conscious-ness; she is attempting something similar to Joyce's *Ulysses* or Gide's *Counterfeiters,* where the same incident is seen from the point of view of several characters. The main weakness of the device is that Mans-field's characters tend to be believable in inverse proportion to their distance from herself. She is excellent in transcribing the thoughts of children and young women, and weaker on mature men, matriarchal old women, and indeed strong characters of all kinds.

Mansfield has a subtle feeling for the power of words; her images are forceful and inevitable, and she possesses a sure touch for dialogue. She is little interested in exposition and often ignores it entirely; the reader is left to puzzle out who is related to whom and what has occurred before the story opens. It is in the use of these two devices — (1) switching the stream of consciousness from one character to an-other, and (2) beginning *in media res* and ignoring exposition — that Mansfield was most influential on younger writers.

In content Mansfield's work is relatively restricted. Most of her stories are built around one of three situations: (1) a sensitive little girl in New Zealand entranced by nature but misunderstood by her elders; (2) an English girl, often a governess, in Germany, disgusted and depressed by German boor-ishness; or (3) a female English writer in France, sometimes engaged in romantic adventures. Her stories are inevitably tragic; even her more whim-sical sketches end in calamity or disillusionment. The world of Katherine Mansfield is one in which the sensitive, the creative, and the good-hearted are tyrannized by the unthinking and animal-like extroverts until they finally destroy themselves like butterflies breaking their wings against a cage.

Life

Katherine Mansfield's life was touched by the tragedy about which she writes. She was born in Wellington, New Zealand in 1888 and spent her childhood in this city and in the nearby village of Karori. In 1903 she went with her sisters to London to attend Queen's College; she became a skillful musician, edited a student magazine, and tentatively began to write fiction. In 1906 she returned to New Zealand, but now found the narrow provincial atmosphere stifling; like Thomas Wolfe she learned that "you can't go home again." She was desperately unhappy until her father allowed her to return to London in 1908 on a small allowance. Back in England she took a cheap flat, joined an informal literary circle, and began to write in earnest. In 1909 she married George Bowden, a young musician, on impulse; she lived with him only a few days. A short time later she journeyed with her mother to Woerishofen, a Bavarian spa, where she gave birth to a stillborn child; her health began failing at this time and continued to deteriorate for the rest of her life.

In 1911 Mansfield met the author and critic John Middleton Murry; the pair were immediately attracted and lived together as husband and wife thenceforth, although they were unable to marry until Mansfield's divorce in 1918. Her first important collection of stories, *In a German Pension,* appeared in 1911. In 1915 she suffered a great shock when her brother Leslie was killed on the Western front; she seemed at this time to turn back nostalgically to her New Zealand childhood, and most of her subsequent stories are laid in New Zealand. In 1917 an attack of pleurisy resulted in a progressive and incurable deterioration of her lungs. She continued to write intermittently, but died in France in 1923, Murry still at her side.

Representative Stories

Three stories will suffice to show the variations in Miss Mansfield's material. "The-Child-Who-Was-Tired" is a typical sketch from *In a German Pension* (1911). A very young girl, perhaps a child, is forced to take care of a squalling lot of babies in a German household. The father is an unfeeling tyrant, and the mother, simply called "the Frau," is a sickly woman half-killed by the endless succession of babies her husband forces her to bear. For her part the child-nurse is almost dead with weariness; she is forced to attend the children all night, and falls asleep on the floor while lighting the oven. She is rudely awakened by the father, who informs her that the Frau is going to have yet another baby. In the evening the family adjourns to the parlour to entertain guests, leaving the child in the bedroom with orders to keep the baby quiet at all costs. Groggy from fatigue, the child smothers the baby with a bolster and then falls gratefully to sleep on the floor. This powerful little sketch is based on a story by Chekhov, whose work Mansfield greatly admired. Her treatment, however, is technically more radical than Chekhov's.

***Prelude* (1918):** This is a long, detailed story, almost a novella. Like many of the stories of her later period, it is laid in the New Zealand of her childhood. Kezia, the youngest child of a family of sisters, is an autobiographical character. The little girl, sensitive and unhappy, is abandoned with her sister on the family moving day because "there was not an inch of room" in the buggy; the drayman is ordered to pick them up later, and they arrive at the confused new country household in the evening. Kezia is dominated by her elder sister Isabel and virtually ignored by her egocentric and neurotic mother. She fearfully seeks admission to the games of the older children; midway in the story she receives a terrible shock when she witnesses the decapitation of a duck. Only the grandmother understands and loves Kezia, and this solace makes her life worth while. The story is viewed successively through the minds of various characters: Kezia, her mother Linda, the father Stanley, and the aunt Beryl each have their turns. "At the Bay" (1914) is a continuation of *Prelude,* although written four years earlier.

Je ne parle pas français **(1919):** This is a long story based on an affair with the French poet Francis Carco, whom Mansfield visited in northern France in 1915. The work was published in book format by Murry and was later included in Mansfield's collected stories. The action is related by the protagonist, Raoul Duquette, an affected and sentimental young Frenchman. On a café blotter he sees the scribbled inscription *Je ne parle pas français,* and this reminds him of a delicious but painful incident in his life; these were the first words spoken to him by a young English girl who had a strange effect on him. The girl, nicknamed "Mouse," arrives in Paris in company of an English friend of Raoul's, Dick. When Dick abandons Mouse, Raoul hopes to become her protector. But her English coolness and her superb savoir-faire intimidate him, and rather than retreat to the humiliating position of a platonic friend, he abandons her as Dick has done. Raoul is well drawn; he is one of Mansfield's few convincing male characters.

JAMES JOYCE (1882 – 1941)

Joyce, like Proust, should be read in his entirety for a proper understanding. His literary development begins with the relatively conventional stories of *Dubliners,* proceeds through *A Portrait of the Artist* to the daring experimentation of *Ulysses,* and finds its climax in the difficult and esoteric *Finnegans Wake.* Furthermore, Joyce's work is consecutive not only in technique but in content. The themes of his earliest work recur in *Ulysses* and *Finnegans Wake,* and actual characters and incidents from *A Portrait of the Artist* are transported bodily into *Ulysses.* Stephen Dedalus, the hero of *A Portrait of the Artist,* appears in an embryonic form in several stories of *Dubliners* and becomes one of the three central characters of *Ulysses.* The reader who begins with Joyce's earlier works and reads through to *Finnegans Wake* will be approaching a difficult subject in easy and scalable steps.

IMPORTANCE

Joyce for years made his living as a professional language teacher. Language occupies a dominant place in his technique; he is familiar with archaic and etymological senses in ordinary words, he is fond of using exotic, archaic, or foreign words for effect, and he often invents his own words when the dictionary is unable to supply him one. Almost blind himself, he was sensitive to nuances of sound, touch, and smell, and continually sought ways to portray such sensations in language. He lingers lovingly over such phrases as "a day of dappled seaborne clouds" or "bronze by gold heard the hoofirons, steelyringing." He uses startling typographical devices to startle the eye, especially in *Ulysses,* yet his work is meant primarily for the ear. This is particularly true of his dialogue; Joyce is a master of vernacular speech and has captured the spirit of everyday conversation with a skill shared by few modern authors.

The term "interior monologue" describes Joyce's method better than the expression "stream of consciousness." His characters often seem to be talking to themselves. Everything is verbalized, even the sounds of clocks, horse's hooves, or surf. Characters who boast of no particular education or culture speak in the accents of Shakespeare or Dante, or form images worthy of a talented poet. The reader of *Ulysses* is submerged under a stream of glittering, closely packed, and highly allusive language, and even with careful attention he is likely to miss nuances upon first reading.

In the area of the structure of the novel Joyce's influence has been enormous. He is not the inventor of the "pattern novel," which follows a disparate group of people about their tasks through a given period of time, but he brought this technique to a radical and supreme climax and provoked a host of lesser imitators who are still striving fruitlessly to surpass him. In *Ulysses* the effect of simultaneity is achieved by switching rapidly from one character to another; in *Finnegans Wake* the dreaming fantasies of the hero are contrived to include a complete picture of his society and indeed of all humanity. In this sense, that is, in structure, Joyce is a naturalist not very different from Dos Passos or Romains; but his highly experimental prose style marks him as an impressionist more closely allied to Proust and Virginia Woolf. *Ulysses,* an experiment in comparative technique, contains passages similar to continental expressionism as well as parodies of classic and medieval scholasticism. Joyce's chief stylistic device, however, is the interior monologue, where the innermost thoughts of the character are combined with stimuli from the external world and the resulting mental processes portrayed in disconnected sentences.

As a youth Joyce was trained by the Jesuits, and he was never able to free himself entirely from the influence of this Catholic indoctrination. In later years he renounced both Catholicism and the Irish nationalism in which he had dabbled in his youth, but he remained emotionally attached to both these influences. His blasphemy is that of a Catholic heretic and not of an unbeliever; likewise his sneers at Ireland are those of a disillusioned and sorrowing native son. His character throughout his career was that of a doubtful rebel; he severed his intellectual ties with his youth but felt bound to it by an emotion more powerful than reason.

Joyce is a highly subjective writer; he invented little he did not experience in his own life. Even his characters, with the possible exception of Molly Bloom, are patterned after persons he knew in his lifetime. *A Portrait of the Artist* is almost totally autobiographical, and *Ulysses* is meticulous in its description of Dublin places, persons, events, and dialect. Joyce is not a highly inventive writer, but he possesses a talent for transforming his own experience into a highly artistic and convincing fiction.

Life

James Joyce, born in Dublin, was the son of a convivial civil servant named Stanislaus Joyce and a devout Irishwoman who set his footsteps carefully in the path of her own Catholic faith. Joyce attended an excellent Jesuit school, Clongowes Wood College at Clane; after three years there he moved to Belvedere College in Dublin. A brilliant scholar, he went on to the Jesuit University College in Dublin; there he mastered virtually every major modern language, became an adept Latinist, and read thoroughly in classic and modern literature. He took his bachelor's degree in 1902 and immediately left for Paris. By this time he had lost his faith both in Catholicism and in Irish nationalism. In 1903 he was called home by his mother's death; the following year he met and eventually married (after they had lived together for many years on the continent and had two children) Nora Barnacle, a charming and witty Galway girl. The couple left almost immediately for Europe, and Joyce found a position teaching language in the Trieste Berlitz school. Most of the stories in *Dubliners* were written during 1905, his first year in Trieste, from notes jotted down earlier; but, although the manuscript was accepted the following year by an English publisher, it did not appear as a book until 1914 because various printers refused to set up in type such objectionable matter as the word *bloody* and an innuendo against Edward VII. This was only the first of Joyce's many struggles with publication and censorship, official and unofficial, but certainly from a later perspective officious. Also at Trieste he began writing *A Portrait of the Artist as a Young Man,* which he finished in 1914 and which was first published in New York in 1916, having encountered the usual obstacles in Ireland and England. He was forced to earn his living by teaching language and by other jobs, however, until after the First World War, when he began to receive aid from certain affluent admirers.

From 1914 to 1921 he labored at *Ulysses* in Trieste, in Zurich, where the Joyces spent most of the war years, and in Paris; the novel began to appear in various little magazines as early as 1918 and was published in its entirety in 1922. *Ulysses* created such a furor that at one time or another it was banned in virtually every English-speaking country; it was finally admitted to the United States only after a famous judicial decision by U. S. District Judge John M. Woolsey in 1933.

The third period of Joyce's literary career extends from 1922 to 1939; during this time he was working on *Finnegans Wake,* at first tentatively titled

Work in Progress. Most of the work on this book was done in Paris. *Finnegans Wake,* extremely esoteric in technique, was well received in avant-garde circles but was not financially successful. By this time Joyce's health was extremely poor. His eyesight had grown constantly weaker throughout his life; he underwent more than ten painful operations on his eyes, but was virtually blind by 1939. In 1940, with the fall of France, the Joyces escaped to Zurich, almost penniless and separated from Lucia, one of their two children. Joyce, worried and weakened, fell ill and was operated on for a duodenal ulcer; he died shortly after.

Chief Works

Dubliners **(1914):** These fourteen connected stories and a novella have the impact of a novel when read in that way through its unities of place, the increasing age of individual protagonists, the nature of its epiphanies, and the recurrent and overriding theme: the paralysis or entrapment and resulting frustration that a modern city, always Dublin for Joyce, imposes on its inhabitants. Joyce thought it represented a chapter in the moral history of the race, the first three stories about childhood, told in the first person by an unnamed boy narrator who is disillusioned in his faith in "The Sisters," in his hopes in "An Encounter," and in love in "Araby"; moving to a second group of four stories about wrong choices of mate and vocation by a young woman, "Eveline," and the young men, Jimmy Doyle in "After the Race," the "Two Gallants," Corley and Lenehan, and Bob Doran of "The Boarding House," which represent a deeper stage than disillusionment, entrapment — Eveline is trapped by not marrying and Bob by letting himself be forced into it; a third group of four stories that show the results of such entrapment in later life: the wasted lives of Little Chandler in "A Little Cloud," Farrington in "Counterparts" (one of the most brutal and brutalized characters in Dublin's hell), the spinster Maria of "Clay" who is pathetic and empty, and it isn't her fault, and the equally empty, but it is his fault, James Duffy of "A Painful Case"; to the fourth group, three stories of public life and the ultimate paralysis that has been produced in politics and love for one's country in the ironic contrast of "Ivy Day in the Committee Room" between the memory of Parnell and the miserable state of politics in a local ward with the buying of votes, in culture and the hopes and ambitions of artists in "A Mother," and in faith with the businessman's retreat in a Jesuit church with the ironic and sardonic "Grace" of Father Purdon. In some of these stories the main character is given an insight into the problem, an epiphany or understanding, but not Eveline, who is too simple, not Farrington, and none of the characters in "Ivy Day," "A Mother," or "Grace." They're too far gone. James had written to his brother Stanislaus, "What's the matter with you is that you're afraid to live. You and people like you. This city is suffering from hemiplegia of the will." After finishing the first story, he declared, "I am writing a series of epicleti. . . .

I call the series *Dubliners* to betray the soul of that hemiplegia or paralysis which many consider a city."

The Dead is the novella coda to the fourteen short stories of progressive paralysis. It is a finely controlled and poetically written story about the man Joyce might have become had he not escaped from Ireland, Gabriel Conroy, and the party given on Twelfth Night or Epiphany by his aunts, the Misses Kate and Julia Morkan. The Dublin and the Ireland that Gabriel distrusts (he takes his vacations on the continent and refuses to join the Gaelic revival espoused by Miss Ivors) is the same Dublin that has emerged in the preceding stories, "brown all over" and stultifying. The party seems lively enough on the surface, but it is forced, and the most vital character in the story is the dead man, Michael Fury, who had been the youthful lover of Gabriel's wife, Gretta, and who died for love. After the party understanding and anguish come to Gabriel in the hotel room at the Gresham, contrasting his own self-conscious heaviness and lust with the lyrical, poetic, emotional attachment of his wife to the memory of Michael Fury; now he looks out the window westward at the snow falling all over Ireland, over the living and the dead.

The events in *Dubliners* take place during a ten-year period from 1894 to 1904, and originally *Ulysses* or the story of Leopold Bloom had been conceived as an additional story to be incorporated into the group. Indeed there are special affinities between *Dubliners* and *Ulysses,* particularly in the precision of place references and the wanderings within the city that make them closer to each other than either is to *A Portrait of the Artist* or *Finnegans Wake.* Stephen's imagination and that of the sleeper H. C. Earwicker have much in common. Leopold Bloom, on the other hand, is clearly a Dubliner with both feet on Dublin ground, although he seems more fortunate than the others — perhaps because of Molly.

A Portrait of the Artist as a Young Man (1916): This novel is relatively conventional in style except for certain idiosyncracies of typography and punctuation — for example, the use of dashes in the French manner in place of quotation marks. The career of the hero, Stephen Dedalus, is followed from his schoolboy days until the moment he determines upon a literary career; thus, the novel corresponds to the first twenty years of Joyce's own life. The major portion of the action takes place in school, in Chapter I the Clongowes Wood College, for the next three chapters Belvedere in Dublin, and for the last chapter University College — all of which Joyce himself attended. Stephen is an apt scholar, but gets into trouble because of his independence of thought and his growing religious doubt. He is also tormented by sensual passions, and because of his training he believes these mark him for eternal damnation. A minor triumph is his skirmish with Father Dolan, a teacher who beats him for accidentally breaking his glasses.

Stephen goes to the head and complains of his treatment, and is later viewed as a martyr and hero by his companions. At sixteen he is enticed into a brothel and is there passively introduced to physical love. Later he hears a scathing sermon on heaven and hell; he is filled with remorse and dismay until he manages to confess to a strange priest. Stephen gradually grows apart from his fellows; he cannot share their Irish nationalism or their naive piety, and at last realizes he does not belong with them. At the end of the novel he recognizes his literary vocation and determines to leave Ireland for some foreign land, there to "forge the uncreated conscience of his race."

Ulysses **(1922):** This pattern novel follows the experiences of certain persons through the day of June 16, 1904 in Dublin. The construction of the novel is superficially parallel to that of Homer's *Odyssey*. The chief characters are Leopold Bloom, a middle-aged advertising salesman of Jewish ancestry; his half-Spanish wife, Molly; their daughter, Millicent or Milly; Blazes Boylan, Mrs. Bloom's lover; Stephen Dedalus, a young intellectual just returned from Paris and now teaching in a small private school; and Buck Mulligan, a medical student and acquaintance of Stephen.

During the day various events, all of which are related, occur in Dublin. Molly Bloom, with the knowledge of her husband, commits adultery with Boylan; Bloom arises late and cooks himself a pork kidney; Stephen quarrels with his friend Mulligan and finally quits his job as schoolteacher; Bloom racks his mind for advertising jingles; one Patrick Dignam is buried and various of the principals attend his funeral; a woman named Mina Purefoy gives birth to a child; and various civic and public events take place.

The novel is organized into three parts and eighteen chapters, each chapter written in a different style. The chapter content may be summarized as follows:

PART I: 1. Stephen and Mulligan breakfast at the old Martello tower where they live. Mulligan taunts Stephen with his Jesuitical ways; Stephen departs to teach his pupils. The style is similar to that of *A Portrait of the Artist*.

2. In Deasy's school. Stephen conducts a lesson and later has a conversation with the tedious schoolmaster Deasy. The style is similar to that of Chapter 1.

3. Stephen goes for a walk on Sandymount Strand, thinking about his family, which is much come down in the world since his mother's death. He muses bitterly upon the ambitions of his boyhood. The chapter is written as an impressionistic internal monologue.

PART II: 1. Bloom is introduced. He prepares a pork kidney for his breakfast. His wife receives a letter from Boylan, and he realizes they are planning an assignation. Style similar to Chapter 1.

2. Bloom goes to the post office, where he receives a letter from his

epistolary sweetheart Martha. Later he visits a church, buys a cake of soap, which he carries about with him all day, and goes to the public baths. Style: internal monologue.

3. Bloom attends the funeral of Dignam and passes Stephen on the way. His friends twit him with allusions to Blazes Boylan. The style is conventional narrative dialogue, interspersed with Bloom's thoughts.

4. Bloom, in his office, gropes for advertising slogans. The action presently shifts to Stephen, who enters the newspaper office and converses with the editors. Style: stream of consciousness interspersed with mock newspaper headlines.

5. Bloom takes a walk; he stops at Davy Byrne's pub for a cheese sandwich and a glass of burgundy and overhears talk of Boylan. Style: stream of consciousness.

6. Stephen visits the library and takes part in a conversation about Shakespeare. The idea of his search for a spiritual father is introduced. Style: dialogue.

7. Various characters, including the Jesuit Father Conmee, Stephen, Boylan, the typist Miss Dunne, and Bloom, are depicted at an identical moment soon after noon. The viceregal coach passes through the streets of Dublin, and is noted by various characters. Style: conventional narrative.

8. Miss Douce and Miss Kennedy, barmaids at the Ormond Hotel, engage in a trivial conversation. Various characters enter; Boylan persuades Miss Douce to snap her garter. Bloom takes liver and bacon and mashed potatoes and overhears more talk of his wife. Boylan departs for his rendezvous. Style: narrative and dialogue and musical *leitmotifs*.

9. Bloom rises above attempted humiliation in a barroom squabble, at the end of which a biscuit box is thrown at him. The story is related secondhand by a pub-loafer. Parodies of medieval romance, scientific reports, and Rabelaisian accounts of an execution are interspersed.

10. Bloom walks to the beach and spies lasciviously on a crippled girl, Gerty MacDowell. She imagines him as a mysterious and handsome stranger. Style: internal monologue, switching from Gerty to Bloom.

11. The maternity hospital, 10 p.m. Mrs. Purefoy's child is born. Bloom and Stephen meet. Parodies of medieval, biblical, and medical styles, as well as the progress of English literature down to and including American slang.

12. Midnight at a bawdy house. Stephen is intoxicated; Bloom is also present, having protectively followed the youth. The meeting of Stephen and Bloom (spiritual son and father) is the climax of the novel. Style: a fantastic nightmare in dramatic form; Stephen's and Bloom's consciousness are mixed.

PART III: 1. Bloom extricates the drunken Stephen from the bawdy house; they take shelter in a cabman's hut. Stephen tells an encountered friend there will be a job available tomorrow at Deasy's school. Gradually Stephen sobers. Style: narrative and dialogue.

2. Stephen and Bloom return to Bloom's home to sleep, but Stephen departs after taking cocoa. Bloom goes to bed with his wife. Style: mock catechism.

3. Molly Bloom, awakened by her husband's entry, falls into a half-dreaming revery in which she recalls her youth and reviews the entire action of the novel. Style: internal monologue unbroken by punctuation.

The above is the framework of the novel. Behind the events of this day, apparently chaotic and disconnected, lies a carefully contrived plan. June 16, 1904 is not a particularly momentous day in Irish history, but Joyce has included in it what he considers a complete crosssection of modern life. Various public and semipublic events occur during the day, and each of them is linked to the private lives of the several characters. In many cases these incidents are seen from more than one point of view as they impinge upon different minds. A knowledge of the events of the day in Dublin is therefore helpful as the novel is read. The most important of these events were as follows:

The day was generally sunny and warm, although a thundershower came up shortly after sundown. In Ascot, England it was Gold Cup Day; Dublin opinion favored the mare Sceptre to win, but the race was actually won by a long shot named Throwaway. Posters and newspapers announced the imminent arrival of Dr. Alexander Dowie, an American evangelist who was to preach in Merrion Hall. A store called Hely's was advertising through a sandwich-board stunt. The newspapers reported the burning and sinking of an excursion boat, the *General Slocum,* in New York with the loss of many lives. The Japanese army won a battle against the Russians at Fuchou in Manchuria; this was also reported in the Dublin papers. Shortly after noon the viceregal coach, recalling to mind England's political control of Ireland, passed through the streets, eliciting comments from several characters. Mrs. Mina Purefoy gave birth to a child, and the funeral of one Paddy Dignam was held. Thus the day included disaster, religion, war, sport, political events, death, and the recurrence of life; it becomes in the novel a microcosm, however banal, of human existence.

From the pattern of the day's activities the personalities of the chief characters and their relations with each other also emerge. Leopold Bloom is the central character; each of the others' destinies is connected to his. Born of a Hungarian-Jewish father and an Irish mother, he feels homeless and uprooted in Dublin. His appearance is not prepossessing; he is pasty and "sinewless," he perspires easily, and wears an unconfident look. His associates treat him with little respect. But he is a sincere Irish patriot, more so, perhaps, than many native Irishmen, and he resents the tendency of his acquaintances to treat him as a foreigner or as a Jewish outsider. He suffers inwardly from sexual frustration; he still has tender feelings toward his wife, but he has too little courage to interfere in her acts of adultery. He writes love letters under an assumed name to a girl he has never seen, but this brings him little satisfaction. Meanwhile his erotic inclinations are subconsciously diverted toward his daughter Millicent; he is attracted by her resemblance to Molly as she was in her youth. A painful spot in his memory is his lost son, Rudy, who was born after Milly but who lived only eleven days. Bloom seldom holds a job very long, and at present is doing poorly in his position as an advertising canvasser.

Molly Bloom, his wife, is the daughter of the British Major Tweedy and a Spanish Jewess; she grew up in Gibraltar, but Bloom wooed her on the hill of Howth near Dublin. She is talented as a singer, and considers herself more sensitive and artistic than Bloom. She is promiscuous not out of lust but through a restless yearning after romance; she has a healthy sensualism, and Bloom's middle-aged deterioration leaves her indifferent. Her true character, and many of her subconscious attitudes, are revealed in the final chapter of the novel, an interior monologue in a half-asleep state. The chapter begins and ends with the word "yes"; its theme is a passionate affirmation of life. She recalls the "Poldy" Bloom she once knew and the ecstasy of their first days together. At heart she still loves the Leopold Bloom of those days, and longs desperately to recapture the experience of the past. The recording of Siobhan McKenna reading Molly's soliloquy is already a classic interpretation.

Stephen Dedalus, the hero of *A Portrait of the Artist as a Young Man,* is here seen after his return from Paris, for which city he had left the shores of Ireland at the end of *Portrait* two years earlier. Somewhat more sophisticated, he has not changed basically. He has rejected both the Irish nationalism and the Catholicism of his youth; yet he still feels resentment over England's domination of Ireland, and traces of Catholic training are evident in his speech and thoughts. He is well read and intellectually mature; he knows Church theology thoroughly and is conversant with world literature and philosophy. In many respects he resembles Joyce himself; there are elements of Joyce in Bloom, but Stephen is an autobiographical character to a much greater extent. Stephen has little affection for his father, the indolent and convivial Simon Dedalus, and thus feels a gap in his life, which he tries subconsciously to fill. He loved his now dead mother greatly, and feels a secret guilt because he refused out of principle to pray with her as she lay on her deathbed.

The principal minor characters are Malachi (Buck) Mulligan, Stephen's good-natured medical-student friend, and Blazes Boylan, the flashy and cocky man-about-town who sneers at Bloom and openly commits adultery with Molly.

The dominant symbolism of the novel is the mythological parallel to the *Odyssey;* like Mann and Eliot, Joyce utilizes the concept of the recurrence of myth in modern life. Bloom (Odysseus or Ulysses) is a wanderer and alien who passes through many adventures, some of them erotic, before returning to his "faithful" Penelope (ironically, Molly). Stephen (Telemachus) is searching for his spiritual father; he mentally connects the Hamlet story with a legend of Shakespeare's short-lived son Hamnet. Likewise Bloom is searching for his faithful son, and subconsciously believes he has found him when he encounters Stephen in the bawdy house scene.

The structural parallel to the *Odyssey* is also important. The correspondence between the action of the novel and the incidents of the *Odyssey* has been interpreted as follows:

Ulysses chapter	*Odyssey* incident
I. 1	Telemachus
2	Nestor
3	Proteus
II. 1	Calypso
2	The Lotus Eaters
3	Hades
4	Aeolus (the cave of winds)
5	The Lestrygonians
6	Scylla and Charybdis
7	The wandering rocks (non-Homeric)
8	The Sirens
9	Polyphemus (the Cyclops)
10	Meeting with Nausicaa
11	The Oxen of the Sun
12	Circe's island
III. 1	Greeting by Eumaeus
2	Arrival in Ithaca
3	Reunion with Penelope

Finnegans Wake (1939): This is a less conventional and much more difficult work than *Ulysses*. Where *Ulysses* attempts to transcribe the thoughts and impressions of certain persons through the course of a certain day, *Finnegans Wake* purports to reveal the subconscious mental processes of a single sleeping individual, and to weave racial, mythological, and psychological symbols into this fabric. In order to convey such material, Joyce is forced to invent a virtually new language. It is rich in foreign words, puns, and "portmanteau words"—neologisms containing elements of several words and subject to ambiguous interpretation. The language follows a disconnected, ungrammatical, and spontaneous pattern intended to convey the processes of the sleeping mind; it is similar to the prose experiments of Virginia Woolf or Gertrude Stein but much more radical. Many of the neologisms used contain foreign elements—German, Scandinavian, Gaelic, French, old German, Anglo-Saxon, and others—and a knowledge of languages is virtually essential to a full appreciation of the book.

The title of the novel refers to the Irish ballad of the hod carrier Tim Finnegan, who was killed in a fall off a scaffold but who revived at his wake when whiskey was spilled on the corpse. The protagonist, however, is an Irish-Scandinavian pubkeeper named Humphrey Chimpden Earwicker; in his dream he also converts his name to Here Comes Everybody (symbol of identification with all mankind) and Haveth Childers Everywhere. He keeps a pub called the Bristol in Chapelizod near Dublin, located on the edge of Phoenix Park and near the River Liffey; the birthplace of the mythical heroine Iseult or Isolde is said to be nearby.

Earwicker's subconscious ramblings, however, are of a curious sort; he evokes images which one man alone would not be likely to have in his memory. He has, rather, a racial memory, a command of all mythology, of history, of literature, and of most modern and classic languages. He, too, as Joyce would say, was once "Jung and easily Freudened." The reason for this is that in a broader sense the dreaming protagonist *is* all mankind; Earwicker's mind partakes of the store of universal human memory. The chief myths that pass through the dreamer's mind are that of Tristram and Iseult; and, more important, the Adam-Eve-Cain-Abel story; with Matthew, Mark, Luke, and John running in on the side with another story of resurrection besides Finnegan's. His wife Anna is sleeping next to him, and he also has two sons, Kevin and Jerry, and a daughter, Isobel. He imagines himself as Tristram in pursuit of Iseult, who is partly his wife but who sometimes becomes his daughter Isobel; his dream involves incestuous desires which his "censor" represses during waking consciousness. Freudian theory is evident here. His daughter is connected with the mythical heroine through the linguistic transition Isobel-Iseult-la-Belle; at one point the connection is stated specifically. The River Liffey enters this set of mental associations and is personified as "Anna Livia Plurabelle." Earwicker's attitude toward his son Jerry (also called Shaun) is likewise incestuous; in his waking hours he does not realize that his preference for Jerry includes a homosexual element. These relations are never presented in a lucid form, but may be inferred from the recorded mental associations.

The concepts of the novel are greatly influenced by the work of the eighteenth century Italian philosopher Giambattista Vico, who postulated the evolution of civilization through three distinct phases. These are (1) the stage of belief in polytheistic gods; (2) the stage of mythology, in which euhemeristic heroes are evolved; and (3) the naturalistic stage, in which society is viewed from the point of view of man and man's mentality. A second idea of Vico is that history, in fact all human activity, tends to move in cycles and to repeat itself periodically. Thus Joyce utilizes the theme of the alternation of life and death (the cycle of existence), which also interested Mann and Eliot. In structure also Joyce follows Vico: *Finnegans Wake* begins with a fragmentary sentence, and the beginning of this sentence is found in the last line of the novel. Thus the novel itself is an endless cycle; and Earwicker's dream, on a naturalistic level interrupted by morning, symbolically continues forever.

JOYCE CARY (1888 – 1957)

Joyce Cary is a novelist somewhere between the new and the old. He has clearly read and been influenced by the discoveries of such writers as D. H. Lawrence, James Joyce, and Virginia Woolf; but he seeks to return to the novel something of its old traditional form of a Dickens or a Fielding while holding on to the immediacy of psychology, analysis, impressionism, and stream of consciousness. At his best he suceeds and may be viewed as a "post-modern" writer. His most effective discovery is a new kind of novel trilogy, one novel for each of three characters who view essentially the same series of events from their particular and peculiar perspectives. It's something like the technique of the Japanese movie, *Rashomon,* the retelling of the same story from such divergent views that it no longer seems to be the same story. It's also as if *Ulysses* had become three separate and congruent novels, one for Stephen, one for Leopold, and one for Molly. But Cary is quite himself, and his first success in this triangular presentation is in *Herself Surprised* (1941) with Sara Monday looking at things, *To Be a Pilgrim* (1942) with Tom Wilcher's view, and *The Horse's Mouth* (1944) with the painter Gully Jimson as the "other" man of the triangle who has an artist's vision — and a very sensuous, sensitive one at that. The filming of this story with Alec Guinness in the role of Gully Jimson was a masterpiece of characterization.

The form of this particular approach seemed to open up a new vein of ore for Cary. He turned from art to politics in a second trilogy: *Prisoner of Grace* (1952), *Except the Lord* (1953), and *Not Honour More* (1955) featuring Nina Nimmo, Chester Nimmo, and Jim Letter. There are other novels of interest by Cary, but his most distinctive work seems to lie in his two trilogies. One can see from the titles that there is an undercurrent of religious dimensions running through this novel sequence. As William Van O'Connor suggested, "In another century, Cary might have been a preacher." But it is hard to go as far as he does in suggesting that his (Cary's) "God-driven men are grotesque vessels of grace, something like Flannery O'Connor's grotesque saint Hazel Motes, in *Wise Blood.*" True, each seeks his own salvation, but hardly in the Catholic framework of a Flannery O'Connor or a Graham Greene or an Evelyn Waugh. This is no hound of heaven pursuit; if anything it's the reverse.

Life

Arthur Joyce Lunel Cary was born in Derry in Ireland in 1888, but his parents, Arthur Pitt Cary and Charlotte Joyce, lived in London. They traveled back and forth a good deal, even after the death of Joyce's mother when he was eight. Uncle Tristram Cary and his household in England became the family center. After preparatory school and Clifton College in Bristol, Joyce went off to Paris at seventeen to become a painter. It didn't go well in Paris, so he went to study art in Edinburgh for three years, giving it up to do some work in law at Trinity, Cambridge. With the Balkan War of 1912 – 13, Cary went out to see what he could do, was arrested briefly as a spy, and joined the Montenegrin army as a cook. Upon his return he joined the government service and went to Nigeria in 1913, serving there until 1919, although on leave in 1916 marrying Gertrude Ogilvie. During this time he tried to write, finally sold some stories in New York, and settled down with his family in Oxford to devote himself to writing. For ten years he wrote and destroyed novel after novel. Finally his first book, many times rewritten, was published in the early thirties, *Aissa Saved,* about a young African convert who leads her fellow Christians in a holy war against human-sacrificing pagans and is finally eaten alive by ants.

Other African novels followed until Cary turned to an entirely English setting in *Charley Is My Darling* (1940), which with *A House of Children* (1941) led him into his first trilogy and a place among the best English novelists. Finally he had public attention and acclaim. During the war he worked on Civil Defense at Oxford, prepared a film on Africa, *Men of Two Worlds,* and following the war traveled to India and America. His wife died in 1949, and the children were grown; but he stayed on in the big house in Oxford to continue writing. The second trilogy appeared from 1952 to 1955. Joyce Cary was ill for a long time with an incurable progressive paralysis. He kept writing from his wheelchair, then from his bed, and then by dictation after both hands had become useless and even after his speech became impaired. *The Captive and the Free,* the last novel he was working on, was published in 1959. Cary had died in Oxford on March 29, 1957, admired for his personal courage as well as for his artistic accomplishment.

Chief Novels

***Herself Surprised* (1941):** The story of a cook who marries her master and rises in the world, herself is Sara Monday, one of the great characters of the modern novel, generous, loving, feminine, full of guile yet naive — life is living for the moment. She has been called a modern Moll Flanders, with justice, and seems clearly a sister under the skin to Molly Bloom. Chiefly she loves men and domesticity, would welcome any lonely stray into her warm bed (Gully and Wilcher both make it). Described as Nature, Love, "female flesh and female season" (that's close to Molly), Sara is nevertheless very English, very London, and full of infinite variety and connivings.

***To Be a Pilgrim* (1942):** Second in the trilogy, it is about Sara's employer, an old conservative who hates change, Tom Wilcher. He too is very English, in the old sense, mindful of the family estate at Tolbrook, place and tradition, inhibited, dedicated, sensitive. In spite of his love he allows Sara, who has stolen to help Gully Jimson, to be arrested, although he knows that she has "saved" his soul. He hopes for their reunion when she is released from prison; he has learned from her that life is motion and subject to change, watching her in the kitchen and creeping into her bed. But he learns too late as death approaches.

The Horse's Mouth (1944): A fitting climax to the trilogy, it is the story of an artist who seduces Sara and then abandons her. Gully Jimson is a social rebel as well as an artist, who gets into a succession of predicaments, an old man who can make love at sixty-seven with delight and imagination, fraudulent, irreverent, kleptomaniac, dream-haunted, but always with an artist's eye: "I was walking by the Thames. Half-past morning on an autumn day. Sun in a mist. Like an orange in a fried fish shop." The artist, and a man, needs total experience to express the conflicts and commonplace joys of life in minute concrete particulars and so to work through toward meaning. Art can clarify life's confusions. Gully is a scoundrel, a picaro, and a romantic. There is no restraint or moving toward peace. Life must be taken in with open arms, with its injustice, anguish, hardship, and, as O'Connor points out, "no modern fictional characters, with the exception of some of Faulkner's, show this better than Cary's." Even after his stroke, Gully Jimson argues with the nun in the hospital. Sara and Gully both bear it out to the end, their respective ends, with gusto and without whimpering. There is a lot of Joyce Cary in many of his characters.

LAWRENCE DURRELL (1912 – 90)

If Graham Greene in publishing *The Quiet American* in 1955 and Saul Bellow with *Mr. Sammler's Planet* in 1970 were being in some degree timely and opportunistic, it could be said somewhat more favorably of Lawrence Durrell that the publication of the novels that make up *The Alexandria Quartet* from 1957 through 1960 was both prophetic and contemporary. Conspiracy in the Arab-Jewish world with Alexandria as a city of intrigue could be related either to the Suez crisis of 1956 or to Israel's "short war" in 1967 or probably to any number of events that may appear in tomorrow's newspaper or tonight's newscast. Remembering how other writers of the twentieth century have focussed on particular cities as symbolic of modern man's predicament, as a paradigm of the world, the hub of the universe — Dos Passos with New York, Joyce with Dublin, Hemingway with Paris and later Madrid ("The Capital of of the World"), Döblin with Berlin, Camus with Oran and later Amsterdam, William Carlos Williams with Paterson, to mention the most important — Durrell's choice of Alexandria was brilliant (of course he had E. M. Forster's *Alexandria: A Guide Book* to help him, and the Greek poet, Cavafy or Cavafis, both of whom he makes use of; but he *did* make the choice). His fiction has forced the world to take a long look at Alexandria as the focus of its history and its dilemma. With this work Durrell has become an English novelist the world takes seriously. The French have acclaimed him a successor to James Joyce and D. H. Lawrence. Alexandria is deeper in history than any of the cities mentioned above; its decadence and detritus and omphalic geographical location give it specific relevance to an age encumbered by its own history.

The influences on Lawrence Durrell are many (his literature is built largely on the literature before him, as all good books are, according to Michel Butor), to list only the most important in an effort to find him a temporary place: Henry Miller, Sigmund Freud, Albert Einstein, D. H. Lawrence, James Joyce, André Gide, Marcel Proust, Ford Madox Ford, Eliot and Rilke, and Robbe-Grillet. First of all, Henry Miller. Durrell had read the *Tropic of Cancer,* first published in Paris in 1934, shortly after the appearance of his own first novel, a potboiler, in 1935. "*Tropic* opened a pit in my brain," he wrote to Miller, "It freed me immediately . . . to write about people I knew something about." The correspondence between Miller and Durrell became a volume (published in the sixties), and they became fast friends. Indeed Durrell did learn to use similar material in his fiction, but at his best the naturalistic detail is included in a frame of reference that lifts it out of the near-to-pornography category. He had also studied Freud carefully and found that one of the psychologist's best insights was that "the nuclear structure of all anxiety" is in "the sexual preoccupation of childhood." This leads him to what has been referred to as "the unmapped landscape" explored by Freud and Jung and Adler, the private, internal complement to the external, public landscape of modern Einsteinian physics. Freudian discoveries can offer us, Durrell explains, "a new territory inside ourselves in which each one of us who is seeking to grow, to identify himself more fully with life, will feel like Columbus discovering America." This is from his *Key to Modern British Poetry* (1952), in which he discusses also the other landscape developed by Einstein, Eddington, and Whitehead, the principle of indeterminacy and the theory of relativity.

The new physics, he says, "is founded upon the theory that we cannot observe the course of nature without disturbing it." "Under the terms of the new idea a precise knowledge of the outer world becomes an impossibility. This is because we and the outer world (subject and object) constitute a whole." This necessitates reorientation of the modern writer toward his art, himself, his world, and his audience; and it shows up in Joyce and Virginia Woolf, the characters of Gide, the structure of T. S. Eliot's "Gerontion" and in metaphor, imagery, symbol, and sentence structure as well. The "Continuum" of Einsteinian physics (space-time) is a metaphor for the new art. Durrell writes

> I do not think it is stretching a point too far to say that the work of Joyce and Proust, the poetry of Eliot and Rilke, is an attempt to present the material of human and supernatural affairs in the form of poetic continuum, where the language no less than the objects observed are impregnated with the new time. . . . In Proust and Joyce you see something like a slow-motion camera at work.

Their books do not proceed along a straight line, but in a circular manner, coiling and uncoiling upon themselves, embedded in the stagnant flux and reflux of a medium which is always changing yet always the same. This attitude towards the material of the work has its effect on character also. Characters have a significance almost independent of the actions they engage in: They hang above the time-track which leads from birth to action, and from action to death: and, spreading out time in this manner, contribute a significance to everything about them.

In *The Alexandria Quartet* Durrell tries to use the continuum, both Einsteinian and Freudian "landscapes," the "inherent duality in things, and an acceptance of it as part of the human limitation . . . both in the relativity-view and . . . 'ambivalence' in Freud," "as one of the most important cosmological formulations of the day to do a poetic dance upon." He added that "if you have all four books held in your cranium, you should get a notion of the continuum." In a 1970 release the experiment was made to transfer *The Alexandria Quartet* to the screen under the title of its first novel, *Justine.* Opinions as to its relative success differ widely. But the novel tetralogy itself is likely to remain significant for some time to come. G. S. Fraser is probably wrong in finding *Tunc* (1968) Durrell's best novel (the overlay of "science fiction," particularly the "Abel" device, removes it from that category, and sex here seems somewhat more gratuitous, less well integrated); but it is not negligible, the satire of the super Merlin cartel and the suggested Benedicta-Julian diabolism as a modern emergence of the principle of evil are effective in their own right, and the reader is disturbed and alarmed by sharing in Felix Charlock's attempt to escape in a world where there is no place to hide.

In 1970 Lawrence Durrell published *Tunc's* sequel, *Nunquam,* and gave us the epigraph from Petronius' *Satyricon* (which has also provided Fellini with his film of the late sixties): *"Aut tunc aut nunquam"* ("Either then or never"). And there are probably additional reasons for his choice of title. Quite accurately he analyzed this work in an authorial postscript as a sort of a two-part "novel-libretto based on the preface to *The Decline of the West"* and Freud very much there with Spengler. Preposterous, sometimes outrageously nauseating incidents and commentary are casually introduced into the excitingly artificial and moving narrative, but then modern culture, big business, science, technology, media for the masses, also does precisely the same kind of offensive thing. *Nunquam* is centrally about the creation of a robot film star Iolanthe (who died miserably in *Tunc*), a robot that would pass for human, which is not so difficult in a world where most human beings would pass for robots. This is science fiction with a satiric sting, social relevance, and a very sharp thrust. The major characters of *Tunc* reappear: Felix Charlock; the Merlins, Jocas, Julian, Benedicta; Marchand, Hippolyta, Caradoc, Nash, Vibart and others. Julian at one point seems less real to the robot (with Abel's works in her) than the robot does to Julian. The identity crisis, the Kafkan nightmare, Pirandellian relativity all return with a crash. Durrell, with amusement it is to be hoped, refers to himself in a footnote as "the best of our modern poets." His chances of being recognized as the best of the English novelists of the second half of the twentieth century are better.

Life

Much more reticent about his private life than his friend Henry Miller, Lawrence Durrell has contributed little to biographical information about himself. He was born of an English father and an Irish mother in India in 1912 and remembers a childhood in the shadow of the Himalaya mountains. At the age of eleven he left the College of St. Joseph in Darjeeling and was taken to England to continue his schooling in St. Edmond's School in Canterbury. There were two brothers, Gerald and Leslie, a sister Margaret, and his widowed mother. Hating England, he later wrote to Henry Miller of his young manhood, "I hymned and whored in London, playing jazz in a nightclub, composing jazz songs, working in real estate. Never really starved, but I wonder whether thin rations are not another degree of starvation." In 1935 he married his first wife, Nancy Myers — "We struck up an incongruous partnership: a dream of broken bottles, sputum, tinned food, rancid meat, urinals, the smell of the lock hospitals" — and he published a "cheap novel," *Pied Piper of Lovers,* which failed artistically and financially. His second novel, *Panic Spring,* was published two years later under a pseudonym, Charles Norden, so that it might not be swamped by association with the first.

In the middle thirties Lawrence pressured his mother into pulling up stakes and moving the whole family to the Mediterranean island of Corfu, an experiment in expatriation; like James and Joyce and Henry Miller he had decided that the only way to deal with his country, to write about it objectively, was to leave it. During the Corfu years he wrote poetry and the first Milleresque novel about London, *The Black Book,* which Faber and Faber couldn't touch without expurgation (although T. S. Eliot liked it) and which finally came out in Paris, pushed through by Henry Miller, subsidized by his wife Nancy, in 1938, and published in New York in 1960. Durrell island hopped in the forties and fifties, Corfu to Crete to Rhodes and finally to Cyprus from 1953 to 1956. He produced a trilogy of island portraits in the "style of diaries," *Prospero's Cell* (1945) (primarily about Corfu), *Reflections on a Marine Venus* (1953) about Rhodes, and *Bitter Lemons* (1957) about Cyprus.

During the war Durrell had taught briefly at the British Institute in Athens, was a Foreign Press Service Officer in Cairo, and Press Attaché in Alexandria. His first marriage broke up: Nancy and their daughter Penelope Berengaria went to Palestine. In Rhodes as a Director of Public Relations, he married his second wife, Eve Cohen, an Alexandrian who brought him material for the *Quartet.* After separation from Eve, he met Claude, a married woman, in Cyprus; they fell in love and after respective divorces were married in 1961. This was a period of great literary activity for Durrell; a book of poems, *Cities,*

Plains and People (1946), was followed by others, including *On Seeming to Presume* (1948); verse plays, not successful in the English theater but tried out on the continent: *Sappho* (1950), *An Irish Faustus* (1963), and *Acte* (1965); translations, light novels, essays, sketches; and most important, *Justine* (1957), *Balthazar* (1958), *Mountolive* (1958), and *Clea* (1960) — which together make up The *Alexandria Quartet. Tunc,* supposedly the first of two novels to make up a "double-decker," was published in 1968, and the other half, *Nunquam,* in 1970.

In 1974 Durrell became Mellon Professor of Humanities at the California Institute of Techonology. His five-part novel series, *The Avignon Quintet,* appeared over the course of the next two decades: *Monsieur,* or *The Prince of Darkness* (1978), *Livia,* or *Buried Alive* (1978), *Constance,* or *Solitary Practices* (1982), *Sebastian,* or *Ruling Passions* (1983), and *Qunix,* or *The Ripper's Tale* (1985). These works center on the search some years ago for the lost golden treasure of the Knights Templar and, by extension, the quest for wisdom through escape from individual ego. Some of Durrell's poetry appears in *Vega and Other Poems* (1973) and *Lifelines: Four Poems* (1974).

Chief Work

The Alexandria Quartet **(1957 – 60):** *Justine,* 1957; *Balthazar,* 1958; *Mountolive,* 1958; and *Clea,* 1960 are mostly about a city, Alexandria, "the great wine-press of love," seen through the eyes of the modern Greek poet Cavafy (1863 – 1933), with assistance by E. M. Forster, but related in each novel except the third by a first-person narrator, a young Irish schoolmaster and poet, Darley, who tries to find out the "truth" about a woman with whom he has had a passionate affair, Justine. The events covered are practically the same in all four novels, but the angle of vision is constantly changing. There are separate and discrete layers of truth, and the personalities of people are made up of many roles or masks. There are many symbols or themes, which Durrell is said to use in "heraldic" fashion, chiefly wounds and healing, mirrors, masks, letters, intrigues, and novels within the novel. The style is lush, almost excessively lyrical, sometimes fragmented, with the "work-points" that dribble off at the ends of Darley's novels, suggesting further possibilities (and reminiscent of the endings of some of Eliot's poems, like "The Wasteland" — "These fragments I have shored against my ruins").

Consider the beginning of *Justine:* "The sea is high again today, with a thrilling flush of wind. In the midst of winter you can feel the inventions of Spring. A sky of hot nude pearl until midday, crickets in sheltered places, and now the wind unpacking, the great planes, ransacking the great planes. . . . I have escaped to this island with a few books and the child — Melissa's child." And immediately he thinks of the city with "a thousand dust-tormented streets. Flies and beggars own it today — and those who enjoy an intermediate existence. . . . Five races, five languages, a dozen creeds: five fleets turning through their greasy reflections behind the harbour bar. But there are more than five sexes and only demotic Greek seems to distinguish among them. The sexual provender which lies to hand is staggering in its variety and profusion. You would never mistake it for a happy place." Alexandria, "the great wine-press of love; those who emerged from it were the sick men, the solitaries, the prophets — I mean all who have been deeply wounded in their sex."

The other important characters should be introduced: Melissa, the mistress of Darley (among others), a Greek cabaret dancer; Nessim Hosnani, a rich Coptic banker and merchant; Justine Hosnani, his Jewish wife; Narouz, his brother on the estates outside the city; Mountolive, the English Ambassador to Eygpt (formerly in Russia); Pursewarden, a subordinate officer in the embassy; Liza, his blind sister; Leila, the mother of Nessim and Narouz, formerly loved by Mountolive; Johnny Keats, the journalist; Arnauti, a French-Albanian novelist and Justine's first husband; Scobie, an old philosopher-homosexual and sometime transvestite; Toto, another but young; Balthazar, a doctor and occultist friend of Darley, and seemingly bisexual; Amaril, another doctor; Capodistria, a one-eyed sexual athlete who had raped Justine in childhood; Pombal, the French diplomat; and Clea, a painter. The list is long and the interrelationships are often complex.

The action of the novel takes place during the struggle for Egyptian independence, having at its center a conspiracy of the Copts (Egyptian Christians of an ancient church) and the Jewish nationalist movement to outwit the world of the Arabs and their supporters, France and Britain. Curiously the plots and counterplots have a continuing validity not limited to specific time. Love and politics become inextricably intertwined. "The politics of love, the intrigues of desire, good and evil, virtue and caprice, love and murder, move obscurely in the dark corners of Alexandrian streets and squares and brothels, moved like a great congress of eels in the slime of plot and counterplot."

In *Justine* Darley, obsessed with the city of Alexandria, tries to get his impressions down on paper before they vanish. His love affair with Justine as the wife of Nessim, who is deeply involved in the conspiracy, draws him into a whole network of exotic relationships. Very early in the novel Justine, sitting in front of a dressmaker's multiple mirrors, speculates on approaches to fiction: "Look! five different pictures of the same subject. Now if I wrote I would try for a multidimensional effect in character, a sort of prism-sightedness. Why should not people show more than one profile at a time?"

In *Balthazar* Darley discovers more pieces to the puzzle of the events and people already presented. The doctor Balthazar, a former lover of Justine, comes to the island with notebooks and manuscripts. "The really horrible thing is that the compulsive passion which Justine lit in me was quite as valuable as it would have been had it been 'real'; Melissa's gift was no less an enigma — what could she have offered me, in truth, this pale waif of the Alexandrian littoral? Was Clea enriched or beggared by her relations with Justine? Enriched — immeasurably enriched, I should say. Are we then nourished only by fictions, by lies? I recall the words Balthazar wrote down somewhere in his tall grammarian's handwriting: 'We live by selected fictions.'" The device of variant accounts of a single story is similar to Gide's in *The Counterfeiters* and Faulkner's *Absalom, Absalom.* The major difference comes with the insertion of the third novel into the series.

Mountolive is a straightforward third-person narrative, sweeping backward in time, and concentrating not on the private masks but the "public false faces of political action." Much of the history of Mountolive, the British diplomatist, told through letters he had written to Leila, mother of Nessim and Narouz, with whom he had been in love all during his career in Europe, Russia, and England, reveals interconnections and new aspects of characters. He thought the Hosnani family his friends, unaware of the secret conspiracy against his country. But even he comes to see Pursewarden as a "security risk" and that the main motive in Nessim's marrying Justine was to unite Copts and Jews in an anti-British plot. Ostensibly an "objective history of events," *Mountolive* nonetheless has pitfalls for the reader. Are other motives and interpretations less true? Not necessarily.

Clea presents not the last word on the problem, but the last we have, and a corrective vision, or more properly another corrective vision. Darley again probes, this time in a "book of wounds," damaging but life-giving wounds that can be healed only by proper questions of concern for others, by compassion. The story moves forward in time, gathering momentum with an ebbing movement as well to resemble the sea itself washing Alexandria. Time has dealt harshly with characters, bringing Justine a stroke, Nessim the loss of eye and finger, Balthazar the loss of all his teeth, Clea the loss of her painting hand. There are many blind or half-blind people stumbling through the novel, at least four one-eyed and the totally blind Liza. But there is the promise of happy endings and the thwarting of them. Clea, the painter, apparently intended like Virginia Woolf's Lily Briscoe in *To the Lighthouse* to add the stroke that will illuminate the canvas, never gets to do so with the loss of her hand, or does she after all? For all its cruelties, horror, macabre maimings and deaths *The Alexandria Quartet* does not end on a tragic note. Even the dead have ironic and/or comic victories. Pursewarden's suicide has permitted his sister, Liza, whom he had loved incestuously, to marry Mountolive and relieved him of the traitor's role to country or friends simultaneously. Scobie, the old fairy kicked to death, has been resurrected as a saint, El Scob. There is a life force that persists. Justine finds ultimately relative peace in a Kibbutz. Even Darley, Clea, and Balthazar find enough acceptance of things as they are and understanding to go on with the tenderness of human affections, some wit and humor, and a sense of the absurd. There are weaknesses in *The Quartet:* perhaps it was too hastily written; the letters of Pursewarden to his blind sister Liza are never really explained; there seems to be an excessive number of would-be writers and artists. But the fullness and inconsistency of life have been communicated with vitality, eloquence, imagination, and depth.

7
THE IRISH RENAISSANCE

The expression "Irish Renaissance" (sometimes "Irish revival" or "Gaelic Renaissance") is used to refer to the revival of interest in Irish legend and folklore that began in the late 1890s and continued well into the middle of the twentieth century. Mainly a literary movement, it is closely connected with, but by no means identical to, the resurgence of Irish political nationalism that began in the same era.

As a literary movement the Irish Renaissance took the form of a romantic reaction against the English and continental theaters of the time. The Irish National Theatre, the focus of the movement, abandoned both the "well-made play" of the French popular theater and the stark naturalism of the Ibsen-Zola school, at that time at the height of its triurnph in England and Germany. The original patent application for the Irish National Theatre described the purpose of the group as the production of "romantic plays." By this term its founders meant, not a revival of the artificial and melodramatic romanticism of the early nineteenth century, but an imaginative and nonrealistic drama that would penetrate farther into the essence of human experience than the superficial materialism of the naturalistic school. The enthusiasm, energy, and productivity inspired by the movement are remarkable. Although it sprang from a nation of less than 5 million inhabitants and was hampered by the opposition of both the British crown and the more fanatic nationalist elements, it produced at least a half-dozen authors of world literary rank and a good-sized body of plays, novels, and poems that deserve to take their place with the best of world literature.

The Irish National Theatre

In 1896 Edward Martyn, a young Irish poet, introduced W. B. Yeats to Lady Augusta Gregory at the home of the latter. From this meeting sprang the Irish Literary Theatre, which began producing Irish plays in the Ancient Concert Rooms in Dublin. The first drama produced was Yeats' *The Countess Cathleen*, presented on May 8, 1899. The original organization included Yeats, Edward Martyn, Lady Gregory, and George Moore; Sean O'Casey, J. M. Synge, Padraic Colum, and Lord Dunsany became associated with the group in subsequent years. The original funds were raised by subscription, but the theater soon became self-sustaining. In 1904 the company, renamed the Irish National Theatre Society, moved to the Abbey Theatre in Dublin; the society is often referred to as the "Abbey Theatre group." The company travelled to England in 1903 and on several subsequent occasions. In 1911–12 it made its first tour of America, which was on the whole successful and triumphant, although fanatic Irish nationalists sought to break up several performances and the whole company was arrested in Philadelphia on charges of presenting an immoral drama.

The opposition of certain nationalist elements, especially the Sinn Fein and the rural Gaelic League, to the National Theatre was based primarily on its attitude toward the Irish peasant. The new dramas, especially those of Synge, showed the peasant not as the romantic, carefree, goodhearted leprechaun of Irish folklore but as a mundane toiler given to drunkenness and laziness and often deluded by his own empty rhetoric. The British crown, on the other hand, on several occasions sought to revoke the society's patent on grounds of sedition; certain of O'Casey's dramas and a 1909 performance of Bernard Shaw's *The Shewing Up of Blanco Posnet* marked especially violent skirmishes in the "Fight with the Castle." After the First World War and the achievement of Irish independence the society continued its triumph, and has since become something of a national institution.

The Irish Renaissance of 1900 to 1940, with its interest in legend and folklore, "spilled over" into a renaissance more interested in the Irish people of the present (about 1930 to 1970). Sean O'Casey is already of this group, followed in drama by such writers as Brendan Behan, Hugh Leonard, and Brian Friel. The new poets include Austin Clarke (not so new), Patrick Kavanagh, Thomas Kinsella, Richard Weber, James Liddy, Michael Harnett, Seamus Heaney, and McDara Woods. The new fiction is best represented by Frank O'Connor, J. P. Donleavy, and Mary Lavin. Lord Dunsany, who was active with the Abbey Theatre from 1909 to midcentury, sponsored Mary Lavin's entry into letters.

WILLIAM BUTLER YEATS (1865–1939)

W. B. Yeats, along with Lady Gregory the founder of the Irish Renaissance movement, is one of the most important literary figures of the twentieth century. His work is molded by two chief influences: the Symbolist-Aesthetic movement of the fin de siècle, which he encountered during his formative years in London, and Irish folklore and history, which he extracted directly from its Gaelic sources.

Yeats' career was a long and productive one; he passed through many stages in his literary evolution from the shy County Sligo poet to the Nobel Prize Winner of 1923. His early verses (1888–90) were relatively simple in construction and imagery and mainly concerned with description of nature or pastoral landscapes. In his Symbolist period (1890–1900) he worked under the influence of Pater, Ruskin and the English aesthetes, Blake, and the French Symbolist school. The poems of this period often express the desire for escape into fantasy of the so-called decadent school. The epitome of this style is to be found in *The Wind Among the Reeds* (1899). After his association with Lady Gregory and the Abbey Theatre group Yeats turned increasingly to the drama; his political ideas began to take shape, and he abandoned his aesthetic escapism for the role of a man of action. But after 1928 his poetry again becomes subjective, sensual, and emotionally charged; a sort of pessimism similar to that of Housman is to be found in this later work. A common theme of the later period is the expression of regret for sensual experience unfulfilled in youth; the aging Yeats seemed to regret the shyness and prudery that had restrained the exuberance of his younger years.

In addition to his undeniable significance as a poet and dramatist in his own right, Yeats is important as an inspiration and influence on other members of the Irish literary renaissance. Because of his contact with the French Symbolists Yeats was able to bring to the Irish literary movement a sophistication of technique that it would otherwise have lacked; for this reason his influence on the younger poets of the movement is extremely important. The plays that achieved the greatest success in the Abbey Theatre are his poetic dramas: *The Countess Cathleen* (1892), *The Land of Heart's Desire* (1894), and *Deirdre* (1907).

Another group of plays exciting more attention in the sixties were those modeled on the Noh plays of Japan. Among his best are *Calvary* (1921), *Resurrection* ("Two Songs from a Play" are from this play and gain in depth of meaning when the play is played between them), and *Purgatory* (1939). Ezra Pound had led Yeats to this oriental interest, which gives a spare, strange, haunting quality to these dramas.

Life

Yeats was born in 1865 in Dublin. His ancestral home, however, lay in County Sligo, and it is this region he considered his literary homeland. His family were Protestant by tradition, and he himself remained detached from the Catholic aspect of the Irish Revolution. He was educated partly in Dublin and partly in London, where as a young man he participated in the Pre-Raphaelite and Aesthetic movements of the nineties. He constantly sought to find a connection between religion and art; he belonged at various times to both the Theosophist and the Rosicrucian movements, and his early Symbolist lyrics have a certain transcendental and mystic quality lacking in his later work. Upon his return to Ireland in 1896 he was associated for a time with the Sinn Fein movement. The turning point of his career was the meeting with Lady Gregory in 1898; she offered him advice and inspiration, and with her he founded the National Theatre in 1899. He married in 1917. From 1922 to 1928 he held a seat in the Irish Senate; by this time he had assumed the status of a national hero. In 1923 he received the Nobel Prize for Literature, climaxing his triumph as a world literary figure.

Curiously enough, Yeats' later poetry seems more romantic and spontaneous than his earlier, more affected work; it has been suggested that he is a poet who reversed the usual romantic evolution and enjoyed his literary youth at the end of his career. He died in 1939, as the *New Republic* re-marked, "at the height of his powers and with half his work unwritten."

Yeats' Mystical "System"

In 1917, Yeats married a spiritualistic medium, Georgie Hyde-Lees. She stimulated his long-time interest in esoteric theories regarding the nature and meaning of history, human destiny, and individual development. The prose exposition of these ideas is contained in Yeats' *A Vision, an Explanation of Life Founded upon the Writings of Giraldus and upon Certain Doctrines Attributed to Kusta ben Luka* (1925, revised 1937). In this work, Yeats sets forth (via dictation, he says, from spirits speaking through his wife) a cosmography in radical opposition to the prevailing orthodoxies of his day, including Christianity, Marxism, and psychoanalysis.

For his system, Yeats returns to the idea of a great wheel popularized by Boethius and Chaucer. Each of the twenty-eight spokes in the wheel represents a personal and societal phase of development. Human society requires two thousand years to pass through the complete cycle once. Such development is not purely cyclic, however, each passage through the cycle moves the civilization in spiral fashion toward Yeats' "Great Year," 26,000 A.D., when society will escape the cycle altogether.

Like Blake and Freud, Yeats understood the interior of the human psyche as a battleground of warring forces. He conceives these oppositions as two interpenetrating cones or "gyres." In oversimplified form, one's moral cone drives in opposition to one's aesthetic cone. The personality that emerges is the product of the ratio between these forces.

Yeats also distinguished between the realities of one's private life and the public face or "mask" that one wears to disguise these realities. In Yeats' system, individuals tend to choose the public mask that is most antithetical to the developmental stage (of twenty-eight) that they occupy. The deeply subjective or artistic personality, for example, may well chose a cynical, urbane, and hardened mask as a protection against the otherwise unbearable attacks of critics and others.

What must be appreciated in Yeats' achievement of a new spiritual cosmography or set of relatively self-consistent metaphysical tenets is the renewed power that belief system brought to his later poetry. Like the English Romantic poets, Yeats faced the lifelong challenge of breaking through in his art to materials that had not grown threadbare over the previous centuries of poetry and drama. Certainly the Greek gods and their associated imagery were already in noticeable decline by the time Keats, Shelley, and Byron tried to give them serious roles in Romantic poetry. Similarly, the heroes of British history had been "used up," as it were, by Malory, Shakespeare, Spenser, and others. Milton had done much the same for the Biblical materials of the Judaeo-Christian tradition.

Yeats, in spite of his crucial role in rediscovering Irish folklore and mythic figures for the purposes of poetry and drama, nevertheless felt the necessity for a broader, less historically or regionally confined language for his most prophetic poems. His *Vision,* therefore, can be viewed as the poet's declaration of independence from the influence of Christian, Irish, and English literary traditions.

Terms from and allusions to *A Vision* are found throughout Yeats' last great publications of poetry. In *The Tower* (1928) a winding stair becomes a symbol for Yeats' spiraling gyres. He indicates his deep ambivalence over the approach of the year 2000, at which time he expects some new spirtual force to exert power over humanity. In "Sailing to Byzantium" Yeats captures at once the Unity of Culture he prescribes for an artistic society as well as the balance between the sensual and the ideal. Other stirring poems from this collection include "Nineteen Hundred and Nineteen," a denunciation of civil conflict; "Leda and the Swan," concerning the initiation of a new developmental cycle for mankind; and "Among School Children," a philosopical epiphany about the integrated nature of truth.

The Winding Stair (1929) again incorporates the upwardly spiraling gyres of human and societal development. "A Dialogue of Self and Soul" contrasts the differing agendas of the self and the soul. "Byzantium," a revised version of "Sailing to Byzantium," is a difficult but wildly prophetic vision of the passage through mortal experience and art itself to ultimate transcendance.

Chief Drama

Although *The Countess Cathleen* (lyrical tragedy, 1892) was Yeats' most popular play in Ireland during the early years of the Abbey Theatre, *Deirdre* (lyrical tragedy, 1907) probably has greater lasting merit. The latter play is based on the Gaelic legend of the beautiful child Deirdre, who is found by the king Conchubar and reared in his own household. After a time, however, her budding womanhood inflames him and he takes her in marriage, only to lose her when she runs off with young Naisi. The lovers are captured by treachery; Conchubar offers Naisi his freedom if Deirdre will return to his household. This offer Deirdre refuses; Naisi is killed, and Deirdre in despair stabs herself. The play resembles Maeterlinck in mood; the characters are somewhat stylized, although both Conchubar and Deirdre are more complex figures whose personalities present manifold aspects.

Important Poems

"The Lake Isle of Innisfree" (1890): The best-known lyric of Yeats' youthful period, it expresses a longing to escape from civilization to the idyllic peace of the countryside; the sharp contrast between the serenity of the "bee-loud glade" and the "pavements gray" of the city is reminiscent of Wordsworth.

"The Cap and Bells" (1894): This poem is typical of the exotic Symbolism of Yeats' fin-de-siècle period. The jester (symbolically, the poet) offers first his soul, then his heart, to the Queen who commands his affections; she rejects both these gifts, but accepts the cap and bells (poetry) he sends her at last. Woman, superficial and attracted by outward semblance, is captivated by the least essential part of her lover. Yet after the cap and bells have inspired love in the Queen, the doors are opened, and the heart and soul may finally enter; even a superficial attraction may grow into a lasting love.

"The Wild Swans at Coole" (1916): The swans Yeats observed over a period of many years at Lady Gregory's estate inspired this poem. Swans are a favorite symbol of Yeats, but their meaning varies; here they stand for constancy, immutability, or permanence, especially the permanence of love. When Yeats wrote this poem he probably had in mind Maud Gonne (later Maud Gonne MacBride), a vigorous and politically active Irishwoman whom he courted for many years.

"Leda and the Swan" (1923): Here the swan becomes a symbol of inspiration, of spirit, or of the divine spark present in human imagination. The opening lines (ll. 1–8) present a remarkably evocative physical description of the visitation of Zeus in the shape of a swan to the mortal woman Leda. The final eight lines foretell the consequences of this union: it is Leda's daughter Helen who is to cause the outbreak of the Trojan War; thus the swan is the ultimate cause of the "broken wall, the burning roof and tower" (Marlowe, "Was this the face that launched a thousand ships / And burnt the topless towers of Ilium?"). Symbolically the union of Zeus and Leda signifies the union of spirit and flesh. The ending of the poem (ll. 14–15) doubts whether man has put on God's knowledge (divine wisdom) along with the power vouchsafed him by his Creator's hand.

"Sailing to Byzantium" (1926): Here a profound question is treated in a mood of contemplative romanticism. The "country" referred to in the first line is the domain of the poet, which is essentially the realm of the young. Yeats regrets the passing of the "sensual music" of his youth; now that he appreciates the value of sensual experience, his age has made it unseemly. Since his body is old, his poetic nature must sing the louder to compensate for the weakness of the flesh (ll. 2–4). But there is no "singing school" (inspiration) for the mature soul other than the works of the soul itself; the poet must "sail to Byzantium" (go for inspiration to the regions of intellectual fantasy). Thus Byzantium signifies inward thought, and the poem is a justification and explanation of Yeats' mature excursion into romanticism.

"Among School Children" (1927): A similar theme, with less symbolism, is analyzed more fully. The myth of Leda, a favorite motif of Yeats, also recurs. The poet, passing through a schoolroom in his old age, is struck with the thought that he and his beloved were once young as these children; yet now the children view him only as a "smiling public man." This leads into a discussion of the transitory nature of human existence (Stanza V); the mother would be unable to recognize her son as a man of sixty, yet every human is destined to live out the lifecycle. The reference to Plato (Stanza VI) recalls the Platonic doctrine of Ideals, which holds that all physical matter is merely a transitory reflection of an unseen spiritual permanence. The poem concludes (Stanza VIII) that the intellect of man is powerless to tell illusion from reality, ephemera from permanence. Thus the schoolchildren, suggesting to the poet the continual change of the lifecycle, remind him that man's life on earth is but a temporary vision.

The "Crazy Jane" poems (from *Words for Music Perhaps*): These seven poems, written between 1930 and 1933, were started in Rapallo, Italy, where Yeats was visiting his old friend, Ezra Pound. They are deliberately more earthy and sensual, celebrating the "joyous life," than his earlier work. Yeats wrote to a friend that Crazy Jane was founded more or less "upon an old woman who lives in a little cottage near Gort," loving her flowers and sending some to Lady Gregory, having the gift of audacious speech, and once so in despair of the human race that she got drunk. There are three characters who enter the poems, lyrical though they are, two of them speaking the lines in monologue or dialogue: Crazy Jane herself and the Bishop. The third is Jack the Journeyman, the lover who had Crazy Jane's virginity, was banished through the efforts of the Bishop, and returns now to old Jane as a ghost. Apparently the Bishop as a young theological student had been in love with Jane too, but he advocates spiritual love and denounces the physical love of the body. Crazy Jane argues well, that love must include both body and soul. In Poem VI, "Crazy Jane Talks with the Bishop," she tells him, "Fair and foul are near of kin, / And fair needs foul." And later that "Love has pitched his mansion in / The place of excrement: / For nothing can be sole or whole / That has not been rent."

LADY GREGORY (1852–1932)

Lady Gregory was the chief inspiration and literary godmother of the Irish National Theatre; Bernard Shaw loyally called her "the charwoman of the Abbey Theatre." She was also one of its important contributing authors; her one-act sketches and comedies, less well-known today than the dramas of Synge and O'Casey, drew immense attention in the early years of the movement. As a dramatist Lady Gregory feels a genuine love for the Irish character, yet she is no cultist; her characters are often as irrational and emotionally disorganized as those of Synge. Her style is simple and direct: she lacks the ear for picturesque dialect of Synge and O'Casey, and as a result her dramas are more easily playable by non-Irish actors. In addition her simplicity gives her plays the power of understatement; her more serious pieces, like *The Workhouse Ward*, achieve a powerful emotional effect. She is at her best in describing the daily life of the Irish people in a mixture of comedy and pathos; the audience is often left wondering whether they have witnessed a farce or a miniature tragedy.

Life

Augusta, Lady Gregory was born in County Galway in 1852, the daughter of Dudley Persse, a wealthy country gentleman. Her early life was uneventful; at twenty-nine she married Sir William Gregory, who died in 1892. After the death of her husband Lady Gregory developed an interest in Irish folklore and legendry, and gradually became a warm Irish patriot. The meeting with Yeats in 1896 definitely decided her to embark on a literary career and to aid in the creation of a revived Irish literature. Her first serious drama, *Cuchulain of Muirthemne*, appeared in 1902, and an important set of dramatic sketches in 1909 under the title *Seven Short Plays*. From 1899 until her death she was involved in the affairs of the National Theatre; she accompanied the group on its tour of America in 1911–12 and fought in the vanguard of the battles against the Sinn Fein and the British crown. She died in 1932 at the age of eighty.

Chief Dramas

Although Lady Gregory considered her historical pieces such as *Cuchulain of Muirthemne* (tragedy, 1902) her most important work, there is no doubt that she will be remembered chiefly for her dramatic sketches of Irish lower-class life.

Of these, *The Rising of the Moon* consists primarily of an encounter between an Irish constable and a revolutionary he has been ordered to arrest. The two meet on a gloomy quay where the revolutionary plans to embark to safety in a boat; he manages, by appealing to the officer's latent sense of kinship with his people, to persuade him to wink at the escape. The chief interest lies in the conflict in the mind of the constable, an outwardly officious but inwardly romantic Irish type.

Spreading the News (one-act comedy, 1904) is a humorous sketch portraying the working of gossip in a small Irish town. An entirely unfounded rumor arises that Bartley Fallon, a meek husband and respectable citizen, has murdered the red-headed farmer Jack Smith with a hayfork and run off with Smith's wife Kitty. Fanned by gossips, the rumor spreads like a forest fire through the little community. Fallon is arrested, and even when Smith appears on the scene alive and hearty the villagers are more willing to believe rumor than reality. A comically pedantic magistrate, suspecting conspiracy, flings both Fallon and Smith into jail, where Smith will probably kill Fallon for tampering with his wife. This comedy makes effective use of the villagers *en masse* as a sort of chorus.

The Workhouse Ward (one-act comedy, 1907) involves two querulous old paupers who have been "imprisoned" for life next to each other in a poorhouse, although they bicker incessantly and do nothing but make life miserable for each other. At length a female relative of one arrives; she proposes to take him home where he can sit in the kitchen, stir the stirabout, and keep her company until the end of his days. At first the old man is enthusiastic over this picture, but after a moment he reflects he would have to leave the roommate who has been his sole preoccupation for so many years. He sends the would-be benefactor away, and as the curtain falls the two old men continue their quarreling. The half-pathetic, half-farcical mood of this playlet is typical of the best Lady Gregory comedies.

JOHN MILLINGTON SYNGE (1871–1909)

IMPORTANCE

Synge is one of the most original and creative writers of the Irish school; Freedley calls him "undoubtedly the greatest Irish dramatist who ever lived." His work is more radical in technique than that of either Lady Gregory or Yeats; at the same time his preoccupation with poetic effect does not divert his attention from the content and meaning of his plays. All his dramas, and especially his tragedies, are marked by a strange and disquieting poetic mood; there is a note of the supernatural about them. His scenes of beauty are never without a hint of the ominous. It has been suggested that this quality of Synge's work is due to his life-long illness; he views the world, not naturally and exuberantly, but through the dimmed and tormented eyes of a sick man.

Nevertheless Synge has a powerful sense of comedy; his humor proceeds out of character and situation and is never achieved through low jokes or tricks. Synge is a cynic in the manner of Rabelais or Swift; he can seldom admire anything wholeheartedly because he sees the sham that surrounds every human ideal. It was his penetrating insight into human weaknesses that caused his comedies, especially *The Playboy of the Western World,* to be attacked by nationalist groups; the fanatic patriots and Sinn Feiners were unable to accept the fact that the Irish peasant was occasionally credulous, bombastic, or untruthful. Yet there is no doubt that Synge felt a genuine love for the Irish people; he devoted his lifetime to studying and reproducing their folklore, and he was saddened rather than angered by the attacks on his comedies.

Life

J. M. Synge was born on Shaw Street in a Dublin suburb in 1871 of middle-class Protestant parentage. He took a B.A. at Trinity College in 1892, then wandered for several years in Germany, Italy, and France without any particular plan or project in mind. At various times he was inspired to become a musician or a literary critic. In Paris in the late nineties he fell in with the fin-de-siècle Bohemian society of young English and Irish expatriates, and took part in it for a year or two. In 1898 he met Yeats, and the older poet persuaded him to return to Ireland and take up the study of his own literature and folklore. He did so, and became an enthusiastic devotee of Irish lore; he twice visited the remote Aran Islands, off the Donegal coast in the west of Ireland, to learn Gaelic and study Irish society in its most primitive form. Except for short trips to Paris the rest of his life was spent in Ireland. The return to Ireland, however, also marked the beginning of his physical decline; his lungs were never healthy after 1898, and he soon became an intermittently bedridden invalid.

His first drama, *The Shadow of the Glen,* was produced by the Irish Literary Theatre in 1903; it was felt in some circles to be derogatory toward Irish womanhood, and organized demonstrations were held against it. *Riders to the Sea* (1904) and *The Well of the Saints* (1905) provoked little reaction, but the storm broke in full with the production of *The Playboy of the Western World* (1907). A full-scale riot greeted its first performance; the actors were treated to catcalls and whistles and pelted with vegetables, and nationalist newspapers printed diatribes in their editorial columns. When the Abbey company toured America in 1911–12 every attempt to perform this play elicited outraged yells, stamping, custard pies, and concerted fits of coughing from Irish-American nationalists in the audience. Synge himself remained detached from the controversy; he was not belligerent by nature, and preferred to let the fight be carried on by hardier souls. In addition his health was fast declining. He worked on *Deirdre of the Sorrows* (1909), but before this legendary tragedy was finished to his satisfaction he died of tuberculosis. He left a fiancée, Maire O'Neill, an actress in the Abbey company whom he had long planned to marry.

Chief Dramas

Riders to the Sea **(1904):** This one-act drama is a simple but moving folk-tragedy based on Synge's researches in the Aran Islands. There are only four speaking parts, and the action takes place in a single setting. Maurya, an old woman, has lost her husband and four of her six sons to the sea. Now Michael, the fifth, is missing, and the islanders search the beaches for his body. Her two daughters, Cathleen and Nora, console her and try to prevent Bartley, the sixth son, from sailing off to the mainland in stormy weather to sell their last animals for food. All during the play the boards for Michael's casket stand in the corner awaiting the finding of his body. But Michael is washed ashore far to the north and buried by strangers, and the casket is made for Bartley, who is drowned as he attempts to load the horses on the ship. Maurya has suffered the worst that a woman can know, and is now resigned. The only message conveyed by this play is the grotesque hopelessness of human existence; yet there is a certain beauty in the crushing and inevitable calamity, and the final impression is one of exaltation. The chief technical flaw in *Riders to the Sea* is its excessive brevity; in attempting to observe unity of time Synge has compressed an impossible number of events into the short duration of the action.

The Playboy of the Western World (1907): In this half-farce and half-melodrama the audience is never sure whether to laugh, to cry, or to throw vegetables at the actors. Christopher Mahon, a nimble-tongued and cocksure young peasant, arrives cold and hungry at a country pub on the coast of Mayo. He confesses that he is a fugitive from justice; he has slain his own father with a single blow after an argument, and has walked for days from the scene of the crime without eating or sleeping. The villagers are overcome with awe at this anecdote; they acclaim Christy with a fervor approaching adulation, treat him to drinks, and agree to hide him in the pub until the furor over his crime dies down. The cynical and crafty young widow Quin makes advances to him, and Pegeen Mike, the publican's daughter, throws over her spineless suitor and begins to vamp Christy with enthusiasm. "I'm thinking this night wasn't I a foolish fellow not to kill my father in the years gone by," remarks Christy.

But as he basks in his newly won glory, entering and winning all the local sporting contests including the mule races, hailed as the "Playboy of the Western World," Old Mahon, his father, arrives on the scene; he has been merely stunned by his son's blow and has come to wreak revenge on him. Christy's prestige falls to zero; he breaks into an altercation with the old man and chases him outside, where he "kills him for good" a second time in a furious battle to the shouts and screams of the villagers. He returns to the pub, and finds himself in danger of betrayal to the police by frightened local citizens. As Pegeen points out, there's "a great gap between a gallous story and a dirty deed." Old Mahon crawls in the door on all fours; again he has only been stunned. Father and son, more or less reconciled, with Christy asserting the independence of manhood, walk off together back to the farm, as Pegeen Mike laments the loss of the only suitor manly enough to deserve her.

The characters of the Widow and Old Mahon are notable in this play, as is the highly poetic brogue Synge attributes to the Mayo farmers. The title, of course, is an ironic allusion to the popular stereotype of the Irishman as a cocky and goodnatured hero; the "Western World" is also Connaught, the western part of Ireland as opposed to Ulster, Leinster, and Munster, north, east, and south. The theme is related to the Oedipus myth and Jack the Giant Killer in a Jungian, racial way; at least Christy doesn't have Kafka's father-complex—he matures through "murder" even if it's comically un-true.

SEAN O'CASEY (1880 – 1964)

IMPORTANCE

O'Casey is the most talented of the generation of Irish playwrights who began writing after the First World War. He differs from the other, more literary authors of the Irish movement in that he writes directly from life. He himself sprang from the lower-class city milieu he portrays; he knew the dialect of the slums as a child, and was not forced to go about learning it with a notebook in hand. Thus he writes from the inside; his dramas have a sincerity and authenticity achieved by no other Irish playwright. Like most other members of his school, he is adept at shifting from tears to laughter; his characteristic plays are neither totally tragic nor totally comic. His principal interest is in characterization and dialogue, especially in the speech of lower-class Dubliners. His work has been criticized for its lack of form. Although some may object to this amorphous quality, however, his feeling for language and his gift of characterization carry his work across the footlights. His later plays were generally well received by audiences.

Life

Sean O'Casey was born in Dublin in 1880 in a large and struggling proletarian family; he was self-educated and earned his own living from the time he was a boy. He worked at backbreaking manual labor for many years, although he was far from robust, and was able to write only in his spare time. His first play to be accepted by the Abbey Theatre was *The Shadow of a Gunman* (1923), when O'Casey was over forty, followed by *Juno and the Paycock* (1924), which reportedly saved the Abbey from bankruptcy. Nevertheless in 1926 when the same theater presented *The Plough and the Stars,* a riot broke out, almost as violent a controversy as had greeted *The Playboy of the Western World* nineteen years before. The action of *The Plough and the Stars* concerns the famous Easter Week rebellion of 1916, an outbreak in which O'Casey himself had taken part. His socialistic and pacifistic principles, however, led him to deplore the violence of this incident, and even to question the motives of some of its leaders. The play was therefore attacked by nationalist groups to whom the Easter Rebellion had become a hallowed legend. Yeats was furious and addressed his countrymen: "You have disgraced yourselves again. Is this to be an ever-recurring celebration of the arrival of Irish genius? Synge first and then O'Casey."

But O'Casey was angry and left Ireland never to return. Shaw among others befriended him in London. His next play, *The Silver Tassie* (1928), was refused by the Abbey Theatre, which didn't help patch up the quarrel.

O'Casey had been left wing in principle all during his career; a later play, *The Star Turns Red* (1940), was attacked even in Ireland as Communist propaganda. Actually the play's message is liberal rather than radical; the objections were principally provoked by its untactful title. Sean O'Casey enjoyed a long popularity in America (except among Irish nationalists), where he was fervently championed by the critic George Jean Nathan. Both *Purple Dust* (1940) and *Red Roses for Me* (1943) enjoyed good runs in addition to those plays already mentioned.

The stormy relationship with Ireland continued. Cyril Cusak produced another O'Casey play, *The Bishop's Bonfire*, in 1955 at the Dublin Gaiety Theatre, where it was hissed and booed by the audience—"more stage Irishmen in the house than in the cast," wrote Kenneth Tynan of the first night's performance. For a scheduled International Theatre Festival in Dublin in 1958 the Archbishop of Dublin refused to permit an O'Casey play, *The Drums of Father Ned*, or a dramatization of Joyce's *Ulysses*, or Samuel Beckett's *All That Fall* to be performed. O'Casey, as a Protestant rebel in Catholic Dublin, would have trouble there to the end. In September of 1964 at the age of eighty-four and still a rebel, he died of a heart attack at Torquay on the southwest coast of England, where he had lived for some years, writing memoirs and an occasional play.

Chief Drama

Juno and the Paycock (1924): This is O'Casey's best-known play. The action follows the decline and disintegration of the Boyle family in the slums of Dublin in 1922. Jack Boyle, an impractical, alcoholic loafer, has ceded the management of the family to his wife Juno, a magnificent symbol of long-suffering motherhood. There is no money in the house; a son, Johnny, crippled in revolutionary fighting, is confined to bed, bitter and cynical. As for Boyle, the "Paycock," he does nothing but cavort and dissipate with his crony Joxer Daly, a hypocritical windbag, parasite, and flatterer. Whenever a job appears on the horizon Boyle's legs begin to hurt. At the last moment Boyle inherits a fortune from an obscure uncle. The money turns the heads of the whole family; they buy gramaphones, furniture, and fine clothes on expectation, Boyle throws over Joxer, and his daughter Mary accepts the attentions of Bentham, the lawyer who is arranging for the inheritance. But their hopes are betrayed; the inheritance is lost through a technicality. Boyle, refusing to believe the obvious truth, retreats into alcohol with Joxer, and Bentham abandons the now-pregnant Mary. At the lowest ebb in the family fortunes, the revolutionaries arrive to kidnap and murder Johnny for suspected treachery; this rather unconvincing *deus ex machina* is the weakest point in the play. As the action closes, Juno and Mary sadly abandon Boyle to his dissipation and go off to seek their fortunes elsewhere. *Juno and the Paycock* is a typical deterministic tragedy of the decline of bad blood; if it were not for its highly poetic mood it would be a model Naturalistic drama.

LORD DUNSANY (1878–1957)

Lord Dunsany (Edward John Moreton Drax Plunkett) was born of Irish parents in 1878 but was reared and educated in London. He served in the British army during the Boer and First World Wars, and was associated with the Abbey Theatre from 1909. His plays, mostly one-act comedies or fantasies, are imaginative and original; it has been remarked that he performed the striking feat of creating his own mythology and then making it believable. His work is never grim or naturalistic; the whimsy is occasionally countered with a touch of irony, but the total effect is innocuous.

Dunsany's plays were popular with amateurs because of their simplicity, but his success was rather less in the commercial theater. He is the least indigenous of the authors associated with the Irish movement; his work is Irish more in mood and attitude than in content.

The Glittering Gate (1909), a one-act fantasy, is his best-known play, and typical of his work: a pair of deceased burglars, arriving before the Pearly Gates, find them closed and set about jimmying them according to the art of their profession.

PAUL VINCENT CARROLL (1900–68)

P. V. Carroll is another of the Irish dramatists who began producing after the First World War. He was educated at St. Patrick's Training College in Dublin, where he first encountered the aristocratic class of churchmen he was later to depict in *Shadow and Substance.* He served as a schoolteacher in Scotland for some time, and began writing only in his late twenties. After the acceptance of *The Watched Pot,* a grim Tolstoyian drama, by the Abbey Theatre in 1931, he devoted his energies to full-time writing. *Shadow and Substance* (1934) was an immediate success; it was brought to America in 1936 and was enthusiastically received by critics. Carroll's works differ from those of most other Irish dramatists in they are frequently laid in educated, middle-class, or intellectual environments; he has little gift for the idiom of the slum or the countryside. In 1943, having removed to Scotland, he helped found the Glasgow Citizens' Theatre, did some work with Sir Alexander Korda in the films *(Saints and Sinners),* and travelled. He died in 1968.

Chief Work

Shadow and Substance **(1934):** This play is a character study of Canon Skerritt, a proud churchman steeped in the classical traditions of Epicureanism and scholasticism. He despises the vulgar Irish folk to whom he is forced to minister, and he browbeats his two easy-going Irish curates, Father Corr and Father Kirwan. He loves his Irish housekeeper Brigid, however, in a paternal sort of way, and seeks to rid her of the imaginative reveries in which she sees visions of her patron, St. Brigid. In an allegorical sense Brigid is a symbol of Ireland herself and the Canon a personification of the Church that has come to minister to the nation without understanding its Celtic atavisms.

The plot comes to a head when the parishioners attack a liberal schoolmaster, O'Flingsley, whom the Canon has long excoriated. Brigid, going to the rescue of O'Flingsley, is killed, and the Canon realizes too late that O'Flingsley (the Irish intellectual class) was really his sort of person and that the two might have become fast friends. The Canon's admiration of classic culture, his rigid decorum, and his loathing of the vulgar have made him completely unfit to be a priest to the Irish townfolk, and only tragedy has come from his high ideals. The play contains fine portraits of the Canon, the simple but unconsciously poetic Brigid, and the two athletic and insouciant curates.

JAMES STEPHENS (1882 – 1950)

James Stephens is one of the few modern Irish writers who wrote no drama and was in no way connected with the Irish theater movement. His work falls into two main groups: whimsical novels based on Irish folklore, and short lyric poems somewhat in the style of Housman or Hardy. He was born in Dublin of poor parents and was virtually self-educated; he spoke with a pronounced brogue and had a native flair for Irish idiom. He studied Gaelic language assiduously and made himself an acknowledged expert on Irish folklore; he served capably as assistant curator of the Dublin National Gallery. His first and most famous novel, *The Crock of Gold,* won the Polignac Prize in 1912. Although he lived extensively in Paris, Stephens contributed actively to the nationalist movement and served as a Sinn Feiner before the achievement of Irish freedom. He died in 1950.

Chief Novel

The Crock of Gold (1912): This is an amusing fable cast in burlesque fairy-tale style. The story is told in the flattest possible manner; some of the irony appears almost unconscious. The chief characters are two philosophers who live in the pine wood called Coilla Doraca; they are married to two quarrelsome wives, but their skins are so thick they never notice when their wives are pinching them. After one philosopher commits suicide in an improbable and whimsical manner, the other philosopher is accused of his murder. Meanwhile the children of the two families are kidnapped by the leprechauns, who thereupon lose the crock of gold that, according to tradition, they guard in their woodland lairs. The leprechauns are forced to return the children in order to recover their treasure, and the surviving philosopher, who has been held in thrall in the city, is rescued by the "Three Absolutes," a set of abstract deities who watch over the Irish people. "And they took the

Philosopher from his prison, even the Intellect of Man they took from the hands of the doctors and lawyers, from the sly priests, from the professors whose mouths are gorged with sawdust, and the merchants who sell blades of grass . . . and then they returned again, dancing and singing to the country of the gods." The chief interest in *The Crock of Gold* lies in its half-veiled irony and in the circumlocutious and moronic discussions into which the Philosopher inveigles everyone he encounters.

Poems

"The Goat Paths" is a light lyric in tetrameter quatrains which rises to a slightly more serious note at the climax. Stanzas 1–5 describe the goats that clamber peaceably about the hills cropping the grass, but bound away if a civilized stranger approaches. In Stanza 6 the poet expresses a longing to live a life like theirs; had he the wisdom of the goats he would flee from the city to "stray apart and brood" in the "silence of the furze." Thus he would have time for contemplation and would be able to think out the intangible idea which lies "in the bottom of my mind." Thus Stephens rejects the city and longs for a return to the placid and uncomplicated life of the country, where true wisdom is achieved through contemplation.

"What Thomas an Buile Said in a Pub" is a whimsical snatch of folk dialogue illustrating the expressive bombast of the Irishman under the influence of drink. Thomas swears to his fellow topers that he saw God with his hand resting on a mountain; the "Almighty Man" was about to smash the sinful earth into oblivion, but was stayed when He heard the protesting voice of his dear child Thomas, whom He had thought dead.

"The Red-Haired Man's Wife" is a comment on marriage; the lines are spoken by a bride to her husband. In the first six stanzas the wife protests against the law and custom which make her the virtual chattel of her husband. Yet in the final two stanzas she warns him that she possesses the mysterious power of woman, which man can never entirely conquer; she resolves to retain a part of her individuality in spite of his effort to crush it. He may possess her body and mind, but there is an inner essence which she can never surrender to anyone.

"Righteous Anger" is devoted almost entirely to an eloquent and heartfelt curse. The poet, refused a "loan" of a glass of beer by a barmaid, calls upon her head a long list of Irish imprecations, climaxed with a hope that "the High King of Glory permit her to get the mange." This poem well illustrates Stephens' adroit command of Irish vernacular; its simplicity is combined with a shrewd and colorful poetic expression.

BRENDAN BEHAN (1923–64)

Brendan Behan is a typically Irish phenomenon. He made a very big flash in a relatively small pan. As a dramatist he follows a kind of Sean O'Casey tradition, adding touches of the Theater of the Absurd and more certainly the anger of the Angry Young Men of Britain who clustered around John

Osborne. He has to his credit one powerful play, *The Quare Fellow,* described as a comedy drama and published in 1956; one somewhat less effective play, *The Hostage* (1958); two books of novelized autobiography, *Borstal Boy* (1958) and its sequel, *Confessions of an Irish Rebel* (1965); a collection of articles he wrote for the press, *Hold Your Hour and Have Another* (1963); and an incredible number of anecdotes and legends surrounding his personal life. The play about him based on *Borstal Boy* was a hit of the 1970 season in New York, where the Irish population is still high. It has the attraction of *Dylan,* based on the life of Dylan Thomas, for both men drank themselves into an early grave. In a sense they lived their best dramatic scenes and played them to the hilt.

Life

Brendan Behan was born in Dublin in 1923. His father, Stephen Francis Behan, has been described as "a roundy little man" with a "bouncy personality," whose zest for life can be diminished only by "the consumption of enough alcohol to render him literally comitose." And that is probably a good deal. Brendan inherited both the zest and the desire. If you have it, spend it, first on necessities like drink, and if there's anything left, then on luxuries like food, clothing, and shelter. That seems to be a generally accepted code among the proletariat in Dublin, and Behan's literary success killed him. As long as manual labor and a small paycheck kept him relatively healthy, he was all right. But Behan started making money, typing out the kind of wit and wisdom his father had been distributing free for fifty years in Dublin bars and selling it to the papers. His mother, the former Kathleen Kearney, had been married before and had two sons when she married Stephen Behan. Their firstborn, Brendan, arrived while his father was in Kilmainham Jail in February 1923 for "political" reasons. Three more brothers and a sister, Carmel, arrived to fill the tenement on Russell Street and later the house at 70 Kildare Road. Times were hard, but there was always something for a drink, a song, or a fight. In 1939, at the great age of sixteen, Behan was arrested in Liverpool in connection with IRA activities (the Irish Republican Army, that is). After his release from a British Borstal Institution (reform school of a sort) and deportation back to Ireland, Behan spent some time in the home penal institutions (excellent background for *The Quare Fellow*) before he was set free in Dublin in 1945. His first publication was some Irish language verse in IRA papers, and then in English a short story called "A Woman of No Importance" in the magazine *Envoy.*

On his release Behan entered the Bohemian life of Dublin, which for him meant mostly "MacDaid's crowd," gathering at a bar in a cul-de-sac off Grafton Street. He got a job as a columnist for the *Irish Press* and started transferring witty and outrageous bar talk to paper. He wrote a radio script called *The Twisting of Another Rope,* then made it a one-act play; still not able to sell it, he made it into a three-acter and after hawking it about placed it in 1954 in the hands of Alan Simpson, who with others had opened a small theater in Dun Laoghaire southeast of Dublin proper. Simpson then recommended a title change to *The Quare Fellow,* and the play opened later the same year at the Dublin Pike Theatre. Two years later it was performed at the Theatre Royal in East London as directed by Joan Littlewood, and rave reviews launched Behan into orbit. Adding to his image and to the box-office success of *The Quare Fellow,* Behan made an almost historic, alcoholic television appearance in 1956 on Malcolm Muggeridge's BBC show, an almost sure way to gain public interest.

Behan, married by now to Beatrice Salkeld, daughter of an Irish artist, was commissioned to write a play in Gaelic by the Gael Linn, supplied with funds from a football pool. The result, *An Goill,* was a success in Dublin as performed in 1957 in Damer Hall, the little Irish language theater in St. Stephen's Green; but when translated into English and done later at the Abbey it was met by shocked protests for its blasphemy and mockery of the far-out nationalism and other absurdities of Irish life. This was *The Hostage,* which had productions in London in 1958 and 1959 and at the Cort Theater in New York in 1960. *Borstal Boy* had been published in 1958, and Behan could not be held down; he went on the wagon and off the wagon. In 1964 he died.

Chief Work

The Quare Fellow (1956) takes place in Kilmainham Jail on the banks of the Royal Canal in the northern part of Dublin City. The "Quare Fellow," which is Dublin prison jargon for a condemned man, is to be hanged in the morning, "the twisting of another rope." There are two groups of characters (most of them known as A, B, C, D, E, Young Prisoner 1, Young Prisoner 2, Lifer, the Other Fellow, Neighbor, and one by name, Dunlavin, an old operator who has spent most of his life in jail) and the warders, or guards (almost equally anonymous, except for the sensitive Crimmin, the young "screw" who faints when the trap is sprung, Warder Regan, the most understanding of the guards who manages to communicate in a human way both with other guards and with the prisoners too, and Holy Healey, the inspector from the Department of Justice). It is the reactions of these and the interplay of their feelings to the imminent hanging of the next day that make up the play. Along with the expressionistic anonymity there is a good deal of naturalistic detail in the prisoners' daily existence, drinking the linament intended for rheumatism, the betting, the language, the references to particular Dublin pubs and streets, and a rather practical view of the sacraments. There is a real struggle to keep the "quare fellow" from taking his own life before he can be hanged in the morning. But even the sorriest prisoner of them all finds life "a bloody sight better than death any day of the world," which has to represent the most affirmative statement of the play.

FRANK O'CONNOR (1903–66)

Although virtually self-educated, Frank O'Connor became one of the great short story writers of modern Irish literature. He fell into some remarkable friendships that aided his literary development. As a young man in Dublin he met A.E. (George Russell, 1867–1935), who took a real interest in him and soon introduced him to W. B. Yeats and Lady Gregory. A.E., who made his pen name initials (really the Greek digraph Æ) famous, was a poet, a mystic, and a character about Dublin for more than forty years, although he held somewhat aloof from the Abbey Theatre group and the "movement," preferring one of his own more esoteric with Madame Blavatsky the spiritualist in the ring. Joyce gives a memorable picture of him in *Ulysses* with Stephen Dedalus remembering in the library, Æ, I O U. A.E.'s son, Diarmuid Russell, emigrated to America and became the literary agent for a host of writers. It was A.E. who accepted O'Connor's earliest stories for publication in the *Irish Statesman.* His first volume of collected stories, *Guests of the Nation,* appeared in 1931.

Yeats "took up" the young Frank O'Connor too and in the mid-thirties engineered his appointment as a member of the Board of Directors of the Abbey Theatre to replace Brinsley MacNamara who had verbally attacked O'Casey. As a director of the Abbey, O'Connor served through many stormy sessions, even carpentering a few plays sometimes in collaboration, for example, *In the Train* and *The Invincibles,* both of 1937, until after Yeats' death in 1939. There are memorable and antic anecdotes of these years and personages (including passages of friendship with Yeats' wife George) in the second volume of O'Connor's memoirs, published posthumously as *My Father's Son* in 1968. The first volume, *An Only Child* (1961), deals with the first twenty years of his life, mostly in Cork and in the "troubles" (chiefly with the Irish Republican Army) from 1914 through 1923.

O'Connor also published two books of literary criticism and appraisals, largely as a result of his tours of duty as a teacher in creative writing in America (at Harvard, Northwestern, and Stanford in particular), one on the novel, *The Mirror in the Roadway* (1956) and one on the short story, *The Lonely Voice* (1962). He wrote two novels of his own, *The Saint and Mary Kate* (1932) and *Dutch Interior* (1940), and poetry as well.

IMPORTANCE

Frank O'Connor is chiefly remembered and anthologized as a writer of the short story. Many of his stories appeared in the *Atlantic Monthly* and in the *New Yorker.* Yeats said that O'Connor was "doing for Ireland what Chekhov did for Russia." Rather than dealing with problems and their solutions, his typical story "just states the human condition"; it has a sense of humor and a sense of reality.

Life

Born Michael O'Donovan, and assuming much later as a pen name his own middle and his mother's maiden name, O'Connor-O'Donovan recalls, "As a matter of historical fact I know that I was born in 1903 when we were living in Douglas Street, Cork, over a small sweet-and-tobacco shop. . . . My memories begin in Blarney Street, which we called Blarney Lane because it follows the track of an old lane from Cork to Blarney. It begins at the foot of Shandon Street, near the river-bank, in sordidness, and ascends the hill to something like squalor." He speaks of himself so often as "Mother's Boy," and she lived with him for such long periods in Dublin and elsewhere while his father remained alone in Cork that he does find fictional detail in autobiographical memories. The relationship between the child and the mother and the father is a central concern in the stories. The family was poor, and young Michael received only an elementary education at a Christian Brothers School in Cork (remembering what Simon Dedalus says of the Christian Brothers as opposed to the Jesuits in *A Portrait of the Artist as a Young Man,* such an education might not have been much). But one schoolmaster, Daniel Corkery, made a firm and lasting impression on the boy. He learned Gaelic and wrote verses.

After a course of training O'Donovan worked in County Cork as a librarian and then in the same capacity in Dublin, which allowed for his self-education — the only way he could get access to enough books. In Dublin in the twenties O'Donovan, now O'Connor, began to get his stories into print through A.E.'s influence, and under the wings of A.E. and Yeats reached 1940 and an expanded reputation with six books published and several influential years in the life of the Abbey Theatre. After several terms of teaching in the United States, although without degrees of his own, and publishing another ten or a dozen volumes, Frank O'Connor returned to the world of Dublin. He had had two sons and a daughter by a first marriage to Evelyn Bowen, and in 1953 married Harriet Rich, an American girl from Annapolis, Maryland, by whom he had another daughter. He was always a great man for friendships, and Harriet accompanied him one December day in 1965 to Mary Lavin's studio house in Lad Lane, Dublin, at tea time for a little Irish and conversation. V. S. Pritchett and his wife were there too. The old wit and sparkle came through, but the mark was on him. In March 1966, a little over three months later, he died.

Representative Short Stories

"My Oedipus Complex": Often anthologized, this is one of a group of stories about the fictional family of Larry Delaney, his Mummy, his Daddy, Mick Delaney, and the young baby brother Sonny. They live in Cork, approximately where the O'Donovans lived, and many of the incidents are reported in the autobiographical memoirs although shorn of the narrative details and development that make them effective stories. This effectiveness depends in part upon the I-narrator's being five years old and convincingly so even if Larry is endowed with strong personality traits. He is possessive, perfectly egocentric, but capable of some compromises however difficult and absurd they seem. The father has been away at war, and the child has seen little of him during his first five years; he remembers him only like Santa Claus, coming and going mysteriously. Most of the time he has had his mother's attentions all to himself. But they pray for Father's safe return from the wars, and return he does. "The irony of it," says Larry, as he finds himself displaced in Mother's attentions, affections, and bed. When he crawls in with the two of them, he has to be quiet and he wants to talk—"Whose house was it, anyway?" He staggers his mother by saying firmly, "I think it would be healthier for Daddy to sleep in his own bed."

Open warfare breaks out between Larry and Daddy. When the second baby Sonny arrives, however, both Larry and Daddy find themselves similarly displaced. Larry is trapped into saying, "If another bloody baby comes into this house, I'm going out." Father and Larry develop a working understanding—that kid Sonny "only cried for attention"—and finally make affectionate gestures to each other in their isolation.

"The Drunkard": Another Delaney story, with a new twist. For Father Mick, drink was a great weakness, and he looked forward to the funeral of his friend and talk-companion, Mr. Dooley, because that would be the excuse for liquid refreshment afterwards. He had been on the wagon for some time and had a great thirst. But Mother has to work and sends Larry to the funeral with Daddy, hoping that the boy will act as a brake on any excesses. Afterwards, joined by a drinking companion, Peter Crowley, they reach the pub. "Dadda, can't we go home now?" "Two minutes," says the father, as he always does on such occasions, "Just a bottle of lemonade, and we'll go home." He orders one lemonade and two pints. Larry drinks up, but Father prepares leisurely for enjoyment, filling his pipe and talking. Larry still thirsty and getting bored experiments with Father's glass. It was a terrible disappointment but "I took a longer drink and began to see that porter might have its advantages. I felt pleasantly elevated and philosophic." Finishing the glass, the boy gradually becomes "The Drunkard," through the stages of embarrassment, giggling, melancholia, roaring, and nausea. Father wonders who has drained his glass while his back was turned, realizes the truth, helps the boy vomit, and with the aid of Crowley gets him home and to bed but not before a cut on Larry's face from lurching into a wall and the stern disapproval of gossipy neighbors leaning over fences. The boy at that point is mad drunk, shouting "ye bloddy bitches!"—a carbon copy of a more adult "Drunkard's Progress." But the mother on her return, after tongue-whipping her husband, saves a word of praise for Larry, "You were his guardian angel."

"News for the Church": This story is one of what might be called a series on the clericals in modern Ireland. O'Connor is neither as cuttingly satirical as James Joyce nor as warmly kind as Mary Lavin in his picture of church figures, but somewhere between with a detached curiosity. All are free with touches of caricature as only born Catholics can be. "News for the Church" is quite simply a confession by a young, very modern woman of nineteen to a

Father Cassidy, who is not easily shocked but is pushed pretty far by the penitent, whose repentance seems somewhat limited. He is an easy and understanding confessor as she confesses being drunk and passed out (she is a teacher in a convent school, and doesn't often get the chance), but is startled at carnal intercourse and more at her not wanting to marry the man. The priest makes her see the act as beastly, browbeating her for details, and assigns the penance one would give a child. After the confession he has the chance to see that his psychology may be having the effect he had hoped for.

MARY LAVIN (1912 –   )

The importance of Mary Lavin as a writer was probably first recognized by Lord Dunsany in 1942 when he wrote a preface for her first collection of short stories, *Tales from Bective Bridge.* Even at that time he speaks of "reading the work of a master," of a "piercing eye" into "the hearts of women and children and men." From the very beginning he reports that he was able to help her only with her punctuation. He is right in placing her with the Russians, particularly Chekhov; but he might also have mentioned Joyce, when he says, "She tells the stories of quiet ordinary lives, the stories of people who many might suppose have no story in all their experience." Then the small detail. "It may seem too tiny a thing to notice, and the man's life, which turns in another direction from that moment, may seem tiny and unimportant too, to any who may not reflect how hard it is for any of us to say what is important and what is not." This is close to the technique of *Dubliners,* the Joycean epiphany, and Mary Lavin carries on the tradition with the addition or modification of feminine intuition and vision.

Besides a host of short stories, many first published in *The New Yorker* (that's the Lavin style), ten volumes from the Bective stories through *Happiness and Other Stories* published in 1970, there are two novels, *The House on Clewe Street* and *Mary O'Grady.* Frank O'Connor and V. S. Pritchett have both praised her fiction with distinctive comment; the first said, "She fascinates me more than any other of the Irish writers of my generation because more than any of them, her work reveals the fact that she has not said all she has to say." Pritchett called her "one of the finest living short story writers."

Life

Mary Lavin was born June 11, 1912 in East Walpole, Massachusetts (near Boston), the only child of Thomas and Nora Mahon Lavin. She was a pupil at Bird School in East Walpole and ten years old when the family went on a visit to Ireland. From that time on except for travel visits to England, America, and Europe, Mary Lavin has remained in Ireland and Irish. Her father was put in charge of Bective House, an estate in County Meath just north of Dublin, when Mary was fourteen, which began her long association with that region, including the banks of the upper reaches of the Boyne.

Mary continued her schooling at the Loreto convent on St. Stephen's Green, Dublin, and took an M. A. from the National University of Ireland in 1937, with honors for a thesis on Jane Austen. She began the study of Virginia Woolf for a doctorate but interrupted her program to visit the United States. In 1938 her first story, "Miss Holland," was published in *Dublin Magazine.* Lord Dunsany invited her to send other stories and her first collection was put together in 1942, receiving a James Tait Black Memorial Prize in England.

Lavin's first novel, *The House on Clewe Street,* was published in 1945 and her second, *Mary O'Grady,* in 1950. She was married to William Walsh, a Dublin lawyer, and became the mother of three daughters: Valdi, Elizabeth, and Caroline. They lived in Bective House, on a farm near Navan and not too far from Dublin. Mary Lavin was made a member of the Irish Academy of Letters. Her husband died in 1954, and the young widow continued writing, caring for her daughters and her mother who had become an invalid.

In 1965 Mary Lavin had a studio home in Dublin, hidden away in a kind of mews at 11 Lad Lane near the crossing of the Grand Canal and Upper Leeson Street. She found time to display Irish hospitality there. Several times in the sixties Mary Lavin was a writer in residence or gave readings at various American colleges. She read in good voice, was charming both as guest and hostess, and was likely to be unreliable as a correspondent. For a literary portrait see the Maura of Elizabeth Cullinan's "Maura's Friends."

Chief Works

The House on Clewe Street **(1945):** This novel is the story of three generations of an upper middle-class Irish family with some aristocratic pretensions living in the town of Castlerampart (King John's castle and rampart, both in ruins), which, although fictional, must be close to Navan. There are later scenes in Draghead (which again may well be Drogheda at the mouth of the Boyne), and the last quarter of the novel is in Dublin.

The grandfather of the story is Theodore Coniffe and the family house is on Clewe Street. "As near as it is ever possible to say when a story has its beginning, this story began when Theodore Coniffe's wife, Katherine, was still alive." They had a maid Mary Ellen and two daughters, Theresa and Sara, who were in their teens when they discovered to their surprise that another child was on the way. They hope for a boy. Katherine dies in childbirth. It's a girl, and she's named Lily.

Family continuity hangs by a thread as Theresa and Sara grow into spinsters. Lily, however, in her teens meets and attracts a young solicitor, Cornelius Galloway. They are married and Cornelius is killed by a horse at a hunt — he hadn't been bred to it. Lily is with child and Gabriel is born. Once more Theresa and Sara take over the bringing up of another child — their own and not their own — as if he were a Coniffe. However, when Gabriel grows up, with grandfather dead and mother unable to resist Theresa's domination, he is sent to Draghead to Technical School instead of to Dublin, where his friend Sylvester has gone to study art. Lily dies suddenly, and Gabriel is more than ever under his aunts' direction. Sara is softer toward him than Theresa, but both are shocked when he runs away from home with Onny Soraghan, very low class, who had worked in their house on Clewe Street after Mary Ellen had been let go some time before.

The love affair may be romantic but it is not romanticized, as Onny and Gabriel go to Dublin to live, still unmarried and with little money. They share a studio apartment with Sylvester who is now a painter living on Kildare Street near St. Stephen's Green and live on his charity while Gabriel unsuccessfully looks for a job. The aunts arrive one day, but Onny refuses to let them in. She shows her lack of sensitivity and taste on several occasions. Sylvester and his artist friends who have some rather bohemian parties are surprised and amused to discover that Onny's real name is Honor. She becomes pregnant but refuses to marry Gabriel, who tries to insist. Apparently having sought out an abortion, she is found in a state of collapse in Stephen's Green, dies, and is taken to the city morgue. Gabriel identifies her from the newspaper description, remembers the old days, the miseries and securities of Castlerampart, but decides to follow the Coniffe way of true honor and face the consequences of an inquest.

This is a quiet but highly effective family chronicle, with large doses of felt life and carefully observed details.

Mary O'Grady **(1950):** This is another family novel, but about one generation only this time and all in Dublin. We follow Mary, a young country woman from Tullamore, who marries a Dublin man, Tom O'Grady, a tram conductor met on her first and only trip to Dublin to visit an aunt, from the early years of the twentieth century as a young bride through the births of five children: Patrick, Ellie, Angie, Larry, and Rosie. Mary goes every day to the tram shed to take Tom a hot dinner; it gives her a chance to linger on her return near the open fields by the Grand Canal at the end of Fitzwilliam Street—the grasses there remind her of Tullamore and her old home.

The children grow up quickly, and we watch the passing of time through successive deaths and catastrophes: first Tom, suddenly, when Larry and Rosie were still small children, with burial in Glasnevin Cemetery; then Patrick's wanting to go to America to make his fortune and going; then the coming of the airplanes to Dublin, the first, for sightseeing rides from Phoenix Park, and then with the deaths of Ellie and Angie and their country-bred fiancés, Bart and Willie, in a plane crash on the North Strand. Mary, still a young widow with her husband's small pension, is rocked but tries to hold her family together and protect them. Her failures are a measure of her courage.

But Mary is not long-suffering and noble, doing God's work with the consolation of religion and family affection. She is not sentimentalized at all. She is frequently sharp and bitter, saying things she didn't mean to say. She is rather irascible and spends but little time thinking of religion—at least until

Larry is persuaded by a priest that he has a vocation at the age of fourteen and goes away to a seminary. Mary, like a good "Irish mother," is pleased, but she is intelligent enough to know that poor Larry has little aptitude for anything, that it is almost as if "he were blemished or weak." But off he goes, at some sacrifice, and Mary is alone with Rosie.

We are then aware of 1929 with vague news of a stock market crash in America followed by depression. Patrick, after a long silence, comes home mentally deranged, having lost whatever fortune he had made in America, and has to be taken to an "institution." As Rosie grows up, Mary worries about her association with the high-living Esmay family, and instead of succeeding in sending Frank "packing," pushes Rosie and Frank into what she considers an unfortunate marriage. Not all the blows have fallen. Larry is refused for the priesthood shortly before he was to reach ordination, and decides to go off to Foreign Missions. Years continue to pass, and Mary gets visibly older, less careful of house and person. Rosie and Frank come to an impasse in their long childless marriage; and Rosie comes to tell her mother that she is leaving him, paying little attention to her mother's fatigue and illness. They express some asperity to each other; the only note of hope as Mary dies quietly is that Rosie may finally be pregnant. All other hopes have been dashed in a series of blows that almost, but never quite, break down the humanity and dignity of the girl from Tullamore, Mary O'Grady.

Representative Short Stories

"The Living" (first published in *The New Yorker,* Nov. 22, 1958) is a companion story to Joyce's *The Dead,* probably not intentionally so; it is a short coda to the coda of the *Dubliners.* It too takes place in Dublin, and there is a family, the family of the narrator, a seven-year-old boy, his mother, father, and brother. The story opens with the boy's friend, eight-year-old Mickser, asking an abrupt question, "How many dead people do you know?" Corpses, that is, not ghosts. Mickser, proud of his superiority because he has seen corpses, talks the boy into attending a wake across town near the railroad tracks. But when the grief-stricken widow, a little off her rocker, asks the boys to stroke the hands of the corpse and comb his hair, Mickser flees with his friend behind him. He reflects that "That one oughtn't to count"; he was sort of dead when he was alive, not being right in the head.

The boy decides to leave Mickser for now and go home. There are questions to ask Mother, a pretty woman and very much the center of the family. The father clumsily tries to make gestures of love toward her, but suddenly wonders if she's feeling all right, with intimations of her possible death. The boy can't question her now but thinks of the nightly prayers: ". . . the living and the dead . . ." They are suddenly terrible words. As they excitedly go into the parlor for tea, the last paragraph says: "And in the excitement I forgot all about the living and the dead. For a long time." The epiphany has occurred, and the boy has taken a step toward growing up — or down; but the Dublin of the football matches and the wake is not as depressing as the gloom of the Christmas party and Gabriel's view of the snow falling "upon all the living and the dead."

"Happiness" (the title story from the volume of that name, 1970) is typical of Mary Lavin's use of common, almost trivial, material to present character in the round. "Mother" has the secret of happiness, but it doesn't corrrespond to Father Hugh's definition with sorrow as a necessary ingredient. The story is told by one of three daughters; Bea and Linda are her younger sisters. Their father died suddenly after a short illness. Mother treats the priest as if he were "a human being — that's all!" But that doesn't prevent gossip, which is one thing that can never touch Mother's happiness. She thinks she inherited the capacity for it from her father. Certainly her own mother doesn't possess it; as an invalid she makes constant, insistent, never satisfied demands on her daughter Vera. Father Hugh said of Grandmother, "God Almighty couldn't make that woman happy."

Mother remembers how she carried a huge armful of daffodils from the country to Father in a Dublin hospital. The nun had chastised her, "Where are you going with those foolish flowers, you foolish woman? . . . Don't you know your husband is dying?" As Mother dies, she is still thinking about putting those daffodils in water. Foolish, perhaps, but happy. One suspects that the secret of this beautiful story is simply honesty, that Vera is Mary Lavin looking ahead as well as back, that the narrator's name should be Valdi. But this is not intended to be biography hunting — only a word of praise for sincerely recorded precise details in a fictional frame. It is close to the secret ingredient for success.

Note: For other Irish authors see George Bernard Shaw and James Joyce.

HISTORICAL BACKGROUND (1939–55)

Germany had risen as an industrial power from the ashes of the First World War. Hitler wanted to expand German territory to the east, and therefore attempted to destablize the Czech government in the Sudeten region. To prevent the outbreak of war, British Prime Minister Neville Chamberlain struck an agreement with Hitler, Mussolini of Italy, and Daladier of France at Munich in 1938. The agreement allowed Germany to take over additional eastern territory and let Hungary and Poland divide large portions of Czechoslovakia. His actions were condemned by many English leaders as a cowardly attempt to placate, and thereby strengthen, a potential foe, but they were supported by many who wanted peace above all.

Hitler quickly seized control of Czechoslovakia for Germany, and thereafter the Danzig and Polish Corridor regions of Poland. The British government demanded that Germany retreat from Poland. When Hitler refused, Prime Minister Chamberlain declared war, in alliance with France. Italy joined forces with Germany. The Second World War began.

In the early phases of the war, Germany swept across Poland as far at its capital, Warsaw. As the British under Churchill scrambled to assemble an alliance among its commonwealth, the Germans invaded and captured Denmark, Norway, Belgium, and the Netherlands. By early summer, 1940, France had accepted an armistice with German and Italian forces. Germany now turned its attention to the bombing of England and a future invasion.

After the Japanese attack on Pearl Harbor, December 7, 1941, the United States entered the war. Together with British forces, the United States succeeded in driving German and Italian forces out of Northern Africa. American and British forces landed on the coast of Normandy in June 1944, and by the end of that year had reclaimed French, Belgian, and Dutch territory. Germany itself was invaded by Russian, British, and American forces. Berlin fell in May 1945, and Japan shortly thereafter, following the dropping of the atomic bomb on two Japanese cities.

After the war, reconstruction began in England under the leadership of the Labour Party and Prime Minister Clement Attlee. He promptly converted England to what amounted to a socialist state by nationalizing civil aviation, the railroads, mining, telecommunciations, and the Bank of England. Social security and medical benefits plans were made available to all under the terms of the National Insurance Act of 1945 and the National Health Service Act of 1946. These social enthusiams had cooled by 1951, however, when the Conservatives again returned to power under Winston Churchill and undid much of the Labour Party's socialist legislation. In May, 1953, George VI died and his young daughter was crowned Elizabeth II on June 2, 1953.

In the years following the Second World War, English leaders played an active role in the development of the United Nations. In 1946, the Assembly of the United Nations met in London to elect its first president and to select a permanent meeting site (in New York).

REVIEW QUESTIONS

THE REACTION TO REALISM

Multiple Choice

1. _____ The dialogue in Ivy Compton-Burnett's novels
   a. expresses the conflict between conversation and subconversation, what is said and what is meant
   b. is almost nonexistent, since the novels are devoted almost entirely to the characters' thoughts
   c. expresses the conflict between men and women
   d. is used to express the characters' fear of solitude

2. _____ E. M. Forster, D. H. Lawrence, and Christopher Isherwood
   a. shared a radical political outlook
   b. wrote about characters from the upper middle class
   c. used their travels as backgrounds for some of their books
   d. were philosophically alike in their pessimistic view of humanity

3. _____ Joseph Conrad considered himself to be
   a. an adventure writer
   b. a novelist of human nature in its deepest manifestations
   c. primarily a poet
   d. a crusader against the evils of imperialism

4. _____ Impressionism, stream of consciousness, and internal monologue were used
   a. in reaction against the high moral tone of the Victorian era
   b. in reaction against the overly analytical phychological novel
   c. to express doubt about the validity of the vision of reality presented by Realists and Naturalists
   d. to make literature less accessible to the average reader

5. _____ Ford Madox Ford's *Parade's End*
   a. is a series of novels about society before the First World War
   b. is a series of novels about the British Empire
   c. has a hero who finds himself out of step with the modern world
   d. satirizes the British aristocracy

6. _____ Which of these premises was NOT shared by impressionistic and stream of consciousness writers?
   a. The true existence of individuals lies in their mental processes, not in the external elements of their lives.
   b. The internal life of an individual is not sharply logical.
   c. Psychological associations help to form people's emotional attitudes.
   d. Physical love is a negligible and often immoral part of human existence.

7. _____ James Joyce's works
   a. are increasingly experimental in their use of language
   b. require the reader to be familiar with Irish history

c. express his Irish nationalism

d. have had little influence on other writers, since they are so idiosyncratic

8. _____ The literary movement of the Irish Renaissance first took the form of

a. dark and gloomy poetry

b. stark naturalism

c. romantic plays

d. patriotic, nationalistic novels

9. _____ The symbolism Yeats developed in *A Vision* and other works is used

a. to enable him to make universal statements about the human condition in his poetry

b. to create a new religious movement, Theosophy

c. to express revolutionary sentiments that would otherwise have been censored

d. to create romantic verse drama based on Irish mythology

10. _____ Frank O'Connor's short stories can best be characterized as

a. slice-of-life glimpses of degraded humanity

b. biting satires

c. nationalistic propaganda

d. realistic but kindly visions of ordinary life

True-False

11. _____ Characters in E. M. Forster's novels strive to overcome social conflict and convention.

12. _____ D. H. Lawrence believed that sexual realization was a necessary part of the wider struggle toward self-realization.

13. _____ Christopher Isherwood thought of himself primarily as a poet, and wrote prose only to support himself.

14. _____ Ford Madox Ford's novel *The Good Soldier* was one of the first antiwar novels to come out of the First World War.

15. _____ Although a supporter of the British Empire in his youth, Rudyard Kipling came in later years to embrace pacifism and socialism.

16. _____ Lawrence Durrell's *Alexandria Quartet* was a failure when it first appeared because its comic irony did not appeal at the time.

17. _____ Impressionistic authors are primarily concerned with the social, political, or ethical problems of their characters.

18. _____ Virginia Woolf's characters are often autobiological.

19. _____ The content of the plays produced by the Irish National Theatre often antagonized Irish nationlists.

20. _____ In old age, Yeats returned to the romanticism of his early poetry.

Matching

21. _____ D. H. Lawrence   a. *The House at Clewe*
22. _____ James Joyce   b. "My Oedipus Complex"
23. _____ Christopher Fry   c. *The Horse's Mouth*
24. _____ John Millington Synge   d. *The Quare Fellow*
25. _____ Mary Lavin   e. *To the Lighthouse*
26. _____ Frank O'Connor   f. "Ivy Day in the Committee Room"
27. _____ Lawrence Durrell   g. *The Playboy of the Western World*
28. _____ Brendan Behan   h. *The Lady's Not for Burning*
29. _____ Joyce Cary   i. *Sons and Lovers*
30. _____ Virginia Woolf   j. *Mountolive*

Fill-in

31. The title of E. M. Forster's novel _____ symbolizes the need for wider human horizons.
32. The final words of James Joyce's _____ begin the sentence that occurs at the start of the work.
33. A young man whose failure to live up to his own ideals of honor and courage determines his subsequent actions is the central character in Joseph Conrad's _____ .
34. Short stories dealing with a sensitive young girl in New Zealand are typical of the work of _____ .
35. Realistic dramas depicting working-class Dubliners were written by _____ .
36. Verse dramas, popular in the 1940s and early 1950s, were written by _____ .
37. D. H. Lawrence's novel based on his own youth is _____ .
38. Berlin during the Weimar republic is depicted in Christopher Isherwood's _____ .
39. _____ , by Virginia Woolf, depicts a single day in the life of several characters in London.
40. Plays based on the Japanese Noh dramas were written by _____ .

Answer Key

1.	a	5.	c	9.	a
2.	c	6.	d	10.	d
3.	b	7.	a	11.	T
4.	c	8.	c	12.	T

13.	F	23.	h	32.	*Finnegans Wake*
14.	F	24.	g	33.	*Lord Jim*
15.	F	25.	a	34.	Katherine Mansfield
16.	F	26.	b	35.	Sean O'Casey
17.	F	27.	j	36.	Christopher Fry
18.	T	28.	d	37.	*Sons and Lovers*
19.	T	29.	c	38.	*Berlin Diary*
20.	F	30.	e	39.	*Mrs. Dalloway*
21.	i	31.	*A Room with A View*	40.	William Butler Yeats
22.	f				

Part 4

THE REALM OF IDEAS: INTELLECTUAL AND IDEOLOGICAL LITERATURE

WORKS AT A GLANCE

Aldous Huxley

1921	*Crome Yellow*	1949	*Ape and Essence*
1928	*Point Counter Point*	1959	*The Genius and the Goddess*
1932	*Brave New World*	1962	*Island*
1945	*Time Must Have a Stop*		

Evelyn Waugh

1930	*Vile Bodies*	1952	*Men at Arms*
1945	*Brideshead Revisited*	1955	*Officers and Gentlemen*
1948	*The Loved One*	1961	*The End of Battle*
1949	*Scott-King's Modern Europe*		

G. K. Chesterton

1904	*The Napoleon of Notting Hill*	1914	*The Wisdom of Father Brown*
1908	*The Man Who Was Thursday*	1926	*The Incredulity of Father Brown*
1911	*The Innocence of Father Brown*	1927	*The Secret of Father Brown*

Graham Greene

1932	*Stamboul Train*	1951	*The End of the Affair*
1936	*A Gun For Sale*	1953	*The Living Room*
1938	*Brighton Rock*	1955	*Loser Take All*
1939	*The Confidential Agent, The Lawless Roads*	1957	*The Potting Shed*
1940	*The Power and the Glory*	1959	*The Complaisant Lover*
1943	*The Ministry of Fear*	1961	*A Burnt-Out Case*
1948	*The Heart of the Matter*	1966	*The Comedians*
1950	*The Third Man*	1969	*Travels with My Aunt*

William Golding

1954	*Lord of the Flies*	1959	*Free Fall*
1955	*The Inheritors*	1964	*The Spire*
1956	*Pincher Martin*	1965	*The Hot-Gates*
1958	*The Brass Butterfly*	1967	*The Pyramid*

George Bernard Shaw

1892	*Widowers' Houses*	1903	*Man and Superman*
1894	*Mrs. Warren's Profession*	1905	*Major Barbara*
1895	*Candida*	1906	*The Doctor's Dilemma*
1894–98	*Arms and the Man*	1912	*Pygmalion*
1897	*The Devil's Disciple*	1921	*Back to Methuselah*
1898–1907	*Caesar and Cleopatra*	1923	*Saint Joan*

H. G. Wells

1895	*The Time Machine*	1916	*Mr. Britling Sees It*
1896	*The Wheels of Chance*		*Through*
1897	*The Invisible Man*	1920	*Outline of History*
1905	*Kipps*	1926	*The World of William*
1909	*Ann Veronica, Tono-*		*Clissold*
	Bungay	1934	*Experiment in*
1910	*The History of Mr. Polly*		*Autobiography*

George Orwell

1934	*Burmese Days*	1946	*Animal Farm*
1938	*Homage to Catalonia*	1949	*Nineteen Eighty-Four*

John Osborne

1956	*Look Back in Anger*	1965	*Inadmissible Evidence*
1957	*The Entertainer*	1968	*The Hotel in Amsterdam*
1961	*Luther*		

Harold Pinter

1957	*The Birthday Party, The*	1960	*The Caretaker*
	Dumb-Waiter	1965	*The Homecoming*

Caryl Churchill

1972	*Owners*	1979	*Cloud Nine*
1975	*Objections to Sex and*	1982	*Top Girls*
	Violence	1987	*Serious Money*
1976	*Vinegar Tom, Light Shining*		
	in Buckinghamshire		

David Storey

1960	*This Sporting Life, Camden*	1969	*In Celebration, The*
1963	*Radcliffe*		*Contractor*
1967	*The Restoration of Arnold*	1970	*Home*
	Middleton		

Samuel Beckett

1934	*More Pricks than Kicks*	1957	*All That Fall*
1938	*Murphy*	1958	*Krapp's Last Tape,*
1951	*Molloy* (English, 1956)		*Endgame*
1952	*Molloy Dies* (English,	1961	*Happy Days*
	1956), *Waiting for Godot*		*Act Without Words I*
1953	*The Unnamable* (English,		*Act Without Words II*
	1960)		

Doris Lessing

1952–69	*Children of Violence*	1963	*A Man and Two Women,* "How I Finally Lost My Heart"
1957	"The Day Stalin Died"		
1962	*The Golden Notebook*		

Edna O'Brien

| 1960 | *The Country Girls* | 1981 | "Sister Imelda" |

Susan Hill

| 1973 | "How Soon Can I Leave" | | "The Springtime of the Year" |

8
THE RETURN TO TRADITION AND FAITH

As a part of the general reaction against materialism that took place around 1900 there occurred a small but important revival of mysticism and religious idealism in literature. The general disillusionment with regard to science and democracy contributed to this movement, as did a reaction against the late nineteenth century fads of evolution, agnosticism, and socialism. In England the movement was heralded by the Pre-Raphaelites, the chief of whom were Dante Gabriel Rossetti (1828–82) and John Ruskin (1819–1900). In France there were two important predecessors: the conservative and traditionalist novelist Paul Bourget (1852–1935), whose novel *Le Disciple* (1889) attacked the skepticism of the Naturalistic school; and Maurice Barrès (1862–1923), who in *Les Deracinés* (1897) called for a return to the patriotism and Catholicism of France's classic age. Although three of these four authors lived into the twentieth century, their influence was exerted chiefly on the generation that reached maturity before 1914. In their wake appeared a school of novelists and poets who formed around 1914 what is known as the Catholic Revival movement. Much of the work of this group is mediocre, but it did include at least four important authors: G. K. Chesterton and Evelyn Waugh in England; François Mauriac and Paul Claudel in France. A number of English writers besides Chesterton and Waugh became converts to Catholicism, Graham Greene and Muriel Spark among them, turning their literary talents to the service of their convictions.

Aldous Huxley arrived at a similar goal through a different process. Equally antagonistic toward modern technology, he ignored medievalism and Catholicism to turn instead toward the mysticism of the East. Thus he speaks not for a return to any extant Western church, but for a reawakening of the common mystical heritage of all mankind. Like the rest of the group, however, Huxley argues that the salvation of humanity is contingent upon its abandonment of materialism for some more spiritual creed.

The authors in this group tend to be conservative in politics, although usually not in a partisan sense. Waugh is the only one to take up his stand specifically by the conservative banner; Mauriac and Claudel are "conservative humanitarians" who often find themselves on the liberal side when questions of human welfare are at stake. Their attitudes toward morals vary. Chesterton is frankly a Catholic Epicurean; he detests Puritanism, teetotalling, and vegetarianism. Huxley is the enemy of debauchery, especially sexual excesses; and Waugh, especially in the later part of his career, takes a similar position. Claudel, however, is free from any form of Puritanism. His respect for sainthood is heartfelt and genuine, but he affirms the comforts of marriage and materialism just as heartily for those whose vocation lies in that direction. Where Claudel's Catholicism is typically French, Mauriac's takes a Jansenist, almost a Protestant, hue. In literary technique these authors tend toward romanticism and fantasy, although the novels of Huxley and Waugh are realistic or satirical.

William Golding seems to be more like the American William Styron, revitalizing a Protestant rather than a Roman ethic. T. S. Eliot, who may also be considered in this group, advocated a traditional and conservative Anglicanism, however high church. There are, then, multiple traditions and faiths to which modern writers may return.

ALDOUS HUXLEY (1894–1963)

Huxley, in many ways a typical product of the British tradition, is nevertheless totally opposed to the spirit of the twentieth century. He is suspicious of science, scornful of progress, and saddened by the secularism and skepticism of modern intellectual life. In his eyes modern man has sold his divine heritage for a mess of gadgets — refrigerators, airplanes, cannon, and vitamin pills. Huxley views the modern Western man as a creature hopelessly addicted to materialism, one who spends his lifetime in a chimerical pursuit of possessions and comfort and in a lurking fear of the death that must inevitably exterminate his identity. Huxley respects individualism, but not egocentricity; he seeks freedom, but not democracy — which he views as mob rule. Although he is in a sense the enemy of Puritanism, he condemns the lustful and adulterous sexual life of the intellectual and upper-class strata in Western society, and along with it the middle-class cult of comfort — the cushions and innerspring mattresses, the warm rooms and soft food, and the aversion to whatever is natural, unsynthesized, stark, or elemental. These things considered, it is no surprise that Huxley is deeply impressed with Oriental society, and especially with Hindu philosophy. His is the spirit of a yoga incongruously born into twentieth century British society.

IMPORTANCE

As an author Huxley is less revolutionary. He writes essentially in the tradition of Swift, Sterne, and the eighteenth century satirical novelists; his characters are stylized and his style salty. He has a talent for ludicrous characterization and for inane and preposterous conversations; there is nothing of the stuffy saint about him. His characters are usually dominated by a single obsession. The old millionaire Stoyte in *After Many a Summer,* depravedly erotic and obsessed with a fear of dying, is the epitome of the Huxley protagonist.

Life

Huxley's antecedents are distinguished: he is the grandson of the biologist T. H. Huxley and the brother of the scientist Julian Huxley, and his mother was a niece of Matthew Arnold. Born in Surrey in 1894, he was educated at Eton and Oxford. At eighteen he was stricken entirely blind; he recovered his eyesight gradually, but remained partly blind for many years. After Oxford he became associated with J. M. Murry on the *Athenaeum,* and soon turned to criticism and essay writing. He began to write fiction around 1920 and turned out about one novel a year from 1921 to 1931, when his production began to drop off. Two of his best novels, *Eyeless in Gaza* and *After Many a Summer,* however, date from the period 1936–1940.

Huxley spent most of the twenties in Italy; he also visited India and the Orient during this era. He was friendly with D. H. Lawrence in Italy up to the time of Lawrence's death in 1930. In 1938 he established himself in America, and after that spent most of his time in California. In the forties and fifties he devoted much attention to exercising his eyes through the Bates method and improved his eyesight greatly; he was also active in Vedanta and other religious circles in Los Angeles. He continued to publish novels, *Time Must Have a Stop* (1945), *Ape and Essence* (1949), *The Genius and the Goddess* (1955), and *Island* (1962). Other writings turned toward commentary (much of it on religions of the East) and biography.

On November 23, 1963, Aldous Leonard Huxley died in Los Angeles, at the home of friends where he and his wife had been staying since their house had been destroyed by fire the year before. This was the time of President Kennedy's assassination, and the Huxley obituary notices received only slight attention.

Chief Novels

Crome Yellow (1921): In this, Huxley's first successful work, the action is laid chiefly at Crome, the old country house of Henry Wimbush and his wife. A house party is planned: the chief guests are Denis Stone, in love with Wimbush's niece Anne; Gombauld, an eccentric artist; Mary Bracegirdle, an amateur Freudian; and Ivor Lombard, a "painter of ghosts and spirits." The guests cavort in the typical manner of the abandoned twenties. Mary is seduced by Ivor, who then departs and leaves her heartbroken; Anne throws herself at Gombauld, and Mr. Wimbush bores the entire party with his interminable histories of Crome. Denis, unable to take a decisive step, allows his wooing of Anne to become hopelessly confused. Encouraged by the bitter

Mary, he concocts a telegram calling himself away from the estate; when it arrives he learns too late that Anne has secretly loved him for some time. This novel is a satire of upper-class manners in the twenties, including the fad of Freudianism of the time.

***Point Counter Point* (1928):** This experiments with technique suggested by Gide's *Counterfeiters.* The chief devices borrowed from Gide are the trick of showing the same incident from various points of view, and the "Quaker Oats theme"—the novel within a novel, in which the chief character is writing a novel much like that in which he appears (the term is drawn from the successive receding motifs on a popular breakfast food carton).

The central figure of the novel is Philip Quarles, a novelist, contemplative and introspective rather than aggressive. His wife Elinor is the daughter of John Bidlake, a crusty and egocentric old artist. Another of Bidlake's children, Walter, is growing bored with his mistress, Marjorie Carling, and plans an affair with Lucy Tantamount. Since Marjorie is pregnant and Lucy increasingly indifferent, however, this affair comes to nothing.

A subplot concerns the enmity between Everard Webley, an admirer of Elinor's and leader of a pseudo-fascist movement, and Spandrell, a liberal but cynical young playboy. Spandrell, in order to justify his existence in some decisive way, murders Webley, writes a confession of his crime, and is then himself killed by Webley's thugs. Elinor, in whose house the first crime is committed, is away at the time at the bedside of her son Philip, who eventually dies of meningitis in a heart-rending scene. The only characters in the novel who seem to derive any satisfaction from life are Burlap, an eccentric editor, and his mistress, Beatrice Gilray. At the end of the novel these two, free from repressions and childishly playful, present a gay picture of Bohemian hedonism.

Mark Rampion, a young painter, is based on the figure of Huxley's friend D. H. Lawrence; he serves as a mouthpiece of the author's own ideas in the novel. Also interesting are the passages from Philip Quarles' notebook, in which he sets down remarks on the technique of the novel embodying Huxley's own literary principles. One of the key themes of the notebook is the principle that the ideas of the novel must be personified in characters rather than presented in essay form.

***Brave New World* (1932):** In this nightmare utopia, a picture of civilization in the twenty-fifth century, science and technology have achieved a complete tyranny over humanity. The action takes place chiefly in the Central London Hatchery and Conditioning Centre, where human beings are produced from chemically preserved sperm and "conditioned" for life in bottles. The process can produce humans of any desired intellectual capacity: Epsilons, strong and stupidly content, are raised for menial labor, and a few creative Alphas are produced for leaders. There are numerous intermediate castes, and each group is conditioned psychologically to remain in its station. Discontent is alleviated through "soma," a drug much like alcohol in its effects but producing no hangover. There is no passion, no frustration, and no deviation from the normal in this ultra-scientific society.

Bernard Marx, an Alpha, is believed by his colleagues to be slightly imperfect due to alcohol damage during his embryonic formation. He has vestiges of individuality and questions many things he finds in utopia. With Lenina Crowne, a normal young Alpha, he journeys to New Mexico, where a few Indians are still allowed to live a "savage" life on a fenced-in reservation. There he meets John, a young savage, and brings him back to London. Actually John is of English extraction; his mother is a former utopian who was lost in the reservation during a visit. John, whose attitudes are those of the twentieth century, is astonished at what he sees in the London Centre and lashes out bravely in an attempt to free the masses from their tyranny. They become enraged at his efforts, however, and he is almost killed. At the end of the novel he goes away to live a life of contemplation in a ruined lighthouse tower and there eventually dies by his own hand. Bernard, attempting to aid John in his revolt, is banished to a remote post in Iceland, and the life of utopia proceeds as before.

It is noteworthy that many of the futuristic devices depicted in this 1932 novel — for example, television and helicopters — are already in operation, and that psychological conditioning of the masses has been widely used in totalitarian countries.

EVELYN WAUGH (1903–66)

IMPORTANCE

Waugh was an energetic conservative and Catholic convert whose main concern was the decline of faith in Western civilization. Of aristocratic inclination, he felt that the finer values of civilization could be transmitted only by a minority of breeding and education, and that this class, specifically the aristocratic and intellectual element in Britain, was growing successively more unfit to carry out such duty. Therefore he "flayed" the English aristocracy. The deterioration of morals so characteristic of the twenties was one of his favorite subjects. His early novels treated this subject descriptively and objectively, but in later years he tended to become more critical of modern materialism and more concerned with the return to faith that he felt to be the sole recourse of civilization. His early work is typified in *Vile Bodies* (1930), which in prose style somewhat resembles Scott Fitzgerald; his *magnum opus, Brideshead Revisited* (1945), climaxes the later movement in his work.

Like Proust, Waugh is mainly preoccupied with the leisure classes, sometimes branching out to include their relations with lower strata. He is neither a naturalist nor a sociologist; he feels that the most interesting fictional characters are those who have ideas, and that in our time ideas are the virtual monopoly of persons of culture. Thus Waugh may justifiably be accused of snobbery, although it should be added that he assumes this attitude consciously and for the highest of purposes. The bourgeois in his novels are vulgar moneygrubbers or self-made men, and the plebeians either deferential servants or hopeless ruffians. Stylistically too Waugh is aristocratic. His dialogue is sparkling but shows overtones of irony; it somewhat resembles that of Oscar Wilde. His characterizations are effete, and he seldom interrupts the stream of his prose to explain things to his less acute readers. His wide popularity, curious when his aristocratic prejudices are considered, is a tribute to his talent as a skillful and witty novelistic technician.

Life

Waugh's background is respectable but thoroughly middle class. He was born in London in 1903, the son of a publisher and editor. A brilliant student at Oxford, he appears to have felt thoroughly at home there; the University is present in one way or another in almost all his novels. At one time he hoped to become a painter; his year of art-school training is apparent in his characterization of Charles Ryder in *Brideshead Revisited.* An early intimacy with the wealthy British Guinness family made it possible for him to move in fashionable circles, and provided him with a valuable source of data for his fiction. His writing began in 1928 with a biography of Rossetti. The year 1930 marks an important turning point in his life: his reception into the Catholic Church. The same year he divorced his first wife, and in 1937 he married Laura Herbert, daughter of a conservative M.P. He was active in Anglo-Catholic circles following his conversion. During the Second World War Waugh served capably and bravely in a Commando group.

After the war Evelyn Waugh turned his satiric pen against the American scene, particularly California and the morticians, in *The Loved One* (1948), and wrote an equally brilliant satire on postwar Europe in *Scott-King's Modern Europe* (1949). In three war novels Waugh showed a romantic obsession with the past, with chivalric honor, and with medieval Catholicism: *Men at Arms* (1952), *Officers and Gentlemen* (1955), and *The End of the Battle,* also called *Unconditional Surrender* (1961), constituting a Ford-like trilogy for the Second rather than First War. A character named Guy Grouchback is the latter-day Christopher Tietjens.

In April of 1966 Waugh died at his Taunton home in Somerset outside of which he had posted a sign: "No admittance on business." He is described as having had a "prickly," if shy, personality. Once when an interviewer asked him how he wrote, he is supposed to have answered, "I put the words down and push them around a bit." He did not, apparently, suffer fools gladly.

Chief Work

***Brideshead Revisited* (1945):** Waugh's chief novel, it treats a typical Waugh theme: the decline of a proud but degenerate family of British aristocrats. The Marchmain clan consists of the old Marquis, head of the family; his wife, the ardently Catholic Lady Marchmain; and their four children, Brideshead, Sebastian, Julia, and Cordelia. The story is related by Charles Ryder, a painter who meets Sebastian at Oxford and whose life becomes intricately involved with the history of the Marchmains.

Before the action opens (1923), the Marquis has abandoned his wife and gone to live with his mistress Cara in Italy. The children are brought up as Catholics and are given the finest rearing the enormous wealth of the famliy can provide. In spite of this each of the children spoils his life in a different way. Brideshead, the stolid elder son, thinks of becoming a monk, but eventually marries a homely widow older than himself who will never provide him with any children. Sebastian, sensitive and witty, goes to Oxford, becomes a close friend of Ryder, but turns to drink and becomes a hopeless alcoholic. He ends as a lay brother in an African monastery. Cordelia, a naive and childish enthusiast, grows into a plain and consecrated social worker. Julia, more intelligent than the rest, marries Rex Mottram, a vulgar parvenu, out of boredom and spite. Later she falls in love with Charles Ryder, who by this time has been abandoned by the alcoholic Sebastian. Charles begins to realize it was Julia he was seeking all along in his attraction to Sebastian. Julia, who has lost her faith, proposes to divorce Rex and marry Charles. At the last moment she attends at the deathbed of her father and sees the dying man, a lifetime skeptic, receive the sacrament and make the sign of the cross. This gesture so moves her that she rejects Charles and begins to grope toward a reawakened faith.

The outstanding merits of this novel are the superb characterization of the insouciant and talented Sebastian, and the carefully drawn pictures of dissipation among the British upper classes.

***The Loved One* (1948):** This short and pointed satire presents two mortuaries in the Hollywood-Burbank area: Whispering Glades for humans and the Happier Hunting Ground for pets. It was referred to as an Anglo-American Tragedy. Dennis Barlow, a young Britisher, works for the Happier Hunting Ground, which provides at good prices innumerable services: interment or incineration, religious services with the release of a white dove over the crematorium at the moment of committal, and every anniversary a remembrance card mailed to the pet's owner, reading "Your little Arthur is thinking of you in heaven today and wagging his tail." Similar solicitude for appropriate fees is available at Whispering Glades, with special attention for those who work in films; Mr. Joyboy is Senior Mortician and Aimée Thanatogenos is a junior cosmetician and a hostess. Dennis and Mr. Joyboy become rivals for the hand of Aimée; when she is torn between them, she consults her Guru who advises suicide. Her body is an embarrassment to Mr. Joyboy, and Dennis for a thousand bucks offers to help him dispose of it in the pet incinerator. Dennis is left thinking of the postcard that would go to Mr. Joyboy every year: "Your little Aimée is wagging her tail in heaven tonight, thinking of you," as he prepares to leave Los Angeles headed for home.

G. K. CHESTERTON (1874–1936)

During the latter half of his long career Chesterton, assisted by his friend Hilaire Belloc, was the undisputed leader of the Catholic movement in English letters. He came to Catholicism only very gradually; his views were pronouncedly High Church before the First World War but he was formally accepted into the Catholic Church only in 1922.

Chesterton viewed Catholicism as the traditional religion of England, a faith from which the nation had perversely and tragically deviated in the sixteenth century. Although he admitted that Catholicism seemed an exotic faith to the average Englishman, he himself considered it genuinely British. Unlike Belloc, he himself was thoroughly British in inclination and attitude; his views inclined toward nationalism rather than toward the cosmopolitan. Yet his nationalism was of another sort from Kipling's; there was nothing of imperialism in it, and little of the racial superiority with which Kipling regarded the "lesser breeds without the law." As a nationalist Chesterton continued to believe in the Brotherhood of Man. His politics were likewise humanitarian. He was opposed to both Capitalism and Socialism; both, he felt, subdued the individual to the group by concentrating large amounts of wealth in supreme authorities. He called for a return of private property to the little man, a redistribution of wealth restoring the English worker to his rightful position as a free and propertied yeoman.

IMPORTANCE

Chesterton's novels, that part of his work most likely to persist, incline toward the fantastic and allegorical. His erudition is great, yet his knowledge seldom shows through the perfectly finished exterior of his work. His moralities and allegories carry the reader along even when he is hostile toward the author's message; this is the secret of his effectiveness as a literary moralist.

Life

Gilbert Keith Chesterton was born near London in 1874. His background was middle class and comfortable; he was educated at St. Paul's boys' school and at the University of London. As a young man he met Hilaire Belloc, witty, half-French, and Catholic in sympathy; the two men remained friends to Chesterton's death. They shared each other's ideas enthusiastically; both detested Puritanism, socialism, free love, prohibitionists, and vegetarians. Considering these antipathies, the long quarrel of the pair with Bernard Shaw is understandable.

During the early part of his career Chesterton made his living as a journalist, writing book reviews, essays, and political pieces. By 1905, however, he emerged as an important novelist. His major novels, of which the two most important are *The Napoleon of Notting Hill* (1904) and *The Man Who Was Thursday* (1908), appeared long before his official conversion; their religious tone is an adumbration of his later decisive act. In 1930–31 Chesterton came to America to lecture at Notre Dame, and received an honorary degree from the University. He died at his Chiltern Hills estate in 1936.

Chief Works

Chesterton's best-known novel is *The Man Who Was Thursday* (1908). The story opens in Saffron Park, a London suburb, where Lucian Gregory, an affected poet, is arguing that poets must be anarchists and vice versa. Gabriel Syme, a police officer disguised as a poet, taunts him into proving his anarchistic ideas are serious. After swearing Syme to secrecy, Gregory takes him to a meeting of anarchists in a fantastic London cellar. The group is about to elect a new delegate to the central council. Each member of the council is named for a day of the week; the newly elected dignitary is to be called Thursday. Syme cleverly outwits Gregory and wins the election himself, and is conveyed off to a meeting of the full council. The presiding official is Sunday, a mysterious and imposing figure who appears in a different light to each man. Gradually the identity of each member is revealed; most of them turn out to be detectives like Syme. Sunday himself remains an enigma, and all together approach him and demand to know who he is. He escapes in a variety of odd vehicles including a balloon, but they pursue him; at last he reveals himself as Divinity, personified in the Peace of God. Gregory is an agent of the Devil, and the official who appointed and guided the six detectives, it appears, is Divinity personified as the Church. Divinity is proclaimed as the bearer of order to the universe, which otherwise would fall into a diabolic chaos.

In a lighter vein are the famous Father Brown stories, comprising *The Innocence of Father Brown* (1911), *The Wisdom of Father Brown* (1914), *The Incredulity of Father Brown* (1926) and *The Secret of Father Brown* (1927). The hero of these fantastic detective stories is a mild Catholic priest, a bumbling amateur sleuth who solves crimes through perceptive intuition rather than through clues and logic. The stories incidentally contain a good deal of innocuous Catholic polemic.

GRAHAM GREENE (1904 – 91)

Graham Greene was a prolific writer and a popular novelist whose major work began to appear in 1940 and continued into the sixties, although he began writing as early as 1929 and produced almost a book a year with very few years off. He is another Roman Catholic convert, and his best novels make use of his Catholicism rather than his Catholicism making use of his novels. He has had some rather remarkable critical insights into his own work, calling many of his early novels, after the first three apprentice works (two of which were "withdrawn"), "entertainments" rather than ascribing to them more serious intentions. Very good entertainments they are, making good film scripts and television fare, *Stamboul Train* (1932), *A Gun for Sale* (1936), *Brighton Rock* (1938) and *The Confidential Agent* (1939) among the best; but it would be pretentious to consider them more. He continued this kind of writing in *The Ministry of Fear* (1943), *The Third Man* (1950) and *Loser Takes All* (1955). His craftsmanship and ability to tell a story carry over into his more serious work (there are melodramatic elements in both); and the Catholic framework emerges in some of the thrillers too, especially *Brighton Rock,* where it is something of a sore thumb.

Frank Kermode refers to the fable of the jeweler, ingenious maker of jeweled eggs, in *A Burnt-Out Case* (1961) as fitting Greene himself as well as Querry, the Catholic architect of the novel to whom it is applied. "Everyone said he was a master technician, but he was highly praised too for the seriousness of his subject matter, because on the top of each egg there was a gold cross set with chips of precious stones in honour of the King." Greene seems to have become partially conscious or self-conscious of this in the sixties.

IMPORTANCE

In many ways, stylistically at least, Greene is an old-fashioned novelist; stream of consciousness is not congenial for him, nor the objectivity of authorial impersonality. He prefers to comment both on his characters and their actions, although he tries to find less obvious ways to do so than Fielding or even nineteenth century novelists. There are recurrent themes in his novels: the impact of childhood experience (as in Tolstoy); death as a desirable end (and a relationship between the death-wish and the will to live); treachery and betrayal (a Judas complex); fascination with squalor and failure; pursuit (the hunter and the hunted, or the technique of "Westerns"); dentistry and dental decay;

and the rather seedy, homeless heroine. There are also, of course, conversion, a return to faith, a framework of Catholic religious symbolism, and the use of miracle in a nonmiraculous age.

In the novel *The End of the Affair* the novelist character Bendrix predicts of his critic Waterbury, "Patronizingly in the end he would place me probably a little above Maugham," which may be, in spite of the slur, Greene's perceptive self-evaluation. In any event he will probably come to rest somewhere between Maugham and Mauriac. His enthusiastic supporters ask where one can find his equal among his own generation of British novelists, but seldom wait for an answer. William Golding might be considered his equal, perhaps even C. P. Snow. But many consider him good; and *The Power and the Glory* (1940), *The Heart of the Matter* (1948), probably *The End of the Affair* (1951), and possibly *A Burnt-Out Case* (1961) and *The Comedians* (1966) will, it seems, last as long as *Of Human Bondage* and *Le Noeud de Vipères.*

Life

Graham Greene was born October 2, 1904, the son of English public (that is, private) school headmaster, C. H. Greene of Berkhamstead, where he himself went to school before attending Balliol College at Oxford. He started with poetry, then journalism in Nottingham where the conversion from Anglicanism to the Roman Catholic Church took place in 1926; the next year he married Vivien Dayrell-Browning. His first novel, *The Man Within,* was published in 1929, since which time Greene was a freelance writer, except for important occasional work as a journalist and government service during the Second World War. After the "entertainments" referred to above, Greene's first novel that appeared as serious fiction with the dimensions of thought, felt life, and realized characters, *The Power and the Glory,* resulting from a trip to Mexico in 1938 (and the record of the journey, *The Lawless Roads,* 1939), was published in 1940, although the war years delayed critical recognition of its new values for a number of years. Following this success with another, *The Heart of the Matter* (1948) set in British West Africa (Greene had been in foreign service for the British government in Freetown, Sierra Leone, during the war), Greene came up with his third Catholic novel, *The End of the Affair* (1951) set in London. Péguy and Léon Bloy furnished epigraphs for these novels and with Greene's confessed admiration of Mauriac and Bernanos represent the culmination of French Catholic literary influence on the British novelist.

Greene tried his hand at writing for the theater with *The Living Room* (1953) and *The Potting Shed* (1957); but, although they were competent and represented another attempt to write Catholic ideas into his work, they were little more, the plots creaked in their naked "well-made play" context—and even with the somewhat more successful comedy, *The Complaisant Lover*

(1959), Greene did not become important in British drama, where much more exciting things were happening. While working on *The Quiet American* (1955), rather uncomplimentary to the American character, the author researched his material and setting by making four trips to Indochina, staying twelve months. The background is the French war in Indochina, with Pyle the quiet American working on a medical mission in Saigon. The novel is actually somewhat prophetic in suggesting that American intervention there would be both futile and unjustifiable. It has been suggested that Greene had "worked out" the vein of tragic conflict between human and divine values in *The Power and the Glory* and *The Heart of the Matter,* that he was trying to find a new *modus operandi* in terms of comedy and irony from *The End of the Affair* through *The Comedians* (1966) and *Travels with My Aunt* (1969); but if so, he may have lacked the necessary comic vision and the gift for irony, say that of a Gide or a Mann.

Chief Novels

***The Power and the Glory* (1940):** Some consider this Greene's masterpiece. Its Catholic views are almost completely integrated in a wonderfully convincing character, the whiskey priest, who is set over against an opponent and a double (like Conrad's "Secret Sharer" grafted onto Dostoevsky's doubles), the Police Lieutenant. Neither of these two, the hunted and the hunter — with an odd reversal of roles in a spiritual sense — is named. The anonymity suggests allegory. The Mexican setting helps one overlook simplicities (one can swallow almost everything except the American gangster Calver as Calvary; shame on the critic who first pointed it out). At the beginning the whiskey priest is trying to escape from that part of Mexico where a socialist state is persecuting the Church (priests are forbidden to practice their sacraments); he comes into contact with the dentist Dr. Tench; Coral Fellows, a precocious child; Luis, a boy bored by his mother's reading of a conventional saint's life; and the Chief of Police and his lieutenant, representing the power structure. The escape by ship having failed, the priest returns to his native village, where he has an illegitimate daughter Brigitta, narrowly escaping detection by the lieutenant. Back in town looking for communion wine, the priest is arrested for bootlegging, not recognized, and released. On the point of escaping from the territory, he is called back to give last rites to a dying gangster, a trap and a duty. He is betrayed, apprehended by the lieutenant, and executed; but his martyr's death has an effect on other characters: on Luis, who sees a real "saint's" death instead of the artificially sentimental "Life"; Dr. Tench, the dentist, who decides to return to England to set his house in order; and the lieutenant himself who has seen the possibility of salvation.

***The Heart of the Matter* (1948):** Set in the steamy heat of British West Africa, it deals with sexual sin and damnation. Henry Scobie, a tired, middle-aged Assistant Commissioner of Police, had become a Catholic in order to marry a devout Catholic woman, Louise, who, childless since the death of a daughter, has become a rather unlovable wife. Scobie has an overdeveloped sense of pity and responsibility, keys to his character; he is honest and just, the incorruptible man in the midst of corruption. His wife despises him as mediocre and a failure; but, having promised her a holiday in South Africa, he borrows imprudently from a trader (and suspected smuggler) named Yussef. Soon the honest man is entangled in corruption; pity for the captain of a Portuguese trading vessel leads him to suppress information about a contraband letter found during a routine inspection. His duties require his receiving the survivors of a ship torpedoed in the Atlantic, including a young widow, Helen. His wife away, Scobie's fall continues. He and Helen fall in love and find happiness together, introducing the adultery in conflict with his faith. Scobie is troubled as he looks at the tide, "Somewhere on the face of those obscure waters moved the sense of yet another wrong and another victim, not Louise, not Helen." Greene does not have to tell us that it's God.

Scobie is sucked deeper into sin by deception, blackmail by Yussef, even conniving at murder. When Louise returns, he is forced to take communion in a state of sin and to keep up the deception, "his damnation was being prepared like a meal at the altar," a shocking awareness for him and preparation for his suicide to cut the Gordian knot. The story is tight, the character well drawn (if somewhat hypersensitive to spiritual agonies), and the world of tropical heat and corruption is both symbolic and real. The question of the hero's damnation or salvation may be irrelevant. The Péguy epigraph says, "No one is as competent in the matter of Christianity as the sinner. No one, unless it is the saint."

***The End of the Affair* (1951):** This novel explores an old theme, religion in terms of sex and adultery (Hosea did it first and beautifully sometime before Christ), but it has new shock value when set in wartime and postwar London. The main character is a woman, Sarah Miles, who has had an adulterous love affair with a middle-aged novelist, Maurice Bendrix. When she broke off her affair with him shortly after he had escaped death in a wartime bombing, he assumed the existence of another lover and experienced more jealousy than would have been possible to her husband, Henry. The novelist arranges to have a private investigator spy on Sarah, and he eventually comes into possession of her diary, where he learns that she still loves him but, having believed him killed in the air raid, had prayed and promised to God to give him up in exchange for his life. Convinced of a miracle, she has moved steadily toward a firmer belief in God through the Catholic faith. Bendrix, a disbeliever, tries to persuade her to return to him, but she sickens and dies soon after. The rival for Sarah's love is not another man, not her husband, but God—and that is an endless affair. The novelist learns after her death that without her knowing it she had been baptized a Catholic, and we are led through a series of phenomenal miracles that strain credulity and weaken the ending. Up to Sarah's death, however, the detective mystery coupled with spiritual mystery and physical love is provocative and intriguing.

WILLIAM GOLDING (1911–93)

IMPORTANCE

It is commonplace to say that any author worth writing about is difficult, if not impossible, to classify, but the problems of where to place William Golding are particularly interesting. He is clearly a novelist of ideas. He has acknowledged indebtedness to H. G. Wells, particularly in *The Inheritors* (1955), although he rewrites *The Outline of History* from a rather different perspective. He is no longer optimistic, nor does the shadow of the Victorian idea of progress hang over him; and he is neither liberal nor humanitarian. He seems to have inherited ideas of existentialism, and frequent comparisons have been made of his work to that of Sartre, with the character Sammy Mountjoy of *Free Fall* (1959) as a kind of "baptized Roquentin" *(Nausea),* and the more obvious comparison of *Free Fall* with the Camus novel, *The Fall;* but Golding apparently acknowledges no debt. One interesting influence on him that is discernible is a debt to the antinovel and to Robbe-Grillet, in particular in *Pincher Martin* (1956) and *Free Fall* among other works, although one can find the plot in a Golding novel without too much frustration. But he is a traditionalist, even a conservative; *Lord of the Flies* has been hailed by Francis Kearns as the conservative's answer to *The Catcher in the Rye.* More importantly, perhaps, Golding views the evil in modern man and his society as a part of man's own nature, and he presents it in all its degradation and disgusting circumstances as vividly as Francois Mauriac, Evelyn Waugh, and Graham Greene (and somewhat more succinctly). A knowledge of that, of man's own nature, grounded in evil, or an awareness of original sin, is a prerequisite for faith; although Golding will hardly lead the reader to any particular doctrine, he will make him rethink moral assumptions. Additionally one may say that Golding is halfway between the arts and sciences (it has been suggested that he writes "science fiction"). Bernard Dick thinks he may "take up the theme of the scientist and produce the kind of novel C. P. Snow should, but unfortunately cannot, write—a novel in which men are more than working hypotheses."

Life

William Gerald Golding was born in Cornwall in 1911, the son of another headmaster (like Greene) of the Marlborough Grammar School, Alec Golding and his wife Mildred, an active worker on women's suffrage. Relative isolation in childhood persisted in a kind of secluded private life as an adult. He reported having been fascinated by words in wide reading as a child, "I had a passion for words in themselves, and collected them like stamps or birds' eggs." Homer's *Odyssey* in Greek was a great and moving experience for him, as for so many others, although often in translation. From his father's grammar school he went to Brasenose College in Oxford to read science, after two years switching to English literature; the dichotomy between rational and religious man was already exhibiting its tensions. There was the usual book of undergraduate poetry. In the late thirties he did some writing, acting, and producing for a small non-West End London theater, and in 1939 married Ann Brookfield and became a teacher at Bishop Wordsworth's school in Salisbury. During the war in the British Navy he participated in D-Day Normandy landings and from his experiences came to reject his father's confident scientific humanism. He returned to teaching in Salisbury after the war and finally, after twenty-one rejections, published *Lord of the Flies* in 1954. Two more novels followed in succeeding years, *The Inheritors* and *Pincher Martin,* each highly original and inciting critical attention.

Before going on with the novel Golding prepared a play, *The Brass Butterfly* which was produced at the Strand Theatre in London with Alistair Sim in the leading role in 1958. Besides essays and reviews, no longer teaching, three significant novels have appeared: *Free Fall* (1959), *The Spire* (1964), and *The Pyramid* (1967). In 1961–1962 Golding did become, in a brief American public appearance, a writer-in-residence at Hollins College in Virginia and made a lecture tour in the American university circuit. *The Hot-Gates* (1965) is a collection of his reviews and essays. In 1979, Golding's novel *Darkness Visible* appeared. The work earned unfavorable reviews and sold poorly. More critically acclaimed was his trilogy *Rites of Passage* (1980), *Close Quarters* (1987), and *Fire Down Below* (1989). Set in the nineteenth century, the trilogy recounts a voyage from England to Australia as recorded by a young aristocrat.

Chief Novels

Lord of the Flies (1954): This book very quickly became a "classic" in the schools, theoretically expressing "the alienation of modern youth," and was made into a highly effective film by Peter Brook. It began as a reworking of an 1857 book by Ballantyne called *The Coral Island* with characters Ralph Rover, Jack Martin, and Peterkin Gay, who live in harmony and happiness when shipwrecked on a Pacific island; from a cynical "post-two-world-wars" view Golding decided, "People don't do things like that" — its morality was unrealistic, therefore false. The subject of *Lord of the Flies* is moral evil, the darkness in the human heart, made more terrifying because the characters are young children, school boys wrecked on a desert island during the war, who gradually make the natural paradise into a hell as they degenerate into primitive and bloodthirsty savagery. They try at first to do things the English civilized way, elect as a leader Ralph, have a meeting place with a conch shell (symbol of reason) to summon them; but civilized standards of conduct fade with frightening ease. First appear imaginary, irrational fears, of the dark, of monsters, "something behind you all the time in the jungle." The boys split into two groups, one the hunters, the other trying to remain civilized. The lapse into barbarism comes with pigsticking, and painting their faces with colored clay. Jack, the leader of the hunters, feels safe from shame behind the mask. At last with the ritual chant, "Kill the pig!" they howl, dancing around the corpse, and it is only a matter of time until they find a human victim, Simon. The hunting of the pig, the discovery of the dead airman, the taunting of Piggy with his glasses are vivid scenes. A rescue ship arrives to end the nightmare, but there is no relief from the darkness or Original Sin in the human heart. The ambiguity and irony of the ending is in the arrival of an adult naval officer, with cap and revolver, cruiser waiting in the view of the "rescued." Fable and fiction are united.

The Inheritors **(1955):** This takes off from the H. G. Wells' account of Neanderthal man in *Outline of History* and his story *The Grisly Folk*. Neanderthal man, in this novel represented by such characters as Lok and Fa, the innocent ones, is being baffled, defeated, and forced to yield to a superior, more intelligent, more corrupted race. Without being able to use a logical sequence of thought, Golding with considerable skill shows Neanderthal man thinking in pictures. Lok looking at Fa sees "the water run out of her eyes," rather than weeping. The superior man who succeeds him is self-conscious and reflective, seen as an aspect of human guilt. Loss of innocence is what we pay for knowledge and human consciousness; Lok and Fa, hiding in a tree, witness orgies of drunkenness, lust, and cannibalistic cruelty in postlapsarian (or post-Neanderthal) man—innocence destroyed by experience.

Pincher Martin **(1956):** Another *tour de force,* this time the action of a whole novel, a whole lifetime, is seen in the moment of stretched-out consciousness in a drowning man, Christopher or "Pincher" Martin. Actually he dies on the second page of the book, "But the man lay suspended behind the whole commotion, detached from his jerking body. The luminous pictures that were shuffled before him were drenched in light but he paid no attention to them. . . . There was a kind of truce, observation of the body. There was no face but there was a snarl." But there is enough ambiguity in the flashbacks that follow, parallel to the technique of Alain Robbe-Grillet's film script for *Last Year in Marienbad* and reminiscent of Hemingway's "The

Snows of Kilimanjaro," so that we can't be sure until we have been led through the novel. Martin presents us initially with the heroic picture of a will for survival, but this is undercut if not eliminated by the emergence of an antiheroic image of man's guilt, greed, and egotism. Prometheus on the rock is whittled down to less than life size. Pincher with the claws that cling becomes a reversal of Eliot's symbol at the end of "Prufrock,"—the crab that is at least "alive," "Scutling across the floors of silent seas"; he represents Man's first fall, a self-centered creature indifferent to any claims beyond the greed for life. But ambiguities remain as one contemplates the meanings of damnation and heroism.

Free Fall **(1959):** Its title has a double meaning, scientific and religious, and for the bridge between them, as Golding later remarked, most of us have an unexpressed faith that it exists, "even if we have not the wit to discover it." As a part of our contemporary scientific "myth" it means that state of neutralized gravitational pull that space travellers experience. As a religious concept, of course, it means the fall from grace, the garden lapse from innocence to guilt. The main character is Sammy Mountjoy, born in a slum in Kent, orphaned, who discovers two "parents not in the flesh," Nick Shales with his science and Rowena Pringle with her religion. They are alternative, potential solutions to the problems of existence but how can both be true? As he grows up, Sammy seduces one girl, marries another, becomes a Communist, quits the party, takes up art, and goes to war; but the reader does not find out these things in this order. There is a series of flashbacks, like talks from a psychiatrist's couch, an attempt to find out the first moment of sin, the fall from innocence. In the novel's structure space and time are somewhat chaotic (in the direction of, if not as far as, Robbe-Grillet's *In the Labyrinth,* or, perhaps, Lawrence Durrell's *Alexandria Quartet*). The book imitates to a degree the incoherence of life, but suggests an approach to design. Events are not recorded according to chronology but according to relative importance for the character, Sammy, recalling them. The lack of pattern is as much his life as it is the book, and that brings a certain terror with it. Sammy is not greatly successful in his self-analysis; his world remains unpredictable and chaotic, but his understanding increases and he becomes more fully alive in it. The comparison with *The Fall* of Camus is inevitable with the parallels of guilt, retribution, and confession, but Mountjoy doesn't have the intellectual strength or ironic perspective of Jean-Baptiste Clamence and his adventures seem both more banal and more sordid. It still seems fair to say that Golding is one of the most provocative novelists now writing, who can break his own patterns from novel to novel but still give us basic insight into the human condition, because, as he says, "Modern man is appallingly ignorant of his own nature." *The Spire* (1964) is an "historical" novel, putting the spire on Salisbury Cathedral, with more than a touch of Ibsen's *The Master Builder,* and the fable built around the idea, "There is no innocent work. God knows where God may be."

9
LIBERALS AND HUMANITARIANS

In contrast to the religious and conservative authors treated in the preceding section, a more typical body of authors in the twentieth century are secular, humanitarian, liberal, and iconoclastic in attitude. The liberal movement among European intellectuals, which began to gain momentum in the middle of the nineteenth century, was still the most powerful force in the European battle of ideas a hundred years later. Many of its characteristics had altered in this time, but its basic principles were the same.

There are two chief sources of this liberal-socialistic ideology. The first is the classic liberalism of Locke and Jefferson and of the American and French revolutions: the concept of the brotherhood of man, of the "certain inalienable rights" of the American constitution, and the principles of freedom and justice contained in the American Bill of Rights. The second source is the proletarian movement, which began with the Chartist and socialist movements of the early nineteenth century and found its culmination in the writings of Karl Marx. Some modern authors, like Anatole France, lie chiefly under the influence of the earlier doctrines, and others, like Malraux, write in the proletarian-Marxist tradition.

A minority, of which Bernard Shaw and Jean Giraudoux are the best examples, disclaim affiliation with any doctrine or ideology, and claim to speak from original impulse. In some cases these authors assume attitudes incompatible with what is ordinarily considered liberalism; Shaw's antipathy toward vaccination and inoculation is an example. In the main, however, these authors are in one camp: They attack the capitalistic state as it is presently constituted, they demand greater rights, benefits, and privileges for the common man, they are vigorously pacifistic, and they insist upon more or less drastic revision of the economy and political structure of the modern state.

The group also shows certain resemblances from a literary point of view. They tend to lie under the influence of Ibsen, Tolstoy, Zola, and the Naturalists in general, and they are often as iconoclastic in style and technique as they are in content.

GEORGE BERNARD SHAW (1856–1950)

Bernard Shaw is first and foremost a dramatist. His nondramatic works — novels, essays, criticism, and correspondence — must be considered as secondary to his work in the theater. Moreover, his drama is essentially drama of ideas; the elements of melodrama, personal conflict, suspense, and wit are intended merely to support and convey the intellectual content. In his literary criticism Shaw finds Racine inferior to Brieux and Shakespeare inferior to himself, not because he fails to recognize the genius of the two classic authors, but because he believes the social effect of a drama is more important than its incidental poetic merit.

Shaw's ideas are today neither highly original nor highly revolutionary, although they may have seemed so in 1900. He was a liberal and socialist, but of a peculiar cut. He cannot be assigned to any literary school, political party, or philosophical movement; his ideology is highly individualistic, although no part of it is totally unique. The more important of Shaw's ideas may be summarized as follows:

1. *Socialism:* At one time an active member of the Fabian Society, Shaw remained throughout his career an advocate of public ownership of resources and of a more equitable division of social wealth. He is antagonistic toward the capitalistic class not because he believes it to be inherently wicked, but because he believes it must be disenfranchised before any worthwhile social amelioration can take place. He subscribes to the Proudhon-Marxist theory of surplus value, along with the Ricardo theory of wages, yet he is not an orthodox Marxist. He departs from the Marxist-Communist line chiefly in his attitude toward the working classes: He regards them not as the virtuous heroes of a coming social upheaval, but merely as a brutalized and uneducated mass of humanity inherently intelligent but incapable of unaided rational thought. He is a humanitarian, but not a democrat; his ideal state is one in which educated leaders are supported by popular franchise but remain independent of the whims of the masses. Because of his belief in the planned state and his admiration of the superior man, Shaw was frequently attacked as a sort of proto-fascist. This he was not; he had a more sincere respect for individuality than many a self-professed champion of the masses.

2. *The Life Force:* From Bergson and from the Lamarckian school of evolution Shaw derived a belief in a sort of *élan vital*, a motive spirit that drives mankind onward to successively higher forms of evolution. The Life Force takes many forms. The most common of these is the reproductive drive, manifested especially in women. The highest form, however, is Mind — the incredible organ that man has evolved in his effort to rise to purer forms of existence. The doctrine of the Life Force is especially prominent in *Back to Methuselah* and *Man and Superman.*

3. *Feminism,* derived chiefly from Ibsen. Although Shaw was not prominently involved in the organized feminist movement, he felt that society as it

was arranged in the nineteenth century was perversely unfair to women, and that it had thus suppressed an untold quantity of genius and energy that might otherwise have been contributed to the benefit of humanity. Shaw's women are talkative, energetic, intelligent, and imaginative; often they are cleverer than the men who attempt to keep them in their place. Shaw also admires women as the particular agents of the Life Force, against which men strive constantly but in vain. He does not precisely conceive of women as intellectually superior to men; theirs is a subtle power beyond intellect and in the end more potent than mere mind.

4. *Antiscientism:* In his work Shaw often claims to view society with a scientific attitude; at the same time he vigorously derides what he calls "scientism," or the slavish adulation of the scientist and the doctor plus the instantaneous public acceptance of any doctrine alleged to be scientific. Shaw, who objected to being dictated to by anyone, naturally balked at being parcelled out the truth by some lesser mind who happened to wear a white coat and possess a medical degree. This led him into such escapades as deriding the statement of scientists that the sun was 93 million miles away, and declaring that he himself had calculated it to be only thirty-seven miles away. It also led him into his well-known campaigns against vivisection and compulsory vaccination. Shaw, a vegetarian and a sort of nature crank on a superior plane, objected to the introduction of anything into the body other than its natural sustenance — which did not include "dead bodies." He objected to vivisection on the grounds that if a man is allowed to bake a dog in the interests of science, he will soon arrive at the point of baking his mother in the same cause.

IMPORTANCE

Shaw is an interesting and effective propagandist for these ideas mainly because he is an unusually skillful manipulator of language. His style is polemical; his talent is devoted almost entirely to demonstrating the wrongness of the opposing cause. He is a master of paradox, antithesis, and irony; he has an unerring sense of diction, and the force of his style can make even a preposterous thesis seem plausible for the moment.

His dramatic technique is likewise highly individual. He performed a veritable revolution in the theater by abandoning the nineteenth century emphasis on plot that characterized the school of Sardou and Bulwer-Lytton and turning to the drama of discussion, or talking play. Here he owes much to Molière and to his master Ibsen. A typical nineteenth century melodrama consisted of an exposition, a complication, and a dénouement; Shaw retained the first two of these elements, but abandoned the dénouement in favor of a discussion.

Life

George Bernard Shaw was born in 1856 in Dublin on Synge Street. His father, George Carr Shaw, was an idler and drunkard who contributed little to the family; Shaw's antipathy toward drinking was formed at an early age. His mother, an aggressive and dominant woman with fine musical taste, was important in inspiring his feminist views in later years. After a brief secondary education Shaw was apprenticed to a real estate firm. In 1876 he revolted against this career and went to establish himself in England, which remained his home for the rest of his life. As a young man he worked as a dramatic critic and reviewer and as a music critic. During this period he became interested in socialism, and in 1884 he helped to found the Fabian Society, an intellectual debating and propaganda circle which included Beatrice and Sidney Webb and, somewhat later, H. G. Wells. Many of the ideas of the Fabians, including some of Shaw's own ideas, later found realization in the program of the British Labour Party.

In 1898 Shaw, stricken by a serious illness, was nursed back to health by a woman who forthwith became his wife: Charlotte Frances Payne-Townshend. Earlier and later affairs with such notable ladies as Ellen Terry and Mrs. Patrick Campbell remained on a totally intellectual basis.

The first of Shaw's plays to be produced was *Widowers' Houses* in 1892. From then until the time of his death he continued to pour out a stream of plays, essays, novels, and pamphlets on every imaginable subject. He was adept at creating a public legend, a sort of caricature of himself in the eyes of the man on the street; he even contrived the adjective "Shavian" to describe his own personality. The legend of Shaw as a brilliant but irascible old man, based mainly on newspaper interviews, has unfortunately obscured his real importance as a serious dramatist. During both world wars Shaw incurred public displeasure by speaking his own mind freely and caustically; as might be expected, he failed to view either war as a clear-cut struggle between black and white. The height of his prestige occurred in 1925 when he was awarded the Nobel Prize for Literature. He donated the entire proceeds of this award to a fund for popularizing Scandinavian literature. His final will was written in the same spirit: the major part of his estate was to be devoted to propaganda for a phonetic English alphabet. He died at his Ayot-St.-Lawrence estate in 1950.

Chief Dramas

***Mrs. Warren's Profession* (1894):** This play proved so shocking to nineteenth century propriety that it was not actually performed until thirty years after it was written; it helped, however, to pave the way for frank discussion of the problem of prostitution. The action opens as Vivie Warren, a sensible, highly educated young lady, comes to take a study vacation in the country. She is visited by her mother, Mrs. Warren, and two of her mother's friends, Sir George Crofts, a sophisticated gentleman, and Mr. Praed, a rather naive artist. Unknown to her daughter, Mrs. Warren is a former prostitute, now in partnership with Crofts in the management of a chain of houses of ill fame. Crofts is attracted to Vivie but is secretly afraid of the possibility he might be her father. Praed admires Vivie as a person but is horrified at her practicality and her aversion to art. Frank Gardner, a young man of the neighborhood, is in love with Vivie, but has no money of his own to marry her. His father, the Reverend Samuel Gardner, is a pretentious windbag who commands no real respect. He had once had an affair with Mrs. Warren, and she still preserves some letters he wrote her at that time. This admits the possibility that Frank may be Vivie's brother. Vivie is repelled by her mother and Crofts, although she finds Praed attractive. In a conversation with her mother, Vivie learns half the truth, but is left believing that this unsavory aspect of her mother's life is long past. Crofts, proposing to her, reveals that the business is still flourishing; when Frank takes umbrage at this and threatens him with a gun he alleges that Frank is Vivie's half-brother. Completely disgusted, Vivie goes off to London and installs herself in an office. Frank and Praed visit her there, both learning for the first time the truth about Mrs. Warren's profession. Frank, who now feels unable to accept Mrs. Warren's money as a dowry, withdraws as a suitor and tries to prevent Mrs. Warren, who has just arrived, from staying for an interview with her daughter. The meeting takes place, however, and leaves Vivie determined never to see her mother again and to accept no money from her.

Shaw's point in *Mrs. Warren's Profession* is that prostitution is an inevitable result of the capitalistic economic system; the answer to the evil is not suppression but socialism. Vivie takes a rather high-minded line toward her mother's disgrace, yet her own education and comfort proceed from the money she finally rejects at the end of the play. Shaw wrote this drama specifically to tear down the romanticized picture of prostitution presented by such dramas as Dumas' *Camille*.

Candida (1895): The most playable of Shaw's early comedies, the plot is outwardly banal. Morell, a devoted young clergyman in a poor London parish, has been boosted to success by his clever wife Candida. An impassioned young poet, Marchbanks, falls in love with her and proposes to rescue her from the banality of her marriage. Morell learns of the affair, and for the first time his comfortable little world is threatened. In a long conversation with Marchbanks, however, Candida explains that she can offer him only innocent affection; her true love, and her life, must be devoted to her husband, who needs her more. The theme of the play is that sexual love is not the only compelling force in determining human action.

Arms and the Man (1894–98): In this witty satire on war and militarism, Captain Bluntschli, Swiss by birth but an officer in the Serbian army, flees from a battle with the Bulgars, climbs into a convenient window, and throws himself on the mercy of Raina Petkoff, daughter of a proud Bulgarian aristocrat. In a conversation with Raina he scoffs at her naive chauvinism and argues that the first duty of a soldier is to save his own skin. He also eats quantities of chocolate creams, which earns him the title of the "Chocolate Soldier." Later Bluntschli meets Major Petkoff and Raina's fiancé Sergius; the latter tries to pick a fight with him, but Bluntschli talks his way out of it in a most unmilitary manner. As the play ends he inherits nine hotels in Switzerland and becomes engaged to Raina himself. The chief interest of the drama lies in the satirical contrast between the thick-headed heroism of the Bulgarians and the unheroic common sense of Bluntschli.

The Devil's Disciple **(1897):** This satirical melodrama with philosophical overtones is laid in the time of the American Revolution. The chief theme is the hypocrisy of Puritan society. Timothy and Peter Dudgeon, brothers but opposite in character, have both died as the action opens. Peter, a profligate and black sheep, has been hanged by the British as a hostage, and Timothy, a respectable citizen, has died after disinheriting his wife and leaving his possessions to his son Richard, who resembles Peter in character. The family is scandalized when Richard, the "Devil's Disciple," comes to the house for the reading of the will and speaks arrogantly to everyone present, including the local minister Mr. Anderson. Only Essie, the ill-treated illegitimate daughter of Peter Dudgeon, respects Richard; he sees a kindred soul in the friendless waif.

In the second act, set in Minister Anderson's house, the minister sends for Richard to warn him the British are likely to arrest and hang him as they did his uncle. During the interview Anderson is called away, and British soldiers shortly enter to arrest him. Richard pretends he is Anderson and allows himself to be taken away in the minister's place, first forcing Judith, Anderson's pretty wife, to take part in the farce and kiss him goodby. Judith is indignant, but after Richard leaves, she realizes the sacrifice he has made for her husband.

When Anderson returns and discovers Richard's act of heroism, he gallops off madly to some mysterious destination; Judith imagines he is fleeing from the British, and in her disgust her love is transferred to the condemned Richard. But just as Richard's execution is about to take place, Anderson, who has taken command of an irregular colonial troop, arrives as an emissary with a British safe-conduct in his hand. The Americans have captured a nearby town and now menace the British position; Richard is saved. Both Anderson and Richard have found their true vocations: Anderson abandons his cloth and becomes a soldier, and predicts that the "Devil's Disciple" Richard, who in a moment of danger showed himself to be an idealist and a man of character, will soon be preaching from the abandoned pulpit. Thus *The Devil's Disciple* argues that the truly good are not always those who make an outward profession of virtue, and that a man who scorns formal religion may nevertheless be an unselfish idealist. The Puritan concept that virtue consists entirely of abstinence is also satirized. Through the portraits of the British soldiers Major Swindon and General Burgoyne the play ridicules the military mentality; the British strategy in America is hopelessly muddled, as General Burgoyne remarks, and the army is no match for the enthusiastic and determined American amateurs of war.

Caesar and Cleopatra **(1898 – 1907):** A character study of a great man, it attempts to debunk the legend surrounding the figure of Caesar and reveal the true nature of his genius. In a prologue the Egyptian god Ra addresses the audience, setting the themes of the play and filling in the anterior action. He describes Caesar's defeat of Pompey at Pharsalia and his pursuit of Pompey to Egypt, where Lucius Septimius kills Pompey to curry favor with the Emperor. An "Alternative to the Prologue" takes place in Cleopatra's palace on the Syrian border of Egypt. A messenger arrives to announce that the Romans, led by Caesar, are coming. Cleopatra has fled the palace, and her half-sinister, half-comic nurse Ftatateeta does not know the Queen's whereabouts. Actually she has gone to the Sphinx, in the direction from which the Romans are to come.

As Act I opens Caesar hails the Sphinx and is warned by Cleopatra, who pretends to be the voice of the statue, that the "Romans are coming." Identifying himself only as a Roman, Caesar persuades the Queen that Caesar will not eat her if she is courageous; he then leads her back to the palace. An interesting conversation, one of the key dialogues of the play, ensues. Caesar proceeds to educate Cleo in the duties of royalty; he urges her to put the insolent Ftatateeta in her place and to assume her rightful authority as Queen and Priestess. To aid her in this he coaches her in the Machiavellian political strategy that has made him Emperor of the world. He finds Cleopatra a prankish and irresponsible child and leaves her at the end of the play a mature queen, confident in the authority of her position.

Act II takes place at the Palace of Ptolemy in Alexandria. The child Ptolemy, aided by his guardian Pothinus, announces that he will not allow Cleopatra to steal his throne from him. Then Caesar and his staff arrive; Caesar orders Ptolemy and his court out of the palace. He is horrified when he is told that Pompey was murdered by Egyptians who now claim his gratitude. In a conversation with Caesar, Cleopatra recalls with longing the visits of Mark Antony several years before; she confesses that she has been in love with the young Roman ever since. The middle-aged Caesar promises to send him back sometime. Then Caesar learns that the occupation army that has been stationed in Egypt since those days is marching on Alexandria; he orders the ships burned to prevent the escape of his own troops as well as the seizure of the vessels by the rebels. He also directs the capture of the famous Alexandrian lighthouse, a key tactical point.

Act III is laid on the edge of the Alexandrian quay. Cleopatra, still full of adolescent romanticism, has herself smuggled in to Caesar wrapped in a carpet; but the troops surround the quay, and she finds herself besieged along with the Romans. Caesar persuades the group to follow him in swimming across the harbor to the safety of some loyal ships; Cleopatra is learning something of the courage necessary to rule properly.

In Act IV, before the Alexandrian palace, Cleopatra has an interview with Pothinus, the guardian and supporter of Ptolemy, in which she wins his respect for her newly won wisdom; he berates her, however, for her loyalty to Caesar. Then, as Pothinus, a guest, leaves a banquet with Caesar, she puts her new Machiavellianism to work by having Ftatateeta murder him in the street. Ftatateeta is presently slain herself by Rufio, one of Caesar's staff, because he fears her sinister ways.

Act V also takes place before the palace. Leaving for Rome, Caesar appoints Rufio as governor of Egypt. Cleopatra, full of vengeance for the murdered Ftatateeta, protests, but when Rufio explains the murder as an act of preventive strategy rather than as a deed of vengeance, Caesar approves. To cajole Cleopatra Caesar promises to send her the young and handsome Mark Antony when he reaches Rome.

This drama is built around the character of Caesar, who is presented as the model of the man of action. He is completely cynical, yet straightforward and honest; he treats the responsibility of his crown as a job like any other. He never allows his emotions to interfere with the task at hand; he is as free from the emotions of hatred and vengeance as he is from fear. He is totally independent of petty scruple and convention: here he is sharply contrasted with his slave Britannus, who is a personification of the English temperament with its undue awe of propriety. Shaw's Caesar is more human than any previous portrayal of the man, yet the cause of his greatness is clearly and convincingly demonstrated.

Man and Superman (1903): This is a key play, expressing most of Shaw's personal philosophical ideas. The plot is based on the Don Juan story as found in Mozart and elsewhere. Ann Whitefield, the heroine, is a vehicle of the Life Force; a self-directed young woman, she achieves her ends by ascribing her machinations to her father, her guardian, or to some other duly constituted authority. As the play opens her father's will is read, and John Tanner, a young revolutionary, is revealed as one of her guardians. The other is Roebuck Ramsden, a man of "advanced ideas" who is none the less scandalized at Tanner's politics. Actually Ann has shrewdly suggested Tanner's guardianship to her father; she is secretly determined to marry him. Another suitor is Octavius Robinson, a poetic young man who idolizes Ann.

Irate when he learns the situation, Tanner flees to Spain in an effort to escape Ann's wooing. Captured by brigands, he has a dream (the interlude "Don Juan in Hell") in which he becomes his spiritual ancestor Don Juan and the other principals likewise assume historical costumes. Finding herself in Hell, "Ana" objects, but Don Juan tells her that Hell is the true haven of seekers after happiness. He also explains the Life Force, of which Ann, its living manifestation, has been unaware. In the final act Tanner, restored to his proper identity, finds himself snared by Ann and her Life Force. He capitulates gracefully, recognizing the omnipotence of the force that motivates her. Octavius resigns himself to bachelorhood, while continuing to worship Ann. The most important secondary character is Henry Straker, Tanner's chauffeur, who represents the "New Man," educated in trade schools and proud of his technical competence. A subplot involves Octavius' sister Violet and her clandestine marriage to Hector Malone, a young American whose father wishes him to marry a "title"; Violet brings the father neatly to heel.

***Major Barbara* (1905):** The play has three sets (and acts): the first, the very upper-class library of Lady Britomart Undershaft's house in Wilton Crescent; the second, a Salvation Army Shelter in a very poor section of London at the "sign of the cross" in West Ham; and the third, the Undershaft Munition Works at the "sign of the sword" in Perivale St. Andrews. Lady Britomart, her son Stephen, one daughter, Sarah, and her fiancé, Lomax, are all very upper class and dedicated to not much of anything. The other daughter, Barbara, is a major in the Salvation Army and a vigorous one. Her fiancé, Adolphus Cusins, a professor of Greek, has followed her into the army for love. Andrew Undershaft, the munitions king, hasn't lived at home for some fifteen years; he is looking for an adoptable foundling to whom he can leave the Undershaft business and name, because it has been done that way since James the First. His wife has long been furious, having hopes for Stephen, but now needs her husband's help for doweries. He is agreeable, but the only member of the family who interests him is Barbara. They make a bet. She tries to convert him to the Salvation Army but gives up when she finds that the Army will exist on funds from Bodger the whiskey maker and Undershaft the cannon maker. He tries to convert her, claiming that poverty is the only sin, and discovers that technically her fiancé Cusins is illegitimate and can be adopted as the "foundling." In the end Barbara will devote herself to saving the souls of the Undershaft workmen living in neat, clean homes. The filmed version with Wendy Hiller as Major Barbara was a classic of the early screen.

***The Doctor's Dilemma* (1906):** Here is Shaw's chief pronouncement on the medical profession. In addition to a gallery of comic medical supernumeraries, the cast includes Louis Dubedat, a satirical young artist; his wife Jennifer; Blenkinsop, a tubercular young doctor; and Ridgeon, a famous tuberculosis specialist. The plot revolves around the dilemma that Ridgeon can save the life of either Blenkinsop or Dubedat, but not both. He chooses Blenkinsop, mainly because Dubedat admits to being a bigamist. Dubedat dies, and shows in the manner of his death that he is not only a talented artist but a man of character as well. The play's thesis is that private practice is obsolete and that only through socialization can medicine properly care for mankind's ailments.

***Pygmalion* (1912):** In this witty study in the conflict of social classes as well as analysis of certain individual problems, Henry Higgins, an arrogant

Professor of Phonetics, takes up an ignorant flower girl, Liza Doolittle, and attempts to make her into a fine lady to win a bet. He improves her manners, obliterates her Cockney accent, and dresses her in impeccable fashion; eventually he passes her off as a Duchess at a garden party. Liza, however, has developed a sense of human dignity along with her elegance; she bitterly resents Higgins' objective and arrogant attitude toward her and demands to be treated as a person. In the end, she puts him in his place and flounces out, the winner of the encounter. The social thesis of the play is that the alleged intellectual and moral superiority of the upper classes is purely the result of education and rearing. The musical *My Fair Lady* is based on Shaw's play but substitutes a more romantic, less Shavian, ending.

Back to Methuselah (1921): Along with *Man and Superman,* this is one of Shaw's most important plays. It is also his longest. The action is divided into five parts, each symbolic of a stage of human evolution. In the first Lilith tears herself apart to create Adam and Eve; the two invent birth and death, then bear Cain, who invents murder.

The second part takes place in our own times. Conrad Barnabas, a biologist, offers a disquisition on the immaturity of mankind, and predicts higher forms of humanity to come. In the third part the date is 2170 A.D.; the human life span has been stretched to three hundred years, and England is governed by Chinese scholars. Many labor-saving devices have been invented, including television. Part four takes place in 3000 A.D. Human beings are now classified as primaries, secondaries, or tertiaries, depending on how many centuries they have lived. The naive primaries, less than a hundred years old, are treated as children.

The fifth and final part leaps to 31,920 A.D. Humans now produce offspring in eggs, which hatch full-grown adults after seventeen years. For the next four years the offspring love, dance, and play games; then they become mature and pass into the higher realms of mental activity. The theme of the play, especially the latter parts, is that physical life and indeed every activity connected with the body is only a temporary stage, which humanity will presently leave behind in its striving toward bodiless perfection.

Saint Joan (1923): In this iconoclastic portrait of the famous French heroine of the fifteenth century, Shaw's Joan is a healthy, shrewd, yet genuinely pious girl of bourgeois origin. Her "voices" actually originate in her own head; they are merely the dictates of good sense. The drama opens as she comes before the rural lord Robert de Baudricourt to request horse and armor to go to aid the Dauphin in raising the seige of Orleans. Robert, who at first scoffs at her demand, is soon won over by her sincerity and her air of authority. Provided with the needed equipment, she sets out to go to the Dauphin; when she reaches his court she immediately picks him out of a crowd of retainers. He too is carried away by the force of her conviction; he puts her in charge of the French army. Joan joins the commander Dunois, who has been waiting for some time for a favorable breeze to cross the Loire and attack the British at Orleans; with Joan's arrival the wind undergoes a "miraculous" change. Soon success comes to the French cause under Joan's leadership.

But Joan has powerful enemies, both English and French; the Earl of Warwick and the Bishop of Beauvais cooperate to plot her undoing. In addition she alienates many of her own followers through her unfailing accuracy of judgment; the world grows weary of a saint who is always right. Arrested and taken before the Inquisition, she receives what Shaw points out is a perfectly fair trial considering the laws and customs of the time. Her inquisitors do their best to save her body and soul; they exhort her to recant her heresies and accept the absolution of the Church. But she refuses to deny that she derives her authority directly from God without the intervening agency of the clergy. At one point she temporarily recants, but soon recovers her faith in her own convictions; now, as a relapsed heretic, salvation is impossible for her. She faces death courageously, convinced that she is right and all the learned authorities of the Church wrong.

In an epilogue Joan returns twenty-five years later for a posthumous conversation with the Dauphin, now Charles VII of France; by this time the Church has reversed its stand and declared her to be innocent. Suddenly the year changes to 1920; Joan has now been canonized, yet her inquisitors and executioners still maintain that, since heretics are always a menace to the Church, they did right in condemning her in the fifteenth century. Thus the message of *Saint Joan* is the artificiality of all churches and ecclesiastical systems and the validity of naive individual faith, which in the end is nothing but the individual's subconscious trust in the dictates of common sense.

H. G. WELLS (1866–1946)

The literary work of H. G. Wells falls nicely into three groups. His first important novels were the "scientific romances" written around the turn of the century. Here Wells took up a genre that had been only sketched out by Edward Bellamy and Jules Verne and established it firmly as an acceptable literary type; the later utopian novels of the twentieth century were built partly on his example. Wells' scientific fantasies demonstrate a thorough foundation in physics and biology; they are the work of a gifted novelist who was forced to labor in his youth as a science teacher and writer of scientific textbooks. At the same time they have literary qualities lacking in earlier authors like Verne; their characterizations are adept and memorable, and they are full of sensitive and imaginative description. The best of them are *The Time Machine* (1895) and *The Invisible Man* (1897).

Around 1900 Wells turned to a pure comedy of character somewhat in the manner of Dickens or Meredith. (*The Wheels of Chance,* the first novel of this group, actually appeared in 1896.) In this period his typical plot involved a contemplative but idealistic character something like himself—Mr. Polly, Mr. Lewisham, or Kipps—who abandons his mundane clerk's life, and sometimes a mundane wife along with it, and strikes out to seek more dangerous ecstasies. The great merit of these books is to be found in the portrayals of their chief characters, and the best of these is the dyspeptic but perennially cheerful merchant Mr. Polly. Although the heroes of these novels sometimes return to wife, home, and virtue, the theme is more commonly the superiority of the dangerous life over complacent domestic vegetation.

Third, Wells turned shortly before the First World War to a set of discussion novels in which the chief characters are mouthpieces for his own political and economic ideas. *Ann Veronica* (1909) is a predecessor of these books, and *The World of William Clissold* (1926) marks the climax of the period. In addition to these three styles there must be mentioned Wells' scientific and pedagogical works (*The Outline of History,* 1920) and his remarkably candid *Experiment in Autobiography* (1934).

IMPORTANCE

Wells, like Bernard Shaw, was a lifetime socialist and sometime member of the Fabian Society. Unlike Shaw, however, he is not a practical political propagandist; his talents lie in the realm of long-range planning and conjectural fancy. As a Briton Wells supported the First World War; in the long view his pacifistic and socialistic ideas are more utopian than those of Shaw. In literary style as well the two differ. Shaw's method is that of the public-meeting platform; his attitude is rhetorical and propagandistic. Wells, more detached and less brashly confident, writes in the tone of a leisurely and objective scientist. Consequently Shaw is most successful in the theater, whereas Wells writes best in the area of personal prose.

Life

Herbert George Wells was born at Bromley, Kent, in 1866. His mother, Sarah Neal Wells, was a housemaid at the nearby manor of Up Park, and his father was a gardener on the same estate. Shortly after the birth of their son the couple attempted to establish a china shop, but the venture was a failure. After a time the mother was forced to go back into service; Wells' father made small sums of money as a professional cricketer until an injury forced him to retire. The boyhood of the author was passed in the bitterest poverty, made even more miserable by the attempts of his mother to maintain a respectable front.

The parents endeavored to make Wells into a draper's clerk, but three or four years as an assistant demonstrated to him that he had no aptitude for this.

He took a job as a private tutor and studied in his free hours; dogged by sickness and poverty, he nevertheless turned out a biology textbook which proved to be his start in life. Frank Harris, the editor of the *Saturday Review,* lent him a helping hand, and by 1895 he was established as a novelist. His early career, however, was further handicapped by an unfortunate and short-lived marriage to his cousin in 1891. A second marriage, to Amy Catherine Robbins, lasted until her death in 1927.

Wells joined the Fabian Society in 1903; he did a good deal of writing for the group, but eventually abandoned it. His own reserved personality and scientific objectivity little fitted him for the company of such impassioned exhibitionists as Bernard Shaw and the Webbs. In addition, his faith in political socialism seemed to dwindle as time went by. He abandoned his pacifism for the second time during the Second World War, and by 1945 seemed to have relapsed into a hopeless and melancholy pessimism. His last published book, *Mind at the End of its Tether* (1945), saw nothing ahead for humanity but misery, destruction, and oblivion. He died shortly after in 1946.

Chief Works

The Time Machine (1895): In this novel, the hero, the "Time Traveller," invents a machine that can transport him into any desired era of history, past or future. He forthwith travels to the year 802,701 A.D., by which time all humanity has been divided into Eloi, aristocratic vegetarians who lead a life of leisure, and Morlocks, subterranean carnivores who labor to support the Eloi but themselves live virtually at a bestial level. The Time Traveller rescues a young girl, Weena, from drowning, and she becomes his companion. Together they have many adventures, including a narrow escape from attack by the Morlocks.

On a later journey the Time Traveller moves forward thirty million years into the future; by this time the sun is growing cold and virtually all life has ceased to exist.

Kipps (1905): One of Wells' most skillful works from a literary point of view, it contains less didactic content than most of the romances of the early period, and its economy of style recommends it to readers who find his later novels diffuse and talkative. The hero, Arthur Kipps, is partly autobiographical but in another sense is the antithesis of Wells himself; he is pugnacious and high-spirited as a boy and grows into a likeable but not very thoughtful adult. Orphaned in his infancy, Kipps is reared by his lower-class aunt and uncle, who teach him little but a strict morality and an incorrect accent. He plays wild and adventurous games with Sid, the boy next door, and experiences puppy love with Sid's sister Ann. Then he is sent off to be a draper's apprentice in Folkstone; Ann is forgotten while for seven long years he drudges in the dry goods shop. This dismal period almost, but not quite, quenches his constitutional optimism. Conscious of his lack of education, he resolves to "improve himself" by taking a woodcarving class, but only succeeds in falling in love with the teacher, Helen Walshingham. He senses that Helen, who has gone to college, is far above him, and he begins to wonder where his life is leading. Then he reads his name in the paper; to his astonishment he learns that his grandfather has died and left him the staggering fortune of twelve hundred pounds a year.

At first he has no idea how to spend this money; he buys a banjo he cannot play, and lends five hundred pounds to a ne'er-do-well actor friend, Chitterlow, to produce a play. Soon he becomes aware that he is much too gauche and rude in his manner to be taken for a gentleman, and tries bravely to rise to the challenge life has thrown at him. He studies an etiquette book, but only becomes horribly confused; he attempts to correct his cockney accent, and sets about doggedly learning the rules of gentlemanly deportment. Helen and her parents learn of his good fortune and lay snares for him; soon he finds himself engaged, and Helen criticizes his speech and dress and does her best to make him presentable in high society. Kipps accepts the principle that being miserable is a part of gentility. Then, at a party, he recognizes one of the housemaids as his childhood sweetheart Ann; he abandons Helen and high society to marry this girl of his own class. For a time he and Ann are happy, but the two begin to quarrel over Kipps' determination to live on a plane commensurate with his wealth. When it develops that Helen's brother, a lawyer who has been handling Kipps' affairs for him, has absconded with most of his money, the young couple are at first bitterly pessimistic. But Kipps, with the remnants of the fortune, opens a bookstore, and the future begins to look brighter. When Chitterlow's play becomes a hit and returns two thousand pounds on Kipps' investment, he and Ann realize that providence has at last established them in a rank of life where they can find true happiness.

This novel is primarily a witty and masterful character study of its hero, but it contains as well a latent criticism of the British concept of gentility and the system that produces it. The poverty of Kipps' youth is degrading, but even worse is the stuffy hypocrisy of the genteel class into which he is admitted by his inheritance. When he finds his niche as a bookseller he strikes a medium between parisitical wealth and poverty; he is his own master, and he is performing a service useful to society. This is Wells' ideal of social service as he expressed it in his own life.

Tono-Bungay **(1909):** This discursive first-person narrative is built around the theme of modern commerce and its effect on traditional English society. George Ponderevo, the narrator, grows up in the magnificent country estate of Bladesover, where his mother is a servant. Here he observes English life as it was lived in the eighteenth century. His social consciousness is first aroused when he falls in love with Beatrice Normandy, a little girl belonging to the "upstairs gentry"; when this affair results in his banishment from the house, he begins to feel an intense resentment toward the class system. He goes to London as a student, and for the first time encounters the real England, the England of the twentieth century with its blatant commercialism and its sharp contrasts of poverty and wealth. Later he goes to Wimblehurst to become a pharmacist's apprentice under his uncle, Teddy Ponderevo. The uncle is the central figure of the novel. Ambitious and energetic, he is a personification of "American" efficiency. Yet he is curiously romantic; he associates himself with Napoleon and indulges in wild dreams of financial triumphs. His preoccupation with impractical schemes ruins his provincial pharmacy, and he and his wife Susan go to London to live in lodgings. George comes to London too, and resumes his studies in science and engineering. An interlude relates George's friendship with the eccentric sculptor Ewart and his marriage to Marion Ramboat, attractive but, as it turns out, somewhat prudish. When George finds himself temperamentally incompatible with her, he arranges for divorce proceedings.

Meanwhile his uncle has come forward to offer him a job. He has concocted a patent medicine he calls Tono-Bungay, which he represents as a virtual panacea; and this product is making money so fast he needs George's help to run the business. Although George knows Tono-Bungay is worthless, he accepts; and soon they have become rich on human credulity. The novel then describes Teddy's effort to buy his way into aristocratic society; he buys a country house and begins building a huge and pretentious annex to it, and George amuses himself by building experimental flying machines (the novel was written shortly after the first successful flights of the Wright brothers). At the height of his success George meets Beatrice again, and the two renew their childhood love. She promises to marry him in spite of the social gulf separating them. But Uncle Teddy's affairs take a bad turn, and a new venture is necessary to recoup. George sails to West Africa to acquire, by shady means, a shipload of "quap," a tremendously valuable radioactive mineral. The scheme is an ill-fated one; the ship sinks on the return trip, and George arrives in England to find his uncle bankrupt and under prosecution for fraud. In an ironically fantastic chapter George loads his uncle on his newly-built flying machine and carries him to the South of France, where Teddy shortly dies of pneumonia. George returns to England, but now that he is penniless, a marriage with Beatrice is out of the question. The lovers part in sadness, and George turns his talents to the building of destroyers for any government willing to buy them.

The theme of this novel is the passing of the traditional English way of life and its replacement by a brash new commercial aristocracy. George's uncle produces nothing and improves nothing; he is sheer personality and ballyhoo and nothing more. He gains immense wealth at the height of his career, but this wealth is false; and George fails in an equally synthetic attempt to corner a valuable mineral. Wells begins by delineating the decadence of England's traditional aristocracy, but he shows it as vastly preferable to the shoddy commercialism that is replacing it. It is only through genuine production and a fair distribution of its products that society can find true prosperity and happiness.

***The History of Mr. Polly* (1910):** This is the most famous of Wells' Dickensian comedies. The hero, Mr. Polly, begins like Wells as a draper's assistant and eventually becomes the proprietor of a small shop. His life, his work, and his wife, however, become insufferably dull, and he is continually tormented by dyspepsia. He tries to commit suicide by burning his shop down, but botches the job and ends up rescuing a deaf old lady from the flames. Acclaimed as a hero, he flees the town in disgust and settles down in a far region as a handyman in a country inn. After five years he returns secretly to find his wife living cozily on the insurance money; he realizes she would be horrified at his return. Fate has shown Mr. Polly his path; henceforth he continues to lead the life of an indolent, carefree ne'er-do-well.

In this novel, as in *Kipps,* Wells shows his sympathy for the British white-collar class as individuals. Mr. Polly, a typical retail clerk, rebels against his dull life as Wells himself did; his revolt is not only a rejection of middle-class respectability but an affirmation of a hedonistic ethic. After his rebellion he strives only to enjoy himself; he has no more interest in being "proper." Thus the novel implies a latent criticism of the Puritanical middle-class moral code; Wells is sympathetic toward the individual British clerk but not toward the mores of his class.

A second theme is the superiority of happiness over truth. When Mr. Polly is legally dead, both he and his wife are happy, and to disclose the truth at this point would only cause misery to everyone but the insurance underwriters. Mr. Polly in his bliss harms no one, and Wells considers his "dishonesty" in respect to his wife of little importance.

***Mr. Britling Sees It Through* (1916):** This novel treats a similar character in much more serious circumstances. The novel is actually a disguised autobiography relating Wells' evolving attitude toward the First World War. Mr. Britling is at first an isolationist and pacifist who believes the war will not take place. He expounds his views to Mr. Direck, an American visitor, at the very moment the Archduke Ferdinand is being assassinated. When the war becomes imminent, Heinrich, the Britlings' German tutor, leaves for mobilization and Hugh and Teddy, Britling's sons, volunteer for service. Hugh is killed and Teddy reported missing, and Mr. Britling does some grave thinking about the war. He decides that, although neither side is right and no immediate good will come from the war, the world will eventually be improved through the tremendous cathartic effect of the tragedy. When Teddy turns up alive Mr. Britling becomes almost optimistic. He learns that Heinrich has been killed and tries to write a letter to his parents, but finds words inadequate to express what he feels. The novel ends as day dawns and Mr. Britling looks forward to better times in the future.

GEORGE ORWELL (1903–50)

IMPORTANCE

Orwell's liberalism stands at the opposite pole from that of Malraux; he argues consistently and effectively for the rights of the individual as opposed to the demands of the group. He has a profound mistrust of political parties right or left; his liberalism is personal rather than political. At one time or another he has attacked most of the forms of organized tyranny of our era: British imperialism in the East, the Spanish fascist dictatorship, Communist power politics in Spain, the Soviet Russian regime, and even the stupid and impersonal cruelty of French public hospitals ("How the Poor Die" in *Shooting an Elephant*). Orwell is a thinker who consistently continued to defend the right of the individual to go his personal way, a rare argument in this age of parties and organization.

As a stylist Orwell is more skillful than original. His best-known work, *Nineteen Eighty-Four,* owes its effectiveness to the author's ability to create moving and shocking situations rather than to any stylistic ingenuity. His prose is that of the cultured and restrained British man of letters; it resembles the style of E. M. Forster or the early Somerset Maugham. Much of the power of *Nineteen Eighty-Four* proceeds from understatement, as well as from its tongue-in-cheek irony. This second quality is dominant in *Animal Farm* and *Shooting an Elephant.*

Life

George Orwell (pen name for Eric Blair, who maintained a curiously British reticence about his identity) was born in Bengal in 1903 in a family of colonial Britons. He was sent to England to be educated at Eton (1917–21), then came out to Burma to serve in the British security police. He was not very efficient at this job, and began to have doubts about the moral justice of the whole Empire system; eventually he gave up the position and went to Paris to make a living as a writer. These early years were hard, and had a telling effect on his health. He held a series of odd jobs in France and England until 1935, when his writing began to pay enough to support him. *Burmese Days* (1934), a novel based on his colonial experiences, was his first successful book; the quality, however, is not up to that of his later works.

In 1936 Orwell, newly married, went to Spain to cover the Civil War as a correspondent. When he arrived, however, he was impressed and excited by the enthusiasm of the Catalonian loyalists, and soon joined the POUM militia, an anarchist organization, as a common soldier. His experiences in this outfit he described in *Homage to Catalonia* (1938). The POUM incurred the displeasure of the Stalinist high command, and when the Communists assumed total power in the area, Orwell found himself a hunted criminal. Still suffering from a battle wound, he was forced to flee Spain for his life; the collapse of the Catalonian front occurred soon after. This experience only served to confirm Orwell's mistrust of organizations of all kinds.

Although Orwell wrote a periodic column for the *Partisan Review,* he became well-known to the American public only with *Nineteen Eighty-Four* (1949). He died unexpectedly soon after its publication, in 1950.

Chief Novels

***Animal Farm* (1946):** A witty parable of the "betrayal of the revolution," it argues that violent social upheavals are always followed by a reactionary tyranny acting in the name of revolutionary ideals. The plot closely follows the history of the USSR since 1917, although the allegory could just as easily be applied to post-Revolutionary France. The novel begins as the animals on Manor Farm revolt and drive out their human masters (the Czarists). Seven laws are promulgated, of which the most important are "Two legs bad, four legs good," and "All animals are equal." For a time all goes well; then a quarrel breaks out between two boars, Napoleon (Stalin) and Snowball (Trotsky). After Snowball is expelled, tyranny becomes rife. The laws are distorted to allow Napoleon certain comforts, and the most important law is amended to read, "All animals are equal, but some animals are more equal than others." The more important pigs begin walking on their hind legs; the Revolution has come full circle. When at last Napoleon contracts an alliance with nearby human farmers (the Molotov-Ribbentrop pact of 1939) no animal dares raise his voice in protest.

***Nineteen Eighty-Four* (1949):** A powerful nightmare of human society has appeared in the year indicated by the title. The nations of the world have been reduced to three superstates: Eurasia, Eastasia, and Oceania, in the last of which the action is laid. Oceania, comprising England, North and South America, Antarctica, and several other regions, is governed by a system called English Socialism ("Ingsoc"), which actually means total control of human activity, thought, recreation, and economics by a small party elite. War has become permanent; Oceania is always at war with either Eurasia or Eastasia. The symbol of patriotism is "Big Brother"; no one knows his exact identity, but posters everywhere proclaim that "Big Brother Is Watching You." In every inhabited room a "televiewer" projects propaganda and also provides a camera through which spies can watch anyone's activity. In short, personal rights and personal existence have been virtually wiped out.

The hero of the novel, Winston Smith, is an employee of the propaganda bureau ("Truth Ministry"). His job is to revise newspaper and magazine files when it is necessary to change the past for party purposes. As an official explains to him, the past exists only (1) in public records, and (2) in the memories of living persons. Both these repositories being under the control of the party, it can change the past at will. As a result no one really knows any more what happened before the inception of Ingsoc.

The complications begin when Winston falls in love with Julia, another employee of the ministry. Since such affairs, along with all private exercises of emotion, are strictly forbidden, their meetings must be carried out with the utmost stealth. Gradually the pair become increasingly resentful toward Ingsoc, and seek about for some means of rebellion. They think they have found this when O'Brien, a member of the elite Inner Party, invites them to join a revolutionary Brotherhood. O'Brien is a spy, however, and Winston and Julia are arrested at a rendezvous. Winston is tortured so ingeniously and thoroughly that he at last begins to believe, actually and literally, in the dogmas of party propaganda; he is released shattered in body but loyal to Big Brother. This novel apparently owes a good deal to the Russian novel, *We*, by Evgeni Zamyatin, published in 1922, a long satiric novel about a collective utopia (in 1931 Zamyatin left Russia and spent his last years in Paris). There are more than incidental parallels.

10
EXPERIMENTS IN THEATER AND THE NOVEL

More and more critics are coming to agree that May 8, 1956 is a date in the British theater roughly equivalent in importance to 1066, for this, the first performance of *Look Back in Anger* by John Osborne, inaugurates the era of the new British playwrights and a revitalization of English drama, the like of which had not been seen since Shaw. Until this time West End theaters (the British equivalent of Broadway) had been filled with competent and relatively insipid plays of upper-middle-class drawing-room comedy (Terrence Rattigan and J. B. Priestley are usually named and blamed, plus the audience that fed on such pablum). There had been aborted hopes in the poetic plays of Christopher Fry and others who tried the same kind of thing in the forties and early fifties, but they didn't seem to lead to anything beyond. By 1960 people in search of exciting theater stopped going to Paris and Rome and gathered in London; this impetus continued at least into 1971. How did all this come about?

Among other explanations there was certainly a fortuitous combination of theatrical groups, imaginative directors, seasoned and talented actors, experimental and original dramatists, and at least a sufficient number of people to make up audiences to carry the word. New theatrical companies came into being to challenge the theatrical establishment. The English Stage Company was formed by George Devine and Ronald Duncan, director and poet-dramatist, among others to present the work of new playwrights as well as foreign plays and revivals. Its home was the Royal Court Theatre in Sloane Square, and it also ran a club, the English Stage Society, for private performances not subject to the censorship of the Lord Chamberlain. Its first big find was John Osborne. *Look Back in Anger,* accepted for production, was directed by Tony Richardson and received mixed reviews from the critics. But Kenneth Tynan in his review built his own reputation along with Osborne's, and several careers were launched. His next play, *The Entertainer,* in 1957 had the added advantage of Sir Laurence Olivier in the title role of Archie Rice. Although the next three plays (the third for television) were not equally impressive, they were good enough not to damage the playwright. In 1961 he turned on a full Brechtian treatment of *Luther,* played by Albert Finney, who later acted in Osborne's film script of *Tom Jones.* He has continued to produce, and he gave the name if not the identity to the generation of Angry Young Men. The English Stage Company made other discoveries as well: Arnold Wesker and John Arden, whose *Serjeant Musgrave's Dance* has been called "nearly as important as *Look Back in Anger*," among the more important. The Royal Court Theatre in the late sixties made another find, a new lode, in David Storey, who seems ready to be as ingenious and productive as Osborne has been.

The Theatre Workshop, another company created almost single-handedly by one of the most vital talents in modern drama, the director Joan Littlewood, had grown out of her earlier Theatre of Action, and was founded in 1945, setting up shop in London's East End. She could turn almost anything into live theater, *Oh, What a Lovely War* and the film *Sparrows Can't Sing*, for instance — both Joycean and Brechtian but coming out Littlewood. Her Workshop breakthrough was the production of Brendan Behan's *The Quare Fellow* two weeks after the premiere of Osborne's *Look Back*. She later worked out the production of Behan's *The Hostage*. Shelagh Delaney's *A Taste of Honey* is the workshop's other major discovery.

The Royal Shakespeare Theatre Company, which came out of the Stratford-upon-Avon Memorial Theatre, with Peter Hall as its director from 1960, annexed the West End Aldwych Theatre and began building Harold Pinter as "the crest of the British new wave," or *Nouvelle Vague* west of the channel, although it had not discovered him.

A fourth group must be mentioned, the National Theatre Company, which assumed its new name in 1963, formerly the Old Vic Theatre Company, Sir Laurence Olivier director and Kenneth Tynan, critic for *The Observer*, as literary manager. Its fare is largely Shakespearian, Jacobean and Restoration plays, modern continentals, and "one bright Britisher," Peter Shaffer (*Five Finger Exercise, The Royal Hunt of the Sun, The Private Ear* and *The Public Eye*).

No view of the activity of the London stages in the sixties would be complete without reference to Robert Bolt (*A Man for All Seasons*), to Peter Nichols (*A Day in the Death of Joe Egg* and *The National Health* or *Nurse Norton's Affair*), and to Tom Stoppard (*Rosencranz and Guildlenstern Are Dead*). And in 1971 a young Oxford student in his twenties hit both the London and New York theaters. Christopher Hampton found himself talked about with keen interest for his comedy, *The Philanthropist*, which basically turns inside out Molière's *The Misanthrope* in a modern English university town. The English theater was moribund no longer, and it was in fact the most active and alive theater operating anywhere in the world circa 1970. Brecht, the Theatre of the Absurd, and the English Music Hall tradition (roughly equivalent to American vaudeville) seemed to be the most important influences operating in the new British theater.

JOHN OSBORNE (1929–)

John James Osborne, born in the year of the stock market crash and brought up during the depression in a suburb of London south of the

Thames, was sent to "a rather cheap boarding school in the west of England," where he was mostly unhappy. Leaving school at sixteen he drifted into work with a touring stage company, acting for the first time at Sheffield in 1948. These years of acting into the fifties gave him practical stage experience, and he began to write plays on his own and in collaboration with others (what turned out to be the *Epitaph for George Dillon* was written with Anthony Creighton). After the relative success of *Look Back in Anger* (1956), Osborne engaged in occasional polemics with British censorship but remained on the whole a private rather than a public person.

In twelve years he wrote twelve plays, and although critical opinion is divided on which ones are his best after the first, they would be found among *The Entertainer* (1957), *Luther* (1961), *Inadmissible Evidence* (1965), and *The Hotel in Amsterdam* (1968). Living quietly with his fourth wife Jill Bennett, mostly in London, Osborne seemed mellowed without becoming reactionary as is sometimes charged. His film script for *Tom Jones* in 1964, with a fine blend of Osborne and Fielding, certainly broadened public recognition of his dramaturgy. In the 1970s Osborne wrote several important plays and dramatic adaptations, including *West of Suez* (1971); *Hedda Gabler* (1972), an adaptation of Ibsen's play; *A Sense of Detachment* (1972); *The Picture of Dorian Gray* (1974), an adaptation of Oscar Wilde's novel; *Watch It Come Down* (1975), and *The End of Me Old Cigar* (1975).

Chief Plays

***Look Back in Anger* (1956):** This play was breezily but happily reviewed by Kenneth Tynan with the now-famous opening: " 'They are scum' was Mr. Maugham's famous verdict on the class of State-aided university students to which Kingsley Amis' Lucky Jim belongs: and since Mr. Maugham seldom says anything controversial or uncertain of wide acceptance, his opinion must clearly be that of many. Those who share it had better stay well away from John Osborne's *Look Back in Anger,* which is all scum and a mile wide."

A fairly traditional play in three acts with a realistic-naturalistic approach and dialogue, it is set in a slovenly attic flat rather than a middle-class drawing room. This represented a major shift in English drama, the discovery of a new world that had been there all the time under the surface. The vitality and emotional life of the English people were found in very common men and women, who had not previously been on stage. The protagonist or anti-hero is Jimmy Porter, rough, brutal, obscene, but alive and interesting. Born of working-class father (whom he adored and had watched die after his return from the Spanish civil war all shot up: Jimmy says, "Anyone who's never watched somebody die is suffering from a pretty bad case of virginity."), he scorns and attacks the Establishment in all forms; he is equally disillusioned with causes, completely frustrated in the world of 1956, of the Suez crisis, the H bomb, and the Russian suppression of Hungary.

Jimmy, although university-educated (red-brick and white-tile) and knowing T. S. Eliot, Gide, Wordsworth, and Vaughan Williams, has chosen to make a bare living running a sweet stall (candy concession) in a provincial factory city somewhere in England. Married to Alison, he constantly attacks her upper-class parents and brother Nigel and friends, baiting her for reactions. Living with them is a true proletarian lodger, Cliff, who has real affection for and understanding of them both. The boredom of the English Sunday afternoon is broken when Helena, an actress friend of Alison's, arrives to share digs for a few days. She talks the recently pregnant Alison (Jimmy doesn't know and would presumably be angry) into going back to her family for a while. Prig though she is, she falls into Jimmy's arms and bed at the end of the second act.

Alison has well understood the differences between her father, Colonel Redfern (a surprisingly sympathetic character who had served in India from 1914 until after the Second World War and India's independence), and Jimmy. Jimmy obviously both despises and envies the Edwardian past he attacks. She tells Daddy, "You're hurt because everything is changed. Jimmy is hurt because everything is the same." This is a profound observation of different points of view of precisely the same situation, our world. After a miscarriage Alison returns ready to crawl for Jimmy's affection; and Helena having had enough leaves. Jimmy and Alison come together, as they always have, in a squirrels-and-bears fantasy that is the solace and cement in their continuing battle of the sexes. The prognosis for their marital happiness has not significantly changed, although Alison has suffered.

Tynan said that *Look Back in Anger* presents postwar youth as it really is, a signal achievement, in a first play a minor miracle. All the qualities are there — "the drift towards anarchy, the instinctive leftishness, the automatic rejection of 'official' attitudes, the surrealist sense of humor, . . . the casual promiscuity, the sense of lacking a crusade worth fighting for, and, underlying all these, the determination that no one who dies shall go unmourned." It has been thought in some circles that the play has "dated"; to be sure 1956 has receded into the past with great rapidity. But the position of Jimmy Porter, who remains terribly alive, angry, a frustrated idealist, with attacks on the Establishment but nothing to put in its place, intelligent and vulgar, tender and brutal, all at the same time.

The Entertainer (1957): This play, employing half-hearted and half-assimilated ideas of Brechtian staging, produced for Sir Laurence Olivier one of his greatest studies in Archie Rice, the broken-down music hall comic, whose sleazy routines symbolize the rottenness of society. In his traveling stage company Britannia is a buxom and sagging nude: the establishment in decadence and horror. The structure of the play parallels a variety bill with a succession of alternating scenes and interludes with thirteen numbered "turns," the scenes of Archie's domestic life with naturalistic family cross talk, the interludes of Archie's "on stage" corny patter with song and dance routine. The plot merely brings out Archie's failure: his father Billy, a former music hall great, meets life with elderly stoicism; his daughter Jean, with youthful liberal assurance; not so Archie. The fourth major character is Archie's wife Phoebe, repetitive in her misfortunes. They all drink a lot of gin. In the family Archie is very much alone. His son Mick in the army has been captured by freedom fighters in Cyprus. News comes of his imminent release and return, and then of his death in reprisal for the shooting of a terrorist. Billy is sacrificed in his son's attempt to force him into a stage comeback, and Archie himself is pulled off the stage by the man with the hook, his last words: "You've been a good audience. Very good. A very good audience. Let me know where you're working tomorrow night — and I'll come and see YOU." The music hall is dying.

As Simon Trussler points out, Archie is an irrelevant anachronism, caught between "cross-currents of contemporary history. He cannot react simply, and yet he simplifies endlessly, reducing his life to a search for draught Bass and available barmaids. That one can discern his actual complexity in spite of his own simplification is a mark of Osborne's success." And the mark of good and essential theater lies precisely in such a relationship between simplification and complexity under the control of the playwright. It is Archie who says of the music hall theater, or by extension of England or even of the world, "Don't clap too hard, we're all in a very old building." The metaphor works. There's something almost infinitely sad about that.

Luther (**1961**): This historical drama has often been compared with Bertolt Brecht's *Galileo*. There are some obvious similarities: the episodic scenes ranging widely in time (twenty-four years) and place (twelve scenes in nine places), the confrontation of reformer-thinker and the Pope with demands for recantation (although Galileo gives in and Luther does not), the deliberate hindrances placed in the way of seeing the hero as heroic, the dramatic impact of the human, flawed sides of the "hero." But the shock value of Luther's speeches (to conservative Lutherans and to those with tender sensibilities in the audience) and his epileptic fits and constant constipation are based on his own writings, the most historical elements of a plain-speaking age in a plain-speaking play. Like Jimmy Porter, Martin Luther is an apparent iconoclast condemning the Establishment, yet with a nostalgia for a more secure past. The anal obsession in this psychoanalytic study is no bar to (and may even be necessary for) religious fervor and spiritual insight. Some of Luther's greatest illuminations come at stool. The characters of Martin's father Hans and the indulgent supersalesman Tetzel are perforce somewhat caricatured but effective nonetheless. As Martin moves from the insane rigors of cloistered monastic life, sweat-soaked self-castigation (the guilt complex he always carried with him), into a broader-based society at Wittenberg and beyond, he is transformed from a questioning Catholic into an active

Protestant. As Martin says, "If I break wind in Wittenberg, they might smell it in Rome."

Pope Leo X appearing briefly refers to him as a double-faced German bastard! "Why can't he say what he means?" "There's a wild pig in our vineyard and it must be hunted down and shot." But Martin, unlike Galileo, refuses to recant. Show me where I'm wrong in the Scriptures is his repeated demand. The cross-examination of Luther by Cardinal Cajetan in the Fugger Palace in Augsburg, October 1518, is a highly dramatic exchange between two relatively equal antagonists. Political troubles in the Peasants' War make it clear that Luther's vision is no panacea. The play refuses to simplify the historical process.

In the last episode Luther has married the nun Katherine and has produced a son, finally doing something his father could approve. Albert Finney performed the role of Luther with brilliance, according to all accounts of the 1961 production.

HAROLD PINTER (1930 –   )

IMPORTANCE

Harold Pinter is variously considered an absurdist dramatist or an existentialist, although he prefers no label. He has clearly learned some of his techniques from the theater of the absurd but has made them so very English (dialogue, for instance) that they seem quite his own. His characters do have the major existentialist problem of searching for an identity, but they do so in a debased, illogical language that is absurdist, where objects or trivial things *(chosisme)* are likely to communicate more than words, in situations rather than in the sequence of events that forms a plot. There is always a sinister evil hanging over his characters that seems more active than the negative void of a Beckett. His work has been called a "comedy of menace." That the threat is never spelled out for the reader or viewer makes it that much more universal; it is whatever you feel is threatening you.

The difficulties of finding the truth, or in Pinter's case security, are insurmountable. In his plays he adds one characteristic recurring symbol — a room, four walls, representing both a minimal security and oppressive limitation, almost claustrophobic. He says himself, "Two people in a room — .... What is going to happen to these two people in the room? Is someone going to open the door and come in? ... Obviously they are scared of what is outside the room. Outside the room there is a world bearing upon them which is frightening. I am sure it is frightening to you and me as well." Reportedly a reader of Kafka and strongly influenced by *Waiting for Godot* the year before he started writing his own plays, Pinter brings Gogo and Didi indoors, an English interior, and they do their waiting there — not for Godot but for whatever menace they feel coming. He is also anti-Establishment but milder than the Angry Young Men.

Life

Born October 10, 1930, the son of a Jewish tailor, in Hackney, East London, Harold Pinter attended the Hackney grammar school, where he played Macbeth. He left school at sixteen to train for the stage initially at the Royal Academy of Dramatic Arts, then acting with repertory companies between 1949 and 1957 under the stage name of David Baron. Between "jobs" he worked as doorman, waiter, dishwasher, and book salesman traveling from door to door. He was excused from military service as a conscientious objector. In 1956 he married the actress Vivien Merchant.

The next year, at twenty-six, he began writing plays, mostly for private performance and for radio and television. *The Birthday Party,* his first full-length play, written in 1957, was not much of a success in its first London production in 1958; but later *The Caretaker* was a different story with a record run at the Duchess Theatre and an award from *The Evening Standard* as the best play of 1960.

Since that time Pinter has done much work for the films, including *The Servant, The Pumpkin Eater, The Compartment, The Quiller Memorandum,* and *Accident.* In 1965 *The Homecoming* began a run, which in New York produced the biggest controversy since T. S. Eliot's *The Cocktail Party* in 1949 and Beckett's *Waiting for Godot* in the fifties — everyone asking, What does it mean? And almost everyone, including self-appointed critics, volunteering an answer. Pinter's literary production in the last two decades has alternated between stage- and screenplays. Among the former are *No Man's Land* (1975), *Betrayal* (1978), *The Hothouse* (1980), *A Kind of Alaska* (1982), *Victoria Station* (1982), *One for the Road* (1984), and *Mountain Language* (1988). Pinter has become more widely known, however, for his screenplays such as "The Last Tycoon" (1975), "The French Lieutenant's Woman" (1981), "Turtle Diary" (1986), and his screen adaptation of Margaret Atwood's *The Handmaid's Tale* (1990).

Chief Plays

***The Birthday Party* (1957):** There are six characters, the central one being Stanley Webber, a man in his late thirties whose "birthday party" may be the critical one at forty when life is supposed to begin but doesn't. Lulu, a girl in her twenties, is only a potential escape for Stanley ("Shall we go?" "There's no place to go.") and the least important. Petey and Meg in their sixties run a not very successful run-down boarding house by the sea in a seaside town, any town as long as it's English, where Stanley is staying. The menace is brought into the living room of the boarding house by a strange pair: Goldberg (in his fifties) and McCann (a man of thirty).

Stanley apparently used to play the piano in professional concerts; now he does nothing but stay in the boarding house and sleep late. Goldberg and McCann arrive in a big black car and "they" are his enemies, strangers pretending to be friends. Who are they? Gangsters who come to take Stanley "for a ride"? Possibly. Hospital attendants who come to take Stanley to a sanitarium? Or back to a booby-hatch? Possibly. Or agents from another world calling Stanley to account for his sins? We never find out. Stanley tries to defend himself, to drive them away; he pushes himself into a nervous breakdown, becomes violent. In one of the most sinister gestures McCann breaks Stanley's glasses, snapping them quite deliberately. He is led away by Goldberg and McCann; the black car is heard driving away at the end of the play.

A series of questions fired at Stanley by McCann and Goldberg earlier in the play obfuscates rather than clarifies their identities and purpose: Why do you behave so badly, Webber? What did you wear last week? Why did you leave the organization? What would your old mum say, Webber? Who do you think you are? When did you last have a bath? When did you last wash a cup? Why did you kill your wife? Why did you never marry? Do you recognize an external force, responsible for you, suffering for you? When did you last pray? Is the number 846 possible or necessary? And so on. One bit of humor comes when McCann the Irishman tells Goldberg the Jew, "You've always been a true Christian." And he answers, "In a way."

The Dumb-Waiter (1957): This one-act play begins with two characters in a basement room, evidently professional hired killers, Ben and Gus, Ben on a bed reading, Gus in clown-like pantomime action, going off-stage, the pull of a lavatory chain but no flush, returning. Ben then reads aloud newspaper items having to do with death. Gus asks a lot of questions. They have come to "do a job." An envelope with matches but no message slides under the door; they bring out revolvers; there is a feeling of menace and hostility. Suddenly a dumb-waiter begins to work; messages arrive to send up exotic foods; they send up what they have, not much, but authority from above is not satisfied. Gus, increasingly annoyed shouts into the speaking tube "We've got nothing left! Nothing! Do you understand?" In the last few minutes Ben lies down again, more clichés; when Gus leaves the room, Ben receives his orders; when Gus returns *he* will be destroyed because he refuses to continue as a "dumb waiter." The door opens; an unarmed, dishevelled Gus stands there; the curtain falls.

The Caretaker (1960): This three-act play has three characters, again in the basement room of an abandoned building, this time cluttered with junk. Aston, a kindly but slow-witted man about thirty, brings home a visitor, Davies, an old tramp who is very talkative, who has used an alias and is anxious to prove his identity. He is vain, quick to anger, evasive and prejudiced, but hopes to stay with Aston and his younger brother Mick, owner of the place, as caretaker. But he discovers that Aston had once received electroshock treatments in a mental institution and pits the brothers against each other. Mick throws him out. Davies had needed "a place in the world," but his lying, assertiveness, inability to resist being "superior," lack of humility (Man's original sin or pride) has resulted in his expulsion from even this dilapidated Eden.

The Homecoming **(1965):** This play shows Pinter's development toward emerging story line and the addition of sex as an element of both security and menace. The setting is a large drawing room in an old house in North London, a shabby middle-class room with little furniture and no comforts. Characters, angry and self-centered, talk past each other with venomous cutting remarks (the kind one finds in an Ivy Compton-Burnett novel but lower class). This is a strange household: Max at seventy had assumed many "maternal" roles even before the death of his wife; two sons at home, Lenny, a quick-witted pimp, and Joey a slow-witted would-be boxer; and Max's brother, the chauffeur Uncle Sam. After an absence of six years Teddy, the oldest son, a professor of philosophy in an American university, returns with his wife Ruth, married just before leaving England. They left three sons behind for the "homecoming" to introduce Ruth to the family.

Teddy and Uncle Sam (American overtones) consider themselves successful but are really more dead than alive. The three other men, failures on the surface, are very much alive (particularly sexually). But the most vital of all is Ruth, a kind of modernized Lulu from Wedekind's *Earthspirit,* a woman controlling men through the power of sex. She establishes her authority over Lenny, who is used to being in charge, in a grotesque scene with a glass of water. Later, as Teddy packs his things to return to America, sons, and teaching, Ruth accepts the proposition of Max, Lenny, and Joey to stay with them, ministering to their needs and earning her keep as a part-time prostitute. Ruth, more than real, is a realist; being a wife and mother doesn't keep her from being also a whore. But it is implied that the Family is a "ghastly" institution in its modern frame of reference. What do we have to go home to, when primitive human relationships have been debased by the world around us? There are enough ambiguities in *The Homecoming* to provide multiple questions and multiple answers.

CARYL CHURCHILL (1938–   )

Caryl Churchill was born to a middle-class family in London. During the war her family moved to Montreal, where she lived until she attended college in England. She received her degree in English literature at Oxford. Throughout this early part of her life she admits that she lived her life as she was expected to. She did the appropriate intellectual things in college and then married and had children. But still she struggled to maintain her dream of being a writer. In college she wrote plays that were produced by other students, but she found it difficult to pursue her dream amidst what she saw as the dullness of middle-class life. Much of the satire in her plays is directed at this life style.

The style of her works is farcical, satirical, and experimental. She lampoons the middle-class values of capitalism and material success. She herself is a socialist and a feminist, beliefs that are evident in most of her work. She examines the relationship of violence and sex roles in *Objections to Sex and Violence* (1975), and, in *Vinegar Tom* (1976), she demonstrates that women were convenient scapegoats for societal ills during the witch hunts of the seventeenth century.

Chief Dramas

Caryl Churchill's first major play, staged at the Royal Court Theatre, was a farce about the materialism of the middle class called owners. *Owners* (1972) critiques values that capitalists often take for granted like getting ahead at all costs and the ends justify the means. The play demonstrates how ownership destroys potential relationships between people. *Owners* has loosely connected scenes and a loose plot that gives it a dream-like quality.

Vinegar Tom and *Objections to Sex and Violence* are two plays in which her feminism are very evident. Her companion piece to *Vinegar Tom* is *Light Shining in Buckinghamshire* (1976), which focuses on feminism during revolutions. Her most successful farcical play was *Cloud Nine* (1979), which treated the subject of colonialism. Set during the Victorian era in colonized Africa, the play makes analogies between the relationships of colonist and native, master and servant, and man and woman. A unique aspect of this play is her use of cross-gender casting in which a woman plays a delicate school-boy and a man plays the part of an unsatisfied wife to illustrate artificial gender distinctions. The effect of this is both comical and illuminating.

Top Girls (1982) is a play about the effect of poverty on women, and *Serious Money* (1987) is a verse play about the stock market crash of October 1987, a satire about greedy people who want to "get ahead."

DAVID STOREY (1933–)

Americans returning from the London theater season in 1970 and 1971 seemed most excited by the play *The Contractor* by the young dramatist David Storey. Many were astounded that their attention had been held by a group of actors who did nothing but put up and take down a tent on stage for two hours. Of course for theatergoers who had been only waiting for Godot, this was a great deal of action. They were watching something happen and it satisfied a need. With Storey's second great stage success in the year following the opening of *The Contractor,* they were back in Beckett no-action territory in *Home.* But again the magic of characterization and theme worked.

Life

David Malcolm Storey had been born the son of a coal miner July 13, 1933 in Wakefield, Yorkshire, and educated there in the Queen Elizabeth Grammar School. Later, 1953 to 1956, he put himself through the Slade School of Fine Arts in London while playing professional rugby for the Leeds city team and commuting back and forth. This seems a highly unlikely combination and may even be unique. The professional football gave Storey the material and observed detail for his first literary success, the novel *This Sporting Life* (1960). The Slade School permitted him to win a scholarship and to have his work shown in many London exhibitions. *This Sporting Life* had a phenomenal first novel success. In the revived tradition and technique of naturalism, it was soon associated with and hailed by the Angry Young Men like Alan Sillitoe, author of *Saturday Night and Sunday Morning,* and John Braine, author of *Room at the Top.* It won the Macmillan Fiction Award and was made into a film by the Rank Organization starring Richard Harris and Rachel Roberts that won the International Film Critics Prize at the Cannes Film Festival in 1963.

In 1956 David Storey married Barbara Rudd Hamilton, and they had two sons and two daughters. Storey published two more novels on the strength of *This Sporting Life: Flight into Camden* (1960), and *Radcliffe* (1963). These are not in the style of the first novel. *Radcliffe* is something of a surrealistic, grand guignol murder story, heavy on symbolism (red necktie and cut throat) with some antinovel overtones. Although not an entirely successful novel, *Radcliffe* does contain the seeds of the later play *The Contractor:* Ewbank and the workmen, the putting up and taking down of tents. Storey taught art for a time and studied in Paris during 1964. In 1967 he began a new career for himself by turning to the theater. His first play, *The Restoration of Arnold Middleton,* was called by Harold Hobson of the *Sunday Times* the best first play produced by the English Stage Company since *Look Back in Anger.* His second play *In Celebration* was produced in 1969 and also received good reviews: "profoundly moving play," "front rank of today's playwrights," "rich and deeply satisfying," "greatest strength . . . his eye for social detail." Then in the same year came Storey's "best play so far," *The Contractor.* It was staged by the Royal Court in October 1969 and returned to the West End in April 1970 in response to public demand. It had what is for England a long run, and in July 1970 Storey's fourth play *Home* opened at the Apollo Theatre with Sir Ralph Richardson and Sir John Gielgud in the major roles. The same cast brought *Home* to New York City for a limited engagement at the Morosco Theatre in November of 1970.

The influences of the Theater of the Absurd, of Pinter's comedy of menace, of simple British understatement, the national character of reticence, may be seen in the drama of Storey. But the menace is softened to uneasiness, to something we have lived with so long we're getting used to it, like our absurd universe. We neither cry nor groan nor moan. We may stutter like Glendenning in *The Contractor* in the great difficulty of attempted communication, and we shall have tea. As D. A. N. Jones said in the *Listener,* "David

Storey's plays become ever more refined, as austere as Pinter or even Beckett, but nearer to common experience, almost naturalistic." This then was a new combination, highly selective realism combined with the insights of absurdism.

Since 1970 Storey has written several plays and novels, with the latter occupying more and more of his attention. The most autobiographical of his plays is *The Changing Room* (1973), based in part on his four years as a professional rugby player. *Sisters* and *Early Days* followed in 1978 and 1980 respectively. Among his most recent novels are *Saville* (1976), *A Prodigal Child* (1983), and *Present Times* (1984), a biting political satire of social trends, including feminism.

Chief Works

***This Sporting Life* (1960):** This novel is a fairly straightforward naturalistic narrative about a professional rugby player in his early twenties on the Primstone City Rugby League Club, Arthur Machin, who had started as an ordinary factory worker on a lathe at Weaver's plant. The narrative device of first presenting Art Machin on the field when he gets his front teeth knocked out during a game just before Christmas, the difficulty of finding a dentist to fix him up, the big Christmas party at Weaver's (part owner and director of the football club) — and then having Art remember his past up to this point while under gas at the dentist's may not be very original but it works reasonably well with the sweaty, sometimes painful details involving a number of characters, teammates Mellor, Maurice, Frank, and George Wade in the bath and dressing room at the stadium, Johnson the pusher who had helped Machin get on the team, Weaver and his unsatisfied wife, and the other big voice and owner of the Primstone Club Mr. Slomer.

Art has been boarding with a Mrs. Hammond, widow with two small children, for a very low cost to him, helping around the house. After some time and persuasion she is willing to satisfy him sexually but somewhat furtively. Art seems genuinely fond of the children and tries unsuccessfully to get Mrs. Hammond to return his developing love. He spends money on them all. Involved accidentally in a paternity case, which traps his teammate Maurice, Machin is thrown out of Mrs. Hammond's, goes to his parents in the country, who dislike her intensely, and returns to football very much alone and defeated. When word comes to him that Mrs. Hammond is very ill and hospitalized he goes to her, getting her a private room and flowers. She is expected to die, gets better, recognizes her children when Art takes them to see her, and a week later dies. As his world seems to be coming apart, Arthur Machin keeps going on the football field. The novel ends in the dressing room, almost where it began but with a greater sense of futility.

***The Contractor* (1969):** This play is a perfectly realistic, photographic slice of life, or it is an allegory, or it is shades and blends of both. It was G. K.

Chesterton who pointed out the significance of basic metaphor, that all great literature has always been "allegorical of some view of the whole universe," that the *Iliad* is great because all life is a battle, that the *Odyssey* is great because all life is a journey. *The Contractor* offers at least two basic metaphors. All life may be the putting up and taking down of a tent, construction and dismantling, with a wedding in the middle, a gold and green streamer-hung marquee reception in the garden. Or life, our life, may be viewed as a contract: business with labor and management taking suspicious sides, each apparently out to take advantage of the other, or marriage contract—which is something of a business. The salesman has already become the symbol of our business-oriented world in Kafka and Arthur Miller, the small-time clerk in many pieces of fiction (Gogol's *Overcoat*, Joyce's "Counterparts," for example), but here the contractor with his relationship to client and organization becomes the new symbol. None of this, of course, is stated or explicit. Storey is too clever and too English to hit you over the head with his ideas. You *have* to listen, to infer, to feel. But he does imply.

Workmen putting up the tent make for something to watch. There is activity—and inactivity (workmen goldbricking, only pretending to work), but the tent does go up. There are two things almost everybody will stop to watch—a parade and a construction project. This is an exceedingly clever device, prestidigitation: while you watch what the right hand is doing the left hand slips you the business. In this play the contractor is the client; Ewbank, Frank "by name but not by nature," is a self-made Yorkshire businessman; the tent is being erected for the tent-maker on the lawn of his estate as a marquee for the wedding of his daughter Claire to her betrothed Maurice—a society affair that reminds one of a kind of *nouveau riche* Katherine Mansfield "Garden Party." His wife and his parents (the old generation, guests for the wedding) wander in and out, but one of the most important characters is his son Paul (the new generation) who might have become a good workman —he wants to—if new social position had not made his university-educated life dilettante and almost worthless. The other characters are workmen: the foreman Kay, and laborers representing quite individual attitudes toward their jobs, their boss, their lives—Marshall, Irish, pleasant, easy-going, with no great appetite for work; Fitzpatrick, shrewd, independent, clowning, picking and probing at others rather than working; Bennett, anonymous, preferring to be inconspicuous, will do what is asked of him but no more; and Glendenning, a young, good-natured, stammering half-wit, constantly eating, the butt of others' jokes but exacting sympathy. Although not respecting the son —"never done a day's work in his life," the workmen know and basically respect Ewbank who, having been a laborer in the beginning, understands them well. But they believe he has built his wealth from "the money he never paid us," as Fitzpatrick says. Ewbank is somewhat uncomfortable in his acquired position, doesn't take easily to wearing his clothes. His father, an old artisan, drags an old piece of rope around, remembering his past as a rope maker; now there are only machines.

The workmen talk about wives and women and family responsibilities, ragging each other with mild malice as the tent goes up. They get in digs at Ewbank's family; with a wife like that, instead of making tents he should make concrete shelters. Mrs. Ewbank, coming out to look around, re-members a workman who got a splinter in his hand, turned septic, had to have a finger off. Frank has hired all sorts of workers (perhaps he doesn't have to pay them so much?), handicapped, some who have been jailed. Threats almost emerge as tempers rub each other, but by the end of the second act the tent is raised, the floor is in with tables, chairs, and flowers. It is declared lovely. Between Acts II and III the wedding takes place, presum-ably with three or four hundred guests and a string orchestra.

The morning after the intervening day the tent has "suffered a great deal," muslin drapery hanging loosely, tables and chairs overturned, bottles lying around with discarded napkins, streamers, general mess. The workmen have returned to take the tent down. The talk gets sharper with accusations, with references to trade unions, loss of jobs. Ewbank comes on in time to save Fitzpatrick from being fired. There's talk of the future, the up-and-coming generation, the ferment of ideas, but it looks hopeless, the debris of society, that's us. When the tent is down it has left a few marks. Ewbank says, "Aye . . . You pay a price for everything." The son has left on his travels as well as the honeymoon couple; the modern world has left us behind. The old folks are about to depart. The workmen and Ewbank have a drink together and the workmen leave. Summer is over.

The estate could be England or the world and the tent erected some period of its glory, Victorian or Edwardian perhaps; the morning after with its bottles and debris sounds like the Thames' banks in Eliot's "Wasteland" — "empty bottles, sandwich papers, / Silk handkerchiefs, cardboard boxes, cigarette ends / Or other testimony of summer nights." But it doesn't have to be. It can stand by itself. Ronald Bryden saw *The Contractor* as a subtle and poetic parable about the nature and joy of skilled work, the meaning of community, and the effect of its loss." Harold Hobson found it "about a work of art, how it is fashioned, what regrets and happiness it enshrines, and the poignancy of its contrasts with human experience. . . . There is no superfi-cially dramatic incident, yet it wakens in us a sense of infinite mystery." Perhaps its chief virtue is to tease us out of and into thought.

Home (1970): This play is more restricted and astringent than its predeces-sor. There are only five characters: Harry and Jack, the two women Marjorie and Kathleen, and Alfred the would-be wrestler who carries chairs around. The setting, a decaying balustrade and a flagpole, chairs and table in a scruffy garden, is frightening in an austere Charles Adams way. Harry and Jack, in roles created by Sir John Gielgud and Sir Ralph Richardson respectively, are two middle-aged to elderly gentlemen who open the play by talking with each other with half-wary civility, exchanging well worn talk about weather, politics, war, school, and Empire that they have acquired in a lifetime. They are very correct, Harry with hat, leather gloves, and folded newspaper, Jack with handkerchief in jacket pocket and an elegant cane, but are obviously trying to become friends since it's never too late for that. Sometimes they hold back on a private memory or grief even when moved to tears. Reticence is after all English. Only very gradually do we begin to realize that Home is a Mental Home. The two men are eventually joined by two ladies, one randy, stout and coarse in speech (Kathleen), the other sourly suspicious of others, particularly men (Marjorie). They finally pair off, Harry with Kathleen, Jack with Marjorie, and go off to lunch at the end of the first act.

In the second act they return and dawdle away the afternoon with some gossip about fellow inmates, particularly Alfred, who has had a prefrontal lobotomy and who annoys them in a business of moving the chairs. They are not unfriendly to him, however, since he is one of them; they are all at home in the home. One is aware, though, that they think of their former homes and wonder about absent and perhaps-to-visit relatives. Time passes. They are waiting (not for Godot) for teatime.

This is a comedy on a tragic theme written with grace and warmth. Brendan Gill said of it in the *New Yorker,* "We are prompted to laugh, never without compassion, in the presence of what is obviously an intolerable misery of body and spirit. . . . Mr. Storey is an artist, and takes far too serious a view of life to be content with the frivolities of making us weep. Not the least taint of sentimentality stains his unfinished, seemingly vagrant, and at last incantatory lines." Harry and Jack may seem somewhat like Didi and Gogo in *Waiting for Godot,* but they are English, they are much better dressed, and they are eager to live, reach out for sun and food and companionship. The basic metaphor is a starker one here; perhaps all England or our world is a vast public mental institution. We wait from one meal to the next and make what connections we can. Home is thus a concept with double-edged irony. Remember Hawthorne's nostalgia for England as our old home; *You Can't Go Home Again* might become *You Can't Leave Home Again;* Pinter's *Homecoming,* however grim, is more flexible and less dead-end than Storey's. British reviews stressed the tone and understanding of the play: "As a study of human unhappiness *Home* is touching, humane, dignified and universal"; "As a view of crippled lives and wintry tenderness possible between them, the play is beautifully spare and sustained in tone"; "A sad, gentle, misty nocturne."

SAMUEL BECKETT (1906–   )

Life

Beckett was born in Dublin into a relatively well-to-do Protestant family able to provide him with a privileged education at Portora Royal School and then Trinity College, Dublin, where he studied Romance languages. After graduation in 1928, he taught English at the university level in France. His earliest literary hero and model was James Joyce; Beckett's first published work, in fact, was an essay on Joyce (1929). Beckett was also deeply influenced by French philosophers. By the early 1930s he had established himself as an important young writer with a series of short stories (*More Pricks than Kicks,* 1934). Settling in Paris, Beckett wrote a novel (*Murphy*) on the typically Irish themes of a poverty-stricken external life and a richly textured internal life.

During the Second World War, Beckett was active with the French Resistance, often to the point of risking his life. During a particularly dangerous two-year period, he hid himself as a farmhand in a rural French village. Following the war, he returned again to Paris and began writing primarily in French. During the five years following the war he produced his "trilogy": *Molloy, Malone Dies,* and *The Unnamable.* These novels center on personality types that we would now label "compulsive-obsessive." The protagonists typically feel a mixture of *ennui* and anger toward society and seek out ways to exist, however primitively, on their own terms.

After 1950, Beckett turned in earnest to the writing of drama. *Waiting for Godot* (1952) was produced in France, England, and the United States. For a postwar world weary of moral idealism and patriotic appeals, Beckett's offbeat and sometimes whimsical style struck an immediate and positive response. A radio play, *All That Fall,* and the popular *Krapp's Last Tape* followed in 1957 and 1958. Other plays of that period included *Endgame,* a quirky vision of the end of the world, and *Happy Days,* an even stranger musing on postmodern human relationships. Beckett also wrote mime plays (*Act Without Words I* and *Act Without Words II*).

IMPORTANCE

At heart, Beckett dramatizes the themes of French existentialism, particularly as espoused by Albert Camus and Jean-Paul Sartre. Beckett poses the central problem of achieving worth, identity, and joy in an essentially absurd world. His characters typically achieve no large or lasting victories, but instead small internal conquests over despair, panic, boredom, and loathing.

Important Works

***Waiting for Godot* (1952):** Two tramps amuse themselves with tricks while ostensibly waiting for Godot to appear. They put the best face possible on their interminable waiting and wondering, often with self-directed humor and fellow-feeling. But the pathos of their dilemma is apparent to the audience; like children, the tramps somewhat naively cling to the hope that Godot will keep his promise and appear. At one point in the play, Godot sends a boy to assure the tramps that he is on his way. But the play ends without Godot's arrival.

Popular commentators quickly made the play out to be a cynical statement about the cruel hoax of religious promises in an absurd, unheeding world. Beckett resisted this explicit reading of his play, however, and carefully avoided the narrow role of a religion-basher. *Godot,* he seemed to imply, is a larger phenomenon in human wish-development than merely an allegorial stand-in for religious figures.

After a first-night performance that stunned and confused both theater-goers and critics, *Godot* ran for more than three hundred performances in Paris. It is important to note that the play in its original draft existed as early as 1947, demonstrating how directly the experiences of the Second World War influenced Beckett's themes and character materials in the play.

In the United States, the play opened — and quickly closed — in its premiere run in Miami. It had much more success, however, in a long run in New York, where both critics and playgoers apparently were more prepared to deal with the play's intellectual implications and drastic departures from past dramatic conventions.

Happy Days (1961): This play introduces the talkative Winnie as an aging woman literally and figuratively up to her neck in life's problems, including the problem of a silent and often sullen mate, Willie. Winnie, nevertheless, carries on as best she can, filling her "happy days" with chatter, memories, and quizzical speculations. She talks at Willie, not to him, and has a steady stream of suggestions for his improved comfort or prospects. As the external circumstances of the couple grow more extreme, Winnie rises to the challenge in spirit, though hardly in the mode of traditional heroism or nobility. Like *Waiting for Godot,* the play ends with a hauntingly ambiguous dramatic statement as Willie extricates himself from his earthen burrow and climbs slowly up the hill, gun in hand, toward the point where Winnie is buried up to her neck.

Beckett handles these apparently simple materials with great complexity and frequent flashes of humor. The audience recognizes in Winnie a survivor who, with a touch of the Irish, can talk herself through dilemmas she cannot think herself through. Beckett holds back from direct statements of theme in this play, as in his others; but the spirit of *Happy Days* is not one of despair over the hopelessness of the human condition. Rather, Beckett seems to be celebrating, at least in a modest way, the power of the human spirit and language itself to create a bearable, if not ideal, environment for the brief period of mortal existence.

DORIS LESSING (1919 –   )

Doris Lessing was born in Persia to English parents and lived for her first twenty-five years on a farm in Southern Rhodesia. She moved in 1949 to England, where she began a series of linked novels under the general title

Children of Violence. These works make up a psychological autobiography involving the complex and often cruel relationships between African blacks and whites. A later novel, *The Golden Notebook* (1962), explores gender inequities and oppression as well as moral questions implicit in political choices. Other themes common in her writing are the problems of aging, loneliness, alienation, and generational misunderstandings. Some of her best short stories are contained in the collection *A Man and Two Women*.

Important Work

"How I Finally Lost My Heart" (1963): This short, Kafka-esque, tale is told in the first person about a woman in mid-life. She stands at her window, contemplating past, present, and future loves. This very day, in fact, she plans to meet her first "serious" love (now a past love) for lunch, then another male friend for afternoon tea. But she focuses most of all on her date with "serious love C," a man she will meet for the first time that evening for a date.

As she looks out her window, she imagines that he, too, is looking out his window, wondering what the evening will bring. She resolves to call him with the caution that they not fling their wounding hearts at one another. Just as she is about to do so, her own heart plops into her left hand. Amazed at first, she sits down to contemplate it, including its layers of memories. Then she tries to remove the heart from her hand, without success.

She wraps her hand and heart in tinfoil and covers both with a sweater, then goes out onto the street and toward the subway. As she sits unnoticed in an almost empty car, she notices another woman, apparently poor and miserable, moaning to herself about a betrayal of love. The narrator suddenly feels the heart fall loose from her hand. She places it beside the distraught woman, who clutches it as if it were a precious gift. The narrator gets off the subway, laughing. She is free of her heart, and with it, her pain.

"The Day Stalin Died" (1957): This complex story features the narrator and several of her female friends, all of them involved in local Communist politics. Amid the routine doings of the day, the narrator finds herself accompanying her Cousin Jessie to a photography studio in the company of Jessie's mother, Aunt Emma. Jessie has purchased new clothes in which to be photographed.

On the way to the studio, the narrator notices a newspaper headline telling that Stalin is critically ill. The news hardly has time to settle for the narrator before she is plunged into a highly charged interpersonal duel between Jessie and her mother, culminating in the cancellation of the photography session altogether. When the narrator returns home, she receives calls from two friends, who convey the news that Stalin is dead. The narrator takes the news in stride, but is urged by one friend to "be worthy of him." The narrator agrees unenthusiastically.

EDNA O'BRIEN (1930 –   )

Edna O'Brien was born in County Clare, Ireland, and was educated at the National School in Scarrig, the Convent of Mercy at Longrea, and at the Pharmaceutical College in Dublin. Edna O'Brien's fiction stands out as a counterpart to James Joyce's. Whereas James Joyce writes about the responsibilites and experiences of growing up male in Irish society, O'Brien focuses on the experiences of women. Her own life mirrors that of characters in Joyce novels and her writing reflects that. She grew up with a violent father, turned to her suffering mother for comfort, and first exerienced the world outside her home through a convent school. The autobiographical element of her writing gives it its realistic quality. In her short story, "Sister Imelda" (1981) she expresses a troubled adolescence of awakening sexuality conflicting with shame.

Edna O'Brien eventually needed to escape from Ireland to express herself as a writer. In her first month away from Ireland she wrote her first novel *The Country Girls* (1960). Since then she has written seven other novels as well as four collections of short stories and a variety of other works. Through all of her writing, love plays an integral role expressing pleasure and pain, gain and loss. As Joyce depicts fully realized men and shadowy undefined female characters, O'Brien creates female characters with depth and dimension. In her world women are sufferers and survivors.

SUSAN HILL (1942 –   )

Susan Hill was born in Scarbrough in 1942 and was educated at Kings College, University of London. She has become best known for her novels and short stories and she has been awarded the John Llewelyn Rhys Prize, the Somerset Maugham Award, and the Whitman Award.

Her writing is distinctive for the struggling of the characters to gain independence against an oppressive parental figure. The struggle frequently ends in tragedy as in "How Soon Can I Leave" (1973). In this short story the protaganist struggles against a parental figure for an independence that she realizes too late she doesn't want. In "The Springtime of the Year," though, the young woman is able to come to terms with her husband's death before further tragic consequences occur. She must first face a characteristic threat of Hill's fiction, madness and despairing isolation. She must find a renewed connection to the world before madness sets in. Hill's writing is typically unsentimental, but she does not neglect the emotional world.

HISTORICAL BACKGROUND (1955–93)

The year 1955 marked the end of Churchill's leadership as prime minister. In his last four years in power, Churchill had little to offer a recession-plagued England except for a patchwork of economic and social programs. Except for Hong Kong and a group of mostly small Pacific islands, the former British Empire had dissolved itself. In policy and temperament, Great Britain seemed to be settling in to an active retirement of sorts — strong in voice and spirits, but largely withdrawn from the commercial, political, and military field of combat. As Robert Adams has summarized, "Elizabeth II, a respected lady, has presided over no great outpouring of public confidence, no flareup of literary imagination, and least of all over any bold revival of Britain's economic energies."

In the 1960s and 1970s, Britain struggled with prolonged recession, the shrinkage of exports, and high rates of unemployment. At the same time, tourist facilities burgeoned as Britain, for better or worse, became a place where travellers could view former greatness and contemporary pleasantness. The political stalemate in these years pitted Labour, with its perpetual call for more nationalization of industry, against Conservatives, who favored privatization so long as it did not threaten tradition or privilege. Prime ministers in the period included Eden, Macmillan, Douglas-Home, Wilson, Callaghan, and Heath. England's balance of payments and currency reserves, measured in real dollars or pounds, slipped ever lower during the period. Per capita industrial production fell from one of the highest to among the lowest in Europe. By 1980, Britain faced the dilemma of a depleted natural-resource base (with coal and iron largely mined out) and an outmoded industrial infrastructure.

The conservative government of Margaret Thatcher (who in 1987 became the first prime minister in modern history to be elected to three terms) seized upon a bolder public rhetoric and new economic initiatives in the 1980s, including development of the North Sea oil fields and the installation of nuclear power generators. When John Major took office on November 28, 1990, he inherited leadership of a nation on the verge of opening a tunnel corridor to the Continent (the "Chunnel") and wedding its economic destiny to that of the European Community (comprising Belgium, Denmark, France, Germany, Greece, Ireland, Italy, Luxembourg, Netherlands, Portugal, Spain, and the United Kingdom). Import imbalances continue to plague the British economy, with virtually all of its cotton, rubber, and sulphur coming from abroad, 80 percent of its wool, half of its food and iron ore, and large percentages of paper and chemicals. Britain competes primarily against Japan in its production of electronic devices, including radios, televisions, and scientific instruments, and against the United States in arms production, including jets and ground armaments.

REVIEW QUESTIONS

THE REALM OF IDEAS: INTELLECTUAL AND IDEOLOGICAL LITERATURE

Multiple Choice

1. _____ The revival of mysticism and religious idealism in literature was a response to
   a. the prominence of Catholicism in the literature of the Irish Renaissance
   b. the horrors of the First World War
   c. the Victorian preoccupation with convention
   d. the materialism of the twentieth century

2. _____ The main target of Evelyn Waugh's satire is
   a. the loutish behavior of the working class
   b. the inbred aristocracy
   c. the political conservatism of the wealthy
   d. the deterioration of morality

3. _____ Recurrent themes in Graham Greene's novels are
   a. guilt and expiation
   b. death as a desirable end
   c. treachery and squalor
   d. All of the above

4. _____ The authors grouped under the heading of Liberals and Humanitarians are generally
   a. communists
   b. secular
   c. socially conservative, though politically radical
   d. radical in their literary techniques

5. _____ The author considered the first of the Angry Young Men is
   a. H. G. Wells
   b. Harold Pinter
   c. John Osborne
   d. George Orwell

6. _____ Characters with major existentialist identity problems are typical of the plays of
   a. Harold Pinter
   b. George Bernard Shaw
   c. Caryl Churchill
   d. G. K. Chesterton

7. _____ Aldous Huxley viewed modern man as
   a. fair and democratic
   b. hopelessly materialistic
   c. intellectual and concerned about morality
   d. spiritual and enlightened

8. _____ Although in many ways considered a conservative, G. K. Chesterton advocated
   a. socialism
   b. fascism
   c. redistribution of wealth
   d. the abolition of the monarchy

9. _____ In his political views, George Orwell was
   a. similar to H. G. Wells
   b. sensitive to the dangers of dictatorship from both the left and the right
   c. a Fabian socialist
   d. increasingly conservative after his experiences in the Spanish Civil War

10. _____ Characters in bizarre, nonrealistic situations commenting on existential problems are characteristics found in the works of
   a. Evelyn Waugh
   b. Graham Greene
   c. Samuel Beckett
   d. William Golding

True-False

11. _____ Evelyn Waugh approved of the freedom modern society gave to individuals.

12. _____ Aldous Huxley applauded the technological advances of the twentieth century.

13. _____ H. G. Wells was a practical political propagandist.

14. _____ George Bernard Shaw idealized members of the working class in his plays.

15. _____ G. K. Chesterton was fond of employing paradoxes in his writings.

16. _____ William Golding displays an optimistic view of essential human nature.

17. _____ Both Doris Lessing and Caryl Churchill are considered feminist writers.

18. _____ Samuel Beckett wrote a number of works in French, rather than English.

19. _____ Ireland serves as an important setting for both Edna O'Brien and Samuel Beckett.

20. _____ Satire is a favorite weapon for both Evelyn Waugh and Aldous Huxley.

Matching

21.	_____ Evelyn Waugh	a.	"The Springtime of the Year"
22.	_____ Graham Greene	b.	*Endgame*
23.	_____ William Golding	c.	*Major Barbara*
24.	_____ George Bernard Shaw	d.	*The Homecoming*
25.	_____ Harold Pinter	e.	*The Tent*
26.	_____ David Storey	f.	*The Country Girls*
27.	_____ Samuel Beckett	g.	"The Day Stalin Died"
28.	_____ Doris Lessing	h.	*Pincher Martin*
29.	_____ Edna O'Brien	i.	*The Loved One*
30.	_____ Susan Hill	j.	*The End of the Affair*

Fill-in

31. The quintessential drama of the Angry Young Men is _____ .

32. Similar to *Nineteen Eighty-Four* in its vision of the loss of individual freedom in the future is _____ .

33. Children are shipwrecked and isolated on an island in _____ .

34. The importance of the Life Force is a theme in the dramas of _____ .

35. *Point Counter Point,* an experimental novel that portrays incidents from several points of view, was an early novel by _____ .

36. Rooms represent minimal security and oppressive limitation in the plays of _____ .

37. In _____ , H. G. Wells tells of a young man who tries to "improve" himself when he inherits a fortune.

38. _____ and _____ were associated with the Fabian Socialists.

39. South Africa and its racial problems figure in the works of _____ .

40. The existentialism of Jean Paul Sartre was a strong influence on the works of _____ .

Answers

1.	d	5.	c	9.	b
2.	d	6.	a	10.	c
2.	d	7.	b	11.	F
4.	b	8.	c	12.	F

13. F	24. c	33. Golding's *Lord of the Flies*
14. F	25. d	34. George Bernard Shaw
15. T	26. e	35. Aldous Huxley
16. F	27. b	36. Harold Pinter
17. T	28. g	37. *Kipps*
18. T	29. f	38. G. Bernard Shaw, H. G. Wells
19. F	30. a	39. Doris Lessing
20. T	31. *Look Back in Anger*	40. Samuel Beckett
21. i	32. Huxley's *Brave New World*	
22. j		
23. h		

Part 5

TRADITION AND REVOLT IN POETRY

Like the majority of the intellectuals and artists of their generation, the poets entered the twentieth century in a rebellious mood. The century began in one of those periodic revolts against poetic convention which break out whenever poetry becomes too artificial; similar movements, it will be recalled, took place in the Renaissance and at the time of the nineteenth-century Romantic movement. The twentieth century poetic rebels, however, lacked any single philosophy of rebellion around which to rally; the only quality they all shared was an intense individualism. Thus the twentieth century is an era of schools and movements of great diversity: surrealism, imagism, dada, Symbolism, and a score of movements that are none the less distinct for remaining unnamed.

It is nevertheless possible to group these diverse movements roughly under two headings: (1) the poets who abandon artificiality and preciosity of any kind and seek to return to a natural vernacular idiom; and (2) the opposite group who plunge into various forms of Symbolism, obscurantism, experimental reconstruction of language, and esoteric systems of prosody. For convenience we shall term these two groups "verse naturalism" and "experimental verse" respectively, although the second term especially includes techniques of such variety and diversity as to make it virtually a presumption to speak of them under one heading. This second group, however, is by far the larger and more significant of the two, particularly in Europe.

WORKS AT A GLANCE

John Masefield

1902	*Salt-Water Ballads,* "Sea-Fever," "The West Wind'	1912	*Dauber*
		1919	*Reynard the Fox*

Wilfred Owen

1920	*"Dulce et Decorum Est,"* "Disabled"

Gerard Manley Hopkins

1876	"The Wreck of the Deutschland"	1880–82	"Spring and Fall"
1877	"God's Grandeur," "The Windhover," "Pied Beauty"		

Robert Bridges

	"A Passer-By" "On a Dead Child"	1880	"London Snow"
		1929	*The Testament of Beauty*

A. E. Houseman

1896	*A Shropshire Lad,* "Loveliest of Trees, the Cherry Now," "With Rue My Heart Is Laden,"		"When I Was One and Twenty," "Is My Team Ploughing," "Epilogue" "The Carpenter's Son"

W. H. Auden

1940	*Another Time,* "Musée des Beaux Arts," "In Memory of W. B. Yeats" "O What Is That Sound?" "Mundus at Infans" "September 1, 1939"	1947	*The Age of Anxiety*
		1965	*About the House*
		1969	*City Without Walls and Other Poems*
1941	*The Double Man*	In collaboration with Christopher Isherwood:	
1945	*Collected Poetry, For the Time Being*	1935	*The Dog Beneath the Skin*
		1938	*The Ascent of F.6, On the Frontier*

Stephen Spender

1928	*Nine Entertainments*	1939	*The Still Center,* "An Elementary School Class Room in a Slum"
1930	*Twenty Poems*		
1933	*Poems,* "The Express"		
1934	*Vienna*	1951	*World Within World*
1938	*The Trial of a Judge*	1969	*Learning Laughter, The Year of the Young Rebels*

Dylan Thomas

1934	*Eighteen Poems*, "The Force That Through the Green Fuse Drives"
1936	*Twenty-Five Poems*, sonnets
1939	*World I Breathe, The Map of Love*
1940	*A Portrait of the Artist as a Young Dog*
1945	"A Refusal to Mourn the Death, by Fire, of a Child in London," "Do Not Go Gentle into That Good Night"
1952	*In Country Sleep*
1952–53	*The Collected Poems of Dylan Thomas*
1954	*Under Milk Wood* "A Child's Christmas in Wales" "When All My Five and Country Senses See" "Twenty-four Years"

Louis MacNeice

1929	*Blind Fireworks*
1935	"Sunday Morning" "The British Museum Reading Room" "Morning Sun" "Birmingham"
1938	"Among These Turf-Stacks" "Bagpipe Music"
1944	*Springboard, Christopher Columbus*
1947	*The Dark Tower*
1948	*Holes in the Sky*

Edith Sitwell

1915	*The Mother*
1922	*Façade*
1923	*Bucolic Comedies*, "Aubade"
1925	*Poor Young People and Other Poems* (with Osbert and Sacheverell Sitwell)
1929	*Gold Coast Customs*
1930	*Alexander Pope*
1933	*English Eccentrics*
1942	*Street Songs*, "Still Falls the Rain"
1944	*Green Song and Other Poems*
1945	*The Song of the Cold*
1947	*The Shadow of Cain*
1949	*The Canticle of the Rose*
1950	*A Book of the Winter*
1962	*The Queens and the Hive*
1963	*Gardeners and Astronomers*
1965	*Taken Care Of*

David Jones

1937	*In Parenthesis*
1952	*Anathemata*
1967	"A, a, a, Domine Deus"

Philip Larkin

1945	*The North Ship*
1946	*Jill*
1947	*A Girl in Winter*
1955	*The Less Deceived*, "Poetry of Departures," "Church Going"
1964	*The Whitsun Weddings*, "Here"
1969	*All That Jazz*

John Silkin

1954	*The Peaceable Kingdom,*	1965	*Nature with Man,*
	"Death of a Son"		"Dandelion," "Lilies of
1958	*The Two Freedoms*		the Valley," "Peonies,"
1961	*The Re-Ordering of the*		"A Daisy"
	Stones	1966	*Poems Selected and New*

Donald Davie

1983	"Across the Bay"		"To Certain English Poets"

Thom Gunn

1979	"Considering the Snail"	1983	"Human Condition"

Ted Hughes

1972	"Relic"	1979	"A Disaster"

Seamus Heaney

1975	"The Grauballe Man"	1982	"Punishment"

Elaine Feinstein

1976	"Waiting"	1979	"Night Thoughts"

Molly Holden

1979	"Photograph of a	1972	"Some Men Create"
	Haymaker, 1890"		

Stevie Smith

1936	*Novel on Yellow Paper*	1957	"Is It Wise"
1937	*A Good Time Was Had by All*	1942	"Our Bog is Dood"

11
THE VERSE NATURALISTS

One of the important literary aspects of the Renaissance was its revolt against the stultified Latinism of the late middle ages and its attempt to recreate a popular vernacular literature. In the nineteenth century Wordsworth, one of the focal figures of the Romantic movement, was likewise inspired to abandon artificial poetic convention and to return to a diction, if not a content, comprehensible by the ordinary plowman. In America Walt Whitman, in the middle of the century, renounced conventional prosody entirely and wrote simply and sincerely in a sort of unembellished free verse. Each of these attempts represented an experiment in what later came to be known in the twentieth century as verse naturalism. It is noteworthy that all these earlier vernacular revivals were involved with romantic movements. Twentieth century vernacular poetry is connected to a vastly different literary school: the pseudoscientific Naturalism of the late nineteenth century.

For this reason the twentieth century verse naturalists share certain qualities with the prose naturalists of the order of Zola, Dreiser, or Hemingway. In diction they shun artificiality or preciosity; their vocabulary is simple, and they avoid bizarre images or highly complex construction. In content they seek to return to the commonplace, although they often disagree on what this commonplace is to be. In the case of Robert Frost and E. A. Robinson it is the simple rural life that had earlier appeared in the poetry of Wordsworth and Hugo and is represented in the Wessex poems of Thomas Hardy, the Naturalist who most wanted to be known for his poetry. For Carl Sandburg the true commonplace of our century is the world of the factory, the locomotive, the metropolis, and the dynamo. For John Masefield man's common life is related to the sea and sailing. Wilfred Owen had to find his commonplace with soldiers on the battlefield.

In all instances the aim is the same: to abandon the exotic and imaginative themes that so often dominate poetry and to return for subject matter to the interests and activities of the common man.

JOHN MASEFIELD (1878–1967)

In his early career Masefield thought of himself as a vigorous rebel against the poetic artificiality of the Victorians. He renounced the traditional poetic diction of his time to turn to the vernacular of the street, the farm, and the forecastle; he achieved a refreshing simplicity, so much so that his early verse at times approaches crudity. But his rebellion was always tempered by an innate sentimentality; Masefield is by temperament a romantic rather than an iconoclast. Although he is generally thought of as a poet of the sea, his sea experience was small compared to that of Conrad or Pierre Loti; he views seafaring life from a distance, as a landsman does, and casts over it a veil of sentimentalized glamour. His best-known sailor-hero, the "Dauber" of the poem by that name, is not a seaman at all but a sensitive young artist who is unhappy and out of place on a sailing ship. In content Masefield is a typical romanticist; he seeks escape into the archaic and exotic, and views even the squalor of the present through the haze of sentimentality.

It is rather in diction and other technical matters that Masefield is to be classed with the verse naturalists. Like Wordsworth, Sandburg, Frost, and Dehmel, he seeks to confine himself to the diction of the worker and the farmer; he avoids artificial poetic imagery and intricate experiments in prosody. His favorite verse form is the simple iambic pentameter, rhyming in couplets or in *abab* quatrains. Such early lyrics as "Sea-Fever," which appear to be written in a long seven-beat line, are actually adaptations of the traditional English ballad meter of four-foot and three-foot lines in alternation; Masefield's only innovation is to write two lines as one.

One of Masefield's important contributions is that he helped to bring verse narrative back into public favor. Here he performed much the same function as Robinson Jeffers did in America. In his verse narratives Masefield often imitates Chaucer, not only in the spirit and structure of his work but in the meter of such poems as *Dauber* and *Reynard the Fox*. These narratives are for the most part unremarkable in technique and often spotty in quality; sections of rare descriptive power alternate with long stretches of doggerel. He differs from Robinson Jeffers in that his narratives are less symbolically pretentious; he makes no attempt to load his story with psychological meanings and associations as Jeffers does.

Life

John Masefield was born in Herefordshire in 1878, son of a provincial lawyer. After attending King's School, Warwick, he decided at thirteen to become a merchant marine officer; he served as cadet aboard the famous training ship *Conway* and shipped out at fifteen on a sailing ship. He made only one voyage under sail, however, and from 1895 he definitely abandoned the sea as a profession. There followed a period of odd jobs in New York and London; gradually his literary ambitions began to take form, and in 1902 he published his first book, *Salt-Water Ballads*. These simple and blunt sea verses won him widespread acclaim; Masefield's popularity continued to increase through the period of the First World War. After the war, in the new and more radical literary atmosphere of the twenties, those critics who had blamed his crudity and frankness now began to accuse him of excessive conservatism. In 1930 he was appointed Poet Laureate to fill the vacancy caused by the death of Robert Bridges; the laureateship was said to have been conferred chiefly on account of *Reynard the Fox*. In his later years Masefield settled on an estate at Boar's Hill, a secluded district near Oxford. He died in 1967, eighty-eight years old, with official words of mourning by Queen Elizabeth II.

Important Poems

"Sea-Fever" (1902): This is the best-known lyric of the *Salt-Water Ballads*. The long heptameter couplets and the repeated use of participles contribute to the general mood of rhythm and wandering that dominates the poem. The three stanzas are mainly devoted to images of sea life, carefully chosen to accentuate the lonely and carefree qualities of the seaman's attitude. The last line may be interpreted as a death metaphor, although the idea is not explicit.

"The West-Wind" (1902): This poem is similar in meter and mood. This time the sailor, wandering about the world, scents the west wind and is reminded of his inland home, where the blossoms of April are bursting forth. Again there is a hint of a death metaphor (the expression "to go west") but the idea is only latent.

***Dauber* (1912):** This narrative poem is drawn mainly from Masefield's single voyage around the Horn. Dauber, the hero, is a quiet lad of twenty-two who wants to become an artist; he has temporarily chosen the sea as a living in order to gain experience. Since he is not a seaman, he lives in the roundhouse with the other "idlers," and officers and crew treat him with derision. He spends his spare hours sketching and painting, but his companions scoff at his efforts and even break in his cabin to wantonly deface his paintings. At last the mate forces him to join the watch aloft as the ship rounds the Horn in winter; after a few days Dauber begins to get the hang of the job, but accidentally falls from a yard and is killed. The crewmen now begin to feel guilt at their treatment of the boy; they admit "A smart young seaman he was getting to be." After Dauber's burial the wind turns fair; the artist was a Jonah in a ship of tough seafaring men. Yet the men are left with "beauty in their hearts" through their contact with the despised artist. The best passage in *Dauber* is the masterful description of the rounding of the Horn; the weakest are those concerned with Dauber's aesthetic sentimentality.

***Reynard the Fox* (1919):** Another narrative poem, this is a novel and effective poetic story of a rural English fox-hunt. The poem is frankly modelled on Chaucer; it opens with a prologue introducing the characters in the manner of the *Canterbury Tales*. The verse pattern, however, is the tetrameter couplet of the traditional Teutonic ballad *(Knittelvers)*. The first half of the long narrative is devoted to the human participants in the story: the excitement of the hunters as they race after the trace of the fox, the minor mishaps that arrive as they leap fences and brooks, and the technical details of fox-hunting strategy. The poem then shifts to the fox himself; his emotions, as well as his tactics, are shown in their turn. Fleeing madly toward his "home country" where a secure hiding-place awaits him, the fox narrowly escapes the hounds several times. He is finally saved when another fox crosses his trail; the hunters follow this new spoor and Reynard slips away unnoticed. The poem then returns briefly to the human characters and finishes with an idyllic description of night creeping over the countryside.

Reynard the Fox is especially interesting as a documentary picture of an English folk custom. Fox hunting is shown, not as the aristocratic recreation it is sometimes thought in America, but as a democratic country ritual involving all social classes from small farmer to aristocrat. Stylistically the poem is erratic; if it often lacks Chaucer's spontaneity and bluntness, it is successful in its portraits of rural hunters and its sustained mood of excitement.

WILFRED OWEN (1893–1918)

Wilfred Owen illustrates the truth of the Latin phrase *Ars longa vita brevis est* (Art is long, life is short). Cut off at the age of twenty-five by machine-gun fire on the front in France on November 4, 1918 just seven days before the armistice was signed, he had lived a relatively uneventful life of which the last year seems to have been the most exciting with his closest friendship and breakthrough in poetic commitment and production. He published only four poems during his lifetime, the first in a hospital magazine, *The Hydra,* in September of 1917. But following his death a series of English poets of stature in their own right dedicated willing efforts to collecting (some from scraps of paper in his effects), editing, publishing, and analyzing his poems beginning with Siegfried Sassoon and Edith Sitwell who prepared from manuscripts the first collection that appeared in 1920 all the way to Jon Silkin who in the sixties continued the promotion of Wilfred Owen as the greatest of England's First World War poets and including Edmund Blunden, C. Day Lewis, and Dylan Thomas.

IMPORTANCE

Although Stephen Crane with *The Red Badge of Courage* (1895) had begun to take the romance and glory out of war, Owen was the first English poet to present firsthand a realistic-naturalistic picture of what twentieth century warfare meant in human, honest terms, without recourse to religious, patriotic, or other cant phrasing. What came out was good material for pacifist organizations, and, more important, works of art because of his eye for detail and utter truth telling.

Life

Wilfred, the oldest of four children (one a girl), was born March 18, 1893 at Plas Wilmot, Oswestry, Shropshire. His father, tied to a responsible but poorly paying post with a railway company, was never able to bring the family out of poverty. His mother, and Wilfred was Mother's boy, was something of a religious fanatic, conservative and evangelical Established Church. In September of 1911 Wilfred passed entrance examinations for London University, but there was no money to send him. His mother, through clerical friends, got him a place as lay assistant to a vicar, the Reverend Herbert Wigan, in Oxfordshire (the kind of opportunity Hardy's Jude Fawley had envisioned), hoping that he would go on to enter the church. Wilfred reacted in the opposite way, finding confirmation of his earlier doubts of orthodox institutional Christianity. He wrote to his younger brother Harold denouncing the Established Church as departing from the teachings of Christ. He was also ready to abandon Poetry with the capital P for something more sincere and felt.

Having been ill and disappointed in his local environment, Wilfred answered an advertisement by the Berlitz School of Languages and got a part-time teaching job (English) in Bordeaux, France, which he held during 1913–14. (What with Joyce and Owen perhaps someone should investigate the Berlitz patronage of men of letters.) He then became a private tutor in a Bordeaux family and became friends with Laurent Tailhade, a minor French Symbolist poet.

With the advent of the war Owen returned to England and joined up. In 1916 he was commissioned and went on active duty in France. In less than a year as a victim of shell-burst and shell-shock he was transferred to Craiglockhart War Hospital in Edinburgh, where he met another poet who had already published in his own language and nearer his own age, Siegfried Sassoon, a war hero who, as a result of declared pacifism in the middle of the war, throwing his Military Cross into the River Mersey and refusing to return to the slaughter, had been sent to hospital as obviously "shell-shocked" instead of being court-martialled. They talked "poetry," stimulating without seriously influencing each other. Sassoon introduced Owen to a circle of men of letters, including Osbert Sitwell, young Guards officer and poet, H. G. Wells, and Arnold Bennett. Leaving the hospital he was given light duty in training others at Scarborough, where he wrote poetry and letters to his new friends Sassoon and Sitwell. Owen in a burst of enthusiasm planned a collection of poems, with a tentative table of contents and a Preface which begins:

> This book is not about heroes. English poetry is not yet fit to speak of them.
> Nor is it about deeds, or lands, nor anything about glory, honour, might, majesty, dominion, or power, except War.
> Above all I am not concerned with Poetry.

My subject is War, and the pity of War.
The Poetry is in the pity.
Yet these elegies are to this generation in no sense consolatory.
They may be to the next. All a poet can do today is warn. That is
why the true Poets must be truthful.

At the end of August 1918 Owen, refusing efforts of friends to find him a
safe post in England, reembarked for France with premonitions of the end.
For his grave his mother chose his own words from a sonnet called "The
End," which begins:

> *After the blast of lightning from the east*
> *The flourish of loud clouds, the Chariot Throne;*
> *After the drums of time have rolled and ceased,*
> *And by the bronze west long retreat is blown,*
>
> *Shall Life renew these bodies? Of a truth*
> *All death will be annul, all tears assuage?—*
> *Or fill these void veins full again with youth,*
> *And wash, with an immortal water, Age?*
>
> *When I do ask white Age he saith not so . . . .*

And then Earth says:

> *"My fiery heart shrinks, aching. It is death.*
> *Mine ancient scars shall not be glorified,*
> *Nor my titanic tears, the seas, be dried."*

Ironically his mother made two small changes, one capital letter and one
mark of punctuation: "Of a truth / All death will He annul, all tears assuage."
The bereaved mother "reverses her son's intention and imposes her own," to
use the words of Gertrude White in her book on the poet. This may be the
truth, but not as Wilfred Owen saw it.

Representative Poems

"*Dulce et Decorum Est*"from the 1920 volume is one of the most perfectly
conceived and executed of all of Owen's poems. The first stanza describes
the soldiers with one of them speaking in words so exact that paraphrase is
impossible: "Bent double, like old beggars under sacks,/ Knock-kneed,
coughing like hags, we cursed through sludge. . . ./ Men marched asleep.
Many had lost their boots,/ But limped on, blood-shod. All went lame, all
blind;/ Drunk with fatigue; deaf even to the hoots/ Of gas shells dropping
softly behind." In the second stanza one of the soldiers gives the warning:
GAS! and the men put on their masks, but the one that gave the warning
doesn't make it and in the green light "plunges at me, guttering, choking,
drowning." The third stanza is an address to *You*, presumably one safe at
home, if you could see him in the wagon we flung the body on, "If you could

hear, at every jolt, the blood/ Come gargling from the froth-corrupted lungs . . . — My friend, you would not tell with such high zest/ To children ardent for some desperate glory,/ The old Lie: *Dulce et decorum est/ Pro patria mori.*"

Interestingly enough this is almost the identical use made of the same Latin phrase by Ezra Pound in one section of *Hugh Selwyn Mauberley,* also published in 1920:

> *Died some, pro patria,*
> > *non "dulce" non "et decor" . . .*
> *walked eye-deep in hell*
> *believing in old men's lies, then unbelieving*
> *came home, home to a lie, . . .*
>
> *There died a myriad,*
> *And of the best, among them,*
> *For an old bitch gone in the teeth,*
> *For a botched civilization . . .*

It would not do to suggest that either knew the other's work, but Owen's poem can stand beautifully on its own merits. Pound's is a different thing — with the same sentiment — in a different context, bitterly satiric, flippantly ironic, almost self-indulgent in the ode for the selection of his own monument toward which fifty years later he still crawled.

"Disabled" is a deeply felt poem about one of the war wounded, mutilated, legless and without forearms, sitting in his chair "waiting for dark." Boys and girls play and dance in the late afternoon, and the amputee can only remember the past, "how slim Girls' waists are" and an old football injury — "One time he liked a blood-smear down his leg,/ After the matches." Why did he join up? Perhaps to please his girl. A man looks handsome in uniform. It certainly wasn't because he had any enemies, "Germans he scarcely thought of." Now "a few sick years in Institutes." "How cold and late it is! . . . Why don't they come?"

12
VARIETIES OF EXPERIMENTAL VERSE

Authors, especially poets, developed an increasing tendency after 1850 to write for a limited group of *cognoscenti* rather than for the public as a whole. This tendency, which was enormously accelerated during the Symbolist era of the nineties, rose to a second climax in the period following the First World War. Poetry tended to become the exclusive possession of schools, movements, and cults, each self-sufficient and each believing itself to be struggling in the very vanguard of modern literature.

The poetry produced by these various groups shares at least one quality: it is never obvious, and it is quite commonly difficult or esoteric. It is generally the product of highly educated poets who have a wide background in languages, literary history, and philosophy; Eliot, Rilke, Valéry, Auden, and Spender are all men of a highly erudite culture. This is not to say that these poets are academic in attitude; on the contrary they are often antagonistic toward university disciplines and academic criticism. Many of them, it would seem, spend their lives overcompensating for their failure to impress their professors as undergraduates. Their pedanticism, when it occurs, is their own; their allusions and their classic echoes are none the less obscure for the lay reader.

It should be remarked that the most prominent influence on this entire movement is that of the Symbolist school. In the case of the English poets this often means Yeats; in the case of the continentals it is more commonly Mallarmé or Verlaine. From this school the moderns borrowed their interest in sensory associations, which they further refined by the addition of modern Freudian and Jungian psychology. The nineteenth century Symbolists also share with many modern poets a certain morbidity, apparently deriving from a repugnance toward modern materialism and a disillusionment with the ideals of democracy and science.

There seems to be little consistency in the political attitudes of these poets, unless it is the fact that they are all dissatisfied with the *status quo.* Eliot objects to the tendency of modern democracy to become mobocracy, and therefore assumes a royalist and conservative stand; Auden and Spender, blaming capitalism for the vacuity of modern culture, take the opposite course and turn toward the left. The conservative Eliot and the reactionary Pound appear to be exceptions; the more typical poet of the century is a liberal or radical. On the other hand he is wary of parties; he may espouse socialism or even communism sporadically, but his innate individualism makes him a poor group worker.

It is remarkable as well that an unusual number of modern poets are expatriates for one reason or another. Eliot abandoned America for England, Auden moved in the opposite direction, Rilke lived out his life as a permanent wanderer, and a crowd of American poets established in Paris a little expatriate society complete in itself. This tendency of the avant-garde poet to deny his origins stands in sharp contrast to the nostalgia for the homeland of verse naturalists. Hardy and Yeats, considered elsewhere in this volume, are poets of stature and should be reconsidered here. Many critics would view Yeats as the most important of the entire group, the peer of the American-British Eliot, the German Rilke, and the French Valéry. Auden would now probably emerge as his closest competitor, with Dylan Thomas not far behind.

GERARD MANLEY HOPKINS (1844–88)

Hopkins' poems were almost totally unappreciated during his lifetime; they were read only by a small circle of his friends and were not published until 1918, thirty years after his death. Their publication at this time was an important literary milestone; the poems deeply impressed the postwar generation of poets who were deliberately searching about for new techniques. Hopkins' curious metrical system suggested the most radical experiments of the twentieth century, and his vividly condensed imagery was as advanced as that of the formal Imagist school of Ezra Pound and Amy Lowell. Hopkins' difficult and often obscure verse is still unknown to the general reading public, but his acceptance by a half-dozen English and American poets alone would mark him as an important literary figure. Like Gertrude Stein, his chief literary importance lies in his technical influence on younger writers.

Hopkins himself referred to his metrical system as "sprung rhythm." Essentially it is a pattern common to much primitive and archaic poetry, although there are certain original elements in the system as Hopkins utilized it. Its principle is that each line has a fixed number of stressed syllables — usually four or five — and an unspecified number of unstressed syllables. Thus two stressed syllables may come together without any intervening beat or they may be separated by four or five off-beats. This pattern is found in Anglo-Saxon poetry; in fact it is the dominant metrical system in English verse up to the time it began to be influenced by French poetry in the eleventh century. Hopkins also uses alliteration, another device of Anglo-Saxon and Teutonic poetry; he adds to it run-over rhymes, consonant rhymes, inversions, and other iconoclastic poetic devices. His poetry, which seems loose almost to the point of approaching free verse, is actually highly formal;

it adheres to rules of its own as strict as those of traditional iambic verse. The content of his poetry is usually unremarkable, or at least unoriginal; it is in technique that his work is important.

IMPORTANCE

A key concept in Hopkins' work is that poetry should concern itself with "inscapes," which he himself described as limited and precisely delineated images from nature conveyed in language appropriate or equivalent to the image concerned. Poetry is to communicate chiefly the experience of nature, and the flow of language is to match the sensation described in rhythm and general emotional impact. In addition Hopkins sought to rid his verse of particles, relative pronouns, suffixes, and other non-imagistic parts of speech; each word was to contribute to the total "inscape." It is here that his kinship with the formal Imagist school is to be found. Hopkins declared that his verse could not be properly understood unless it was read aloud; his metrical innovations and his imagistic nouns and verbs were intended entirely for auditory impact. Here he adumbrates Dylan Thomas and E. E. Cummings, two poets whose work often resembles his own in technique.

Life

Gerard Manley Hopkins was born in 1844 into a moderately High Church British family; he remained a devoted British patriot all his life. An apt scholar, he won prizes for his verse as a schoolboy. He entered Oxford in 1863; there he came under the influence of the aesthete Walter Pater and the liberal classicist Benjamin Jowett. Before he left Oxford, however, he had surrendered to a new influence: the Roman Catholicism of Cardinal Newman, who had left Oxford in 1845 and was now the focus of an English Catholic revival. He graduated in 1867 and a year later he had become a Jesuit novice; he burned most of his youthful poems upon taking orders.

Hopkins spent the rest of his life as a Jesuit priest. He served in parishes in London, Oxford, Glasgow, and Liverpool; he taught in a Jesuit school, and in 1884 went to Dublin as Professor of Greek at University College. For many years he denied himself the pleasure of writing poetry; he returned to it in 1875 only at the specific suggestion of his superiors. When he began to write again his first production was the difficult and extremely advanced "Wreck of the Deutschland," which was refused by a Jesuit magazine. He continued to write up to the time of his death, but his verse was read and comprehended only by three friends, with whom he maintained a lifetime correspondence later published: the poets Robert Bridges, Richard Watson Dixon, and Coventry Patmore. Always in poor health, Hopkins died in 1888 at the age of only forty-four.

Important Poems

"The Wreck of the Deutschland" (poem, 1876) is Hopkins' first poem in his distinctively original style. The inspiration for the poem came from accounts of a German ship bound for America, which was wrecked on the Kentish coast in the winter of 1875. Among the drowned were five Franciscan nuns, exiles from Germany bound for America to take up a new life. The themes of the poem are two: expression of awe and respect toward the grandeur of God, and wonder that God's ways should include the sacrifice of the innocent nuns who have already been persecuted for their love of God. Stanzas 1-10 are devoted to praise of God and comparison of his grandeur with the pettiness of man. The second part of the poem, beginning with Stanza 11, describes the sailing and destruction of the vessel on a stormy Sunday morning in December of 1875. The pitiable fate of the nuns and their heroic stoicism are especially stressed. Yet the nuns, like all humanity, are mortal flesh. Flesh and spirit are the twin poles of man's existence; "Abel is Cain's brother." Stanza 24 recalls the poet's own comfortable circumstances in a Welsh house on the night of the disaster. The poem then turns to a philosophical treatment of the problem of suffering: why have these five been chosen out of mankind for destruction? Consolation is found in recalling the even more poignant sacrifice of Christ (Stanzas 30-31), and the poem concludes (Stanza 35) with a prayer that these sufferers, as well as ourselves, may be remembered in "the heaven-haven of reward." Thus the nuns' fate seems less cruel in the light of their eventual entry into bliss.

"God's Grandeur" (sonnet, 1877) is one of many Hopkins poems written roughly in the sonnet form. The grandeur of God is inherent in all nature, yet today, in the industrial age, the ugly soil and stain of civilization lie across it: trade and toil have blighted the earth. Yet nature is never spent (ll. 9ff); the Holy Ghost still hovers over the earth and blesses it with the divine spark. The power of this poem lies chiefly in its choice of images: "shook foil" for the grandeur of God, and the image-series "bleared . . . smeared . . . smudge . . . smell" for the ugliness of industrialism and commercialism.

"The Windhover" (sonnet, 1877) is an imagistic study of the soaring bird known also as the kestrel, a type of falcon. The poetic tempo of the poem follows the gyrations of the windhover's soaring; he slips off into a dive "as a skate's heel sweeps smooth on a bow-bend." The poet's heart is touched with awe at "the mastery of the thing"; here Hopkins conveys his feeling for nature as a manifestation of the divine ingenuity of God.

"Pied Beauty" (poem, 1877) reflects Hopkins' admiration of "dappled things," a predilection he also mentions in "The Windhover." All the dappled and freckled things of nature are praised, then contrasted at the end of the poem with God whose "beauty is past change," undappled.

"Spring and Fall" (poem, 1880–1882) is important for its poetic statement of the concept of "inscape." The inscape of each object or creature, the poem explains, is its functional essence: "What I do is me: for that I came." This ontological statement is then applied to man's ethical position; man's duty is to act in God's eye what in God's eye he is, i.e. to follow his divine mold instead of surrendering to his baser fleshly nature.

ROBERT BRIDGES (1844–1930)

Robert Bridges' poetry is a curious mixture of old and new. Steeped in classic culture and in Milton, he is fond of obsolete diction and of the poetic devices of the seventeenth century; and the romantic idealism of his content often resembles that of the mid-Victorians. Yet he was influenced by Gerard Manley Hopkins and others to seek a new and more radical system of prosody, a system with roots in Anglo-Saxon poetry and thus uniquely and characteristically English. He never carried his experiments in meter as far as Hopkins' "sprung rhythm"; he was sufficiently grounded in classic poetry to retain a symmetrical rhythm in his line. The influence of Latin poetry is seen in his return to the hexameter; *The Testament of Beauty* is written in "loose Alexandrines" which combine traditional hexameter construction with a variation in the number of off-beats as in Hopkins. Such innovations are more characteristic of Bridges' later work; his early poetry is usually cast in traditional English pentameter.

In content too his work shows a mixture. Traditional poetic material, including Greek mythology and the love and nature themes of English poetry, are present; but in his later work modern elements are seen to creep in. Bridges was deeply impressed with the theory of evolution, and sought to elevate this doctrine to an aesthetic and ethical plane. Yet this pseudoscientific interest is interwoven with an almost Keatsian respect for abstract beauty; indeed *The Testament of Beauty* postulates ideal beauty as an end or goal of the evolutionary process.

Bridges' popularity and his laureateship, however, are due not so much to the nature of his technique or materials as to the general atmosphere of his verse. Serene and optimistic, he moves on a plane far above the pitched social and literary battles of his time; he is eminently a poet of the middle classes. He is untouched by the socialism and humanitarianism that inspired so many of his contemporaries; in fact he often seems to reflect an ill-concealed dislike of the worker and the peasant. He thus pleased an officialdom and a public that were baffled and antagonized at the radicalism, both social and literary, of the poets of his day; he wrote in a style familiar to readers of Tennyson and Arnold, and the public, which accepted him for his literary conservatism, chose to ignore his modest experiments in prosody and content.

Life

Bridges was born in Kent in 1844 of well-to-do landowning parents; he was educated at Eton and Oxford. After studying medicine at St. Bartholomew's Hospital in London he actually practiced as a physician until 1882. Meanwhile, however, he had turned his hand to poetry, and as soon as his financial situation would permit he turned to a full-time pursuit of literature. His first volume of poems was published in 1873; his dramas, most of them based on Greek mythology, appeared chiefly between 1884 and 1905. Although his work was praised from the first by a small circle of critics and friends, he was virtually unknown to the general public when he was appointed Poet Laureate in 1913. He never achieved a popularity comparable to that of Kipling or Masefield even after he became Laureate; he was a singularly independent official poet, and several times rejected suggestions that he write occasional poems or addresses. During most of his laureateship he was working on the poem he considered the masterpiece of his career: *The Testament of Beauty.* This work appeared in 1929 and was generally favorably received, although most readers found it less enjoyable than his earlier and shorter poems. He died the following year at eighty-six, his creativity still active and unimpaired.

Important Poems

"A Passer-By" is a descriptive piece typical of the lyric power of Bridges' early work. In the first stanza a sailing ship is described as it leaves the harbor for a tropic voyage. In Stanza II the poet's imagination flies before the ship and views its entry into an exotic foreign port; gradually the ship takes on mystery as a symbol of abstract beauty, its crowning white sails suggesting inspiration. In Stanza III the poet begins to doubt whether the actual ship he has seen has "a courage blameless" and is worthy of bearing this symbolism; yet he concludes that the impression of beauty produced by the ship is valid nonetheless.

"On a Dead Child" is a descriptive threnody inspired by the sight of a child at its funeral ceremony. The poem is mainly devoted to pathetic contemplation, but Stanza VI contains a reflection: the poet questions whether the child has passed on to a realm where injustice like its own death is banished. He ends by restraining his prayer that the child be brought back to this more anguished life. This poem is also important for the example it provided for later poems on the same theme, such as those of Dylan Thomas and John Crowe Ransom.

"London Snow" is a lyric description of snow falling over the grimy city and transforming it into a wonderland of whiteness. The poem is technically adroit; the motion and feel of falling snow is suggested in ll. 3–9 by a profusion of participles and by subtle onomatopoeia: "lazily and incessantly . . . Silently sifting." As morning comes and the sun breaks over the city, the landscape gleams with eye-shattering brilliance; but soon the workmen trudging to their toil smear brown paths in the virgin purity. Thus the final thought is the contrast between the purity of nature and the soil of the human city.

The Testament of Beauty (poem, 1929) is an ambitious philosophical treatise divided into four parts: "Introduction," "Selfhood," "Breed," and "Ethick." The meter is a hexameter roughly modelled after Latin poetry; Bridges refers to the pattern as "loose Alexandrine." The poem has been compared to such works as Lucretius' *De Rerum Natura* and Wordsworth's *Prelude;* it was partly inspired by the former.

The theme is the presentation of evolutionary doctrine in the light of Christian revelation, the evolutionary process interpreted as a steady exaltation of mankind toward beauty, truth, and love. Love in its primordial state is a mere bestial lust. But it is purified as the creature evolves; in man it reaches a higher plane, and in exceptional individuals (such as Dante and Beatrice) it may transcend the flesh entirely. Thus the poem, ostensibly based on Christian doctrine, reaches a conclusion not unlike the Platonic doctrine of universal ideals attainable through the pursuit of beauty and culminating in the attainment of the Good, the True, and the Beautiful in the divine purity.

A. E. HOUSMAN (1859–1936)

The publication of *A Shropshire Lad* in 1896 was one of the great literary events of the era, rivalling the effect produced by Fitzgerald's *Rubaiyat of Omar Khayyam.* But Housman's influence was more far-reaching in the end; the unadorned economy of his verse appealed to poets of the twentieth century long after Fitzgerald's oriental preciosity had gone out of date.

IMPORTANCE

In style Housman is eminently a poet of the twentieth century; he resembles the poets of the 1920s more than he does any poet of his own time. The outstanding characteristics of his verse are its directness of expression and its total abandonment of conventional poetic intricacy; its felicity of diction; and its economy of imagery, a sort of starkness which sets Housman off sharply from contemporaries like Yeats as well as from the twentieth century Imagists. It is Housman's extremely sparing use of adjectives and adverbs that gives his verse the power of language composed almost entirely of verbs and nouns.

Housman's content is generally pessimistic. Even in such outwardly serene lyrics as "Loveliest of Trees" the shadow of inexorable death is present in the background. Death, in fact, is one of the chief protagonists of Housman's poetry. Deeply stricken by the death of his mother in 1871, he retained all his life a preoccupation with the end which awaits all human endeavor. Naturally a pleasure-seeking person, he was driven by his sense of the imminence of death to a heightened *carpe diem* attitude; his poetry invites the reader to seize the day with its passing pleasure, for each day that slips away brings the inevitable end closer. Often this thought takes a cynical turn; in "Is My Team Ploughing" the dead lover is assured that his beloved's grief is being assuaged through the attentions of the poet himself.

Life

Alfred Edward Housman was born in the Worcestershire village of Fockbury in 1859. He was the eldest of a family of seven, several of whom (e.g. the dramatist Edward Housman) attained success in their own fields. The poet's mother died when he was twelve; the shock of this grief remained with him all his life. A brilliant student at Bromsgrove School, he won a scholarship to Oxford. Although he failed in "Greats" at the University because of his preoccupation with independent studies, he went on, after a long interlude as Patent Office clerk, to become a professor at Oxford and later at Cambridge. Housman, in addition to his poetic career, was one of the most eminent classic scholars of his time. His emendations on Manilius are still the standard commentary in the field. Meanwhile he had turned to writing verse; during a "continuous excitement" in the spring of 1895 he wrote most of the lyrics published the following year in *A Shropshire Lad.* His devotion to poetry was sporadic; his next volume, almost thirty years later, was *Last Poems* (1922). The posthumous *More Poems* (1936) completed his verse; altogether he published in volume form only slightly over a hundred short lyrics. His sole prose work outside the field of classic studies is the lecture *The Name and Nature of Poetry* (1933).

Important Poems

"With Rue My Heart is Laden" is a lyric of the utmost simplicity; its eight lines are typical of the best of Housman's work. The theme is the passing away of youth and the inevitability of death; the concept is conveyed with the use of only four different adjectives and no adverbs at all.

"When I Was One-and-Twenty" cautions against the dangers of youthful emotional involvement; the wise know that to give one's heart away (to love sincerely) brings only grief. Yet each man must learn this for himself; he will never consent to receive the advice from his elders.

"Loveliest of Trees" is a simple lyric in praise of the cherry blooming in springtime. Yet behind this beautiful image the day of death is always hastening nearer; even at twenty there is little time left to go "about the woodlands."

"Is My Team Ploughing" is spoken by a young farmer not long dead and addressed to his best friend. The friend answers that all the dead man's possessions and pleasures continue as before; even his girl, who was disconsolate upon his death, has found solace in the arms of the friend. This mingling of cynicism and compassion is a characteristic note in Housman.

"Epilogue" (sometimes reprinted under the title "Terence, This is Stupid Stuff") is the chief piece of *A Shropshire Lad;* in this poem Housman reveals, not only his attitude toward poetry, but his essential philosophy including the reason behind his deep pessimism. In the first stanza (ll. 1–14) the healthy Shropshire farmers complain to the young poet Terence that his verse is too sad; they urge him to write "a tune to dance to." The rest of the poem composes the poet's answer. In the second stanza (ll. 15–42) he admits that dancing and ale help one to forget his troubles, "The mischief is that 'twill not last." Some more permanent antidote against the cruelty of the world is needed. In the third stanza (ll. 43–58) this antidote is revealed as pessimistic poetry, which produces in us such a profound cynicism that any good fortune that comes our way seems gratuitously splendid: "train for ill and not for good." The final stanza reiterates the theme through parable. The oriental king Mithridates, fearful of treachery, made himself immune to every poison of the earth by sampling them all in ever-increasing doses.

The structure of this poem is curious in that it presents the example after the message, instead of relating the parable first and then offering its interpretation.

"The Carpenter's Son" is a curious and revolutionary interpretation of Jesus on the cross. Far from feeling exultation at his sacrifice, the young man cautions his friends to follow the path of virtue if they do not wish to end badly as he and the thieves at his side have. "Though the midmost hangs for love" it is no less a calamity to be hanged; the sacrifice of Jesus is in vain.

W. H. AUDEN (1907–73)

Auden's work evolved considerably after he began writing in the early thirties. His early poems, strongly influenced by Gerard Manley Hopkins, were difficult and abstruse. The work included in his 1930 collection is not without resemblance to the later T. S. Elliot: the subjects tend to be philosophical or allegorical, and the style is rich with allusion. In this period (1930–1938) Auden seemed to make a deliberate cult of obscurity; he wrote for a small group of specialists and maintained an air of distant superiority toward the general public. As the decade wore on Auden's poetry became successively more direct and candid. By 1939, the time of his abandonment of Britain for America, he turned deliberately to the task of writing for the general public. The best of the light verse written during this period has the delicate irony of Byron's *Don Juan* or of the *New Yorker* type of verse.

In his verse dramas, most of them written in collaboration with Christopher Isherwood, Auden tended toward the esoteric. He had little interest in plot or characterization; his chief concern was in the presentation of various socio-philosophical problems. He skirted these problems lightly and gracefully without ever coming to grips with them in a decisive manner; one feels that Auden was greatly concerned not to appear too obviously and nakedly lucid before his readers.

Life

Wystan Hugh Auden, born in 1907, was the son of a York army doctor. He was educated at Christ Church, Oxford. Upon graduation he taught for five years in a boys' school at Malvern. Meanwhile he had become involved in a circle of young poets in London and had formed a close connection with his childhood friend Christopher Isherwood. Under these influences he began to produce verse, his first book-length collection appeared in 1930. He spent 1928 to 1929 in Germany, where Isherwood joined him. In 1937 he went to Spain to serve as an ambulance driver for the Spanish Loyalist cause. In 1938 he joined Isherwood in a trip to China, financed by a publishing firm. The following year both young authors came to America with the intent of making their permanent home here.

Auden's political sympathies were distinctly left wing. During the thirties he was sharply critical of the upper middle-class British milieu from which he sprang, and his name was often associated with communist and radical activities. It is doubtful, however, that he was ever a Communist Party member, and the radical element in his poetry attenuated after 1939.

Auden was active as an editor; he edited two separate editions of *Oxford Poetry* (1926 and 1927) as well as the *Oxford Book of Light Verse* (1938). In America he served on the faculties of various colleges including the University of Michigan. His wife was Erika Mann, daughter of Thomas Mann and an author in her own right, although the marriage was probably one of convenience, passport, and citizenship. Auden continued to publish poetry, *Another Time* in 1940, *The Double Man* in 1941, *Collected Poetry,* 1945, and two verse dramas all his own, *For the Time Being,* a Christmas Oratorio in 1945, and *The Age of Anxiety,* a baroque eclogue in 1947. After the war he returned temporarily to England where he took the role of elder statesman of the poets. Among later pronouncements and publications were *About the House* (1965) and *City Without Walls and Other Poems* (1969). Sometimes referred to as the modern Byron, he slowly edged Eliot out of position: the post First World War period was the Wasteland; the post Second World War period was The Age of Anxiety, reflecting the more existential nature of the metaphor and Auden's influence. His satiric view was the temper of the times.

Chief Drama

***The Ascent of F.6* (1936):** The best of Auden's three semipoetic dramas written with Christopher Isherwood, it concerns the efforts of Michael Ransom, a young scholar, to scale F.6, a dangerous mountain in the fictional European country of Ostnia. Three of Ransom's friends lose their lives in the expedition, but Ransom finally achieves his goal. During a pause in the ascent he converses with an Abbot, who explains to him that each human being is dominated by a Daemon who drives him to achieve the goals of his ambition. By opposing our will to the Daemon, we only throw ourselves more completely into its power. Yet to follow the Daemon and conquer our chosen obstacle is also futile, since neither ourselves nor the world will recognize a deed committed under such compulsion. When he reaches the top of the peak Ransom discovers the Daemon is an aspect of his mother. She has always rejected him and forced him to difficult tasks out of her love for him, since "the truly strong man is he who stands most alone." The technique of this work is influenced by the "epic theatre" concept of the German dramatist Bertold Brecht.

Other dramas by Auden and Isherwood are *The Dog Beneath the Skin* (1935) and *On the Frontier* (1938). These plays lack any convincing protagonist like Ransom to give verisimilitude to the action.

For the Time Being (1944): A Christmas Oratorio, it is a long dramatic poem on the advent, with Narrator, Chorus, and characters like Intuition, Feeling, Sensation, Thought, as well as Gabriel, Mary, Joseph, the Wise Men, the Shepherds, Simeon, and Herod. The ancient characters move curiously in the modern world. Joseph is twitted in the barrooms, "Joseph, you have heard/ What Mary says occurred;/ Yes, it may be so./ Is it likely? No." Gabriel offers him no reason, only "you must believe." The satire of the modern world and of the modern Christmas is intense. As the narrator says at the end, "Well, so that is that. Now we must dismantle the tree . . . / So, once we have met the Son,/ We are tempted ever after to pray to the Father;/ 'Lead us into temptation and evil for our sake.'/ They will come all right, don't worry. . . . / In the meantime/ There are bills to be paid, machines to keep in repair,/ Irregular verbs to learn, the Time Being to redeem/ From insignificance." This is a nativity play with a twist.

The Age of Anxiety (1947): A Baroque Eclogue, it was set to music by Leonard Bernstein. It takes place during the Second World War in a New York City bar where four characters come together in a chance meeting and drink loosens their tongues: Quant, an older American born in Ireland; Malin, a medical intelligence officer on leave from the Canadian Air Force; Rosetta, a department store buyer; and Emble, the young man from the Midwest who had enlisted in the Navy and who is conscious that his uniform is attractive to both sexes. They are all lonely and rather cynical, thinking their thoughts. The bar radio interrupts, "Now the news. Night raids on Five cities. Fires started. Pressure applied by pincer movement In threatening thrust." (The verse is modified Anglo-Saxon alliterative verse, and clever.) The four people are brought together and move from stools to a booth, alternately thinking and speaking. Still together they move through a discussion of The Seven

Ages of Man (following Shakespeare), attempting to open to each other the closed shutters of their inner beings, through The Seven Stages, a quest through wasteland uncertainties, and a dirge as they take a cab to Rosetta's apartment, firmly drunken friends now, then a Masque as Rosetta and Emble make overtures to each other before Emble passes out and Malin and Quant leave. They have found no certain answers, but they have probed deeply into their existential anxieties. In these "plays" as in the short poem, "The Unknown Citizen," Auden takes a long and sharply critical look at the modern world.

Important Poems

"Musée des Beaux Arts" is a poetic analysis of the nature of tragedy, inspired by Brueghel's painting *Icarus*. Auden here rejects the Hellenic and Elizabethan concepts of tragedy in which the hero's personal catastrophe affects his entire world, causing plagues, weird marvels, and universal misery. Tragedy, the poem argues, occurs to individuals, not to worlds; its pathos is heightened by the fact that all about it uncomprehending people are going about their ordinary daily activities. The second stanza alludes to the painting of Brueghel; the plunge and death of the Greek hero, an event which later generations were to consider of the greatest pathos, was probably ignored by its eyewitnesses. The structure of this poem, like that of Housman's "Epilogue," reverses the usual procedure by presenting the example after the message.

"In Memory of W. B. Yeats" is a tribute to the poet who influenced Auden greatly. The first section, a conventional eulogy, reflects that Yeats has now passed into the company of the immortals; he is no longer an individual but an idea in the hearts of many individuals. Although the great mass of humanity is unchanged by the event, "a few thousand" will now cherish his memory with the more fervor. The second section remarks that Ireland is still the same as it was before Yeats began to write; poetry cannot change physical nature, but exists in itself. It survives independently as "a way of happening." The third section, in a rhythmic tetrameter startling in a poem on the subject of death, implies that Yeats as a man and a thinker was sometimes less than sublime. Yet good poetry transcends bad thought; Kipling and Claudel are cited as examples. No matter how mediocre his content, the poet can "still persuade us to rejoice" through his voice of inspiration; his is the truly creative vocation. Thus the final and most important section of this poem widens its scope from Yeats the poet to the whole profession of poetry, and sees in it hope for a disgraced humanity.

"O What Is That Sound" is a ballad-form dialogue between a young man and his beloved; the theme is the ominous menace of war. The girl who views the redcoated troops in the distance is filled with anxiety; her lover attempts to reassure her. But the soldiers come, not for the parson or the "cunning" farmer, but for the lover; it is the young and innocent who must fight the wars their crafty elders prepare for them. This poem is one of several Auden pieces in modernized ballad form.

"Mundus et Infans" is a whimsical tribute to a newborn infant. The first three stanzas reflect humorously on the arrogance of babies; the newborn one tyrannically requires his mother to "supply and deliver his raw materials free." In Stanza 4 the infant is compared with the saint; both are exalted above humanity because of their inability to tell lies, their perfect candor. The final four stanzas praise the infant for his innocence and lack of guile. If we object that the baby's love for us is at the bottom inspired by hunger (Stanza 7), we ought to reflect that adults as well have difficulty in distinguishing between hunger (lust) and love.

"September 1, 1939" was written in a New York bar on the eve of the Second World War. The poem, written in eleven-line rhymed stanzas, consists of a deep personal soliloquy on war and on human degradation in general; the poem ends with the conclusion that "we must love one another or die."

STEPHEN SPENDER (1909–)

Spender is often associated in the public mind with W. H. Auden. There was a certain similarity; both were left wing in politics, both revolt against conventional prosody, and the style of both tends toward the esoteric. The two were personal friends, and have no doubt influenced each other to some extent. There are, however, important differences. Spender is more conservative in technique, and thus his poetry is more comprehensible to the ordinary reader. He also lacks Auden's caustic irony; Spender is the more deliberate, the more sentimental of the two. There is a romantic element in Spender quite lacking in Auden; in fact Spender has often been compared to Shelley in both personal mannerism and poetic style.

Spender's sentimentality does not prevent him from attacking social injustice with a sincere and eloquent ferocity. He views society mainly in terms of the class war: the exploiter starves and deprives the poor, meanwhile consoling them with delusory expectations of divine reward. His romanticism is most apparent in his attitude toward the world of the machine. His express trains, his airliners and pylons are animized into marvelous and magical creatures ready to do the bidding of man and heavy with poetic sentiment.

Life

Stephen Spender was born in London in 1909. His father, Edwin Harold Spender, was a journalist and writer; his mother, born Violet Schuster, was of mixed German and Jewish blood. Spender spent a number of years in University College, Oxford, but failed to complete a degree; meanwhile he travelled extensively in Germany. His companions of the period were Auden, Isherwood, and the poet and critic Cecil Day Lewis, who was later to become the champion of the Auden-Spender group. His first important volume of poems appeared in 1933; the work was warmly praised by such important critics as Herbert Read, Gerald Bullett, and David Daiches, and Spender soon found himself a celebrity. In the winter of 1936–7 he became a Communist Party member for a few weeks, but later became disillusioned with the movement. In 1937 he ignored a British government prohibition to attend the International Writers' Congress in Spain; he stayed on to aid the Loyalist cause and to translate the verse of several young Loyalist poets. During the Second World War Spender, disqualified for military service, edited the influential literary review *Horizon* in collaboration with Cyril Connolly.

After the war Spender spent a good deal of time in the United States, teaching and lecturing at various institutions and universities. He effectively assisted in translating such poets as Rilke and Lorca. In 1951 he published his autobiography, *World Within World,* which gives excellent insights into the "Auden group." Besides poetry and criticism in the sixties Spender produced *Learning Laughter* (1969), a first-hand view of social conditions in Israel, and *The Year of the Young Rebels* (1969), a study of current student protest movements.

World Within World came to unexpected prominence in 1993 when Spender sued writer David Leavitt for allegedly appropriating materials from the autobiography for Leavitt's novel, *While England Sleeps.* At the time of this printing, the courts had not yet ruled on Spender's claim.

Chief Works

Spender published two books before 1933: *Nine Entertainments* (1928) and *Twenty Poems* (1930). His first important work, however, is contained in *Poems* (1933). These poems are chiefly vignettes of modern industry and transportation, mixed with occasional leftist attacks on capitalism. "The Express" is a vivid picture of a train that departs from a station amid music "which no bird song, no, nor bough / Breaking with honey buds, shall ever equal." Traditional poetic content is repudiated in favor of the beauty of modern machinery.

Vienna (1934) is a long and somewhat over-earnest polemic inspired by the massacre of the Vienna workers in the Karl Marx Hof in May 1934.

The Trial of a Judge (dramatic poem, 1938) is a "tragic statement in five acts" portraying the persecution of intellectuals at the hands of fascist governments. The theme is similar to that of Kafka's *The Trial,* but the material is treated in a more obvious manner.

The Still Center (1939) includes poems written after publication of the 1933 collection. Many are pieces concerned with the Spanish Civil War. The most famous single poem of the volume is "An Elementary School Class Room in a Slum." Spender first draws a pathetic picture of undernourished slum children miserably bent over their books in a classroom, then begs society to "break the town / And show the children to the fields and all their world."

DYLAN THOMAS (1914–53)

Dylan Thomas was born near Swansea, Wales, in 1914. His father was an English master at Swansea Grammar School, where the poet himself received his schooling. After dabbling briefly in journalism he turned to poetry; his first volume of verse was published when he was only nineteen. He soon became a member of the literary group that also included Auden, Spender, and MacNeice; his poems were praised by critics but almost ignored by the general public. His early work, comprising that contained in *Eighteen Poems* (1934) and *Twenty-Five Poems* (1934) was extremely, perhaps deliberately, obscure; the poems were based on an intricate private mythology and an esoteric system of association which the poet made no effort to explain, In *World I Breathe* (1939) and *The Map of Love* (1939) he moved toward a greater clarity; and in the poems written during the war, many of them inspired by air raids and war news, he gained for the first time the appreciation of that public which appreciates poetry at all. During the war Thomas contributed to the BBC "Third Program" and was instrumental in attracting the radio audience to programs of a higher intellectual content than had before been thought possible.

With the printing of *The Collected Poems of Dylan Thomas* in 1952–53 Thomas came into his own; he was widely acclaimed as one of England's leading poets even by those critics who found in his later poems traces of the obscurantism that had dominated his earlier work. This publication was to climax Thomas' career in more than one sense. Travelling on an American tour in 1953, he was stricken with a brain ailment and died suddenly in New York on November 9th of that year. Such eminent literary figures as T. S. Eliot and W. H. Auden expressed their shock at his death, and it was generally felt that Thomas had been cut off with the greater part of his career still before him. His chronic alcoholism has since become apparent. He was a brilliant reader of his own verse (even impromptu remarks came out "verse"), and every American student should be familiar with his recordings. "A Child's Christmas in Wales" is now as much of a "classic" as Dickens' *Christmas Carol* and Menotti's *Amahl and the Night Visitors* (or should one say *The Wizard of Oz*). He has also written an amusing "autobiography," *A Portrait of the Artist as a Young Dog,* 1940, film scripts, and a play, *Under Milk Wood,* an earlier version of which had been published by Marguerite Caetani in the Roman *Botteghe Oscure* as *Llareggub, a Piece for Radio Perhaps* in 1952.

IMPORTANCE

Thomas' themes are the elemental ones: birth, sex, energy, and death. The chief quality of his style is a boundless exuberance and vitality; even when he treats sordid or morbid subjects his native Welsh energy strikes through. His poetry has great rhetorical brilliance; it is written for speaking, and is at its best when recited aloud. Thomas is no cynical Wasteland poet; his general mood, sometimes dark, is never totally pessimistic. Influenced by Gerard Manley Hopkins, he often expresses a profound religiosity; his theology, however, is less a formal Christianity than a highly personal pantheism. There is a strong Dionysian element in his attitude, growing out of his deep pleasure in physical life.

In technique Thomas' verse is esoteric and difficult, although his later work is somewhat more lucid. Essentially a lyricist, he is fond of delicate nuances of sound, his work is full of half-rhymes, dissonances, and irrational onomatopoeia. His early poems (especially the so-called "altarwise by owl-light" sonnets) are virtually studies in auditory free association. In diction he is elemental; the early poems are written in something resembling Basic English, and even his later work shows the simplicity of vocabulary of a man who is vigorously scornful of formal learning. Yet Thomas is far from cultural naivete; among the influences detectable in his work are those of Freud, Jung, Joyce, Hopkins, and Yeats.

Important Poems

Among Thomas' most difficult and complex poems are the "sonnets" (actually unrhymed poems of fourteen lines) published in 1936 and numbered I–X; they are sometimes referred to as the "altarwise by owl-light sonnets" after the opening phrase of Sonnet I. The poems form an integrated "sonnet sequence"; the dominant symbolism of the entire series is that of medieval astrology. Sonnet I establishes the theme; the "dog among fairies" is Cerberus, the symbol of death, and his biting of the "mandrake with tomorrow's scream" signifies his destruction of the life-hope inherent in the power of reproduction. The "gentleman" mentioned is Hercules; the "halfway house" refers to the autumnal equinox, when the constellation of Hercules sinks to the west. This Hercules-figure, embodiment of mortal mankind, passes through the remaining poems in changing form. In II he muses upon death; the "short spark" of life glows only until it consumes the small stick of the human span. In III a traditional poetic metaphor is utilized: the human life span is compared to the passage of a year. There is small comfort in reflecting that our winter is but the spring of those who come after us (line

14). In IV the protagonist remembers his youth, when he had tormented his faith with questions (line 4); now he sees the image of existence as it actually is (ll. 13-14). In V the stars, still turning in the heavens, pass the autumnal equinox and enter into the region of nightmare; biblical and literary figures pass as in a dream. In VI man and sun are compared to burning candles; the "wound of manwax" refers to the wound of being born, the unhealing blow from which man finally dies. In VII time is shown as illusory; and religious faith, symbolized by the Cross ("tree"), is introduced as an eternal element. Yet in VIII the Cross sets like a star, suggesting the universal myth of the death and rebirth of the god (Adonis, Tammuz, Christ). IX recalls Egyptian embalmment, perhaps the most successful expedient yet contrived for conquering the corruption of death. In X the Cross reappears, symbolizing that religious faith is independent of the passage of time and of temporal events. Thus the series of poems taken together analyses the basic human problem of birth and death, passes through a morbid pessimism, and emerges into a transcendental and quasi-Christian faith in the power of human resurrection.

"When All My Five and Country Senses See" conjectures what would result if all senses shared the clarity and precision of vision. Touch, the sense of love, will see how love ends (ll. 2-5); hearing will observe "love drummed away" until its music ends in discord (ll. 6-7); taste will sense that the beloved wounds of passion are no more, yet will regret their passing (ll. 8-9); and smell will see the breath (of love) burn and perish. Yet (ll. 11-14) the heart is the most acute sense of all; it will still love when the senses warn of the pain and torment that love must inevitably bring.

"The Force That Through the Green Fuse Drives" intricately contrasts love and destruction, birth and death; Thomas' exuberance and Dionysian energy are seen in his exultation in his youth ("green age") and in the blood that the life force drives through his veins. He feels his essential kinship with the rest of animal and vegetable nature (Stanzas II, III); and nature's rhythm (IV, 5) warns him of the incomprehensible death (Stanza V) which is the end of human life and love. This study in elemental passion and death differs from most poems on the subject in its lack of any deep pessimism or morbidity; the final tone is one of awed resignation.

"Twenty-four Years" treats a similar subject in a slightly more lucid manner typical of Thomas' middle period. The connection between birth and death is constantly held in mind (ll. 2, 3-4, 6); the newborn baby, crouching in the "natural doorway" (the loins of his mother) is already sewing the shroud for his journey to death. His life on earth continues only as long as his "money" (allotted span) lasts. Yet again the tone of the poem is contemplative rather than pessimistic.

"A Refusal to Mourn the Death, by Fire, of a Child in London" is an unusual threnody; the poet refuses to mourn the child killed in an air raid because its mortality is only part of the common human mortality. If one is to die at all, there is little difference whether this event occurs in childhood or in old age.

Whoever ordained that man must die is responsible for all, and "after the first death, there is no other" (IV, 6). Thus the child's death is ennobled through the "mankind of her going," her participation in the universal human burden of death.

"Do Not Go Gentle into That Good Night" (1945) is based on the poet's complex emotions related to his father's fatal illness. Thomas presents his father in heroic proportions as one surmounting a peak or setting forth upon an epic voyage. The poet pleads with the ill father not to succumb to depression and spiritual surrender, but instead to fight defiantly (in language reminiscent of Byron) against the coming night of mortality.

The many poems included in the collection *In Country Sleep* (1952) were originally intended as parts of a single long poem. But Thomas died before his plan could be carried out. "In the White Giant's Thigh" is a somberly optimistic poem about the continuity of life forces. "In Country Sleep" a father looks forward to his young daughter's awakening to the full nature of human existence, including the role played by death in the complete cycle of life.

Verse Drama

Under Milk Wood (*A Play for Voices,* 1954) is Dylan Thomas' last completed masterpiece. The central character, narrator, and commentator but not a main "actor," is the blind Captain Cat, who with his extrasensitive hearing can translate minute sounds into visual images. He is something of a metaphor for radio listeners. The setting is Llareggub, a snide pseudonym for Laugharne, the seacoast village in Wales where Dylan was living with his family. The play covers one spring day in the life of the community from before dawn (Captain Cat is sleeping and dreaming of his youth at sea) to nightfall and dark. The characters include Mr. Mog Edwards, draper, and Miss Myfanwy Price, two spinsters in "love" with each other but they'll never marry; Mrs. Ogmore-Pritchard and the ghosts of her two husbands, Mr. Ogmore and Mr. Pritchard, both better off dead, since the Missus won't let the sun in her house unless it wipes its shoes; Willy Nilly, the postman, and his wife who steams open envelopes; assorted drunks, old people, children, animals; and perhaps most sympathetic of all, Polly Garter, who can't say no to a man and has assorted babies by assorted fathers and who says, "Isn't life a terrible thing, thank God?" and the Reverend Eli Jenkins, poet-preacher who loves his town, the good, the bad, and the indifferent. Not much happens but the gossip, as Mrs. Waldo remarks, "Oh, what'll the neighbors say, what'll the neighbors . . . ," and delivery boys, work in the kitchens, work on the farms, and trips to the Sailors Arms pub. But there is the poetry: "It is Spring," says a voice, "moonless night in the small town, starless and bible-black, the cobblestreets silent and the hunched, courters'-and-rabbits' wood limping invisible down to the sloeblack, slow, black, crow-black, fishingboat-bobbing sea."

LOUIS MACNEICE (1907–63)

MacNeice is a member of the Auden-Spender group of younger British poets; his work resembles Auden's in technique, if not in content, and he shares the liberal political tendencies that characterize the group as a whole. He was born in Belfast, Northern Ireland, in 1907; his father was a Protestant clergyman. He read classics and philosophy at Oxford and won a first in "Greats"; he later lectured in classics at Birmingham and at the University of London. He supported the Loyalist cause during the Spanish Civil War, but was too individualistic by temperament to associate himself long with any organized party. Several of his poems, in fact, are pleas for the intellectual independence of the individual with respect to all parties, doctrines, and theories.

In content MacNeice, like Spender, might be termed a modernist or futurist; his favorite subjects are the city, and factory, and the railway. His urbanity enables him to see beauty not only in unspoiled nature but in the complexity, even the banality, of city life. Yet his admiration of the machine is not as complete as that of Spender; he perceives the degradation attendant upon industrial civilization and criticizes it severely by implication. He does not view the evils of urban existence, however, as exclusively due to capitalistic exploitation; he would find urban life in a Communist "utopia" equally unsatisfactory. It is the city's isolation from nature which produces its degradation; in such poems as "Among These Turf-Stacks" he contrasts urban decadence and demagoguery with rural serenity in an almost Wordsworthian manner.

In poetic technique MacNeice is close to Auden, although his language is more specific and closer to the vernacular; in diction he manifests a proletarian simplicity. The general tone of his verse suggests both T. S. Eliot and Edith Sitwell; each of these poets influenced his literary development. Like Auden and Spender, he often uses half-rhymes and dissonances; many lines are made deliberately jerky and rough-edged with juxtaposed consonants ("Cranks, hacks, poverty-stricken scholars"). The best of his verse is sharply ironic; in "Bagpipe Music" he demonstrates his skill at parody and comedy, and a hint of this quality is apparent in most of his verse. His style evolved constantly during his career; the poems written up to *Blind Fireworks* (1929) are delicate but sometimes lacking in strength, and the later work, typified by "Sunday Morning" and "Morning Sun," is more ironic, more powerful, and more deliberate in its statement of theme.

During the 1940s MacNeice published two more volumes of poetry, *Springboard* (1944) and *Holes in the Sky* (1948), indicating a growth in his talent. He also devoted considerable time to the writing of radio plays, *Christopher Columbus* (1944) and *The Dark Tower* (1947), which, as performed with music by Benjamin Britten and with Cyril Cusack reading the part of Roland was a memorable presentation. Among his other activities

MacNeice lectured at Cornell University and translated Goethe's *Faust*. He died in London at the age of fifty-five in 1963.

Important Poems

"Sunday Morning" is MacNeice's best-known poem. The first stanza (ll. 1–10) depicts a typical Sunday morning in the suburbs, a day of relaxation, music, and happy tinkering with cars. The suburban citizen can almost convince himself that workaday Monday will never come, that time has stood still and made this surcease from toil "a small eternity" (line 10). But the suburbanite hears a church bell from up the road; he is reminded, not so much of the eternal religious significance of life, but of the inexorable passage of time which will soon bring back his weekday routine. The implication is that the relaxed pleasure of Sunday is too dearly bought with the six days of sordid toil which precede it.

"The British Museum Reading Room" is a contemplative description of this famous hall in which so many great authors and thinkers have worked. Yet it is not genius that first strikes the eye of the observer; the readers are cranks and hacks, human flotsam who have nothing better to do than pursue their obsessions or dreams in the public shelter of the Reading Room. The final stanza, especially III, ll. 4–8, suggests the universal stream of learning and thought which in a sense passes through the museum; the contrast between "totem poles" and "Ionic columns" (ll. 4–5) hints at the development of humanistic civilization from its beginning in primitive culture.

"Morning Sun" is an impressionistic picture of London in the sunlight; the poem resembles the work of the Imagists more than anything else MacNeice has written. The sunlight enlivens and transfigures the entire city; when it disappears (perhaps the sun passes behind a cloud in Stanza IV) a grayness comes over the city as the ash creeps over the flaming end of a cigarette.

"Birmingham" is a similar impressionistic description; this time the subject is a more comprehensive panorama of a famous English industrial city. Beauty and ugliness, sublimity and banality are found side by side in the city. The general mood is one of sordid monotony; yet the citizen hopes always for a stroke of luck, a vision, a moment of love which will redeem his bleak life (III, ll. 7-8).

"Among These Turf-Stacks" contrasts city with country. The peasant, far from machines and mass production, is ignorant but free from the city's crushing uniformity (ll. 3–6). He is protected by his pastoral environment from the enemies of freedom: the "theory-vendors," the political, social, or religious zealots who seek to make us conform to their way of thinking. The poet and his listener are of those "obsolete" souls who still wish to pursue their private pleasures (II, line 2). The theory-vendors threaten this humble enjoyment, and the poet knows he must soon flee to a less civilized place for refuge.

"Bagpipe Music" is a ribald and rollicking song built of paraphrases of children's jingles and folk ballads. The poem demonstrates MacNeice's fascination with off-rhymes: e.g. "whiskey-fifty" and "culture-puncture." The general theme of this disconnected song is that the vulgar are not attracted to religion, mysticism, or political contemplation; they want only the simple pleasures of a "packet of fags" and a "bit of skirt in a taxi." But (last two lines) this indifference is at the root of the degeneration of democracy; the barometer of culture is falling. It is no good to break the barometer (silence those, like the poet, who indicate this degeneration); the process will go on whether or not the indicator is in working order.

EDITH SITWELL (1887 – 1964)

Edith Sitwell, *grande dame,* was one of the most interesting and colorful personalities in modern British literature. She and her two brothers, Sir Osbert and Sacheverell, comprised a most unusual literary family, three siblings who achieved almost equal if divergent reputations. Of an old landed aristocratic family they were the children of Sir George, fourth baronet, and Lady Ida Sitwell, with ancestry traced back to the Norman chiefs who accompanied William the Conqueror to England. Renishaw Park, the Sitwell estate, had been in the family for over seven hundred years, actually since 1201. Yet her poetry is somewhat satirical of the aristocracy, viewing the past as if it were some faded tapestry, the inhabitants of her world being pushed out of their sheltered, peaceful existence by intrusive commercialism and industry. Edith Sitwell has been seen as an intellectual liberal rather than a conservative aristocrat.

Imposing as a person both in physique (six feet tall) and physiognomy, with what may be the longest aquiline nose ever photographed and resembling not a little certain portraits of William Wordsworth, Dame Edith costumed herself (she was never dressed, always arrayed) in clothes of medieval or Tudor design, wearing huge jewelry — rings, bracelets, gold armlets, necklaces. Her gowns were often of heavy brocade and she liked elaborate hats or turbans. She was quite a contrast to the more dowdy Dame Ivy Compton-Burnett. One famous portrait of her by Cecil Beaton shows Edith in flowered brocade at the harp in front of a kind of medieval tapestry. In a characteristic gesture she posed for another Cecil Beaton photograph as dead on a bier surrounded by flowers and candles. Sitwell generously helped establish the reputation of other poets: at one end of her career working with Siegfried Sassoon on the poems of Wilfred Owen; at the other, giving encouragement to Theodore Roethke.

Her friendships were highly individual, including Gertrude Stein. They met in Paris in the twenties. This first impression is recorded in *The Autobiography of Alice B. Toklas:* "Very tall, bending slightly, withdrawing and hesitatingly advancing, and beautiful with the most distinguished nose I have ever seen on any human being." It was Edith who persuaded Gertrude to give her lecture, "Composition as Explanation," at Cambridge and Oxford in 1926 and, together with Osbert and Sacheverell, entertained Gertrude and Alice in London. Gertrude became very fond of Osbert, said "he was like the uncle of a king."

Publishing well over forty books between 1915 and 1950, Edith Sitwell was for a long time best known as an eccentric, for the reciting of her poetic work, *Facade* (1922), set to music by Sir William Walton (and recorded). The first public performance of this work took place in Aeolian Hall, London, June 12, 1923. With her back to the audience, Sitwell recited through a Sengerphone (to magnify without distorting the voice) over and under Walton's music. The initial reaction of the press and public has been described as savage. One wonders why. The recording gives the impression of gaiety and good fun. While being quite "other," *Facade* can please in the manner of *Four Saints in Three Acts.*

In 1930 came Sitwell's biography of *Alexander Pope* and the developing, more serious, poetry of *Gold Coast Customs* (1929), "an almost savage description of African murder rites that she equated with London slum miseries and the lives of the wealthy and fashionable," Lady Bamburgher, for instance, with Vachel Lindsay-type drum beat insistent in the rhythm. After a pause of more than ten years, the new poetry appeared: *Street Songs* (1942), *Green Song and Other Poems* (1944), *The Song of the Cold* (1945), *The Shadow of Cain* (1947), *The Canticle of the Rose* (1949). The title poems of the last two volumes view the age of the atom bomb with apprehension and the feeling of crisis and cataclysm in man's history. They represent an amazing sensitivity to the new element introduced into our potential material for poetry and its implications: "We did not heed the Cloud in the Heavens shaped like the hand/ Of Man . . . But there came a roar as if the Sun and Earth had come together / . . . the Primal Matter/ Was broken, the womb from which all life began./ Then to the murdered Sun a totem pole of dust arose in memory of Man."

Edith Sitwell continued to publish into the sixties, both poetry and prose: *A Book of the Winter* (1950), *The Queens and the Hive* (about Elizabeth the First, 1962), *Gardeners and Astronomers* (1963) among others, and her autobiographical *Taken Care Of* appeared posthumously in 1965. But one should take a brief look at the brothers as well. Sir Osbert, who wrote stories, poems and essays, is perhaps most remarkable for a running series of autobiographies (about them all): *Left Hand! Right Hand!* (1944), *The Scarlet Tree* (1946), *Great Morning!* (1947), *Laughter in the Next Room* (1948), and *Noble Essences; a Book of Characters* (1950). Sacheverell, the younger brother and also a poet, devoted himself primarily to art, architecture, and music, with several biographies of composers and a fine analysis of Baroque art in Europe.

Life

Edith Sitwell was born in Scarborough, Yorkshire, England in 1887 on September 7, the same day of the month and near the same hour as the first

Queen Elizabeth (as she liked to think). She had a rather unhappy childhood, according to her brother Osbert in *The Scarlet Tree;* extremely sensitive, given to books and music rather than the fashionable pursuits of Renishaw Hall Society, she incurred the opposition and criticism of her mother who showed favoritism to Osbert. It is reported that her father made her wear a painful device "to shape her nose" properly. She did enjoy the occasional company of her two brothers when they were not away in school, received private training of a rambling sort at home until the arrival of a remarkable governess (and translator of Rimbaud's *Les Illuminations*) Helen Rootham, with whom she could share a passion for music and French literature and with whom she travelled in Europe and lived for a time in Paris. Edith Sitwell published her first volume of poetry, *The Mother,* in 1915; in the next year, a volume written with her brother Osbert; and in 1925 Edith, Osbert, and Sacheverell together published an anthology, *Poor Young People and Other Poems* (which is a little like the appearance of Ethel, Lionel, and John Barrymore in a single film, *Grand Hotel* perhaps it was). In the thirties, according to another of Sir Osbert's autobiographical volumes, *Laughter in the Next Room,* Edith spent much time in close attendance upon Helen Rootham who was invalid with a long and mortal illness until her death in 1938, preventing her "from going with us to Italy." She published no new poetry during this period.

Then came the war years, and the bombing of London enters Edith Sitwell's poetry in the now often anthologized "Still Falls the Rain" from *Street Songs* (1942). A flood of production in both prose and verse followed until in the 1954 birthday honors Queen Elizabeth II made Edith Sitwell Dame of the Grand Cross of the British Empire. Asked how she felt in the following year, Dame Edith said, "Dying, but, apart from that, I'm all right." She did die at St. Thomas's hospital in London on December 9, 1964 of a heart attack at seventy-seven.

In one of her fine books of prose biographies, *English Eccentrics* (1933), she had said that eccentricity was particularly English. She once took part in a practical joke, sending a stuffed owl to Parliament addressed to a member widely known as pompous. She was fond of many poets but not of their wives and said, "The wives of poets should be selected by a committee of other poets." When questioned about the stir her early poetry created, she declared, "I am like an electric eel in a pond full of catfish." At the time of her death critics were divided: some placed her in the front rank of twentieth century English poets; some like Louise Bogan preferred her earlier verse; some like Horace Gregory preferred her later verse. Time will no doubt sift the issue, but there is no doubt that a flamboyant personality has left the stage. She believed in poets and in poetry, telling them and quoting Shakespeare's Anthony to Cleopatra: " 'Come on, my queen, there's sap in't yet.' Sap in the event, sap in the heart of man." Sitwell joins Faulkner in leaving a challenge.

Representative Poems

Since *Facade* is so controversial, we might look first at Osbert Sitwell's explanation: "The idea of *Facade* first entered our minds as the result of certain technical experiments at which my sister had recently been working: experiments in obtaining through the medium of words the rhythm of dance measures such as waltzes, polkas, foxtrots. These exercises were often experimental enquiries into the effect on rhythm, on speed, and on colour of the use of rhymes, assonances, dissonances, placed outwardly, at different places in the line, in most elaborate patterns." Nursery-rhyme patterns and drum beats enter Sitwell verse here and persist in undertones throughout. While Gertrude Stein was trying "to paint" with words, Edith was trying to reproduce music. "Fox Trot" is a good example from *Facade* and starts:

> *Old*
> *Sir*
> *Faulk,*
> *Tall as a stork,*
> *Before the honeyed fruits of dawn were ripe,*
> *would walk*
> *And stalk with a gun*
> *The reynard-coloured sun*
> *Among the pheasant-feathered corn the unicorn has torn,*
> *forlorn the*
> *Smock-faced sheep*
> *Sit*
> *And*
> *Sleep. . . .*

But the Tango-Pasodoblè, "When Don Pasquito arrived at the seaside," and the finale, "Sir Beelzebub" are equally effective and charming.

"Aubade" from *Bucolic Comedies* (1923) is a fine picture of a kitchen maid, Jane, as she greets the dawn and feels the morning. It begins: "Jane, Jane,/ Tall as a crane,/ The morning light creaks down again./ Comb your cockscomb-ragged hair;/ Jane, Jane, come down the stair." Rain, light, and kitchen garden come into view, showing "Cockscomb flowers that none will pluck,/ And wooden flowers that 'gin to cluck," as chickens sneak into the picture. "In the kitchen you must light/ Flames as staring, red and white/ As carrots or as turnips, shining/ Where the cold dawn light lies whining." This is the picture of Jane and her morning. In another poem of the period Sitwell writes: "Grey as a guinea-fowl is the rain/ Squawking down from the boughs again." These images startle, which is what poetry is supposed to do. Ultimately they seem exact. And one can detect that Edith Sitwell liked Swinburne as well as nursery rhymes.

"Still Falls the Rain" from *Street Songs* (1942) has the subtitle "The Raids, 1940. Night and Dawn." These are the Nazi air raids during the Battle of Britain when much of London was destroyed and thousands of civilians killed. The rain stands for bombs, for the blood of Christ, for tears, and for rain itself which seems omnipresent in the Sitwell poetry. "Still falls the

Rain — / Dark as the world of man, black as our loss — / Blind as the nineteen hundred and forty nails/ Upon the Cross." Biblical imagery persists, Potter's Field, the Tomb, the brow of Cain, Dives, Lazarus, building up an indictment of the murderous history of mankind, of human responsibility for human misery in the neglect of Christ's sacrifice. The parable of Dives the rich man and the beggar Lazarus with his sores as told in Luke is encapsuled in the line: "Under the Rain the sore and the gold are as one." Here in extended meaning the rain falls on the just and unjust alike. The climax builds up to Faust's lines in his last soliloquy in Christopher Marlowe's play: "Still falls the Rain — / Then — O Ile leape up to my God: who pulls me doune — / See, see where Christ's blood streames in the firmament: / It flows from the Brow we nailed upon the tree. . . ." Faustus is in many ways the modern heroic, tragic figure (Thomas Mann was about to make him the symbol of German responsibility for holocaust and damnation in *Doktor Faustus*), here with the faint, persistent hope of salvation — "One drop would save my soul, Nay, half a drop" — even with the immanent peril of eternal destruction and damnation for having sold his soul to the powers of hell. The question has never been finally solved: Marlowe and Mann condemn Faust; Goethe saves him. The Sitwell poem ends: "Then sounds the voice of One who like the heart of man/ Was once a child who among beasts has lain — / 'Still do I love still shed my innocent light, my Blood, for thee.'" Hope is almost forced to emerge from the hopeless situation. In the paradox the rain that destroys may also save.

DAVID JONES (1895 – 1974)

David Jones was born of Anglo-Welsh parentage in 1895 and became a man fascinated by many things. First by Wales itself, although he knew no Welsh and put himself to learning it. Second by Gerard Manley Hopkins, and Jones became a Roman Catholic convert in 1921. Third by James Joyce, of whom he had a good understanding, even an appreciation of *Finnegans Wake,* which influenced his own work. His original and major artistic effort was in the visual arts, particularly in copper engraving and watercolors. His exhibitions and the reproductions of his work have been numerous. He served in the First World War with the Royal Welsh Fusiliers and later used this personal experience for his first work of poetry. He was variously associated with Eliot, Pound, Yeats, and Auden, and indeed his first book of verse, *In Parenthesis* (1937) was introduced with encomiums by T. S. Eliot. As we find in the Preface the expectation is exciting: the personal experiences of a soldier from December 1915 to July 1916, the First World War viewed with other battles interspersed, those of Roman Britain, the wars of King Arthur as found in Malory, and Shakespeare's Henry V in his French campaign. We are to have a London Cockney soldier serving with Welsh troops in battlefield observations that are expressed in Cockney, Welsh, Latin, and medieval

English language tags. The title refers to this experience, to all human experience, as "the space between." Unfortunately the execution for the unini-
tiated American reader is likely to seem tedious. The best image seems to
come from Malory, the landscape that spoke "with a grimly voice." It would
be interesting to compare this work with Wilfred Owen's poems and with
Ford Madox Ford's *Parade's End,* but it would probably not be to Jones'
advantage. The contents of the parts are indicated as: I. The Many Men So
Beautiful, II. Chambers go off, Corporals stay, III. Starlight order, IV. King
Pellam's Launde, V. Squat garlands for White Knights, VI. Pavilions and
Captains of Hundreds, VII. The five unmistakable marks. The Joycean mixture of languages most lacks the Joycean comic impulse, which of course
would be inappropriate.

Jones' second book of poetry, *Anathemata,* appeared in 1952, praised by
Auden. Its contents are: I. Rite and Fore-Time, II. Middle Sea and Lear-Sea
III. Angle-Land, IV. Redriff, V. The Lady of the Pool, VI. Keel, Ram, Stauros,
VII. Mabinog's Liturgy, VIII. Sherthursdaye and Venus Day. Tony Stone-
burner, in an appreciative article devoted to David Jones' *Work in Progress*
(note the borrowed Joycean term), gives a succinct picture of the content of
the three works: "In *In Parenthesis* the British past is present to soldiers in
France during World War I and in *The Anathemata* the British past with a
number of its contributing factors is present to a worshipper at Mass in Britain
during World War II. In the work-in-progress our own cosmopolitan present
is present by analogy to both Roman soldiers in Palestine and Celtic villagers
in Britain at the time of the crucifixion of Jesus. In *The Anathemata,* the
British Isles are geographically central: Palestine is peripheral. In the work-
in-progress, Palestine is central: the British Isles are peripheral" This is
reading for the hardy and the religiously committed, especially those with a
Catholic imagination. Yet in one brief poem, entitled *"A, a, a, Domine
Deus, "*David Jones strikes fire, such fire that suggests he has done so or will
do so elsewhere. This poem, printed on a single page in *Agenda,* Spring-
Summer 1967, was written according to the poet circa 1938 and 1966. The
title is apparently a stuttering of the worshipper who may feel some hesita-
tion in addressing the Lord God; the worshipper is the poet seeking for a
subject: "I said, Ah! what shall I write?/ I enquired up and down./ (He's
tricked me before/ with his manifold lurking-places.)" The poet looks for
Him in disturbingly modern and mechanical places: textures, contours, dead
forms, pillar, pylon, colours, lights, "I have felt for His Wounds/ in nozzles
and containers./ I have wondered for the automatic devices. . . . / I have
been on my guard/ not to condemn the unfamiliar./ For it is easy to miss
Him/ at the turn of a civilization." The coda of the piece packs the power: "I
have watched the wheels go round in case . . . I might see the Living God
projected from the Machine. I have said to the perfected steel, be my sister
and for the glassy towers I thought I felt some beginnings of His creature, but
A, a, a, Domine Deus, my hands found the glazed work unrefined and the

terrible crystal a stage-paste." One might say that to this attention must be paid.

PHILIP LARKIN (1922–85)

Philip Arthur Larkin, British poet and librarian, was a native of Coventry, where he attended the King Henry VIII School before going to Oxford, where he knew Kingsley Amis and gathered material for his first novel, according to Larkin's 1963 preface to an American edition of *Jill*. After holding posts in various libraries, he became the Librarian of the Brynmor Jones Library at the University of Hull in Yorkshire in 1955, which work he combined with the writing of his poetry. His first book of poetry, *The North Ship* (1945), has been considered negligible in that he had not yet found his own voice. Two novels, *Jill* (1946) and *A Girl in Winter* (1947), are more favorably regarded. His two major volumes of verse are *The Less Deceived* (1955) and *The Whitsun Weddings* (1964). In 1965 he received the Queen's Gold Medal for Poetry. Essays on jazz under the title *All What Jazz,* reflecting a passion from his college days, appeared in 1969.

Two poems from *The Less Deceived* seem characteristic. The first, called "Poetry of Departures" admires those who can leave and go elsewhere, "He chucked up everything/ And just cleared off." The poet thinks they are right, that "We all hate home/ And having to be there: / I detest my room,/ Its specially-chosen junk,/ The good book, the good bed,/ And my life in perfect order/." But, as he continues, "I'd go today . . ., if it weren't so artificial." So there is a tension. To go or not to go, that is the question. And some of us, wanting to go, remain. The second poem, "Church Going," is a somewhat nostalgic but antiquarian and sightseeing going into empty churches, a sadly realistic view that our churches are on the way out. The poet asks, What shall we do with them "When churches fall completely out of use"? "A serious house on serious earth it is, . . ./ And that much never can be obsolete." The first poem in *The Whitsun Weddings,* "Here," is a dramatic, sensuous description of the city of Hull and life in it, but beyond the city "Loneliness clarifies," and the poet keeps his distance.

Larkin was one of the better known members of the Movement, a term coined in 1954 by J. D. Scott, literary editor of the *Spectator,* to describe a loose association of like-minded writers. The group included Kingsly Amis, Donald Davie, Dennis Enright, John Wain, Elizabeth Jennings, and Robert Conquest. In style these writers harkened back to more traditional modes. In tone and content, their works have been characterized as antiromantic, witty, rational, and sardonic. By 1957, most members of the Movement had disowned it, claiming, in Wain's words. "Its work is done."

Larkin's literary production since 1970 has been more impressive in quality than quantity. A new volume of poems, *High Windows,* appeared in 1974 and a collection of criticism, *Required Reading,* in 1982. From 1955 to his death thirty years later, Larkin devoted most of his energies to his responsibilities as a librarian at the University of Hull.

JON SILKIN (1930–   )

Jon Silkin was born December 2, 1930 in London, and was educated at Wycliffe and Dulwich Colleges. In 1947 he was a junior reporter for a small London news agency. He worked for some years as a manual laborer. From 1956 to 1958 he taught English to foreign students at the St. Giles School of Languages. From 1958 to 1960 he held the Gregory Fellowship in Poetry at Leeds University. The second year of the fellowship was also the first year of his honors degree in English, 1960–63. He graduated with a first. In 1963 he did post-graduate research on the poets of the First World War. He founded *Stand,* a literary quarterly, in 1952. It was suspended in 1957 and revived in 1960 at Leeds and is now published in Newcastle-at-Tyne; it is subsidized in part by the British Arts Council and Silkin still edits the magazine.

His publications include *The Peaceable Kingdom* (1954), *The Two Freedoms* (1958), *The Re-Ordering of the Stones* (1961), *Nature With Man* (1965), and *Poems Selected and New* (1966). He was also the editor of *Living Voices* (1960), an anthology of contemporary poetry. Jon Silkin was poet-in-residence at Denison University during the spring terms of 1965 and 1968 and also a member of the faculty at the Writers' Workshop at the State University of Iowa. He gave readings at the YMHA Poetry Center in New York and at many universities throughout America. Jon is a man of short but husky stature with a very full and wildly curling beard, a quiet but resonant voice, and eyes that show a fixed interest in people. In the mid-sixties he was a confirmed vegetarian on the principle of not bringing harm to the animal members of *The Peaceable Kingdom.* He travelled at that time with Kate, a lovely, warm-hearted Irish girl from the west of Ireland. He was firm in his stand against the Vietnam War and against all capitalist oppression wherever it may appear.

Since 1970, Silkin has published four volumes of poetry: *The Principle of Water* (1974), *The Little Time-keeper* (1976), *The Psalms with Their Spoils* (1980), and *Autobiographical Sketches* (1984). He also edited two important literary anthologies, *First World War Poetry* (1979) and *First World War Prose* (1985).

"Death of a Son" (who died in a mental hospital aged one) from *The Peaceable Kingdom* is frequently anthologized. It is so deeply felt as to make the reader uncomfortable—a good thing for a poem to do. It begins, as it continues, very quietly: "Something has ceased to come along with me./ Something like a person: something very like one." The basic comparison of the child is with buildings and by extension singing birds, only in his case mute. "The other houses like birds/ Sang around him." This house of flesh and blood had "flesh of stone/ And bricks for blood." Other "Birds singing crazy," "But this was silence." He never spoke, but as if he could speak "He turned over on his side with his one year/ Red as a wound/ . . . And out of his eyes two great tears rolled, like stones, and he died."

The flower poems that began to appear in *Nature with Man* are possibly Jon Silkin's most original contribution to English verse. He explains that flowers are the "subjects," but they are not flower poems in the traditional Romantic poets' daffodils-daisy-rhodora-globed-peony sense. One part of the approach seems quite objective, detached, scientific, minute — something like Hopkins' "inscape" — taking "one particular species of flower, and to look at the flower quite closely. I also try to characterize the life and process of the flower and, in making all three substantial, to suggest certain correspondences with human types and situations." These poems "hover tentatively" between the flower and the human, but the focus is on the flower. Silkin is trying to draw human life into "a peaceful consortium" with plants, with animals, with nature. Most of his flowers are wild rather than cultivated. If he views a garden it is one "where domestic and undomestic plants sometimes co-exist and sometimes compete. I see the garden, in fact, as a kind of human bestiary, containing in the several plants earlier developed and anticipatory examples of human types and situations. The first poem "Dandelion," for example — sees its subject as a seizer of space, and asks for political parallels to be made." The individual flower for Silkin is almost always a community of the single species, just as he seems more interested, in groups of animals or men rather than in singular identity.

"Dandelion" begins: "Slugs nestle where the stem/ Broken, bleeds milk." Not a pretty picture. The flower, unlike the daisy, has no eye: "the sight is compelled/ By small, coarse, sharp petals,/ Like metal shreds." This is the introduction of machine shapes, or made objects and substances, in the analogy: modern figures for a modern poem. "Formed,/ they puncture . . . / And certainly want to / Devour the earth." The poet sees dandelions as taking hold "On pert domestic strains./ Others' lives are theirs." They infest the grass, "Fatten, hide slugs, infestate./ They look like plates; more closely/ Like the first tryings, the machines, of nature/ Riveted into her, successful." "Successful" here by the poet's building of context becomes a dirty word, which is something of a *tour de force*.

"Lilies of the Valley" and "Peonies" are "female" poems, predatory, not beautiful, the first entrapping with its scent meanly and almost with vulgarity, the second by its assault on our sight "to subjugate and enslave the admirer." But there are poems about benign flowers, "A Daisy," for instance, in its innocence and simplicity. Daisies "Look unoriginal/ Being numerous. They ask for attention/ With that gradated yellow swelling/ Of oily stamens. Petals focus them: / The eye-lashes grow wide./ Why should not one bring these to a funeral?" They have other virtues: "Candid, solid, glad;" "They do not wither;" "Utterly without scent, for the eye,/ For the eye, simply. For the mind/ And its invisible organ,/ That feeling thing." Reading carefully Jon Silkin's flower poems, one walks through a meadow with care; plants, like reptiles, have their venomous members. But he does surely achieve a shock of heightened awareness.

13
CONTEMPORARY POETRY

In *The Burden of the Past,* Walter Jackson Bate (author of the Pulitzer prize winning biography *John Keats* and a recent anthologizer of English and American poetry) makes the valuable point that modern authors are inevitably beset by the problem of how to step from out of the huge shadow cast by the achievements of past writers. At a distance of many decades, the individual paths and contributions of these modern writers become more clear. It is often difficult, however, to define the artistic trajectories of modern writers in their own time. If we cannot pronounce with any finality upon the nature of their unique voices, we can at least call them to the reader's attention by name and general association. More information on each of these contemporary writers can be found in *Contemporary Authors,* a multi-volume set updated each year by Gale Publications.

DONALD DAVIE (1922 –   )

Donald Davie was born in England and graduated from Cambridge University. He became a professor first at Trinity College, Dublin, and later at Cambridge and Stanford. Like many other scholar-poets of his generation, Davie is a teacher, critic, and poet based in an academic setting.

Representative Poems

"Across the Bay" narrates the poet's complex feelings as he visits a beach scene, partly via memory. He recalls pleasure in "the emptiness, the hardness / Of the light, the silence, and the water's stillness," but is called back in feeling by a countermemory of that beach as "the setting for one of our murderous scenes." The personal or social mayhem that occurred there forever brands the otherwise inspiring powers of the natural scene.

"To Certain English Poets" debates the relationship between poetic fury, as contained in the works of now-dead poets, and the social revolutions and political spectacles of the 1960s. The poet is simultaneously put off by such activism yet attracted by its vigor.

THOM GUNN (1929–)

Thom Gunn was the son of a London journalist. He graduated from Trinity College, Cambridge, and studied with the American poet and critic, Yvor Winters. After many years of residence in the United States, Gunn is among the "Anglo-American" poets whose roots lie more in the language than in the locale. Gunn is well-known for his verse experimentation, sometimes preferring syllable count rather than stress as the primary condition for construction of poetic lines.

Representative Poems

"Considering the Snail" takes the poet deep within the snail's "fury" as it "moves in a wood of desire." The poet concludes that the snail's whitish trail reveals no clue as to the intense life-force and purpose evidenced in its groping progress along the grass. By extension (though not by analogy) the poet reflects upon human trails of all kinds, including trails of poetry, and their failure to convey the passion and desire that created them.

"Human Condition" is, in many ways, a modern echo of Pope's *Essay on Man*. Like Pope, Gunn speaks frankly, though imagistically, about his felt dilemmas: a self, an individual, in a world of "fog" where all is "hypothesis" rather than fact. The poet emphasizes the difficulty of maintaining our individuality and our "guard" against the forces that would rob us of mind and spirit.

TED HUGHES (1930–)

Born in Yorkshire, Ted Hughes was educated at Cambridge. He was married to the American poet Sylvia Plath (*The Bell Jar*), who committed suicide at age thirty-one. Hughes acknowledges the influences of Hopkins and Yeats, and his poetry shares the passionate force, yet concern for craftsmanship, of these literary mentors. Like Beckett, Hughes has divorced himself from traditional mythologies in favor of bare, cold images from nature. If Hughes can be said to have cultural heroes, they are certainly the pre-Saxon tribespeople buried in his native Yorkshire, the elemental folk he addresses often in his poetry.

Representative Poems

"Relic," on a surface level, recounts an occasion when the beachcombing poet finds the jawbone of a seacreature. He then meditates upon both the nature of the animal who originally possessed the jawbone and that of the sea that ripped it loose, with the sea itself acting as a giant set of jaws. The poet concludes that the meaning of the experience lies in no imponderable philosophy but in "gripping, gripping" — the instinctual hunger for and holding on to existence — before the inevitable end as a bone on the beach.

"A Disaster" tells of Crow (one of Hughes's key animal figures) as the bird observes the progress and ultimate failure of "the word" in world history. The poet is concerned here with the degree to which previous eras have believed in "the word" and have been disappointed as a result. In the modern world, Crow watches the gradual death of "the word" as it dries from a stagnant puddle to a salty patch of desert. In the end, Crow feels nothing but mild interest at the quaint crystalline shards of salt.

SEAMUS HEANEY (1939 –)

Born in Northern Ireland, Seamus Heaney grew up on a farm and was educated at Queen's University, Belfast. He became friends with Henry Chambers, editor of *Phoenix,* and published several early poems in that magazine. An important transition point came in 1969 when Heaney read *The Bog People,* a book by P. V. Glob telling the story of an early tribe that lived in boglands of northwestern Europe. The idea of a bog as a preserving medium for cultural experience, good and bad, remained a powerful metaphor and vehicle for Heaney.

Representative Poems

"The Grauballe Man" recounts the unearthing in 1952 of the first century man preserved in a bog near the village of Grauballe, Denmark. The poet meticulously itemizes each body part from memory, comparing bones, tissue, and hair to the living natural objects that they most resemble.

"Punishment" focuses on another unearthed body, this time of a first century woman found in a bog in Germany. The poet interprets her manner of death as a punishment of adultery. He sympathizes deeply with her ("I almost love you"), yet admits that, if he had been present at her execution, he too probably would have "stood dumb" as her "betraying sisters" exacted "intimate revenge."

ELAINE FEINSTEIN (1930 –)

Elaine Feinstein (née Cooklin) was born in Lancashire, England, and attended Cambridge University. She married Arnold Feinstein in 1966 and now resides in London. The author of four novels, she began her poetic career as a translator of Russian women poets.

Representative Poems

"Waiting" contrasts the life lived within the repressive and depressive confined world ("the house is sick") with the beckoning but dangerous world "outside" of freedom and space.

"Night Thoughts" depicts the poet's spirit as a wet leaf barely holding on to its branch. By images of dark and dread ("the wet soil of their ghosts") and explicit statement ("I cannot hold on forever") the poet seems simultaneously at the point of despair and of action.

MOLLY HOLDEN (1927 –   )

Molly Holden was born and educated in London. In 1946, she became crippled with multiple sclerosis and, eventually, paralyzed. She married Alan Holden in 1949. The author of four novels, Holden is best-known for her untraditional nature poetry. She uses common nature subjects for uncommon ends and implications.

Representative Poems

"Photograph of a Haymaker, 1890" is a poem about transience. The poet views a photograph of a man pausing from his job of cutting hay with a scythe. The yet uncut hay attracts the poet's attention and meditation. It remains fresh and uncut via the photograph, living on in her imagination as "succulent and straight, / Immediate with moon-daisies."

"Some Men Create" is a poem concerned with unintentional and unmanaged creation. The poet's master image is ivy as it grows untended from gate to wall to bridge. The result, for the poet, is a chance for the eye to "reap with pleasure what / the hand has not sown."

STEVIE SMITH (1902 – 71)

"Stevie" was the nickname of Florence Margaret Smith, who was born in Yorkshire, England. She supported herself as a private secretary to the publishers of several magazines. In later life, she quit her career to care for a feeble aunt and to concentrate on her writing. Her first novel, *Novel on Yellow Paper,* appeared in 1936, and a volume of poetry, *A Good Time Was Had By All,* the following year. These two publications established her reputation and led to the publication of two other novels and eight more volumes of poetry. Her poetry abounds in wit, some of it quite morbid, and frequent stylistic surprises.

Representative Poems

"Is It Wise?" poses the question not whether mortal fears are justified but whether they consort well with our general happiness. The poet concludes three times that "No, it is not wise" to canker living with the truth about dying.

"Our Bog Is Dood" recalls the poet's strange conversation with a group of children, much after the fashion of Wordsworth's "We Are Seven" and "Anecdote for Fathers." The children insist that "our bog is dood," but in spite of the poet's best efforts, it cannot be discovered what the "bog" is or what "dood" means. The poet walks away from the experience to meditate by the sea, itself as insistent yet impenetrable as the children's cries.

REVIEW QUESTIONS

TRADITION AND REVOLT IN POETRY

Multiple Choice

1. _____ The naturalists among the poets of the twentieth century are associated with
   a. free verse
   b. pseudoscientific naturalism
   c. conventional prosody
   d. bizarre images

2. _____ A common element of experimental verse is
   a. clarity
   b. complexity
   c. simplicity
   d. romanticism

3. _____ Gerard Manley Hopkins' poetry made use of
   a. sprung rhythm
   b. alliteration
   c. half rhymes
   d. all of the above

4. _____ Lengthy verse narratives were written by
   a. Stephen Spender
   b. John Masefield
   c. Wilfred Owen
   d. Stevie Smith

5. _____ A poet particularly associated with the avant garde of the 1920s was
   a. Wilfred Owen
   b. W. H. Auden
   c. Edith Sitwell
   d. Louis MacNeice

6. _____ The tone of the poetry of A. E. Houseman is generally
   a. optimistic
   b. pessimistic
   c. satirical
   d. romantic

7. _____ The poetry of W. H. Auden
   a. often deals with social or political themes
   b. typically deals with the relationship between the sexes
   c. depends heavily on its English background
   d. employs frequent classical references

8. _____ The industrialized modern landscape appears frequently in the poetry of
   a. Dylan Thomas
   b. Wilfred Owen
   c. A. E. Houseman
   d. Stephen Spender

9. _____ The use of natural life, particularly animals, is characteristic of the poetry of
   a. Ted Hughes
   b. Philip Larkin
   c. Stevie Smith
   d. Elaine Feinstein

10. _____ A poet who frequently collaborated with other writers was
    a. Robert Bridges
    b. Philip Larkin
    c. W. H. Auden
    d. Dylan Thomas

True-False

11. _____ The poets who came to prominence in the 1930s were generally left wing in their political views.

12. _____ The sound of the language, best appreciated when the poems are read aloud, is particularly important in the poetry of Dylan Thomas.

13. _____ Twentieth century poets rallied around a single philosophy of rebellion.

14. _____ It is easy to classify poets as experimental or naturalist.

15. _____ David Jones is probably better known as an artist than as a poet.

16. _____ Wilfred Owen presented an idealized version of military heroism in his poems about the First World War.

17. _____ Seamus Heaney found a theme for poetry in excavations of ancient peoples.

18. _____ The use of radical poetic techniques is typical of the verse of W. H. Auden and Philip Larkin.

19. _____ The use of poetic diction is characteristic of the verse of Philip Larkin and W. H. Auden.

20. _____ Experimental poets write to attract a large audience for their radical ideas.

Matching

21. _____ Gerard Manley Hopkins
22. _____ John Masefield
23. _____ A. E. Houseman
24. _____ W. H. Auden
25. _____ Dylan Thomas
26. _____ Edith Sitwell
27. _____ Elaine Feinstein
28. _____ Molly Holden
29. _____ Stevie Smith
30. _____ Jon Silkin

a. "Sea Fever"
b. "Death of a Son"
c. "Our Bog Is Dood"
d. "Waiting"
e. "Photograph of a Haymaker, 1890"
f. "Fern Wood"
g. "Musée des Beaux Arts"
h. "Façade"
i. "The Windhover"
j. "When I Was One and Twenty"

Fill-in

31. W. H. Auden wrote a number of dramas in collaboration with _____.

32. "Inscape" was a term coined by _____.

33. Thom Gunn is one of the younger poets who has spent much of his life in _____.

34. A poet associated with Spender and Auden in the 1930s, but less ideologically committed than they, was _____.

35. A writer noted almost as much for her eccentricity as for her artistic accomplishments was _____.

36. Memories of a Welsh childhood figure in the works of _____.

37. The poet who was married to Sylvia Plath was _____.

38. The poetry of Gerard Manley Hopkins was prepared for publication after his death by his friend _____.

39. A series of poems about flowers, with a decidedly nonromantic tone, was written by _____.

40. Robert Bridges, _____, and Ted Hughes were all appointed Poet Laureate.

Answers

1. c	10. c	19. F
2. b	11. T	20. F
3. d	12. T	21. i
4. b	13. F	22. a
5. c	14. F	23. j
6. b	15. T	24. g
7. a	16. F	25. f
8. d	17. T	26. h
9. a	18. F	27. d

28. e	33. the United States	37. Ted Hughes
29. c		38. Robert Bridges
30. b	34. Louis MacNeice	39. Jon Silkin
31. Christopher Isherwood	35. Edith Sitwell	40. John Masefield
32. Gerard Manley Hopkins	36. Dylan Thomas	

GLOSSARY

Allegory: a literary device, in prose or poetry, in which a literal character, event, or object also possesses a symbolic meaning. Thus an allegory may illustrate a philosophical idea, or a moral or religious principle. A work of literature is said to be allegorical if it has more than one level of meaning. (Examples: the *Romance of the Rose,* La Fontaine's *Fables,* Kafka's *The Penal Colony,* Orwell's *Animal Farm.*)

Alliteration: the repetition of a sound, usually an initial consonant, in a line of poetry or prose. (Example: "Walking in a Winter Wonderland.")

Allusion: an indirect or explicit reference to a well-known place, event, or person. Allusion in literature often occurs in a figure of speech. (Example: Keats' "Ode to a Nightingale": "and Lethe-wards [I] had sunk." The poet alludes to Hades, the underworld.)

Antihero: term used to designate the protagonist of many modern plays and novels. The antihero does not possess the classic heroic virtues of power, dignity, and bravery; rather, this character is weak, often ineffectual and passive. (Example: Roquentin, the protagonist of Sartre's *Nausea*).

Archetype: in literature, the critical examination of types of narrative, character, and image that occur in a large variety of texts. Literary archetypes, like the Jungian archetypes of the collective unconscious, are said to reflect a group of elemental and universal patterns that trigger an immediate and profound response from the reader.

Assonance: the repetition, in a line of prose or poetry, of similar or identical vowel sounds.

Bildungsroman: the German term for "novel of formation." This type of novel concerns the development of the mind and character of its protagonist, usually from childhood, through some difficult period and on to higher knowledge or maturity. Included in the genre would be Goethe's *Wilhelm Meister's Apprentice,* George Eliot's *The Mill on the Floss,* and Hermann Hesse's *The Glass Bead Game.*

Catharsis: the purging or purification that occurs, according to Aristotle, through the representation of a dramatic tragedy. It is said to affect the audience, assuaging their guilt and freeing them from fear. Some critics also see it as an integral element of tragedy, attached to the tragic flaw of the hero.

Consonance: the repetition of consonant sounds, with a change in the vowel that follows the consonant. (Example: give-gave)

Denouement: a French term literally meaning "unknotting" that describes the moment when the intrigue or action ends, when the misunderstanding has been explained or the mystery solved. It is used in both tragedy and comedy as well as in novels.

Genre: a French word meaning type, kind, or form. In literature the term is used to designate different literary forms, such as *tragedy, satire, epic,* and more recently *novel, biography,* and the like.

Imagery: literary language suggesting visual (and sometimes auditory) pictures and sensations. Imagery can depict actual scenery or suggest qualities of abstract concepts and ideas. (Example: in Keats' "To Autumn," the abstract idea of Autumn is captured through imagery of Autumn represented as a woman: "Thy hair soft-lifted by the winnowing wind.")

Intentional fallacy: the critical error of evaluating a literary work according to the success or failure of the achievement of the author's intention or expectation for the work. For such critics as W. K. Wimsatt and Cleanth Brooks, the completed work of literary art should stand apart, for purposes of evaluation, from the author's intentions in creating the work.

Irony: a figure in which the explicit meaning of a statement or action differs drastically from its implicit meaning. Types of irony include dramatic irony, verbal irony, and structural irony.

Lyric: a short poem, usually nonnarrative, in which the text expresses the speaker's emotional or mental state. A lyric is written in the first person and is often associated with songs and other musical forms.

Meter: designates the recognizable and repeated rhythms and stresses created by verse form. Iambic pentameter is the most common meter of English poetry.

Metonomy: a figure of speech in which a literal term or attribute of one thing comes to represent another to which it has a contiguous relation. (Example: the use of "crown" to mean king.)

Mimesis: a Greek word meaning imitation, mimesis is the active or dynamic copying or representation of a literal (sensual) or metaphysical (spiritual) reality in a work of art or literature.

Motif: a thematic or structural element used and repeated in a single text, or in the whole of literature. A motif may be a literary device, an incident, a formula, or a reference. (Also *leitmotif* or guiding motif.)

Ode: a lyrical poem of high and formal style, usually rhymed, which often addresses itself to a praised person, object, or quality. (Example: Wordsworth's "Ode: Intimations of Immortality")

Pathetic fallacy: the literary technique (and, for some critics, the literary mistake) of attributing human actions or characteristics to inanimate objects. For example, in Kingsley' phrase "the cruel, crawling foam," the foam cannot be literally cruel, nor does it actually crawl. Many critics, beginning with John Ruskin, condemn the use of the pathetic fallacy as a mark of the author's inability to describe and understand objects in themselves, without immediate resort to human attributes.

Persona: originally the Latin word for the mask worn by an actor in classical theater. The term now denotes the character or set of identifying traits adopted by the speaker or narrator in a work of literature. (Example: the persona of a frustrated, timid, middle-aged figure adopted as a persona by T. S. Eliot in "The Love Song of J. Alfred Prufrock")

Personification: a figure of speech or rhetoric in which inanimate objects or abstractions are given human qualities, or are represented as having human form. (Example: "that lazy old sun")

Satire: a work of literature that attacks society's vice and folly through irony and wit.

Scansion: the analysis of verse or poetry to uncover its meter and rhythmic patterns.

Surrealism: a literary and artistic movement originating in France in the 1920s. Surrealism emphasized the workings of the unconscious mind and the often-strange imagery of dream life in presenting literary, visual, and auditory art. The founder of the movement, André Breton, claimed that through surrealistic techniques the artist could communicate a higher reality by freeing the perceiving mind from the bonds of logic and rational control. (Examples: in art, the weirdly altered images in the paintings of Salvadore Dali and Picasso; in English literature, the flights of imagery seemingly divorced from actual nature description in Joyce's *Finnegan's Wake* and the poetry of Dylan Thomas.)

Synecdoche: a figure in which a part of something is taken to represent the whole. (Example: "ten sails on the horizon" for ten ships.)

Tension: a term of literary criticism popularized by the New Critic Allen Tate. Tension denotes the simultaneous presence of two often-conflicting forms of meaning (literal meaning and metaphorical meaning) in a literary work. In *Moby Dick,* literary tension exists between the literal tale of whale hunting and the metaphorical or spiritual story of the quest for the nature of the eternal or divine.

Theme: an idea presented and expanded upon in a literary work. A theme can be explicit or implicit, and is usually suggested by the narrative action.

SUGGESTED READINGS

This reading list is compiled for the convenience of the student of literature who wishes to make further study of the authors and literary movements treated. It does not pretend to be complete. The list includes selected critical or biographical materials for further reference.

Titles are indicated in English except where no translation exists or where the title is untranslatable. Dates listed, however, are those of original publication.

Especially significant or useful works are indicated with an asterisk (*).

English Literature
*Baugh, Albert C., ed., *A Literary History of England,* New York, 1967.
Harvey, P., *The Oxford Companion to English Literature,* Oxford, 1970.
Moers, E., *Literary Women,* New York, 1976.
Neill, Diana, *A Short History of the English Novel,* New York, 1964.
*Wagenknecht, Edward, *Cavalcade of the English Novel,* New York, 1943.

Thomas Hardy
Bailey, J. O., *Thomas Hardy and the Cosmic Mind,* 1956.
Casagrande, P. J., *Hardy's Influence on the Modern Novel,* London, 1987.
Guerard, A. J., *Thomas Hardy,* New York, 1949.
Howe, Irving, *Thomas Hardy,* 1967.
Marsden, Kenneth, *The Poems of Thomas Hardy,* New York, 1969.
Maynard, K. K., *Thomas Hardy's Tragic Poetry,* Iowa City, 1991.
McDowall, A., *Thomas Hardy: A Critical Study,* 1931.
Morgan, R., *Cancelled Words,* London, 1992.
Reilly, J., *Shadowtime,* London, 1993.
Widdowson, P., *Hardy in History,* London, 1989.
Wing, G., *Hardy,* 1963.

Arnold Bennett
Anderson, L., *Bennett, Wells, and Conrad,* London, 1988.
Broomfield, O., *Arnold Bennett,* Boston, 1984.

W. Somerset Maugham
Forrest, B., *W. Somerset Maugham,* Boston, 1985.
Loss, A., *W. Somerset Maugham,* New York, 1987.
Raphael, F., *Somerset Maugham,* London, 1989.

John Galsworthy
Croman, Natalie, *John Galsworthy: A Study in Continuity and Contrast,* New York, 1933.

Glindin, J. J., *John Galsworthy's Life and Art,* New York, 1987.
Sternlicht, S., *John Galsworthy,* Boston, 1987.

Psychology in Literature, General
Cairns, D., *Aidos,* New York, 1993.
Ginzburg, L., *On Psychological Prose,* Princeton, 1991.
*Hoffmann, Frederick J., *Freudianism and the Literary Mind,* Louisiana State University Press, 1945.

E. M. Forster
Land, S. K., *Challenge and Conventionality in the Fiction of E. M. Forster,* New York, 1990.
Page, N., *E. M. Forster,* New York, 1988.
Warner, Rex, *E. M. Forster,* London, 1950.

D. H. Lawrence
*Aldington, Richard, *D. H. Lawrence, Portrait of a Genius,* New York, 1950.
Feinstein, E., *Lawrence's Women,* New York, 1993.
Sklenicka, C., *D. H. Lawrence and the Child,* New York, 1991.
Tyndall, W. Y., *D. H. Lawrence and Susan His Cow,* New York, 1939.
Walterscheid, *The Resurrection of the Body,* New York, 1993.

Christopher Isherwood
McLaughlin, R., "Isherwood's Arrival and Departure," *Saturday Review of Literature,* December 27, 1947.
Mizejewski, L., *Divine Decadence,* Princeton, 1992.
Moore, G., "Three Who Did Not Make a Revolution," *American Mercury,* April, 1952.
Schwerdt, L., *Isherwood's Fiction,* London, 1988.
Wade, S., *Christopher Isherwood,* London, 1991.

Ivy Compton-Burnett
Baldanza, F., *Ivy Compton-Burnett,* New York, 1964.
Gentile, K. J., *Ivy Compton-Burnett,* New York, 1991.
Johnson, P. Hansford, *I. Compton-Burnett,* London, 1951.
Liddell, R., *Elizabeth and Ivy,* London, 1986.
————, *The Novels of Ivy Compton-Burnett,* London, 1955.
Sarraute, N., *The Age of Suspicion,* New York, 1963.

Rudyard Kipling
Carpenter, Lucile R., *Rudyard Kipling: A Friendly Profile,* Chicago, 1942.
Croft-Cooke, Rupert, *Rudyard Kipling,* Denver, 1948.
Sullivan, T., *Narratives of Empire,* New York, 1993.
Wilson, Edmund, *The Wound and the Bow,* New York, 1941.
Wilson, R. T., *Kipling Reconsidered,* London, 1989.

Joseph Conrad

Carabine, Keith, and Owen Knowles, *Joseph Conrad, Eastern and Western Perspectives,* New York, 1993.

*Gordan, John D., *Joseph Conrad, the Making of a Novelist,* Harvard University Press, 1940.

Hampson, R. G., *Joseph Conrad,* New York, 1992.

Lynn, D. H., *The Hero's Tale,* London, 1989.

Ray, Martin, *Joseph Conrad,* London, 1993.

Vulcan-Erdinast, D., *Joseph Conrad and the Modern Temper,* Oxford, 1991.

Wright, Walter F., *Romance and Tragedy in Joseph Conrad,* University of Nebraska Press, 1949.

Ford Madox Ford (Hueffer)

Armstrong, P. B., *The Challenge of Bewilderment,* Ithaca, New York, 1987.

Cassell, R. A., *Ford Madox Ford: A Study of his Novels,* Baltimore, 1961.

Garnett, D., *The Golden Echo,* New York, 1954.

Gordon, A., *The Invisible Tent,* Austin, TX, 1964.

Hoffman, C. G., *Ford Madox Ford,* New York, 1967.

Judd, A., *Ford Madox Ford,* London, 1990.

Lid, R. W., *Ford Madox Ford: The Essence of his Art,* Berkeley, 1964.

MacShane, F., *The Life and Work of Ford Madox Ford,* New York, 1965.

Meixner, J. A., *Ford Madox Ford's Novels: A Critical Study,* Minneapolis, 1961.

Ohmann, C. B., *Ford Madox Ford, from Apprentice to Craftsman,* Middletown, CT, 1964.

Wiley, P. L., *Novelist of Three Worlds: Ford Madox Ford,* Syracuse, NY, 1962.

Young, K., *Ford Madox Ford,* London, 1956.

Christopher Fry

Hobson, H., "London Hails Mr. Fry, Playwright," *New York Times Magazine,* March 12, 1950.

Leeming, G., *Christopher Fry,* Boston, 1990.

Roy, E., *Christopher Fry,* London, 1968.

Scott-James, R. A., "Christopher Fry's Poetic Drama," *Nation,* October 7, 1950.

Spears, M. K., "Christopher Fry and the Redemption of Joy," *Poetry,* April, 1951.

*Stanford, Derek, *Christopher Fry: An Appreciation,* London and New York, 1951.

Virginia Woolf

Caramagno, T., *The Flight of the Mind,* Berkeley, 1992.

Marcus, J., *Virginia Woolf and the Languages of Patrimony,* Bloomington, IL, 1987.

Mepham, J., *Virginia Woolf,* Bristol, 1992.
Raitt, S., *Vita and Virginia,* Oxford, 1993.

Katherine Mansfield
*Berkman, Sylvia, *Katherine Mansfield: A Critical Study,* Yale University Press, 1951. (detailed, objective)
Gounelas, R. P., *Fictions of the Female Self,* New York, 1991.
Kaplan, S. J., *Katherine Mansfield and the Origins of Modernist Fiction,* Ithaca, 1991.
Kobler, J. K., *Katherine Mansfield,* Boston, 1990.

James Joyce
Beckett, Samuel, et al, *An Examination of James Joyce* (anthology of articles), Norfolk, CT, 1939.
Campbell, Joseph, and H. M. Robinson, *A Skeleton Key to Finnegans Wake,* New York, 1944.
Ellman, Richard, *James Joyce,* New York, 1982.
*Gilbert, Stuart, *James Joyce's "Ulysses,"* New York, 1930–52.
*Levin, Harry, *James Joyce, a Critical Introduction,* Norfolk, CT, 1941.
Ricke, A., *The Sense of Nonsense,* Iowa City, 1992.
Scholes, R. E., *In Search of James Joyce,* Urbana, IL, 1992.
Tindall, William, *James Joyce: His Way of Interpreting the Modern World,* New York, 1979.

Joyce Cary
Allen, W., *Joyce Cary,* London, 1953.
Bishop, A. G., *(Gentlemen Rider) Joyce Cary,* Oxford, 1989.
Bloom, R., *The Indeterminate World,* Philadelphia, 1962.
Mahood, M. M., *Joyce Cary's Africa,* London, 1964.
Makinen, M. S., *Joyce Cary,* London, 1989.
O'Connor, W. V., *Joyce Cary,* New York, 1966.
Wright, A., *Joyce Cary: A Preface to His Novels,* London, 1958.

Lawrence Durrell
Fraser, G. C., *Lawrence Durrell A Critical Study,* New York, 1968.
Unterecker, J., *Lawrence Durrell,* New York, 1964.
Weigle, J. A., *Lawrence Durrell,* Boston, 1989.

The Irish Renaissance
Gonzales, A., *Short Stories from the Irish Renaissance,* Troy, New York, 1993.
Gregory, Lady Agusta, *Our Irish Theatre,* New York and London, 1913.
Marcus, P. *Yeats and the Beginning of the Irish Renaissance,* Syracuse, NY, 1987.

W. B. Yeats

Ellmann, Richard, *Yeats, the Man and the Masks,* New York, 1948.
Finneran, R., *Editing Yeats's Poems,* New York, 1990.
Hone, Joseph M., *W. B. Yeats, 1865–1939,* New York, 1943.
MacNeice, Louis, *The Poetry of W. B. Yeats,* Oxford University Press, 1941.
Meyers, S., *Yeats's Book of the Nineties,* New York, 1992.
Smith, S., *W. B. Yeats,* London, 1990.

Lady Gregory

Olsen, B., *Lady Gregory Fifty Years After,* London, 1986.
*Orwell, George, "The Final Years of Lady Gregory," *New Yorker,* April 19, 1947.
Reynolds, H., "The Greatest Irishwoman of Her Time," *Christian Science Monthly Magazine,* June 7, 1947.

J. M. Synge

Gerstenberger, D., *J. M. Synge,* Boston, 1990.
King, M., *The Drama of J. M. Synge,* Syracuse, 1985.

Sean O'Casey

Armstrong, W. A., *Sean O'Casey,* London, 1967.
Cowasjee, S., *Sean O'Casey, the Man Behind the Plays,* New York, 1963.
Hogan, R G., *The Experiments of Sean O'Casey,* New York, 1960.
Krause, D., *Sean O'Casey, the Man and His Work,* New York, 1960.
Watt, S., *Joyce, O'Casey, and the Irish Popular Theatre,* Syracuse, 1991.

Lord Dunsany

Perkins, D., *A History of Modern Poetry: From the 1890s to the High Modernist Mode,* Boston, 1976.

P. V. Carroll

"The Devil Came from Dublin," *Theatre Arts,* November, 1951.
Doyle, P., *P. V. Carroll,* New York, 1971
"Scotland's Dramatic Genius Is Flowering," *Theatre Arts,* May, 1945.

James Stephens

"Cloca Mora Man," *Time,* January 8, 1951 (obit.).
Davison, E. L., *Some Modern Poets,* New York, 1928.
Frankenberg, L., "James Stephens: Touchstone," *Saturday Review of Literature,* March 22, 1947.

Brendan Behan

Behan, Dominic, *My Brother Brendan,* London, 1965.
Johnson, L., *The Art of Brendan Behan,* London, 1979.
McCann, S., *The World of Brendan Behan,* New York, 1965.

Simpson, Alan, *Beckett and Behan and a Theatre in Dublin,* London, 1962.

Frank O'Connor
Bruce, H. A., *In Our Heritage, New York Herald Tribune Book Review,* Aug., Oct., 1952.
Sheehy, M., ed., *Studies in Frank O'Connor,* London, 1969.
Steinman, M., *Frank O'Connor at Work,* London, 1990.

Mary Lavin
Dunsany, Lord, *Preface to Tales from Bective Bridge,* 1942.
Kelly, A., *Mary Lavin, Quiet Rebel,* New York, 1980.
Peterson, R., *Mary Lavin,* Boston, 1978.

Aldous Huxley
Atkins, J. A., *Aldous Huxley; a Literary Study,* London, 1956.
Buck, Philo M., *Directions in Contemporary Literature,* Oxford University Press, 1942.
Ghose, S., *Aldous Huxley, a Cynical Salvationist,* London, 1962.
Greenblatt, S. J., *Three Modern Satirists,* 1965.
Henderson, Alexander, *Aldous Huxley,* New York, 1935.
Meloni, I., *Aldous Huxley,* London, 1989.
*Muller, Herbert, *Modern Fiction,* New York, 1939.
Nance, G., *Aldous Huxley,* New York, 1988.
Saturday Review of Literature, March 19, 1938.

Evelyn Waugh
Beaty, F., *The Ironic World of Evelyn Waugh,* Dekalb, IL, 1992.
Bradbury, M., *Evelyn Waugh,* Edinburgh, 1964.
Braybrooke, N., "Evelyn Waugh," *Fortnightly,* March, 1952.
Carens, J. F., *The Satiric Art of Evelyn Waugh,* Seattle, 1966.
"The Jesuit Who Was Thursday," *Commonweal,* March 21, 1947.
Myers, W., *Evelyn Waugh and the Problem of Evil,* London, 1991.
Stopp, F. J., *Evelyn Waugh. Portrait of an Artist,* London, 1958.
*Wilson, Edmund, "Never Apologize, Never Explain: the Art of Evelyn Waugh," *Classics and Commercials,* New York, 1950 (also in *New Yorker,* March 4, 1944)

G. K. Chesterton
Attwater, Donald, *Modern Christian Revolutionaries,* New York, 1947.
Belloc, Hilaire, *On the Place of Gilbert Chesterton in English Letters,* New York, 1940.
Coren, M., *Gilbert,* London, 1989.
Jaki, S., *Chesterton, a Seer of Science,* Urbana, IL, 1986.
Ward, Maisie, *Gilbert Keith Chesterton,* New York, 1943.

Graham Greene

Allott, Miriam, and William Farris, *The Art of Graham Greene,* London, 1951.
Atkins, J., *Graham Greene,* London, 1957.
Choi, J. S., *Greene and Unamuno,* New York, 1990.
DeVitis, A. A., *Graham Greene,* New York, 1964.
Kelly, R. M., *Graham Greene,* New York, 1992.
Kunkel, F. L., *The Labyrinthine Ways of Graham Greene,* New York, 1960.
Lodge, D., *Graham Greene,* New York, 1966.
Whitehouse, J. C., *Vertical Man,* New York, 1990.

William Golding

Dick, B. F., *William Golding,* New York, 1987.
Dickson, L. L., *The Modern Allegories of William Golding,* New York, 1990.
Fuller-Dicken, N., *William Golding's Use of Symbolism,* London, 1990.
Gindin, James, *William Golding,* New York, 1990.
McCarron, Kevin, *William Golding,* London, 1990.
Subbarao, V. V., *William Golding: A Critical Study,* New York, 1987.

Liberals and Humanitarians

Bloom, H. *The Anxiety of Influence,* New York, 1973.
Culler, J., *Structuralist Poetics,* New York, 1975.
Harrison, C. Y., "Proletarian Literature Sans-Culottes," *Nation,* March 22, 1933.
Moers, E., *Literary Women,* New York, 1976.
Trilling, L., *The Liberal Imagination,* New York, 1950.
Wilson, Edmund, "Marxism and the Historical Interpretation of Literature," in *The Triple Thinkers,* New York, 1948.

G. B. Shaw

Bentley, Eric, *Bernard Shaw,* Norfolk, CT, 1947.
Ganz, A. F., *George Bernard Shaw,* New York, 1983.
Gibbs, A. M., *The Mind and Art of Shaw,* New York, 1983.
May, K. M., *Ibsen and Shaw,* New York, 1985.
Weintraub, S., *The Unexpected Shaw,* New York, 1982.

H. G. Wells

Anderson, L., *Bennett, Wells, and Conrad,* London, 1988.
Hammond, J. R., *H. G. Wells and the Short Story,* London, 1992.
Murray, B., *H. G. Wells,* New York, 1990.
*Nicholson, Norman, *H. G. Wells,* London, 1950.
Vallentin, Antonina, *H. G. Wells, Prophet of Our Day,* New York, 1950.

George Orwell

Ashe, G., "Note on Orwell," *Commonweal,* June 1, 1951.
Freedman, C., *George Orwell,* New York, 1988.
Matthews, H. L., "Homage to Orwell," *Nation,* December 27, 1952.
Meyers, V., *George Orwell,* New York, 1991.
Rodden, J., *The Politics of Literary Reputation,* New York, 1989.
Siepmann, E. O., "Farewell to Orwell," *Nineteenth Century,* March, 1950.
Stern, J., "Homage to Orwell," *New Republic,* February 20, 1950.

Experiments in Theater

Armstrong, W. A., ed., *Experimental Drama,* New York, 1963.
Betsko, K., and R. Koenig, *Interviews with Contemporary Women Playwrights,* New York, 1987.
Blau, H., *Eye of Prey: Subversions of the Post-modern,* Bloomington, IN, 1987.
Blumenthal, E., *Joseph Chaikin: Exploring at the Boundaries of Theater,* New York, 1984.
Brown, J. R., and B. Harris, ed., *Contemporary Theatre,* Chicago, 1962.
Hayman, R., *Theater and Anti-Theater: New Movements Since Beckett,* New York, 1979.
Kershaw, J., *The Present Stage,* Boston, 1966.
Kitchin, L., *Drama in the Sixties,* New York, 1966
Schechner, R., *Environmental Theater,* New York, 1973.
Taylor, J. R., *Anger and After,* New York, 1962.
Turner, M. R., *Bluff Your Way in the Theatre,* New York, 1967.
Tynan, Kenneth, *Curtains,* New York 1961,
———— *Tynan Right and Left,* New York, 1967.
Wellwarth, G. E., *The Theatre of Protest and Paradox,* New York, 1964.
Whiting, J., *On Theatre,* New York, 1966.

John Osborne

Carter, A., *John Osborne,* Edinburgh, 1969.
Hayman, R., *Contemporary Playwrights: John Osborne,* 1968.
Page, M., *File on Osborne,* London, 1988.
Trussler, S., *John Osborne,* 1969.

Harold Pinter

Esslin, Martin, *The Peopled Wound: the Work of Harold Pinter,* Garden City, NY, 1970.
Gordon, Lois, *Strategems to Uncover Nakedness: the Dramas of Harold Pinter,* Columbia, MO, 1969.
Kerr, W., *Harold Pinter,* New York, 1967.
Merritt, S. H., *Pinter in Play,* Durham, NC, 1990.
Orr, J., *Tragicomedy and Contemporary Culture,* Ann Arbor, MI, 1991.

David Storey

Hutchings, W., *The Plays of David Storey,* Carbondale, IL, 1988.
"Life and Death of the Common Man," *Encounter,* Dec. 1969.

Samuel Beckett

Brater, E., ed. *Beckett at 80: Beckett in Context,* New York, 1986.
Fletcher, J., *Beckett, the Playwright,* New York, 1985.
Gidal, P., *Understanding Beckett,* New York, 1986.
Gontarski, S. E., *On Beckett,* New York, 1986.

Doris Lessing

Brewster, D., *Doris Lessing,* London, 1965.
Pratt, A., and L. S. Dembo, ed., *Doris Lessing: Critical Studies,* London, 1974.
Schleuter, P., *The Novels of Doris Lessing,* New York, 1973.
Singleton, M. A., *The City and the Veld,* London, 1977.

John Masefield

Dwyer, J., *John Masefield,* New York, 1987.
*Strong, L. A. G., *John Masefield,* London, 1952.

Wilfred Owen

Bergonzi, B., *Heroes' Twilight: A Study of the Literature of the Great War,* London, 1965.
Ceasar, A., *Talking I Like a Man,* Manchester, 1993.
Hibberd, D., *Owen the Poet,* London, 1986.
White, Gertrude M., *Wilfred Owen,* New York, 1969.

Gerard Manley Hopkins

Ellis, V. R., *Gerard Manley Hopkins and the Language of Mystery,* New York, 1991.
McNees, E., *Eucharistic Poetry,* New York, 1991.
Mizener, Arthur, et al, *Gerard Manley Hopkins,* Norfolk, CT, 1952.
*Pick, John, ed., *A Hopkins Reader,* Oxford, 1953.

Robert Bridges

*Guérard, Albert, *Robert Bridges, a Study of Traditionalism in Poetry,* Harvard University Press, 1942.
Hamilton, L. T., *Robert Bridges,* London, 1991.
Phillips, C., *Robert Bridges,* New York, 1992.

A. E. Housman

Bayley, J., *Housman's Poems,* Oxford, 1992.
Richards, Grant, *A. E. Housman, 1897–1936,* Oxford University Press, 1942.

W. H. Auden

Blair, J. G., *The Poetic Art of W. H. Auden,* Princeton, 1965.
Boly, J., *Reading Auden,* Ithaca, NY, 1991.
Hecht, Anthony, *The Hidden Law,* Cambridge, 1992.
Nelson, G., *Change of Heart,* Berkeley, 1969.
O'Neill, M., *Auden, MacNeice, and Spender,* New York, 1992.
Replogle, J. M., *Auden's Poetry,* Seattle, 1969.
Spears, M. K., *The Poetry of W. H. Auden,* New York, 1963.

Stephen Spender

Brenner, Rica, *Poets of Our Time,* New York, 1941.
*Daiches, David, *Poetry and the Modern World,* University of Chicago Press, 1940.
O'Neill, M., *Auden, MacNeice, and Spender,* New York, 1992.

Dylan Thomas

Korb, J., *Dylan Thomas,* New York, 1992.
MacNeice, Louis, "The Strange, Mighty Impact of Dylan Thomas' Poetry," *New York Times Book Review,* April 5, 1953.
McNees, E., *Eucharistic Poetry,* New York, 1991.
*Olson, Elder, *The Poetry of Dylan Thomas,* University of Chicago Press, 1954.
Savage, D. S., "The Poetry of Dylan Thomas," *New Republic,* April 29, 1946.
Symons, Julian, "Obscurity and Dylan Thomas," *Kenyon Review,* Winter, 1940.

Louis MacNeice

MacDonald, P., *Louis MacNeice,* Oxford, 1991.
O'Neill, M., *Auden, MacNeice, and Spender,* New York, 1992.
Press, J., *Louis MacNeice,* London, 1965.

Edith Sitwell

Bowra, C. M., *Edith Sitwell,* Monaco, 1947.
Brophy, J. D., *Edith Sitwell: the Symbolist Order,* Carbondale, IL, 1968.
Cevasco, G. A., *The Sitwells,* Boston, 1987.
Lehmenn, J., *Edith Sitwell,* London, 1952.
———, *A Nest of Tigers; the Sitwells in their Times,* Boston, 1968.
Villa, J. G., ed., *Celebrations for Edith Sitwell,* New York, 1948.

Some Younger Poets

Brinnin, Read, McKenna, *The Modern Poets,* New York, 1963, 1970.
King, P. R., *Nine Contemporary Poets,* New York, 1979.
Perkins, D., *A History of Modern Poetry: From the 1890s to the High Modernist Mode,* Boston, 1976.

Perkins, D., and W. J. Bate, *British and American Poets: Chaucer to the Present,* New York, 1986.
Rosenthal, M. L., *The New Poets: American and British Poetry Since World War II,* New York, 1967.
Vendler, H., *Part of Nature, Part of Us,* New York, 1980.

David Jones
Dilworth, T., *The Shape of Meaning in the Poetry of David Jones,* Toronto, 1988.

Philip Larkin
Booth, J., *Philip Larkin,* New York, 1992.
Tolley, A. T., *My Proper Ground,* Ottawa, 1991.

Jon Silkin
Schmidt, M. S., and G. Lindop, *British Poetry Since 1960: A Critical Survey,* London, 1972.

Donald Davie
Bedient, C., *Eight Contemporary Poets,* London, 1974.
Martin, G., ed., *Donald Davie, Charles Tomlinson, Geoffrey Hill,* London, 1976.

Thom Gunn
Press, J., *Rule and Energy: Trends in British Poetry Since the Second World War,* London, 1963.
Schmidt, M., and G. Lindop, ed., *British Poetry Since 1960: a Critical Survey,* London, 1972.

Ted Hughes
Faas, E., *Ted Hughes: The Unaccommodated Universe,* New York, 1980.
Sagar, K., *The Art of Ted Hughes,* London, 1976.

Seamus Heaney
Buttel, R., *Seamus Heaney,* New York, 1975.
Dunn, D., *Two Decades of Irish Writing,* London, 1975.
Morrison, B., *Seamus Heaney,* London, 1982.

Elaine Feinstein
Schmidt, M., and G. Lindop, *British Poetry Since 1960: A Critical Survey,* London, 1972.

Molly Holden
King, P. R., *Nine Contemporary Poets,* New York, 1979.

INDEX